Gifts for Today

DON FANNING

First Edition 2013
Published by Branches Publications
2040 Downing Dr.
Pensacola, FL 32505

Branches Publications was started to publish books to aid in discipleship and missions with the end goal of equipping leaders and teachers how to be strategic with their lives and ministries to fulfill the Great Commission. Publications by Branches are available at www.branchespublications.com and can be reviewed at www.tgcresources.com (i.e., The Great Commission Resources. .

© 2013 Copyright: Branches Publications
Don Fanning
Design: Krista Freeman
All rights reserved ISBN:
All rights reserved. No part of this publication my be reproduced, stored in a retrieval system, or transmitted in any form or by any means without the prior permission of the publisher.
Printed in the United States at SnowFall Press.

The Scripture text used is from the New King James Version, New English Translation, New Living Translation and New American Standard Version as indicated in the text.

Other books by Don Fanning available at Branches Publications can be purchased Online at **www.branchespublications.com** or www.amazon.com

> *Walking His Way: A Devotional Study of the Commands of the NT*
>   Also see one page a day at www.walkinghisway.com
> *What in the World is God Doing? - An Introduction to Missions*
> *Ten Steps of Fruitful Discipleship*
> *Inductive Bible Study Methods*
> *Romans: A Study Guide for Small Group Leaders*
> *Titus*
> *1, 2, 3 John: Know for Certain*
> *Spiritual Gifts: A Survey and Definition of the Spiritual Gifts*
> *Revelation*

Contents

1: Introduction...5
2: Historical Development............................17
3: The Baptism of the Spirit 37
4: Four Aspects of the Baptism of the Spirit.......49
5: How to know if you have received the Baptism of the Spirit.........69
6: The transition in the work of the Spirit........85
7: The Gift of Tongues 101
8: The Gift of the Spirit: by works or by grace?...119
9: Miracles 135
10: Categories and Times of miracles...............149
11: Principles from 1 Corinthians 12 161
12: Ten Arguments for the Inferiority of Tongues..177
13: Ten Rules of the functioning of Tongues.......193
14: Fourteen areas of Evidence for the Ceasing of Tongues...........213
15. Tongues and their Relation to the Canon......233
16: Tongues and their Relation with Christ and the Apostles..........257
17: Tongues and their Relation with the history of the Church........273
18: Devotional Tongues 291
19: A Possible Explanation for the Phenomena of Tongues...........313
20: One Last Word about Charismatics 325
21: The Spiritual Gifts 341
22: Conclusion.....................................357
Bibliography 363

Forward

CHAPTER 1

Introduction

Chapter 1: *Gifts for Today*

Twentieth-century Christianity will be known for various movements (i.e., Fundamentalism, Evangelicalism, Church Planting Movements, Discipleship movements, Bible College and University movement, but most significantly the Pentecostal and Charismatics movements) that have changed the way Christianity is understood and practiced worldwide. Throughout the history of the Church polemic themes sparked controversy in each of its different stages, provoking profound investigations to determine exactly what the Bible has to say about them and how the church should respond. Challenges in different periods of Church History to previously held doctrines and practices made controversies of all the nine clearly defined branches of Systematic Theology (Christology, Bibliology, Soteriology, Ecclesiology, Eschatology, etc.), making them objects of intense study and discussion often resulting in division and criticism.

One of the last branches of theology to be scrutinized by the theological world has been Pneumatology, the study of the Spirit. Even at that, there has been relatively little written on the subject. In the first three centuries of the Church, while theologians were studying the Trinity, the Holy Spirit was declared to be an equal part of the Trinity. However that investigation failed to include a full description of the Spirit and His manifestations. Since then, the Spirit has never been a significant theme or controversy until the twentieth century.

Today Pneumatology has given rise to a variety of interpretations; consequently, it is now vital that every believer be well grounded in what the Bible says regarding the Spirit and His outworking. The evidence in Scriptures is the basis of our faith and practice, so we must constantly be verifying our beliefs. For this reason, the emphasis in this study will be a close analysis of the biblical text, rather than a refutation of other interpretations or reported experiences, in order to see the biblical evidence as clearly as possible. The special focus of this study in the sphere of pneumatology will be the gifts of the Spirit and especially the sign gifts, that is, tongues, interpretation and miracles.

Since the New Testament was written in Greek, there will be references to keywords in the original and also to significant grammatical aspects of the original texts. The main versions that are utilized will be the New English Translation (NET), the New King James (NKJ), the New Living Translation (NLT) and the New American Standard Version (NASV), whichever is the clearest in a particular verse. Only in necessary cases will the author make to a direct translation from the Greek text. All words from the Greek will be transliterated for the convenience of those who do not know the language.

The Importance of the Holy Spirit

The privilege of serving the King of Creation and the Lord of Eternity requires the supernatural capacity that Christ promised His followers. This is possible through the Holy Spirit. Every believer shares a participation in the indwelling of the Holy Spirit and, through Him, is corporately united in Christ. In 2 Peter 1:4, we read that we "may participate in the divine nature" (NIV2 Peter 1:4) by accepting the biblical promises of salvation. We have resident in our lives He who is the power of the resurrection, the maximum internal resource to be able to understand all that He has said and live a victorious life. He is the integral part of our new nature as believers.

The Bible teaches that the Holy Spirit is as essential for service as for salvation. For example: Paul wrote to "be strong in the Lord and in the power of His might" (Eph 6:10). Living for Christ is impossible apart from His power working in and through us.

It would be impossible to serve the Lord while separated from the work and power of the Holy Spirit. God's objective in our lives is to have control of our minds, hearts and bodies through His Spirit, which is resident in every believer.

Three Extreme Positions: Abuse, Negligence and Distortion

From the beginning of the Church, it was easy to distort the true perspective of the work of the Spirit. Such abuses provoked the writing of three significant chapters in the New Testament (1 Corinthians 12-14). Paul was guided to correct the overemphasis on the gift of tongues and the neglect of the teaching and edifying result of the gift of prophecy, that is, the revelation of God's Word. Like the Corinthians, some modern interpreters continue to abuse or exaggerate the truths concerning the Spirit to the extreme that other doctrines are ignored or minimized as though they were less important. Instead of having Christ as the center of the church and of life, the Holy Spirit often occupies this preeminence.

Though equally sincere, other interpreters while guarding against the extremes of hyper-emotionalism, have isolated the doctrine of the Third Person of the Trinity into oblivion, to the extent that it is seen as a divisive doctrine and barely related to practical life. Perhaps because they fear the subjectivism in the teaching or preaching, they make virtually no reference at all to the work of the Spirit. Such ignorance in the churches can motivate a curiosity to discover a personal contact with the supernatural, and many are attracted to any phenomenon that appears to be supernatural or beyond natural explanation.

A final group of interpreters tends to distort the reality of the Spirit, considering Him as merely a force, power or energy to be manipulated rather than a real person to relate to and with whom to live. He is to be treated as a person with a personality, since He can be quenched and offended. This emphasis focuses on the power that the Spirit can provide instead of an intimate relationship with Jesus Christ through the Spirit.

In each of the first major Councils of the Church (Constantinople, AD 381 and Caledon AD 451) they agreed about the person and work of the Holy Spirit, because the basis of their decisions was the revealed truths in the Bible.

What the Church lacks today are believers with a full understanding of the privileges and power that each one possesses through the "divine nature," which we all share. As part of this new nature the character and power of the ministry of Christ are manifest in us, and these are reactivated through the gifts of the Spirit, which now operate in the lives of all believers.

Importance of the Spiritual Gifts

The modern emphasis and variety of opinions on the spiritual gifts in magazines, books, publications, churches, radio and television makes it imperative for everyone to have a clear knowledge of what the Bible teaches, and does not teach, about these gifts. For many people it is difficult to distinguish between the variety of experiences that are announced as supposed genuine results of the Spirit's power and the actual teachings from the Scriptures.

Without a doubt the gifts of the Spirit are very important for the believer. These gifts are the special enabling ability to serve others, a clear indication of the power of God in our lives that can provide the unusual energy beyond normal human strength to contribute to the Kingdom. The disproportionate emphasis that can easily be given to some manifestations of gifts can deviate from the priority that must be given to the biblical text. However important the spiritual gifts are, it must be remembered that there is neither a command to discover your spiritual gift nor a major emphasis on the gifts in the New Testament outside of the corrective chapters in 1 Corinthians 12-14. The majority of the gifts are mentioned only once, and that without explanation. Generally, the believer who is filled with the Spirit and seeks to serve others will "naturally" manifest his spiritual gift, consciously or unconsciously, as he seeks to serve others.

Influence of the Pentecostal/charismatic Movement

Due to its global influence, the most significant twentieth-century movement that influenced beliefs about the gifts of the Spirit has been the Pentecostal and Charismatic movements. The Pentecostal Movement is credited to have began on New Years Eve, 1900, then quickly spread throughout the world. According to Blumhofer, the "Pentecostal denominations boast over 10 million members. If one adds the persons in other Christian churches who embrace Pentecostal-like beliefs and practices [Charismatics], the number more than doubles. In addition, estimates suggest at least 500 million adherents abroad, making Pentecostals the second largest group of Christians in the world, trailing on Roman Catholics." (Blumhofer 2006: 59)

When the Pentecostal experience infiltrated into other Protestant and evangelical denominations at approximately 1960, the Charismatic movement was born. The percentage of believers forming part of this movement is very high in certain countries. In Chile, for example, it is estimated that more than 80% of the evangelicals are Charismatic. The largest churches in Latin America and around the world are often Charismatic churches, many of which claim more than 20,000 active members, and several claim more than 100,000 members. McClung's investigation revealed, "With more than 580 million adherents (growing by 19 million per year and 54,000 per day), the Pentecostal/charismatic movement has become, in just 100 years, the fastest growing and most globally diverse expression of worldwide Christianity. At the current rate of growth, some researchers predict there will be 1 billion Pentecostals by 2025, most located in Asia, Africa, and Latin America (McClung 2006: 30). Some 27 percent of the world's Christians are Pentecostal, charismatic or neo-charismatic, according to the World Christian Database (Alford 2006: 21).

Understanding the Reason for Different Viewpoints

Because of the extensive use of television and publications, many unchurched people think that all evangelicals are Charismatic, principally in other countries, a misconception that skews the public perception of Christianity. This presents a problem for many Evangelicals, especially those who do not have a clear understanding of what the Bible says regarding the gifts of the Spirit. For example, in a church where the majority of the congregation has little or no biblical preparation, the influence of stories about miracles and signs could have such great acceptance that, if the pastor has not manifested such signs, he or any leader could begin to think that perhaps he lacks something or is not as spiritual as those who become known as miracle workers. This type of pressure could obligate a non-charismatic pastor to begin to seek certain signs or gifts in his ministry in order to keep his congregation, or at least to maintain his leadership in the church. Suddenly, the congregation has transformed itself into a Charismatic church. The intimidation factor can become significant.

Common testimonies can include the filling of dental cavities, gasoline tanks in cars being filled, the resurrection of animals, machines that did not function suddenly are "healed," visions of encounters with Christ or angels, or a wide variety of healing and tongue-speaking.

The Pentecostal teaching is that all Christians should experiment miracles on a regular or daily basis. The fear of being excluded from "what God is doing today" obligates many to investigate and accept many phenomena as "miraculous," because they believe that God will leave them out of His program if they do not. Worse is the underlying threat of not recognizing what God is doing, or worse yet, stating that such phenomena is not of God, and thus failing to glorify Him for how He is manifesting Himself.

A common question is, "Why are others having these experiences and I am not?" This problem can get even more complicated when the non-Charismatic churches do not grow as rapidly as the Charismatic churches, as is often the case. Then these leaders begin to feel increasing pressure to imitate

Charismatic practices.

For this reason many are influenced by the "miracles" that are experienced not only by Charismatics by also those experienced in cults, by tribes in the jungle, and even by the Roman Catholic Church. The continual hope is that someday something "good," a miracle, is going to happen in every life. Therefore we must discipline ourselves to seriously search the answers in the Bible as the only final authority in life and to avoid the influences of tradition or impressive stories.

Still, it is sometimes difficult to perceive the difference between the two groups, the Evangelical and the Pentecostal/charismatic, even when biblical truth is taken into consideration. Failure to understand the doctrinal differences is more acute if the hermeneutics, or the processes of interpreting the Scriptures, are not understood. If two groups use the same rules to interpret the Scriptures, the conclusions will generally be similar. When there are two opposing views concerning an issue, one is correct and the other is error. They cannot both be correct according to the Law of non-contradiction.

Among interpreters of the Bible there are two different schools of hermeneutics: the Allegorical and the Literal. The Allegorical school of interpretation tends to spiritualize parts of a narrative or passage to find its "deeper" or "more meaning spiritual. The Literal school of interpretation, also called the Grammatical-Historical-Cultural process of interpretation, seeks to find the original meaning of the writer in the first century and then discern the relevance to the modern day. This study will follow the latter school of interpretation. For this reason, some of the conclusions that are reached may not be the same as those applying an allegorical interpretation.

The major emphasis of this book will be to analyze the biblical evidence regarding the nature of the "miraculous" gifts for two reasons: (1) The Bible has more to say regarding the miraculous gifts than the remaining gifts. Some gifts are only mentioned once, and only in a list. For example, the gift of "helps" is known only by its name, whereas the gift of tongues has three chapters dedicated to its understanding. (2) Great confusion exists in the churches today over the theme of the miraculous. The principal point of this disagreement in the churches today is in the area of the miraculous gifts.

Terminology

To begin the study on the same footing, it is important to be using the same terminology. Often in biblical discussions different points of view may use the same terminology, but actually be referring to different concepts. The author will define the perspectives that will be the basis of the discussion throughout the book. For example,

Charisma: The term is a transliteration (where the actual letters in Greek are carried over to English). It comes from the Greek word that refers to "gift." It is used to describe the "gracious gift" of salvation (Rom 5:15-16;

6:23). The special use of the word charisma is applied to the "gifts" of the Spirit for service (Rom 12:6; 1 Cor 12:4, 9, 28, 30-31; 1 Tim 4:14; 2 Tim 1:6; 1 Pet 4:10). When a believer receives a gift of the Spirit, such as mercy, teaching, exhortation, etc., he has received a *charisma*. This word occurs eight times in the NT (3 refer to the gift of salvation;

The word charisma is a derivation of the word *charis*, meaning "grace," typically defined as "unmerited favor," thus both our salvation and our spiritual gifts are unmerited gifts of God. The following represents a fuller definition: "A spiritual gift is the unique capacity given by the Holy Spirit to empower a special service in the church ministry with the end being that every congregation can progress in unity, maturity and expansion for God's glory."

Tongues: The most controversial of the nineteen gifts of the Spirit is the gift of tongues. There are a variety of interpretations, even within the Charismatic Movement. For example: (1) One form of speaking in tongues refers to the ability to speak in a literal foreign language that is unknown to the speaker, e.g. someone from America goes to Japan and begins to speak in Japanese without any previous study or even having heard the language spoken previously. (2) The other definition of the gift of tongues refers to the gift of speaking in a "celestial language" that is not known to the speaker, nor could it be known from the human perspective. This is not considered an earthly language, thus not subject to linguistic restrictions or analysis according to charismatic believers. This distinction is sometimes made between the "tongues" spoken at Pentecost (Acts 2) and in Caesarea by Cornelius (Acts 10), which is understood as literal earthly languages, and the gift of tongues spoken of in 1 Cor 14, considered by some to be a "celestial" language that sounds like gibberish only understood by God.

Although some testimonies exist of speaking in literal languages, the more common practice is the speaking in a near ecstasy or trance-like state while babbling syllables without any linguistic sense, which is considered a "heavenly language," which communicates more directly to God. At times the person may not be conscious of having spoken in a language, and at other times the person is dominated by the Spirit to the point of losing control of himself.

It is said that this mystical experience produces an intimate and supernatural communication with God that cannot be experienced with a human language. The expression of this "tongue" cannot be understood on earth, only in heaven. This tongue is so heavenly that it cannot be humanly analyzed by linguistics. Larry Christenson, Lutheran Charismatic, author of the book Speaking in Tongues, considers whatever expressions of our sentiments manifested by the most intimate emotions of the speaker "should be classified as a genuine language." (Christenson 1968: 28)

Dennis Bennett, the first Episcopalian priest to publicly announce that he spoke in tongues describes it this way:

To speak in tongues is an act of child-like faith...in the same way that a child begins to babble his first words, to open his mouth and make sounds... With whatever sounds one makes, offering his tongue to God in simple faith, he can begin to speak in tongues... If we do not accept the experience as real (the sounds of babbling), we will not be conscious of the reality, that is to say, any sound should be accepted by faith as the gift of tongues (Bennett 1975, n.a.).

Pentecostals: When certain believers began to "speak in tongues" around 1900, they became known as Pentecostals in reference to similar phenomena that occurred on the first day when the Spirit descended in Acts 2, which happened on a Jewish holiday called the Day of Pentecost.

This is not considered an earthly language, thus not subject to linguistic restrictions or analysis according to the charismatics. This distinction is sometimes made between the "tongues" spoken at Pentecost (Acts 2) and in Caesarea by Cornelius (Acts 10), which is understood as literal earthly languages, and the gift of tongues spoken of in 1 Cor 14, considered by some to be a "celestial" language that sounds like gibberish only understood by God.

The insinuation and objective of the term means that Pentecostals have a similitude with the primitive Church. That is to say, that the Church of the twentieth century should appear in all aspects like the Church of Acts 2. The name and the experiences of the Pentecostals try to demonstrate this continuity.

The Pentecostal experience gave rise to a number of denominational churches beginning in 1901 and springing out of the Azusa Street revival in Los Angeles, CA, including the Assemblies of God, Church of God, Pentecostal Church (with a variety of distinctives: ... Holiness, Four-Square..., etc.). For the first sixty years these churches were marginalized by non-Pentecostal churches, but as their numbers grew and their style of music/worship became more accepted as the norm, the movement has taken a major role in the leadership and direction of evangelical Christianity. The following is a time line of the Pentecostal developments:

Charismatic: Technically, any believer who has received a charisma, a "gift," is a charismatic. However, today the term primarily refers to those who emphasize the gifts of speaking in tongues, signs, wonders and healing. The emphasis on these manifestations in non-Pentecostal churches began around 1959 when an Episcopal bishop in California first spoke in tongues marking the origin of the Charismatic Movement.

There are nineteen distinct gifts (charisma) mentioned in the New Testament. In 1 Corinthians 12:7, the Bible declares that "each one" has been given a gift or "manifestation of the Spirit." By definition, then, every believer is a charismatic person. But in the popular sense, the title is applied primarily to those who speak in tongues and practice healing in non-Pentecostal churches.

Healing: Healing is the capacity to heal or cure sicknesses with a prayer or a command. In the charismatic movement the manifestation of healing is, perhaps, the most emphasized and is the most common characteristic. This emphasis comes from the teaching that Christ carried to the cross not only the sins of mankind but also their sicknesses. Therefore, if a person can ask Christ to forgive his sins, then he can also ask him for healing; in fact, some Charismatics teach that it is part of our salvation. According to this way of thinking, the believer should always have good health just as he always has salvation.

1 Corinthians 12 refers to the spiritual gift of healing and James 5 refers to the ministry of praying for the sick as a function of the elders of the church. Though this area remains a controversy, no one denies that God heals through prayer, but how much priority should healing be given in the worship and ministry of the churches continues to be debated.

Miracles, Signs: Although miracles and signs differ from the healing in the New Testament the manifestation is often the same. A healing is, in fact, a miracle or could be a sign of God's power. In the New Testament, miraculous happenings unrelated to healing are rare. Perhaps it would be casting out demons or raising the dead, but both of these, in a sense, are usually related to some kind of healing.

A miracle is a manifestation of power (*dinamis*), especially as being superior to satanic power (Luke 9:42-43). It seems that the biblical purpose is to demonstrate the power of God as superior to the power of demons.

We will see that there are two types of miracles:

(1) Supernatural miracles that are completely against natural laws (i.e. a hatchet floated in 2 Kings 6:5-6, the sun "stood still" in Joshua 10, and the sun-dial reversed its shadow ten degrees in 2 Kings 20:10-11, Naaman, a leper, was instantly given visibly new skin as of a baby in 2 Kings 5). None of these have natural explanations.

(2) Providential miracles that are the amazing timing of events coordinated by God in order to accomplish an act of provision or protection, etc. Providence acts are events that occur in a natural way but their timing and/or acceleration are too coincidental to have been an accident or good fortune, for example, after a night of not catching fish, Jesus told Peter to drop the nets one more time and the catch of fish nearly broke the nets. Providence does not violate the laws of nature (i.e., a letter arrives in the nick of time with an offering or a tumor gradually shrinks over a 3-day period starting when people began to pray). This does not deny the divine element in providential miracles, because it would not have happened without God's intervention, but there was no creation or phenomenal aspect of these miracles. God used the laws of nature, albeit in an accelerated manner, to bring about His purpose.

Contemporary emphasis on the miraculous gifts (tongues, healing and miracles) has the purpose of convincing the world that the Church today is identical to the Early Church. Reports affirming that the signs of the Apostles and all the miraculous occurrences happen now, just as they happened in the first century, are motivated by the desire to prove that the Pentecostal/charismatic movement is like the Early Church in all its aspects.

The "miracles" of the Bible are related to the apostles more than to believers in general. Because of this they are called "signs of the apostles" (2 Cor. 12:12.) The emphasis on doing miracles today has, in effect, the purpose of declaring that we still have apostles, prophets, etc.

Evangelical: The name itself means "good news." It speaks of one who takes the message of the Gospel seriously and falls in love with the gracious God of the Bible. The "good news" is that man can recognize his sinful nature because he has broken the commands of God (i.e. Ten Commandments) leaving him lost and condemned. Salvation comes when we learn of the finished work of Christ on the cross where Christ's death paid the penalty for all our sins. Salvation is by grace, not by works. Forgiveness from God can only be accepted by faith (trusting in the promises and grace of God). This is the "good news." Therefore, an "evangelical" accepts that salvation by personal faith in the finished and full payment for sin's penalty paid by Christ on the cross without any need to add personal works for acceptance before God. The transformation and good works of every believer come afterward as a result of the new life in expressions of gratitude through the power of the indwelling of the Holy Spirit in every believer.

Some confusion arises when a person "assumes" himself to be a believer. If a person receives healing, has an answer to prayer or some other significant intervention of God he can assume that he must be a Christian, yet has never understood the Gospel. Just because God has been "good" or blessed a person does not mean that person is saved. Salvation must not be "assumed." Salvation begins with hearing and understanding the truth of one's sinfulness and Christ's amazing grace in paying for all our sins. Then as a response to this objective understanding, one makes a specific, personal and heart-felt decision to invite Christ to become a part of his life as his personal Savior and God.

If a person believes that he can do something in order to gain or assure his salvation or acceptance before God, he is not an Evangelical. If he thinks that he must go to confession, do penitence, be baptized, be confirmed or attend a church or mass, that person is not an evangelical because he is not trusting exclusively in the death of Christ as the only payment for all his sins.

Acceptance of the Gospel without works is essential for biblical salvation, no matter what the position on the gifts of the Spirit might be. "For by grace are you saved through faith, and that not of yourselves, it is a gift of God" (Eph 2:8-9).

Where this gets a little confusing is when someone has a strong impression or emotional experience in worship, and then because deep feelings, chills, or other unusual sensations, the conclusion is drawn that he must be saved.

Another type of confusion is drawn when someone has an unusual or miraculous answer to prayer, and draws the conclusion that he must be saved or God would not be answering his prayers. This is deductive reasoning from a false premise. Assurance of salvation is not drawn from experiences or works, but rather from a clear understanding of God's Word regarding our sin and the work of our Savior at that point we consciously and willing put our total trust in Christ's work on the cross as described and promised in Scriptures.

Faith placed in, or conclusions drawn from, experiences, however phenomenal they may be, lead to confusion and false assurances. This is precisely the reason so many will be shocked to find out they had never been saved. Jesus warned that many will think they were saved because of miraculous experiences, but they never were: "Many will say to Me in that day, 'Lord, Lord, have we not prophesied in Your name, cast out demons in Your name, and done many wonders in Your name?'" (NKJ Matthew 7:22).

Each one of these terms and many more will be analyzed in the light of the Scriptures. We will not try to explain every phenomenon in question, but we will attempt to make clear what the Bible teaches and highlight the danger of teaching more than the Scriptures clearly demonstrate.

The Inductive Concept

This study does not begin with a presupposition that a certain theology is correct, then logically and philosophically deduce conclusions. This would be deductive theology, which has led many into diverse conclusions. In our study we will study one verse after another, or concept after concept, in order to accumulate Scriptural evidence. The information in its totality will carry us to a biblical conclusion. There is the possibility that a single verse or an argument may not be conclusive or final when it is isolated from the rest of the evidence. However, when it is taken as part of the accumulated evidence, we will see the clear biblical position with regard to tongues and other sign gifts.

CHAPTER 2
Historical Development

Chapter 2: Gifts for Today

The historical evidence of unusual manifestations, miracles and tongues is much scarcer than one would think, assuming that these miraculous gifts were to be the norm throughout the period of the Church Age. Although there were reports of manifestations of some of the sign gifts, they were not constant, verifiable nor associated with the core leadership of the Church. Instead the doctrinally questionable and radical elements of the Church were the primary groups to report phenomenal activity. This is not to say that it did not happen, but at best, it is suspicious.

Cessation

Although there were some reports of rare manifestations of miraculous events, healings or other phenomena, there were few who doubted the cessation of most of the miraculous gifts near the end of the first century. Pentecostals see the normative pattern "as ceasing and find its cause in the spiritual decline of the church," that is, in developing institutionalism (bishop's office, church sacramentalism, etc.) (Hannah 1992: 2:2).

Whatever the reason may be, the evidence is clear that historically, in general, the apostolic gifts terminated with the apostles. Michael Harper suggests that the gifts ceased when he writes, "But it is possible that at this early stage, the end was already setting in, which led eventually to the temporary cessation of these gifts...The gifts finally did disappear from the pages of history." (Harper 1965: 19)

> One could hardly affirm cessationism if miracles and healing were happening all about him. Experience is the confirming factor in the case of either continuation or cessationism. Ultimately, the Bible must affirm (i.e., either affirm it as true or false) or allow our experience to dictate what is true from what is false. It cannot contradict it (i.e., say it cannot happen) (Powell 1997: 1).

Montanus

Around the middle of the second century Montanism was an apocalyptic movement from the province of Phrygia (A.D. 172) (middle of modern day Turkey) under the leadership of Montanus and two females, Prisca and Maximillia, who supposedly spoke the words of the Holy Spirit in trances. They encouraged ecstatic prophesying and strict asceticism, believing that the Christian who falls from grace could never be redeemed.

Montanus frustrated the Church because he claimed a superior authority arising from his divine inspiration. The major Church leaders, fearing the loss of unity essential to the survival of the persecuted Church, denounced his movement. The sect died around A.D. 220 except in a few small pockets. "But the puristic. anti-intellectual movement had many descendants -- Novatian, the Donatist, the Cathari... and Edward Irving." ("Montanism," 2001-2005)

Chapter 2: *Historical Development*

These movements were generally Gnostic-dualistic in origin, which redefines God, Satan and man, and puts everyone into a conflict for liberation from the material world (ruled by Satan) into the spiritual world (ruled by God). According to theses beliefs, the quest for purity brings liberation from the flesh, thus abstinence is practiced, and the possession of the spirit world is the sign of perfection. Hannah's research showed:

> Montanus used to fall into a kind of transport, during which, without consciousness, but as the passive instrument, as he thought, of a higher power, he announced new persecutions in enigmatical and mysterious expressions. Tertullian, a disciple of Montanus, wrote that a female worshipper at Carthage fell into a trance and the people thought she was under divine inspiration, and sought to gain information from her lips from heaven. (Hannah 1992: 2:3)

Pentecostal writers sometimes appeal to these dubious records to show the continuation of the supernatural elements throughout the early church. After extensive research into the writings of the Early Church Fathers, Dr. John Hannah concludes that by the late third and fourth century the "grace gifts" [sign gifts] all but ceased in the churches and that the main view of the Church was that the gifts had been given for the founding of the Church and had been withdrawn when they were no longer necessary.

John Chrysostom (c. 347-407) wrote in Homilies on First Corinthians, "This whole place is very obscure; but the obscurity is produced by our ignorance of the facts referred to and by their cessation, being such as they used to occur, but now no longer take place." (Chrysostom, 1956, p. 12:168) Michael Harper suggests that the gifts ceased when he writes, "But it is possible that at this early stage, the end was already setting in, which led eventually to the temporary cessation of these gifts...The gifts finally did disappear from the pages of history." (Harper, 1965, p. 19)

The Montanists were considered to be heretics by the early church. In the second century this was pretty unusual. Centuries later such accusations of heresy would mean any disagreement with Rome's interpretation of just about everything, but in the second century the issue was Montanus' radical superiority to the reveal Scriptures. Hoekema's evaluation of Montanus is:

> His position was that the age of the Spirit had come, and that the Spirit now spoke through Montanus. New revelations were received by him, supplementing and augmenting the Bible... Montanus and his followers were excluded from the church because the claim to have received revelations superior to the Bible was judged to be contrary to the finality of Scriptures. (Hoekema 1972: 12)

In spite of overwhelming evidence to the contrary, Montanus is quoted and declared as an example of the proof for the continuance of most charismatic manifestations.

Camisards, Jansenites, Shakers

Throughout the majority of the Medieval Period there are no records of manifestations of the charismatic phenomena in Christian circles and in the period of the pre-Reformation era only a few evidences are apparent. The single exception is the evidence of miraculous healings, especially by the saints or proximity to the relics of the Roman Catholic Church.

In the pre-Reformation period one dissenting group was the Camisards or the French Protestants (also known as Huguenots), who were horribly persecuted after the Edict of Nantes (1598) was revoked in 1685, forcing approximately 500,000 Protestants to leave France for Germany, Netherlands, North America and England where they were known as the "French Prophets." One prophetess, Isabeau Vincent of Dauphiny, a young illiterate shepherdess, began seeing visions and speaking in tongues. "So fanatical were these 'tongues' folks that they declared they were not injured by falls from trees, and that lights would guide them to places of safety in danger. Thousands of them heard voices from heaven in the air, they claimed, and also saw apparitions." (Hannah 1992: 2:7)

The Jansenites or Convulsionaries were another radical group from France within the Catholic Church that was persecuted because of their unusual worship behavior. Devotional mystics were acceptable within the Catholic Church, but ecstatic mystics were discouraged. Speaking in tongues was attributed to them in 1731. This group would later migrate into the Shakers, who manifested visions, prophecy, healing hands, the "power of God" in Ann Lee's touch.

This mixture of popular pagan religious practices in the Christian meetings was the typical characteristic of the Shakers, who broke from the Quakers to be like the French Camisards. They practiced rituals of trembling, shouting, dancing, shaking, jerking and glossolalia, in order to be free from the power of sin and a worldly life. Shaker theology, steaming from their Camisards background, taught the dualism of God as male and female. Among many strange beliefs given in their revelations was that the original sin was sexual impurity; therefore, marriage was not to be practiced among believers, as there will be no marriage in heaven.

The Shakers began in 1747 when James and Jane Wardley, former Quakers, were influenced by Camisards or "French Prophets" to accept their teachings of being possessed by a spirit. The Wardleys moved to Manchester, England, to live with John Tounley, "a mason of considerable means," where meetings where held in his home. Jane Wardley was called "Mother" and functioned as a confessor. The Wardleys attracted Ann Lee to the group in 1757 and she emerged as its leader by 1770. Ann came to America in 1774 traveling in the northeast. Ann claimed to speak in seventy tongues and claimed to be Christ in female form ("Ann, the Word" and "Mother Ann") (Hannah 1992: 2:7). They maintained their numbers through conversions and by adoption of orphans.

Children would make visits to the city in the spirit realm and bring messages they had received from Mother Ann to the community. The gift of tongues was manifested in their groups in 1838, with sacred places in each community with names like "Holy Mount." Their dualistic theology came from the creation of man as male and female "in our image" showed the dual sexuality of the Creator. Jesus was the male manifestation of Christ and Mother Ann was the female manifestation of Christ – she was the Bride ready for the Bridegroom and in her the Second Coming of Christ was fulfilled.

Shaker music was essential to their worship experience, creating music to sing with catchy tunes and great enthusiasm. They taught that revelations could come through spontaneous music creations so they were recorded and treated as inspired, called "prophetic singing." Many lyrics came from words of unknown tongues, a sort of musical glossolalia. Many sounds came from Native American languages and songs of African slaves.

Christie-Murry points out that the revivalist "roots" of the modern-day charismatic movement included not only radical elements of the evangelical revivals and of Wesleyianism, but also the Shakers and the Camisards. One thing that all these have in common is a religious practice and ritual similar to many different mystical religions. In the first American Shaker settlement there were "the charismatic, psychical and spiritualist clairvoyance, telepathy, prophecies, glossolalic singing, dancing and possession by departed spirits." (Christie-Murray 1978: 51-52) This mixture of Spiritism, mysticism and Christianity kept them marginalized from regular Christianity for a while.

An example of this behavior was in 1837 when two girls began to shake and whirl, becoming completely oblivious to their external surroundings. Others would fall to the ground or break out in beautiful unknown songs and tell of being led by angels through heavenly places and of seeing Mother Ann Lee, the founder of the society, but she had died fifty years earlier. Revelations from other departed Shaker leaders were received while in trance-like conditions (Foster 1992: 43-44).

> As heirs both of Quaker and Wesleyan tenets, it is natural to expect that the Shakers would have charismatic leanings... They played a considerable role in the late eighteenth century revivals in Kentucky. Their chiliastic and spiritualistic emphasis lent themselves quite handily to a sort of Pentecostalism. (Schaff 1967: 65-66)

Edward Irving (1792 – 1834)

Meanwhile, in Wales, England, another movement was starting within the Presbyterian Church, which would become the Wales Revival, which would result in the Catholic Apostolic Church. In 1815 the Presbytery of Kirkcaldy licensed Irving. He became very popular such that he had to find a larger church because of his emphasis on prophetic preaching and teaching.

In 1828 he withdrew from the jurisdiction of Presbytery due to charges that he denied the sinlessness of Christ, but equally important to him was the new hope for the church, a renewal of the apostolic gifts of prophecy and healing. He was convinced that these gifts had been quenched in the churches by the lack of faith.

In 1832 the Annan Presbytery withdrew Irving's ordination over his views of the incarnate Christ (a charge of heresy), though by now he had established an independent charismatic church. He was installed as the "Angel" of the group. Irving did not speak in tongues, thus could not be an apostle (therefore was considered inferior). Irvingites believed the gifts were normative, previously withheld for unfaithfulness in the historical churches. "..The Irvingites sought to normalize Acts 2 for every saint and connected tongues to Spirit baptism. They insisted that tongues (and Spirit Baptism) were prerequisite for obtaining the 'grace gifts.'" This became normative in Classic Pentecostalism later, although this is its first recorded appearance in the church. (Hannah 1992: 2:9)

Why is Irving so important to our discussion? Irving became a supernaturalist, a process of altering stories of historical and actual events to describe their supernatural elements. The unusual manifestations within Protestant churches gave some credibility to the movement, though it eventually was rejected and split off into a sect-like denomination.

> "The beliefs and experiences of the various branches of the contemporary Pentecostal Churches are so similar to those of Irving and his followers that one might suspect that they had been handed down by word of mouth or rediscovered like some Deuteronomy of the Spirit." (Strachan 1973: 19)

Mormons or Latter Day Saints

In the Americas, Joseph Smith (1805—1844) was exposed to the Second Great Awakening (1800-1830s) in the Kentucky-Ohio region and the Restorationists, who sought to restore primitive Christianity to the nation, which gave rise to America's new form of religious expression, the camp meetings. It was in a camp meeting that Smith was exposed to the glossolalia, prophecy and heavenly visions, when extempory preaching without preparation became the norm. Many of Smith's immediate family and ancestors experienced numerous visions. Out of these same meetings came the founders of the Seventh-Day Adventists, Campbellitism or the Church of Christ (believing baptism is essential for salvation).

Mixed with this emotional religious expression were elements of folk religion, including seer stones, which could reflect revelations from God or reveal water sources or buried treasure. This was interpreted as the contemporary Urim and Thummim (Ex 28:30; Lev 8:8).

The Mormons, founded by Joseph Smith (1830), state in the seventh article of their creed that they "believe in the gift of tongues, prophecy, revelation, visions, healing, interpretation of tongues..." Furthermore, Grant states that tongues and their interpretation are "one of the evidences of true faith" (Grant 1976:10-12)

A movement evolves

During the twentieth century the charismatic movement transcended all the previous movements in the history of the Church. Normally, one movement gives birth to the next. With each wave of a movement, the one that follows takes with it something of the previous one. It is important to see the development of the unique doctrines and concepts that produced the Charismatic Movement of today. We will briefly examine the following transitions:

Leader or Movement	Emphasis	Dates
John Wesley--	Methodism	(1703-1791)
Charles Finney--	Revivalism	(1792-1875)
The Holiness Movement --	Baptism of Spirit	(1850)
The Pentecostal Movement (1st Wave)	Tongues	(1900)
The Charismatic Movement (2nd Wave)	Tongues	(1959)
The Catholic Charismatic Movement	Tongues for Catholics	(1967)
The Power Movement (3rd Wave)	Healing	(1981)

The Leaders Who Formed the Holiness—Pentecostal—Charismatic Movements and What They Taught

The teaching that caused the birth of the Holiness movement began in England with the ministry of John Wesley in the mid-1700s. It is impossible to understand the Pentecostal/charismatic Movement without knowing the roots of Methodism, Wesleyanism in England and how Finney, in the United States, took the teachings of Wesley to form the movement called The Holiness Movement.

Methodism is the most important of the modern traditions for the student of Pentecostal origins to understand, for eighteenth-century Methodism is the mother of the nineteenth-century American holiness movement, which, in turn, bore twentieth-century Pentecostalism. Pentecostalism is primitive Methodism's extended incarnation. 'The Pentecostal Movement,' concluded a Jesuit student of Pentecostalism in Latin America, 'is Methodism brought to its ultimate consequences.'" (Bruner 1970: 37)

John Wesley (1703 – 1791)

John Wesley studied at Oxford (England) and was ordained as an Anglican priest in 1728. While in college he formed a Holy Club with strict rules of conduct. Later he served in the United States as a missionary in Georgia (1735-1738), but even so, he did not know the Lord. Aboard ship, crossing the Atlantic to return to his country after a difficult time on the mission field, he met some Moravian missionaries from Germany who spoke to him about a personal relationship with Christ. After arriving in England, he traveled to Germany and, with the help of Peter Bohler of the Moravian Church, there received a personal salvation encounter. Later he was introduced to open air preaching by George Whitefield.

The other influence in the life of Wesley was his readings. He read extensively, especially the works of mystics like Thomas A. Kempis and Jeremy Taylor whose books emphasized "the holiness of the heart and life."

It is an interesting fact that Wesley's childhood was steeped in the Mystics. His parents were great fans of the mystical writers and Charles and John grew up in a home surrounded by their works.

> Initially John was wholly accepting their teachings, and they made and left a deep impression on him during the formative years of his life. Eventually, he became involved in a protracted internal struggle with mysticism, which never really abated. John Wesley wrote to his brother Samuel on 23rd Nov.1736: 'I think the rock on which I had the nearest made shipwreck of the faith was the writings of the Mystics'. And in this connection he specifically names Johann Tauler and the Spanish Quietist, Miguel de Molinos (Morrison 2007:17).

From 1738 to 1791 Wesley preached an average of 15 times a week, traveling more that 5,000 miles on horseback each year. He wrote 42,000 sermons and more that 50 books. His influence over evangelicals, even today, is impressive (Hannah 1992:3-3).

Wesley saw salvation as a process by which man passes through a series of successive stages, each stage representing a different and higher level. The first level is called the "Prevenient Grace" which means "all the drawings of the Father -- the desires after God, which, if we yield to them, increase more and more." (Collins 1997: 38)

The second level is "Convincing or Prevailing Grace," which consists of repenting of the reliance on one's self, which is followed by trusting in Jesus Christ for the power to live a holy life. According to Wesley, the origin of this "grace" is when one manifests the good works that are necessary to "retain" salvation. It is not clear exactly when salvation is obtained, but it is clear that Wesley's theology mirrored his experience.

Repentance was preached as a requisite for salvation, as was the continual repentance for sanctification. Wesley taught the impossibility of retaining the grace of salvation without progressing toward sanctification, which is the only level where the heart is completely cleansed from sin.

Complete sanctification is the second work of God in the order of salvation. At this level, it was called "perfection," "the second blessing," "the second work of grace" and "complete sanctification." This second level is granted by God to those who seek it and is the primary assurance that you will be saved, because you have gone on to sanctification. God can interrupt this gradual process with an experience of a special "blessing," which transforms the individual's life, empowering him to live a sanctified life. Wesley called this crisis experience the "second work of grace," later to be called the "baptism of the Spirit" by Finney.

Since Wesley's salvation is a progression, it can be lost in any one of the levels. Only those who continue in the progression toward sanctification will ultimately be saved.

Wesley defined "sin" as voluntary or volitional transgression. He said that the sins of omission are not sins that we are accountable for. According to Wesley, this perfection is not absolute, but it keeps growing according to the knowledge of sin in one's life. Perfection is really more like "maturity." The Christian life is an effort to reach higher and higher levels of holiness. One is always growing in salvation or falling away — there is no neutral ground (Hannah 1992: 3-5).

In an era of rationalism and formalism where there was little emphasis on faith and feelings, Wesley's preaching emphasized the emotional experience of salvation, the necessity that one feels his salvation if it is real. In a sense, a person's "experience" became the authority, even more so than the statements of God's Word for any kind of assurance. Truth was determined by one's emotional experience. Wesley fought for years to obtain salvation, and his personal experience determined his theology of conversion.

> Twenty-five years before Wesley's death Methodism had spread to the American colonies, initially through unauthorized lay-preachers and later by seasoned circuit riders appointed in England. ...After the Revolutionary War Methodists severed any visible ties to Anglicanism, forming the Methodist Episcopal Church with Francis Asbury and Thomas Coke as co-superintendents.
> Methodism experienced phenomenal increases in the first half of the nineteenth century through a detailed matrix of circuits, societies, classes and bands presided over by the ceaseless activities of the now-famous circuit riders...to over a million (out of a total population of 20 million) by 1845 (Ibid.: 4:2).

John Wesley was father to much of the 19th century American religious fervor; and one of his spiritual children was the Holiness Movement, which gave rise to the Pentecostalism of the 20th century.

In spite of his wise insights into many Christian truths, the legacy of John Wesley's teaching on sanctification lived on to become a founding principle in Finney's Revivalism, the Holiness Movement and Early Pentecostalism. As the first half of the 19th century progressed, the old-fashioned idea of revival meetings had gradually turned into revivalism, in which a man-centered emotional experience in conversion became the vogue. (See Revivals & Revivalism by Iain Murray, Banner of Truth) (Morrison 2007: 19).

Charles Finney (1972 – 1875)

Charles Finney studied law in New York and was converted at the age of 28. On the same night of his conversion, Finney said that he experienced the "baptism of the Spirit" and immediately began to preach with amazing results.

Some say that his preaching led to the conversion of more than 500,000 people.

Wesley's perspective on sin was weak, emphasizing the voluntary or intentional aspect alone, but Finney's perspective was even weaker. Finney's doctrine negated the influence of the first Adam's sin in our lives, saying that man was completely free to sin or to repent voluntarily of his own will. In his opinion, a man is a sinner because he sins, a belief that opposes the view that a man sins because he is a sinner. He saw salvation as a change from being consecrated to oneself to being consecrated to God. This change, or repentance, became the prerequisite for salvation. That is, man can live without sin because his intentions toward sin have changed. The result, then, would be that a person makes himself righteous by wanting to do righteous things! This is nowhere near what the Bible teaches about justification. It teaches that we are justified solely through faith in the sacrifice of Christ on the cross.

Charles Hodge gave a serious critique of Finney's view of sanctification:

> "Mr. Finney teaches that full or perfect obedience to the moral law is the condition of salvation, now and ever: 'There is not a passage in the Bible, he says, which intimates that men are saved or justified "upon conditions short of personal holiness or a return to full obedience to the moral law." (p. 366) Any man, therefore, conscious of coming short of perfection, has sure evidence that he is not justified.. "As the moral law is the law of nature, it is absurd to suppose that entire obedience to it should not be the unalterable condition of salvation." (p. 364) Regeneration therefore is declared to be "an instantaneous change from entire sinfulness to entire holiness" (p. 500) (Hodge 1857:. 284).

Complete sanctification, according to Finney, is a possibility because he did not accept that the nature of man is completely sinful, except for when he sins voluntarily. Therefore, perseverance in obedience until the end of one's life is a condition for justification. Because of this, complete sanctification is imperative for salvation. This kind of sanctification is defined as the victory over selfishness and is limited only by our knowledge; hence, we are responsible only for that which we know about God's will.

Since Finney sees no inbred sin nature, he, like Wesley, limits sin to personal knowledge of it in actual behavior.

> "We have seen that repentance, as well as faith, is a condition of justification. We shall see that perseverance in obedience to the end of life is also a condition of justification. Since these are prerequisites to justification they imply an innate ability to repent" (Finney 1994:390).

On the contrary, the Bible asserts that the righteousness acceptable to God is not obtained by our works nor can it be, but rather is granted freely through faith in the death of Christ (Romans 3:19-28; Galatians 2:16-21). Finney insisted in obedience to the law, but Christ redeemed us from the curse of the law (Gal. 3:1-4). The law was to condemn us, forcing us to turn to God for mercy and forgiveness. It was our "schoolmaster" ["disciplinarian, or guide"] to lead us to

Chapter 2: *Historical Development*   27

Christ and the only hope of finding a merciful God (Gal 3:24). The next verse states "after that faith is come, we are no longer under a schoolmaster" (3:25).

By the mid-nineteenth century there had been a huge resurgence of interest in Wesley's sanctification teaching largely due to Finney's revivals. Wesley had referred to this experience as "a still higher salvation...immensely greater than that wrought when he was justified." He and his followers urged people to seek this second blessing experience, and as this experience infected other Protestant groups, the body, which resulted came to be known as the 'Holiness Movement' (Morrison 2007: 19).

Finney declared that the only way a believer can continue and reach this sanctification is through receiving the experience of a crisis moment called the "baptism of the Spirit." In this way he created among evangelicals an attitude or imperative for seeking the baptism of the Spirit that would reach across all denominational barriers. To Finney "Spirit baptism," which inaugurates the higher plane of Christian living, is indispensable to fruitful ministry. He clearly separated Christians from sanctification (second work of grace) when he writes: "Another reason why so many persons are not sanctified is this: they do not receive Christ in all his relations, as he is offered in the gospel." (Finney 1994: 369)

These two, Wesley and Finney, saw salvation as the progressive sanctification with almost none of the truths of our position in Christ, and their concepts about sin were weaker than what the Scriptures teach about our sinfulness. Finney did not admit the existence of carnal believers in spite of the evidence in Romans 7 and Galatians 5, which describe believers struggling with sin in their lives and Eph. 4:30 where the believer "grieves" the Spirit because of his disobedience to the previous verses. According to Finney, carnal believers were simply unconverted, lost sinners.

Thus the "second work of grace" of Wesley became the "baptism of the Spirit" of Finney, an indispensable step toward ultimate salvation. This teaching became a major emphasis for nearly all evangelicals in all denominations through the Holiness Movement for nearly a hundred years or more before the Pentecostal Movement began.

From the Holiness Movement to the Pentecostal Movement

Twenty-five years before Wesley's death (1791) Methodism had spread to the American colonies, initially through unauthorized lay-preachers and later by seasoned circuit riders appointed in England. After the Revolutionary War (1775-1783), Methodism severed any visible ties to Anglicanism, forming the Methodist Episcopal Church with Francis Asbury and Thomas Coke as co-superintendents.

"Methodism experienced phenomenal increases in the first half of the nineteenth century through a detailed matrix of circuits, societies, classes and bands presided over by the ceaseless activities of the now-famous circuit riders...to over a million (out of a total population of 20 million) by 1845 had converted to Methodism in only 75 years of evangelism." (Hannah 1992: 4:2)

Wesley's influence is obvious, but Finney's revivals were responsible for much of the growth. Thousands of pastors and missionaries pleaded with God for the experience of the baptism of the Spirit.

People such as A.B. Simpson, R.A. Torrey (first principal of the Moody Bible Institute in Chicago), and Andrew Murray were among some of the more famous names in this movement. Here in the U.K., it found its counterpart in the Keswick 'Higher Life' Movement. Now although there was clearly a 'devotional spirituality' in this movement, its main problem for the progress of the Church was that it emphasized subjective experience over objective truth. And when that happens, we fall straight into mysticism.
At the beginning of the 20th century, the Holiness Movement gave birth to the Pentecostal Movement which emphasized not only the idea of a second blessing or Baptism of the Holy Spirit subsequent to conversion, but also the evidence of speaking in tongues as proof of it. (Morrison 2007:19-20)

As the popularity of Methodism grew, it resulted in a redefinition of the emphasis of sanctification or perfectionism. As a result the morality of the church began to decline by the end of the nineteenth century. Methodists began to preach more and more about political and social problems like slavery, poverty, workers' rights, and women's rights, while focusing less and less on the principles of the Christian life.

Reaction against the secularization of the Methodists motivated the revivals of Finney in the early nineteenth century. The debate changed the discussions about theology into discussions about experiences and pragmatic concepts. A personal encounter with God became the priority in the preaching with little emphasis on defending its doctrine against the coldness of Calvinism. This was the reason for the growth of Armenianism over Calvinism around the world.

The major vehicle for setting aside of theocentric theology for a warm anthropocentric experience was revivalism; as a result, theology was abandoned for pragmatics (both numerical and social), and the gospel was defined in social and moral change.

"While theologically Methodism has exerted the major influence on the Pentecostal movement, methodologically revivalism, particularly American revivalism, has been the most formative influence. The American predecessor and contemporary of Methodism, the Great Awakening, and its unique child, frontier revivalism, radically transformed America's understanding, appropriation, and application of the Christian faith.

Revivalism's particular contribution to American religion and hence to

Chapter 2: Historical Development

Pentecostalism (again a distinctly American product) was the individualizing and emotionalizing of the Christian faith, alterations which, some have argued, became increasingly necessary in an accelerating depersonalized civilization. Pentecostalism is revivalism gone indoors. In Pentecostalism revivalism has moved from its tents and rented halls into organized Christendom and myriad local churches. Inheriting Wesley's experiential theology and revivalism's experiential methodology, Pentecostalism went out into an experience-hungry world and found a response." (Damboriena 1969: 39)

Synan refers to Wesley as "the spiritual and intellectual father of modern Holiness and Pentecostal movements." (Synan 1971: 13) The principle message of the Holiness Movement, which included the National Holiness Church and the majority of the evangelicals, was the baptism of the Spirit and total sanctification. In the last years of the nineteenth century, following the example of Finney's emotional responses, occasionally there were experiences of ecstasy and even—in rare cases—speaking in tongues, but they were not yet associated with the baptism of the Spirit.

There were two factors with respect to the Holiness Movement that contributed to the growth of next movement, Pentecostalism: (1) In the Holiness Movement, there was practically no reference to speaking in tongues. From 1890-1900 there were only a few manifestations, but in general they were suspect. There was almost an anticipation of some true sign that would make the baptism experience complete. (2) In those days the Holiness Movement was worldwide and interdenominational, which created an open platform for an instant global acceptance of Pentecostalism.

The influence of the Holiness Movement spread throughout all the United States and, through missionaries, throughout the entire world, especially by the conferences of evangelist D.L. Moody in 1880 to 1900, and by R. A. Torrey and the Moody Bible Institute. A.B. Simpson and the Christian and Missionary Alliance Church, the Church of God and many others were products of the Holiness Movement. The factor in common was the seeking of the power of God through the baptism of the Spirit and complete sanctification in order to be assured of one's salvation and effectiveness in ministry.

Other evangelical leaders, without intending to, contributed to the development of Pentecostalism. Men like F.B. Meyer, A. J. Gordon, Andrew Murray and John R. Rice, whose books have been translated into many languages, prepared the way for the Pentecostal experience. None of those men spoke in tongues, but, without knowing the consequences of what they were saying, they gave respectability to the concept of the second work of grace and the crisis experience of the baptism of the Spirit, in order to have the power of God in one's life for victory over sin and an effective ministry.

Although there was a "devotional spirituality" within the Holiness Movement, its main problem for the progress of the Church was that it emphasized subjective experience over objective truth. And when that happens, we fall straight into mysticism.

At the beginning of the 20th century, the Holiness Movement gave birth to the Pentecostal Movement which emphasized not only the idea of a second blessing or Baptism of the Holy Spirit subsequent to conversion, but also the evidence of speaking in tongues as proof of it. (Morrison 2007: 9-20)

The Origin of the Pentecostal Experience (1901)

At the beginning of the twentieth century the largest denomination among the evangelicals was the Methodist church, but it gradually became cold and formal during a period of about one hundred years as a result of the infiltration of liberal teachers who did not believe the Bible, but were more interested in social change and academic credibility. Some of their groups sought the experiences of Wesley and Finney. Some of them also practiced healings.

At a small nondenominational Holiness Bible Institute in Kansas during a 1900 New Year's Eve vigil, a group of leaders and 18 students were fasting and praying as they sought the baptism of the Spirit. Surprisingly some of them "spoke in tongues," which apparently was the first time that the baptism of the Spirit was directly related to speaking in tongues. They began to say that the "latter rains" of Joel 2 had been fulfilled and the news of this new experience quickly swept through the entire world.

> "It was under his [Charles F. Parham] leadership that the Pentecostal/Charismatic movement began. No single individual was more important to the birth and initial growth of the movement than Parham. ...he married Sara Eleanor Thistlethwaite, a devoted Quaker... Influenced by a number of successful faith healers, Parham's holiness message evolved to include an ever increasing emphasis on divine healing. Eventually, Parham arrived at the belief that the use of medicines was forbidden in the Bible. ...In the summer of 1898, the aspiring evangelist moved his family to Topeka and opened Bethel Healing Home. ...Included in the services that Parham offered were an infirmary, a Bible Institute, an adoption agency, and even an unemployment office. Parham also published a religious periodical, The Apostolic Faith. In only a few years, this would become the world's first Pentecostal journal.
>
> After suffering a nervous breakdown in September, 1899, Parham entered a period of study and personal introspection...In the summer of 1900, Parham took a sabbatical from the healing home to embark on a spiritual odyssey throughout the Northeastern United States.
>
> When [Parham] returned to Topeka...he found that the colleagues he had left in charge of the healing home had staged a religious coup d'etat gaining control of the facility. ...Not deterred...Parham relocated...in a castel-like structure...with thirty-four students, Parham began Bethel Bible College, a Bible school that would emphasize Holy Spirit Baptism. ... All students ...were expected to sell everything they owned and give the proceeds away so each could trust God for daily provisions. From this

Chapter 2: *Historical Development*

humble college, a theology was developed that would change the face of the Christian church forever.... On January 1, 1901, Agnes Nevada Ozman, a thirty-year old student, received the Baptism in the Holy Ghost with the evidence of speaking in a language she did not know... In the days following, Parham and a number of other students received the experience and spoke with tongues.

Most church historians agree that the episode at Stone's Mansion initiated the modern Pentecostal revival. ...The experience at Bethel College was unique. Parham and his students reached the theological conclusion that speaking in other tongues was the scriptural evidence of the Holy Spirit Baptism. Earlier, tongues had been viewed as a demonstration of the Sprit similar to weeping, shouting, or shaking. Parham's group received the Baptism with evidential tongues while earnestly seeking the experience. ...Parham taught that those who did not speak in tongues had never received the fullness of the Holy Spirit.

Parham moved his entire enterprise to Houston and opened another Bible College...providing ten weeks of intensive Pentecostal indoctrination. William Joseph Seymour, a Black holiness evangelist, became one of Parham's early students. Because Parham was a strict segregationist, Seymour was not allowed in the room with the white brethren. Parham, nevertheless, accommodated him by leaving the door open so that he could hear the Apostolic Faith message from the hallway. After only five weeks in Parham's classes, Seymour received a call to pastor in Los Angeles, California [at the Azusa Street Mission]. Even though he had not received the Baptism in the Holy Ghost, Seymour was convinced of the reality of this "third blessing." The rest is history (Martin 1997: 14-18).

From Los Angeles Azusa Street revival led by Seymour, the Pentecostal experience spread throughout all the United States and overseas quickly. "Seekers travailed in prayer for the baptism with the Holy Spirit, an experience they expected would be attested by speaking in tongues." (Blumhofer 2006: 59) Anderson writes that "...the Azusa Street revival became a catalyst in the emergence of a new kind of Christianity that would transform the global religious landscape in the twentieth century." (Anderson 2007:9)

"Missionaries from Azusa Street were circling the globe by 1907 with their new message of spiritual power. It has been estimated that this revival movement reached twenty-five nations within two years (Anderson, 2007, p. 9).

The Assemblies of God were organized in 1914 and soon became the largest Pentecostal denomination. During the first 60 years, the Pentecostals were generally considered a little peculiar, but were generally accepted as evangelicals. Even though they put abnormal emphasis on speaking in tongues and healings, their doctrine was basically evangelical.

"...The 'Pentecostal movement' burst forth in 1906 amid unpromising circumstances in a run-down section of Los Angeles. Led by an

African-American preacher with no theological education, its first adherents were poor domestic servants, janitors, and day workers -- black and white -- who had the audacity to claim that a new Pentecost was happening, the New Jerusalem was coming soon, and that they were its designated heralds and grateful first fruits." (Cox 1995: 6)

The Transition to the Pentecostal Movement

The original leaders of this new movement belonged to the Holiness Movement and now had the experience that demonstrated their entry into this higher level of the Christian Life. The news traveled through the churches of the Holiness Movement, convincing many that the evidence of tongues was confirmed to be the "crisis" of the baptism of the Spirit. The transfer was so complete that many of the "Holiness" churches changed their names to "Pentecostal" or "Pentecostal Holiness" churches. For this reason, in just a few years, the tongues-speaking experience created the Pentecostal Movement, especially as many of the Holiness Movement separated themselves from the strange activities of the new movement, like tongue-speaking and rolling in the aisles in a uncontrollable state and other characteristics of the earlier Shaker movement.

In spite of its unusual practices an example of the movement's growth has been phenomenal. In effect, the Pentecostal churches worldwide continue to multiply more rapidly than any other church or denomination.

The Growth of Pentecostalism:

1900:   981,000 Second Blessing Holiness believers
1970: 72,223,000 Pentecostals
2005: 588,502,000 Pentecostal/charismatics
2025: 798,320,000 projected Pentecostal/charismatics (McClung 2006: 35)

The movement has suffered many divisions, caused as much by personality differences and individual inhibitions as by doctrinal issues. Today it is often difficult to define what they believe because of the great variety in their teachings, but there does exist a continuity with respect to the doctrines of the baptism of the Spirit, tongues, healings and the emphasis on the second coming of Christ—the four aspects of the "four square" gospel.

The Pentecostal Movement Produced the Charismatic Movement

In 1960 an event occurred that amplified the Pentecostal Movement forever. A rector of St. Mark's Episcopal parish in Van Nuys, California, Dennis Bennett, experienced speaking in tongues (April 3, 1960). By this time most of the non-Pentecostal churches avoided close contact with the Pentecostal churches for fear of loosing members to this emotional church style. The experience of Dennis

Bennett broke the barrier between the denominations and Pentecostalism. This led to a new wave of participants focusing on the "baptism of the Spirit" accompanied by speaking in tongues, one which invaded churches of many, if not all, denominations. The Pentecostal experience became trans-denominational, thus giving birth to the "Charismatics." The term was coined by H. Bredesen and J. Stone in 1963 to describe a growing trend that later developed in three separate sectors: mainline Charismatic Protestant churches from 1950's, Roman Catholic Charismatic Churches from 1967 and independent Charismatic churches from the late 1960s (Kurian 2001).

The Movement continued adapting itself and evolving through various denominations, including the Roman Catholics, resulting in a variety of forms of expression and doctrines which were not based on an absolute foundation which could be easily analyzed.

> Cardinal Suenens found hope for the future of the Church in a new movement stressing personal Christianity, the Catholic Charismatic Renewal. Leaders traced its beginnings to the spring of 1966 when two laymen on the faculty of Duquesne University, Pittsburgh, Pennsylvania, realized they lacked the power of the early Christians to proclaim the gospel. They gave themselves to prayer. They shared their concern with others on the faculty. Then, in August, 1966, two young men in attendance at the National Cursillo Convention (a Catholic renewal movement born in Europe in the late 1940s) introduced into this circle a book that had intrigued them: Protestant David Wilkerson's The Cross and the Switchblade. After personal contacts with Protestant Charismatics in the Pittsburgh area, several Duquesne faculty members received the Pentecostal baptism, marked by speaking in tongues. By the middle of February, 1967, at what historians of the movement call "the Duquesne weekend," the experience had come to a group of students and faculty on a wider scale (Shelley 1995: 459).

It is hard to imagine how quickly the movement took hold around the world. The world was set up for such a movement, but the continued growth, taking on a life of its own, multifaceted and undirected, has touched every corner of the world. Key dates in the development of the contemporary Pentecostal/charismatic movement:

1887: Christian and Missionary Alliance founded by A. B. Simpson to promote the "fourfold gospel."
1901: Revival in Topeka, Kansas, led by Charles Parham, Agnes Ozman speaks in tongues.
1906-1909: Azusa Street revival becomes global under William J. Seymour
1914: Assemblies of God formed under E.N. Bell in Hot Springs, Arkansas.
1927 International Church of the Foursquare Gospel begun by Aimee Semple McPherson in Los Angeles.
1942: American Pentecostal churches accepted as charter member of the

National Association of Evangelicals
1945: Latter Rains Movement began with William Branham and Oral Roberts began a divine healing movement teaching Restorationism, Fivefold Ministry (Eph 4:11), Laying on of the hands, Prophecy, Recovery of True Worship, Immortalization of the Saints and the Unity of the Faith before Christ returns.
1947: First Pentecostal World Conference is held
1960: Episcopalian Dennis Bennett speaks in tongues in Van Nuys, California. Neo-Pentecostal movement begins.
1967: Catholic charismatic renewal begins at the "Duquesne Weekend" in Pittsburg, Pennsylvania.
1973: Trinity Broadcasting Network cofounded by Paul Crouch and Jim Baker.
1975: Charisma magazine begins publication.
1981: "Third wave" of Pentecostal renewal begins a Fuller Theological Seminary under John Wimber.
1994: The "Toronto Blessing" begins at the Toronto Airport Vineyard Church
1994: Racial reconciliation at the "Memphis Miracle" leads to the founding of a new diverse organization, Pentecostal and Charismatic Churches of North America (McClung 2006: 32-33).

Reasons given for the growth of the Charismatic Movement

Without a doubt the Charismatic Movement is growing more rapidly than all the rest of the evangelical groups put together, assuming that the statistics are valid. In Latin America alone there are more than 200,000 charismatic churches with pastors who do not have academic preparation, rather depending on revelation and prophecy. If the contemporary house church movement pastors were included, this number would pass a million. Some who have studied this phenomenon have come to the conclusion that there are three principle reasons for this growth.

(1) The dead condition of the majority of Evangelical churches
Dead churches are the result of humanistic philosophies and the social gospel of changing society, taught in place of true biblical teachings. In order to seem valid and up-to-date in the twentieth century, many pastors accepted and taught that God "created" the world through evolution, that the Scriptures are not inspired but have acquired that characteristic by the faith of the individual, and that to believe in a divine Christ is not necessary. As a result, formalism and ritualism have made the church to be little more than a social club. Even fundamentalist churches have been infected with the symptoms of a dead church.

These dead churches fall into two categories:
(a) Churches with dead doctrines. A church with dead doctrines teaches

Chapter 2: Historical Development

salvation is obtained through baptism or sprinkling, confession to a priest for forgiveness and following certain rites in order to experience communion and to have hope of going to heaven. These dead doctrines negate that salvation is by the grace of God and obligate people to faithfully follow their rites and ceremonies. Liberal denominations among Protestants, false sects and Roman Catholics fall into this category.

(b) *Churches with dead practices.* These are churches that teach that salvation is by grace, but do not win souls, witness or grow numerically. Their focus tends toward social, worship, moral and political issues to the neglect of clear biblical teaching. The believers who attend these churches receive little spiritual nourishment in the meetings, have little motivation to serve the Lord and become accustomed to great spectatorism, formalism and legalism. Sooner or later they begin to look for something else to satisfy their spiritual hunger.

(2) The promise of joy and power in the Christian life.

The love that is notable among the Charismatics is frequently in contrast with the bitterness, jealousy, critical spirit and in-fighting that has characterized many among the Fundamentalist Evangelicals. How embarrassing! Because of this simple fact, many Evangelical believers are converting to charismatic churches.

Another failure common among many of the Fundamental and Evangelical churches is the absence of any teaching about the Holy Spirit much less practical ways to become a victorious Christian beyond coming to church, tithing, and witnessing. Many church leaders are afraid to touch the theme of the Holy Spirit for fear of alienating church followers, thus leaving believers to feel a deep void which, they are told, only the "baptism of the Spirit" will fill. This takes us to the third reason for the growth of the Charismatic churches.

(3) The declaration of revival or the renovation by the Holy Spirit

It is declared that the renovation of the Spirit has been ignored in the Church for centuries and has only been rediscovered and experienced through the baptism of the Spirit, along with the evidence of speaking in tongues. This causes the followers to feel that they are in the center of what God is doing today. Other people feel attracted because they heard about or saw some miracle or other supernatural phenomenon. The emphasis on being part of a genuine apostolic church with signs and wonders like those of the apostles becomes very tempting.

It has been a tactic of the Roman Catholic Church, the Spiritists, non-Christian sects that emphasize healing, (Mormons, and Adventists) to entice people to try the truth of their claims by experiencing miracles. This approach has become the "calling card" of the Charismatics as well. This does not mean that miracles do not occur among other Evangelical groups, but these groups tend to exploit them. They declare that they are experiencing the power of the Spirit as in the days of the apostles by manifesting especially the two signs of tongues and healing. There are other signs (gift of knowledge, swooning or slaying in the Spirit and different kinds of miracles), but the main ones are tongues and healing.

How wonderful it would be if all churches (1) taught and believed the true doctrines through the exposition of the Scriptures, (2) evidenced joy and victory in the lives of the believers, and (3) communicated a revival of the power of the Spirit, especially in evangelism and in the manifestation of the genuine fruit of the Spirit (Galatians 5:22-23) in lives transformed by Christ. If the members of churches were to live biblical lives, they would not need anything more attractive.

The observations of the "revival" of Azusa Street as recorded by the newspapers created such curiosity that thousands went to see this new phenomenon.

> The Los Angeles Times initially reported the 1906 revival with headlines such as "Weird Babel of Tongues--New Sect of Fanatics is Breaking Loose -- Wild Scene Last Night on Azusa Street -- Gurgle of Wordless Talk by a Sister." Those present were "breathing strange utterances and mouthing a creed which it would seem no sane mortal could understand...devotees of the weird doctrine practice the most fanatical rites, preach the wildest theories and work themselves into a state of mad excitement in their peculiar zeal...pandemonium breaks loose, and the bounds of reason are passed by those who are 'filled with the Spirit,' whatever that may be." (Jenkins 2000: 65)

Since the foundation for this massive movement began and depends upon their concept of the baptism or filling of the Spirit, our study must begin with this doctrine. What does the Bible tell us of the baptism? Can we reach sanctification if we could experience the baptism? Remember: if there are two opposite view on any doctrine, only one can be true; the other must be in error. Any ideas built upon erroneous concepts must likewise be questioned. Thus, the very foundation of the Movement must be examined carefully.

CHAPTER 3

The Baptism of the Spirit

CHAPTER 3: *Gifts for Today*

In spite of the tremendous growth worldwide, we must evaluate the Charismatic Movement in the light of the Scriptures. If its foundational teachings are biblical, we should embrace it; however, if their biblical teachings do not reflect the meaning of the Scripture, we have no other alternative than correct or to reject it. Certain aspects of the movement are still being developed, especially in the areas of worship, spiritual warfare and the redefinition of some of the spiritual gifts, but the basic foundation of the movement has been its concept of the baptism of the Spirit. In this teaching nearly every other doctrine finds its roots. Without exception every Pentecostal and Charismatic writer, leader, teacher, etc., agree that the baptism of the Spirit is essential to the Christian life, but they may not agree on how to receive it. "There appears to be as many suggested conditions for the reception of the baptism in the Holy Spirit as there are, in fact, advocates of the doctrine." (Bruner, 1970, p. 92)

The focus of the baptism of the Spirit begins in the teachings of John Wesley. With respect to this doctrine there is little difference in the interpretation among the different branches of the Pentecostal/charismatic movement. It is essentially the basis of the movement.

Three Viewpoints

Among the Evangelical churches there are two distinct teachings about the baptism of the Spirit.

(1) The baptism of the Spirit is a recurring and perpetual experience after salvation, which must happen in order for the believer to have the power necessary to be holy or reach sanctification in the Christian life.

(2) The baptism with the Spirit, which happens once and with lasting effect, is an essential part of the operation of Christ in every believer's salvation. This view holds that the baptism is different from the filling of the Spirit, and that the gifts of the Spirit are neither signs of the baptism nor of the filling.

(3) Some Charismatics believe that the gift of the Holy Spirit is given to all Christians' (similar to #2), occurring with the experience of salvation. Such Charismatics claim that the gifts of the Holy Spirit -- that is, exercising spiritual power such as speaking in tongues or prophesying, are evidences of a release of the Holy Spirit's power rather than the baptism itself with the Holy Spirit (*The New International Dictionary of Pentecostal and Charismatic Movements* 2001: 465).

Which of the three is biblical? Since they are contradictory, all of them cannot be correct.

The teaching of the Pentecostal/charismatic Movement is generally the first view that the baptism of the Spirit is different from salvation, occurring after salvation with the purpose of preparing the person with spiritual power

CHAPTER 3: *The Baptism of the Spirit*

to overcome sin and, some add, to do supernatural things.

One author stated, "The baptism of the Spirit is the second encounter with God (the first is in conversion) when the believer begins to receive *supernatural power* from the Spirit." [italics mine] (Basham 1969: 10) Therefore, in accordance with this view, the believer has the indwelling of the Spirit at his conversion, but he does not have or experience the power of the Spirit yet.

They teach the regeneration occurs at salvation, while sanctification and power in one's life are possible only through a second work of the Spirit called the "baptism of the Spirit." Some go further and teach that, in salvation, one receives the Spirit of Christ, but in the baptism of the Spirit, he receives the Holy Spirit.

The Apostolic Assemblies of Christ do not believe that all Christians receive the Holy Spirit at the time of their conversion or water baptism, but later when they experience the Baptism in the Spirit.

The importance given to the baptism of the Spirit in the Charismatic Movement is evident in this declaration: "Upon receiving the baptism of the Holy Spirit and showing adequate evidence, the individual is immediately prepared to receive any and all of the nine gifts of the Spirit enumerated in 1 Corinthians 12:8-10." (Dalton 1945: 106)

Historical Beginnings

When the Revivalism of Finney absorbed Wesley's second work of grace as a necessity to conquer sin, the Holiness movement was born. The quest for holiness or "higher ground" could only be attained by the Baptism of the Spirit according to Finney. To him, "Baptism," which inaugurates the higher plane of Christian living, is indispensable to fruitful ministry. He clearly separated Christians from sanctification (second work) when he writes: "Another reason why so many persons are not sanctified is this: they do not receive Christ in all his relations, as he is offered in the gospel." (Finney 1994: 369)

The Holiness Movement of the nineteenth century generally set believers on a quest for the baptism of the Spirit, which would give them the power to be holy or sanctified. Much of the terminology that has become common in the churches is due to a key player in this development named Phoebe Palmer. "While the holiness movement always regarded John Wesley as its great authority the movement owes many of its distinctive ideas and practices to Phoebe Palmer's "altar phraseology." While Wesley saw sanctification in an enduring process, Palmer emphasized a sudden crisis accompanied by emotional exuberance."(Hannah 1992: 4:5) The "altar phraseology" referred to Paul's figure of placing oneself on an "altar" as a "living sacrifice" to represent complete consecration to Christ (from Romans 12:1). The altar is to sanctify the gift. Thus whoever consciously committed himself fully to Christ, "all on the altar is laid," might at that moment believe he was sanctified by faith. This message became the theme of Methodist revivalism and eventually in every major denomination.

Following the Civil War (1865) American Methodism was given a death-blow through four characteristics of the next fifty years: (1) The secularism of society in general, (2) the influence of Higher Criticism eroded confidence in the Scripture's authenticity, (3) the influence of Darwin's "Origin of the Species" and (4) the rise of the social gospel which declared the old gospel preaching was out of place or irrelevant. This "liberalism" motivated new groups to voice their call for repentance and power for victory through the Baptism of the Spirit.

In various parts of the States revival meetings saw special phenomena occurring such as occasional speaking in tongues, falling prostrate, shaking, jerking and other unusual manifestations. These were seen by some as the reality of the divine presence in contrast to growing skepticism in liberal churches. However, there was no relationship yet between the Baptism in Spirit and speaking in tongues. As the movement continued to develop, the Spirit-baptism terminology became common in most denominational meetings. Leaders, such as R. A. Torrey, D. L. Moody, A. B. Simpson, J. W. Chapman and most of the itinerating evangelists unwittingly gave credence to the extreme element of the holiness movement by admonishing their followers to seek the Baptism of the Spirit for power, sanctification and fruitfulness.

Years before the identity of the Baptism of the Spirit with speaking in tongues, several groups split off from the Methodist to form the Nazarene Church, Pilgrim Holiness Church, and the Church of God (1880-1890) in their quest for holiness and faithfulness to the Wesleyan doctrines.

When error exists in any movement, it manifests itself in the fundamental doctrine. Since the primary emphasis of the Pentecostal doctrine is on the baptism in the Spirit, our analysis must begin there. In Article 8 of the "Declaration of the Fundamental Principles and Truths," as given by the General Council of the Assemblies of God, says:

> "The physical sign of speaking in tongues testifies to the baptism of believers in the Holy Spirit initially while the Spirit of God gives them speech (Acts 2:4). Speaking in tongues is, in this case, the same in its essence as the gift of tongues (1Cor. 12:4-10, 28), but different in purpose and use." (Dalton 1945: 81)

According to this teaching, the benefits of the experience after conversion are the following: a permanent, personal and complete indwelling of the Holy Spirit, which gives power to live the sanctified Christian life, the manifestation of the gifts (especially speaking in tongues), and effective fruit-bearing in serving Christ. If this were so, who would not want it? The question is, what does the Scripture say? The purpose of this chapter is to clarify the teachings about the baptism in the Spirit and to examine the meaning of

CHAPTER 3: *The Baptism of the Spirit*

the Scriptural texts. Later the issue of tongues and other miracle gifts will be analyzed. The importance of the meaning, time, medium and purpose of the baptism in the Spirit will be made clear, as well as its three distinct functions.

Biblical References to the Baptism in the Spirit

One would think that if Spirit Baptism were so critical to the Christian Life there would be ample clarity of this teaching. However, in each of the gospels there is only a single reference to the baptism of the Spirit (Mathew 3:11; Mark 1:8, Luke 3:6; John 1:33) always with a future reference. On comparing these references, we find that all four are referring to the same event, which occurred in the beginning of Jesus' ministry. In each one the declaration is, "He will baptize you in the Holy Spirit." Mathew and Luke add, "… and fire." These references anticipated a historic and definite event. In the Bible there is no evidence that the work of the baptism in the Spirit had occurred neither in the Old Testament nor during the entire earthly ministry of Jesus.

It should be noted that the reference to the Baptism of the Spirit is a primary misconception that has spun off a number of other errors. Being careless with the use of a single preposition can lead to mistaken theology. MacArthur states the issue this way:

"The term used often by Charismatics, the baptism of the Holy Spirit, appears nowhere in Scripture. In fact, there is no place in the Bible where the Holy Spirit does the baptizing….Always the Scripture describes Christ as the baptizer; the baptizer is never the Holy Spirit. Charismatic believers often say, "We have had the baptism of the Holy Spirit," and by that they think that the Holy Spirit has done something to them. They may admit that they were baptized by Christ at conversion, but they will insist that the "baptism of the Spirit" came later, after they earnestly sought it. But…the Spirit does no baptizing. The Spirit is the element of baptism. The baptizer is Christ. Just as John was the baptizer using water, Christ is the baptizer who baptizes us into His body with the Spirit of God." (MacArthur 1978: 122-123)

The mention of the baptism in the Spirit in the Gospels and early in Acts refers to a promised baptism, and one of these references (Acts 11:16) states that the promise was already fulfilled, that the Gentiles had received the same promised Spirit baptism that the Jews had received years before at Pentecost (11:17). In no occasion is there an explication of these baptisms, only the declaration that the promise of the Spirit was coming and then a statement several years later that it had been fulfilled. For this reason it would be risky to attempt to extract from these verses an explanation of the nature and purpose of the baptism in the Spirit.

The principal objective of the portion of the New Testament which contains the Gospels and Acts is to present the history of the early Church, not to specifically teach doctrine. For example, Acts 2:42 says that the believers persevered and devoted themselves to the doctrine of the apostles. It never specifies what that doctrine was or what they taught. Acts does not have a record of their teachings, only a few of their public sermons before incredulous Jews and few times before Gentiles (i.e., Athens, Felix and Festus). In order to know what the apostles taught, it is necessary to look at the teaching epistles of Paul and Peter. In the same manner and for the same reasons, we must go to these epistles to find the teaching and meaning of the baptism in the Spirit.

Throughout the rest of the New Testament there are only three references to the baptism in the Spirit, and in each one the objective is to explain its meaning. The three references are 1 Corinthians 12:13, Romans 6:3 and Galatians 3:27. In each place we learn a little more about the nature of the baptism.

The Four Aspects of the Baptism

To begin, it is indispensable to understand how certain scriptural terms were used during the time of the apostles. The word baptize is a transliteration, using the same letters from the Greek word, *baptizo*. During the time of the Classics (600-200 B.C.) the people spoke of a ship being baptized if it sunk. It came to mean "anything submerged," thus carrying the idea of immersion. Another use of the word is to introduce or submerge a person into new surroundings, to radically change his condition and relations. In this way the word came to mean, "being put into something." Thayer gives the definition "to dip repeatedly, to immerge, submerge (of vessels sunk) or immerse into something." (Thayer, 1889, 2000, p. 948) It can also mean to "dye" or to "be totally saturated with" (TDNT) . The result being that the object "baptized" becomes totally a part of or fused together with the new environment.

In the three verses in the Epistles, which treat the theme of baptism, we discover the following areas of focus:

Union or unity through baptism in the Spirit

"For by one Spirit we were all baptized into one body, whether Jews or Greeks, whether slaves or free, and we were all made to drink of one Spirit." 1 Corinthians 12:13 NAU

Through the operation of the Spirit in baptism, the sinner becomes baptized into or put into Christ (1 Corinthians 12:13), thus made into an inseparable union and becomes an intimate part of Christ and such that sinners become "partakers of the divine nature" (1 Peter 1:4NKJ). After the baptism in the Spirit, the believer has a relation of corporate union with

CHAPTER 3: *The Baptism of the Spirit*

Christ. This union is not superficial, mystical, physical or theoretical. It is spiritual; that is to say, a union formed between every believer and the Spirit of God that is real, not imaginary. We are only "in Christ" because Christ joined us to Himself by putting His Spirit within us. Part of Christ is now part of the believer. There are about 90 verses in the NT that use the phrase "in Christ" and an additional 89 verses (NKJ) that refer to this union as "in Him." It is the essence of salvation. The only way to be united to Christ is through having received Spirit baptism. MacArthur puts it this way:

> The body possesses an organic unity. There is a common life principle that brings all of its diversity together so that it becomes a whole, a unit. And Paul realized that the church is no different. The basic intrinsic definition of the church is that it is one organic whole, a plurality of members with a common life principle. And in that plurality of members there is only one kind of Christian. The body of Christ does not possess two or more brands of Christian, some with more of the Holy Spirit than others. We are all members of the body of Christ. We are all a part of the organic whole through which pulses the very lifeblood of Christ Himself (*Ibid.*: 121).

The great emphasis about salvation in the New Testament is the new relation with Christ in the sense that we are part of His Body. We are not just friends or acquaintance with God. Christ is not in a compartment in our heart with a door where He can come and go. In Ephesians 3:6, Paul said that we are the "dwelling place of God in the Holy Spirit." He is part of us just as we are part of Him. So we are literally united with Christ through His Spirit, the Holy Spirit.

Through this union with Christ all the benefits of salvation are available to us. His righteousness becomes our righteousness; His sanctification becomes ours, His glorification becomes ours, and His death, burial and resurrection are ours as well (Romans 6:3). Without this union through Spirit baptism it would be impossible to be saved, because we must personally participate in a death-payment for sins (Rom 6:23) in order for our sin to be forgiven. Therefore, it is impossible to be in Christ and not have the Holy Spirit with all His power living in us from the moment we are saved. It is nonsense to think that the Holy Spirit only partially indwells us at salvation or that He is there, but powerless, until a second work of grace occurs. As someone aptly said, "We do not need more of the Spirit; He needs more of us." For this to occur we need to die to ourselves (John 12:24; Rom 8:13).

Secondly, our union in the Spirit from the moment of salvation brings a unity with other believers. Ephesians 2:22 and 3:6 say that we are "are being built together for a dwelling place of God in the Spirit" and "fellow heirs and of the same body, and partakers of his promise." Consequently, all believers partake of the Spirit, whom they enjoy equally. Without the presence of the Spirit in all believers, there would be no communion among them.

MacArthur explains,

> "If we take away the concept that Christ is the baptizer and that He uses the Holy Spirit to do the baptizing, we destroy the doctrine of the unity of the body. Why? Because we have some people who aren't "in." Where are they? What kind of limbo is it to be saved but not to be a part of the body of Christ? Is it possible to be a Christian and not a part of Christ?" (*Ibid.*: 124)

All of these relationships and unions are the results of the operation of the baptism in the Spirit. The next question is, "When does this baptism occur in the life of a believer?

Timing of the baptism in the Spirit

The word baptism does not appear in the Old Testament, indicating that it never occurred during that era of the Scriptures. In fact, the first time that it is mentioned in the Bible is in the beginning of Jesus' ministry by John the Baptist (Matthew 3:11). Upon investigating the four Gospels, we do not find any additional reference to the baptism of the Spirit during the entire life of Jesus, except this single reference at the beginning of Jesus' ministry. Consequently, it is obvious that the Spirit was working in those days, but apparently there was no "baptism" in the Spirit, because this work of the Spirit had not yet begun. The Body of believers had not commenced.

The next chronological reference is found three years later in Acts 1:5. According to this passage, the first time the baptism in the Spirit would occur would be "…not many days from now." Apart from this verse, there is only one other mention of the baptism of the Spirit in the whole book of Acts. It occurred in 11:15-16, where Peter made reference to the baptism of the first Gentile converts (Acts 10) as an experience equal to the one that the 120 had "at the beginning," a reference back to the Day of Pentecost. The "beginning" must be related to the event, which occurred a few days after the ascension when Jesus baptized His Church in His Holy Spirit.

Chapter 11 of Acts occurred approximately 10 years after that day of Pentecost. Peter testified before the church in Jerusalem that the same experience of Pentecost happened again, except that this time with a Gentile, Cornelius and his family as they all received the Spirit (Acts 10). Though there was no manifestation of the flames of fire, the manifestation of tongues was obvious. This testimony is important for two reasons. First, Peter marked the definite time of the beginning of the baptism in the Spirit: the day of Pentecost, A.D. 30 Then, in Acts 10, more or less in A.D. 40, the first Gentiles were included as recipients of the baptism. Secondly, it is apparent that no other similar events occurred in that ten-year period after Pentecost to which Peter could compare Cornelius' experience. Surely he would have mentioned a more recent event had there been one. Evidently, then, the events of the Day of Pentecost, 30 AD, were not continually repeated in the churches. The phenomenon happened only a few times in history in order to introduce a new step in God's program for the Church, as the burning bush in Exodus marked the beginning of a new revelation of God speaking to man, but it never occurred again.

If Pentecost marks the beginning of the baptism of the Spirit, then when is the end? Many scholars suggest that it will end with the rapture of the Church (1 Thessalonians 4:7). In 2 Thessalonians 2:6-7, Paul made reference to something, which "detains" the manifestation of the "ministry of iniquity," that is to say, the manifestation of the Antichrist. Paul added: "only He who now restrains will do so until He is taken out of the way…" Whatever "it" is, the personal pronoun "He" indicates a person, a divine Person. The presence of the Spirit in the world, living in the bodies of believers, produces the effect of impeding the full manifestation of "that Wicked one" (verse 8). When the rapture of the Church occurs, all those who posses the Spirit will be taken simultaneously, removing the indwelling of the Spirit out of the world. So then, the Day of Pentecost in 30 AD began the baptism of the Spirit, and the rapture will end it.

Means of the baptism in the Spirit

After seeing the what and the when of the baptism of the Spirit, we must ask how? What is the means for receiving the baptism? It must be clarified that Paul is not discussing water-baptism as a means of receiving the Spirit. This is a reference to spiritual immersion into Christ, with the result that His death becomes our death, His resurrection becomes our resurrection, and His righteousness becomes our righteousness. Without this union through the Holy Spirit, none of these benefits would be ours.

> When the Charismatic insists that there is a second experience to be called the baptism of the Holy Spirit, he is actually redefining the doctrine of salvation. He is saying that salvation doesn't really give us everything that we think it gave us. He is saying that we are still lacking, that we need "something more." (*Ibid.*: 125)

Christenson admits that the believer has the Holy Spirit, but not the full power until the baptism (Christenson 1968: 27). In Galatians 3:2, Paul challenged a problem in the churches: some of them were teaching that the Spirit was received by personal merit or efforts. He asked them, "Did you receive the Spirit through the works of the law or through hearing with faith?" (Galatians 3:2). They were "fools" (verse 1) to think that personal works were necessary in order to receive the Holy Spirit, and some still teach that obedience and faith are necessary to receive the baptism of the Spirit. Paul wrote to the Romans saying, "…if anyone does not have the Spirit of Christ, he does not belong to Him" (Romans 8:9). In other words, if someone does not have the Spirit of Christ, he is not saved. Some people want to make a distinction between the "Spirit of Christ" and the "Holy Spirit," but that distinction does not exist in Scripture and such teaching causes serious problems in the concept of the Trinity.

The Spirit is not something that we can earn or deserve through our efforts. In Acts 11:17 the Spirit is called a "gift." Some may not be conscious or aware that the Spirit dwells within them as in 1 Corinthians 3:16, "Do you not know that you are a temple of God and that the Spirit of God dwells in you?" We receive the Holy Spirit from the moment of our salvation, not when we dedicate our lives to Christ or when we get victory over some sin or when we plead with the Father to give us the Spirit. Receiving the Spirit is by faith in Christ, at the moment of salvation, and not earned by any good works, because it is an essential part of salvation by faith. Nor do we know about it by some mystical feeling or experience. We know it from the clear teaching in God's Word.

It does not require a second act of faith or a special petition. One does not put his faith in Christ for salvation, and later his faith the in the Spirit for power to be victorious. For example, one does not have to exercise a second faith to receive the sealing of the Spirit. It is all-inclusive. When Christ is received, He brings all the fullness of God with Him (Col 1:19; 2:9).

Purpose

Is it true that the baptism in the Spirit serves to give us power in the Christian life? If it were so, then the baptism would enter into conflict with the filling of the Spirit. In fact, they would be synonymous as the Pentecostals teach. Later we will see that they are different works of the Spirit. Through the filling of the Spirit the believer receives power to testify, conviction of sin and disobedience, motivation, enthusiasm to serve and joy for worship. The filling of the Spirit can occur many times and without end, but the baptism of the Spirit happens once, with lasting effect. If the filling of the Spirit is the experience of the believer, which brings power, then what is the purpose of the baptism of the Spirit? There are three purposes.

(1)   To make a habitation for God

In 1 Corinthians 3:16, Paul called the believers the "temple of God," because it is within the physical body that the Spirit dwells. In the Old Testament God dwelt among His people in the Tabernacle and later in the Temple. In those days, God decided to manifest himself in places made by men, but since Pentecost (A.D. 30) God has chosen to manifest Himself only in human bodies of those who put their trust in Him. Paul makes this fact the key to understanding our responsibility to protect His new Temple in 2 Corinthians 6:16, "And what agreement has the temple of God with idols? For you are the temple of the living God."

(2) To unify the believers

The thing that all believers have in common is the presence of the Holy Spirit in their bodies. As a result, all believers have an indirect bodily union with other believers; that is to say, we are joined in the Spirit, and because of this the Spirit unites us all. Physical union in families is a reality because they share the same blood line, but the spiritual family of God share the same Holy Spirit. 1 Corinthians 12:13 describes this mutual experience of all believers as we "were all made to drink of one Spirit." Not only have we been placed into His body, but He has been placed into us (through His Spirit) as well.

In Ephesians 2:21 the "building" is the body of believers, or the Church. It says that the building "being fitted together, grows into a holy temple." These expressions communicate the union, interdependence and intimate interrelation of believers in a local church where they can function together through the Spirit's bonding and enabling.

This interdependence is similar to the cells of a physical body. Each one has independent functions, but it is not useful if it is not interrelated with other cells. They must depend on each other as they are linked together. Each believer possesses the Spirit and certain capacities (gifts), to enable him to be useful to other "cells" (people), thus he is useless to God without being "fitted together" with other believers to form a "dwelling for God in the Spirit." For this reason the local church is vitally important in the New Testament.

(3) To unify the sinner with Christ

The purpose that is even more profound about the baptism in the Spirit is the capacity to unify the sinner with Christ in an inseparable and corporate relation or union. Through the baptism, the believer literally participates in the death, burial and resurrection of Christ, which credited to him exactly as if he himself had died, been buried and resurrected in Christ's perfect righteousness. Because of being part of His body (by sharing the same Spirit), everything that Jesus did is passed through to the believer as if he did it. Our union with Christ is how the payment for our sin, which Jesus made on Calvary, is transferred to our guilty account, leaving us without any sins to be condemned. We are made "acceptable in the Beloved" (Eph 1:6).

The law of God is expressed in Romans 6:23: "For the wages of sin is death..." The only pardon for sin is through a death. This shows us how horrible sin is. The options for the sinner are (1) pay the just penalty yourself of an eternal death or separation from God in Hell, or (2) participate in the only death that God accepts as just payment for man's sin, that of His Son on the cross. He gives us the option.

If we accept His invitation, in the same chapter Paul clarified the purpose of the baptism of the Spirit saying, "Or do you not know that as many of us as were baptized into Christ Jesus were baptized into His death?" (6:3-5). Therefore, the only way to participate in Christ's death, as full and just payment for all our sins, is through the baptism in the Spirit. We have to be "put into, or immersed into" the death of Christ to be a participant in the only acceptable payment for sin. We cannot be saved without this baptism [translation, "being place into something"]. It is this baptism, the baptism in the Spirit that, in effect, transmits to us so great a salvation!

The frustration of wrong teaching is to cause people to seek something that is not there or is not real, or to ask them to seek for something that has already been given to the believer. In either case, God is wounded because His Word is not taken seriously. Such actions can open people up to deception, false experiences and disillusionment. In vain we seek what is already given to us.

CHAPTER 4

The four aspects of the baptism of the Spirit

Chapter 4: *Gifts for Today*

The confusion over the Baptism of the Spirit is two-fold: first, on the one hand the word "baptism" is always assumed to be related to water-baptism, which leads to a doctrine of baptism-for-salvation that some churches teach; and secondly, the failure to distinguish between Spirit-baptism and Spirit-filling in the Christian life has marked the Pentecostal-Charismatic movements. The focus of this chapter will deal with the latter of these two misinterpretations.

One of the errors of John Wesley and the movements that resulted from his teachings was the identification of the baptism of the Spirit with the filling of the Spirit. This means that at salvation there is little power for sanctified living, which can only be acquired after a second blessing, a second work of grace or the baptism of the Spirit. The promise of a deeper life, power-filled life, and victorious life is all contingent on having an additional experience according to the Charismatic teaching. Jack Hayford states, "Holy Spirit baptism occurs after salvation. It is here that the person is 'filled with the Holy Spirit.' This is different from and in addition to the entry into a person's life of the Holy Spirit at conversion." (Hayford, 1996, p. 3)

The motivation and quest for such an experience is understandably high. The question is: can the search for more power from an additional experience with God be justified in Scripture? We established in the last chapter that the baptism of the Spirit is the key element of our salvation experience, then seeking an additional baptism is non-existent or in vain. The real question remains, is the baptism in the Spirit the same thing as the filling of the Spirit? To the charismatic the baptism and the filling are synonymous.

> It is a baptism, a coming upon, a filling and a gift. These terms are synonymous when applied to receiving the fullness of the Holy Ghost. The book of Acts *clearly points out* that speaking in tongues was a practice of those who received the fullness of the Holy Spirit. (Roberts 1966:18) [italic mine]

Perhaps someone would say that the difference between the baptism in the Spirit and the filling of the Spirit is not very important, or "what does it matter if it is called the baptism or the filling?" The confusion is caused precisely by not marking a distinction between these two great doctrines dealing with our relationship to the Holy Spirit and secondly, by the emphasis on the baptism that is occasionally transferred to the filling, which causes an imbalance and misunderstandings.

"To put the concept of the filling of the Spirit in context, there are six references to the filling of the Spirit in Acts (2:4; 4:8, 31; 9:17; 13:9, 52) and two references in the Epistles (Ephesians 3:19; 5:18).

A similar expression is found in Col 1:9, "...filled with the knowledge of His will." The word "filling" is used in various contexts, which always results in the control of the individual's behavior. In Luke 4:28 the audience was "filled with wrath (or rage)" and rose up to kill him (v. 29). In Acts 13:45 the Jews were "filled with envy" so they "opposed the things spoken by Paul." Whatever

Chapter 4: *The four aspects of the baptism of the Spirit*

your heart is filled with motivates your behavior (Matt 12:34, "...out of the abundance of the heart the mouth speaks").

As one studies what the New Testament declares with respect to the baptism and the filling of the Spirit, we find at least four differences:

(1) The baptism in the Spirit occurs once for each person, but the filling of the Spirit is a progressive operation without end.

Since it is true that through the baptism of the Spirit the believer is "put into" Christ, then this has to be an event which occurs only once and for all time in the life of all believers. Once this baptism has happened, the person has been put into Christ and this relationship cannot be changed. "For we were all baptized by one Spirit into one body-- whether Jews or Greeks, slave or free-- and we were all given the one Spirit to drink" (NIV 1 Corinthians 12:13).

It is also an immutable and eternal position into which one is sealed by God (Ephesians 1:13; 4:30). Therefore it is impossible that the baptism of the Spirit could be repeated. One cannot be re-immersed into Christ, or un-immersed out of Christ. The biblical purpose for the baptism of the Spirit is to unite us forever with Christ. Our union with Him in Spirit baptism gives us security of our salvation. Roberts writes in the Conservative Theological Journal:

> After Acts 11 there are no further references to the "baptism with the Holy Spirit." There are no commands to be baptized with the Holy Spirit, nor are there any statements of others being baptized with the Holy Spirit. It appears that the baptism with the Holy Spirit explicitly occurred two times, once upon the Jewish believers in Acts 2 and the second time upon Gentile believers in Acts 10. The implication is that the baptism of the Holy Spirit takes place at conversion, and is not to be expected as some sort of "second blessing." (Roberts 2004: 244)

In contrast, after being placed into Christ through the baptism in the Spirit, the believer should begin to continually experience the filling of the Spirit. Throughout the book of Acts the continual experience of the believers was to be "filled" with the Spirit, who had previously baptized them into Christ. "Let the Holy Spirit fill and control you" (Eph 5:18 NLB). Therefore, the baptism must occur first, after which the filling should continue repeatedly throughout the life of the believer. Obviously it would be impossible to receive the filling of the Spirit before having received the baptism in which the Spirit begins to dwell within every believer.

(2) There is no commandment that deals with being baptized in the Spirit, but there is one regarding being filled with the Spirit.

In the first place, it is impossible to be a believer and not have been baptized in the Spirit, because the only way to be "in Christ" is through the operation of the baptism in the Spirit. For this reason there does not exist a commandment in the New Testament asking the person to seek it. If a person is a believer he already has the baptism. The baptism is one of numerous operations of the Spirit that occur simultaneously with the New Birth of Salvation (sealing, regenerating, anointing, etc.) It is not a question of obedience.

On the other hand, the filling of the Spirit is a daily obligation for every believer. He must live being filled continually by the Spirit because it is a commandment; if he does not do it, he will be walking in disobedience. In Ephesians 5:18, Paul wrote, "And do not be drunk with wine in which is dissipation; but be filled with the Spirit."

If this is a command, it is not something that occurs automatically at salvation; instead, it is something we are responsible to maintain through obedience. The present passive tense of the command "be filled" means a continuous action: be repeatedly and constantly filled with the Spirit. The passive voice of the command means that the action is to be done to you, that is, one must constantly be in a position or action where the Spirit can fill or flow through the believer. This command is not in isolation from the rest of Scripture, but rather it is the combination of the obedience to the other commands while trusting that God will empower you to obey them.

Two chapters earlier Paul included these phrases in the same sentence: Ephesians 3:16 "I pray that according to the wealth of his glory he may grant you to be strengthened with power through his Spirit in the inner person,... 3:17 that Christ may dwell in your hearts through faith;...3:19 so that you may be filled up to all the fullness of God, 3:20 ...according to the power that works in us." Summarizing these verses: The Spirit power that works in the believer is because Christ indwells us through faith with the result of being saturated with fullness of God, which is to say, the power that is actively working in us all. How do we know this for sure? He just said it! We trust His Word.

In the context two acts are contrasted with the connective "but," which introduces a contrast, not a comparison. Under the influence of wine a person looses control of himself, but under the influence of the Spirit the "fruit of the Spirit" is self-control (not unconscious ecstasy) is the distinguishing characteristic.

> Ephesus was a center for the cult of Dionysus (Greek, "Bacchus"), the god of wine. Celebrations in honor of Dionysus emphasized fertility, sex, and intoxication. Intoxication would allow Dionysus to control the body of the worshiper. Thus the worshiper would do the will of the deity. Paul was saying in 5:18, "Don't be filled with the spirit of Dionysus through wine, but be filled with the true and living God by his Spirit." Paul's key illustration of being wise was to be filled with the Spirit for all the behaviors he described in 5:19-6:9. Paul described that fullness in several ways: speaking and singing (5:19), thankfulness (5:20), and submission (5:21) (Hughes 1990: 595).

God's power is given to the believer, not for a mystical encounter with God, but to enable the believer to fulfill the commands of the Christian life as described in the NT. The tense of the verb is important: it is imperative present, progressive and passive. All this suggests that the action must be continuous, habitual, and constantly practiced in harmony with God. Although someone is filled with the Spirit today, this is not sufficient for the rest of his life or even for tomorrow. Just as the manna in the desert had to be renewed each day, so it is necessary that we be filled with the Spirit daily. The filling of yesterday is not sufficient for today. We are under orders to be filled with the Spirit progressively and always.

On the other hand, no one was ever baptized in the Spirit more than once and it was never individually repeated. Only the filling of the Spirit was a repeated action.

(3) The baptism in the Spirit is universal among believers, but the filling is not.

If baptism in the Spirit is essential for salvation, by definition it must be the experience of all believers at the moment they believe. In 1 Corinthians 12:13, Paul made it very clear: "For by one Spirit are we all baptized into one body..." Paul explained that exceptions do not exist; it is not possible for some believers to be baptized in the Spirit and others not to be. However, some children of God can be "carnal" (1 Corinthians 3:1-3) or disobedient, and because of it, they are not being filled with the Spirit.

> Even though Ephesians 5:18 is a command to be filled with the Spirit and there are inferences about conditions necessary for being filled, it is surprising that there is no command in Scripture to pray for the filling of the Spirit. Since the command relates to a right relationship to the Holy Spirit, the conditions governing that relationship must have to do with the filling of the Spirit. There are several commands that relate to a believer's being filled with the Spirit (Enns 1989: 279).

Moreover, it is possible for a believer to be baptized in the Spirit, yet not to be filled with the Spirit. The believer who falls into sin and does not confess it or repent becomes a carnal believer. The New Testament gives us three instructions and a fourth warning with respect to our relationship with the Spirit, who has become an integral part of our new being.

(1) Ephesians 4:30 states, "And grieve not the Holy Spirit of God, whereby ye are sealed unto the day of redemption." The sins we commit cause the Spirit within us to be grieved and diminish His potential fruit-bearing in our lives: love, joy, peace, patience, etc. (Galatians 5:22-23). The text in Ephesians 4:31 states that bitterness, wrath, anger, clamor, and evil speaking can cause the Spirit to be grieved. Thus our disobedience to the commands of the Christian life "hurt, create sorrow, or pain" to the Spirit within us. There can be no joy in the Spirit when He is saddened by our disobedience. It is our responsibility to know what to obey through the study of His Word and consciously make a commitment to

obey the commands, imperatives, follow the principles and examples from His Word, and then He empowers our steps of obedience. We grieve him when we react in anger, bitterness, etc. because we were hurt, offended or disillusioned in relationships or situations that God engineered in order to allow us to demonstrate His enabling power to forgive. This seems to be reactionary.

(2) 1 Thessalonians 5:19 says: "Quench not the Spirit." It appears that quenching the Spirit is a step worse than grieving Him. The verb, sbennumi, means "to suppress, stifle," as "to put out a fire." (Thayer, 2000: 4734) The Spirit desires to produce "joy" (1 Thessalonians 5:16) in our lives as a result of an intimate relationship with God (5:17) and thus an attitude of gratitude in all things (5:18), but if we persist in disobeying the Word, we quench the Spirit's conviction, become insensitive to His inner workings in our spirit, then we lose His fruit and influence in our lives. When we say, "No, I will not forgive so-and-so, in spite of what God commands" (or any other command), then we quench Him on purpose. This action seems to be more intentional which makes it worse.

(3) On the other hand, in a positive focus in Galatians 5:16 we read, "I say then: Walk in the Spirit, and you shall not fulfill the lust of the flesh." The power of the Spirit is an enabling power to walk in obedience.

> "If it is possible to grieve and quench the Spirit, it is equally possible to treat the Spirit with respect, to yield and allow Him to work in our lives. We do this by surrendering our wills, our minds, our bodies, our time, our talents, our treasures - every single area - to the control of the Holy Spirit." (MacArthur 1978: 193)

There is so much satisfaction in "walking" in the Spirit (Psalm 16:11; 42:1-2) that the desires of the flesh are not as much a temptation. In 5:25, Paul amplified the concept saying, "If we live in the Spirit, let us also walk in the Spirit," that is, if our dependence, guidance, direction, purpose, motivation and confidence are deposited in that which the Spirit shows us in His Word, we are walking in the Spirit and in harmony with Him. This action is a cooperative relationship: the more I chose to obey, the more the Spirit enables me to obey.

(4) Duffield adds a fourth command: Lying to the Holy Spirit. When one consecrates anything to the Lord, and then does not follow through on that consecration, he is lying to the Holy Spirit. It may be money, time or service. "If a believer does not intend to be faithful to his promise, he had better not make the consecration in the first place. Peter, in verse four of Acts chapter five, tells Ananias, 'thou hast not lied unto men, but unto God.'" (Duffield 1987: 325)

For these reasons the filling of the Spirit is not universal among all believers—it should be, but, sadly, it is not. It is normal that believers learn how not to grieve the Spirit by avoiding overt sins and practicing how to walk in the Spirit. On the other hand those who continue disobeying and ignoring what the Spirit says in the Word will never be filled with the Spirit or enjoy His benefits in their lives. The Spirit's conviction of disobedience is quenched and His illumination of His Word is ignored. Too many believers are filled with themselves, with selfishness, emotional enjoyments, experiences, entertainment, fantasies and other aspects of the flesh, such that they cannot appreciate the joy of being filled with the Spirit.

Paul was not thinking of filling "up" as much as he was thinking of being filled "through" -- permeated by the Holy Spirit's power.
An obvious (and biblical) example is salt. Put salt on food, and it will permeate everything....You possess the divine salt shaker. All you have to do is allow Him to flavor your life."

What, then, goes wrong? Obviously a lot of believers are not filled with the Spirit. They choose not to let the Holy Spirit permeate their lives. They get preoccupied with themselves, with others, or with things. They succumb to pride, self-centeredness, anger, depression, and a dozen other traps that bring spiritual emptiness." (MacArthur 1978:191-192)

(4) The work of the baptism in the Spirit is not an experience, but the filling is experienced.

The baptism of the Spirit is not necessarily an experience that can be felt when it occurs. At conversion, if a person feels something, it is probably relief because of being pardoned from his sins. However, the fact that a person sometimes feels no emotion does not mean that the salvation is not real, nor is the lack of a feeling indicative that the filling of the Spirit is not occurring. The filling is a calm enabling of the Spirit to do the will of God as revealed in Scriptures.

One author cited 32 different things that occur in us at the moment of our salvation. How could we possibly feel each one of them individually? For example, each believer is sealed by the Spirit at the moment of one's personal salvation (Ephesians 1:13). Did you feel it? Then how do you know that you were sealed? The only answer is that the Bible tells us we were sealed, so we believe it. It is not necessary to feel a promise for it to be real. If we believe and depend on it, then it is real whether we feel something or not.

On the other hand, the filling of the Spirit is a daily experience for the believer, if he is walking in the Spirit (Galatians 5:16). The results of this walk are so satisfying an experience (for example, "love, joy, peace...") that the desires of the flesh do not attract us as much. One does not want to ruin what has meant so much to him.

The Six Results of the Filling of the Spirit

After being placed in Christ (through the baptism of the Spirit), an obedient believer should experience the continual filling of the Spirit if he is walking in obedience to the revealed will of God as expressed in the commands of Scripture. We know that we have received the baptism of the Spirit because the Bible teaches it, not because of what we feel. The next question is, how do we know if we have the filling of the Spirit? The Bible gives us six evidences or signs of the filling of the Spirit. Being filled with the Spirit was required of leaders in the early church (Acts 6:3), and, therefore, it had to be evident to those around them. It may well be that others will recognize the filling of the Spirit in our lives more readily than we would notice it ourselves! J. Vernon McGee wrote:

> What does it mean to be filled with the Holy Spirit? We can find the analogy in the man who is drinking, which is the reason Paul uses it here. The man who is drinking is possessed by the wine. You can tell that a man is drunk. In contrast, it is the Holy Spirit who should be the One to possess the believer. It is a divine intoxication that is to fill that need. This is not an excessive emotionalism but that which furnishes the dynamic for living and for accomplishing something for God. When we are filled by the Holy Spirit, it means that we are controlled by the Holy Spirit (McGee 1998: Eph 5:18).

In the following paragraphs there will be little or no disagreement among theologians of different camps. Both Pentecostals and non-Pentecostals agree that the filling of the Spirit produces each of the following elements. Where there is disagreement is whether these evidences are sufficient to indicate if the person is filled with the Spirit or not.

(1) The fruit of the Spirit in daily life (Galatians 5:22-23)

Paul writes what the Spirit's presence in a life will always produce "love, joy, peace, patience, kindness, goodness, faithfulness, gentleness and self-control." These nine aspects of the fruit of the Spirit are one unit, evident by the word "fruit," which is singular. These are not disciplines or goals for the believer. When a person is filled with the Spirit, the nine aspects will begin to be manifested and evident especially to others. The fruit of the Spirit is a brief description of the character of Jesus. When the fruit is manifested today, others get a sense of the presence of Jesus. This type of growth in the transformation of a believer brings glory to God as His character is demonstrated through our lives. It is living proof that God is real.

In order to manifest the fruit of the Spirit and make it evident as a divine reaction and not merely a human ability, God may allow his children to experience difficult circumstances. We should not be surprised when God puts disagreeable people in our lives so that through the filling of the Spirit we may show His love or the patience to suffer injustice. He will place us in bitter, painful circumstances so that we may demonstrate His joy. When the natural reaction is to lose control in anger, he who is filled with the Spirit will respond

Chapter 4: *The four aspects of the baptism of the Spirit*

with long-suffering or self-control. God is interested more in manifesting His character than in maintaining our personal comfort.

If only half of the nine characteristics are manifested, this does not mean that the person is 50% filled with the Spirit. The "fruit" is singular. Therefore, one is either filled with the Spirit or not. There is no neutral ground. The fruit, however, may be manifested in myriads of ways and not all at the same time.

The Spirit-filled walk implies the practice of all the commands for the Christian. Eph 5:19-6:9 lists some of the attitudes and actions that the Spirit enables in the believer's life. The Spirit-filled person loves to sing (inwardly and outwardly) psalms, hymns, and spiritual songs to the Lord. He gives thanks for everything that happens to him or that he receives. The Spirit-filled person is enabled to be submissive to the needs of others and to the authority of his leaders in various areas of his life. Spirit-filled children are enabled to honor and obey their parents, while parents are enabled to avoid provoking them to anger while disciplining and instructing their children. Spirit-filled servants or employees are enabled to obey their employer, boss or authority, while the employer is enabled to be fair and understanding. This is the beauty of the Spirit-filled life. When the Spirit is quenched or disobeyed, all of this harmony is destroyed and the flesh-filled life ruins all relationships.

(2) The power to testify

The second evidence of the filling of the Spirit is the power to testify. The promise in Acts 1:8 is very specific, "But you shall receive power ... and you shall be witnesses to Me ...." In this case, the manifestation of the power of the Spirit is the transformation from a life opposed to God, or fearful of identifying with Him, to a life empowered with liberty to speak of God to others everywhere. Sin in the life of a Christian can quench this desire, but as he delights in his new bond with Christ he cannot help but share his joy.

This has no relationship with the effectiveness of the testimony, but with the boldness to do it. The gospel itself is the "power of God" as it is proclaimed (Rom 1:18), but the promised power of the Spirit is related to the enabling power to overcome our fears and become a faithful witness. For most people the fear of being criticized or rejected by men is greater than the fear that God might send someone to hell if they do not hear and believe the gospel.

When the flesh controls the life, there is no liberty to speak of the things of God. The person is more preoccupied with what others will think of him than with the importance of communication the message of God to those who need to hear it. The flesh is offended with and ashamed of the Word of God.

In Acts 4:31, the relationship is clear: "...when they had prayed...they were all filled with the Holy Ghost, and they spoke the word of God with boldness." These are sequential or coincidental events. I prefer to see it as coincidental, that is, as they "began to speak" [an ingressive imperfect action], they were filled with the Spirit. The filling coincides with our initiative to be obedient. The manifestation of the filling of the Spirit is the boldness to communicate the Word of God.

(3) The victory over the flesh

In Galatians 5:16, the New Testament says that he who walks or lives in the Spirit should not satisfy [*teteo*: "fulfill, bring to completion, act out"] the desires of the flesh. It is as if he were so satisfied with his communion with the Lord that the desires of the flesh do not compare.

The dative *pneumati* [pneumatic] suggests both origin and instrumentality ("by the Spirit"), and therefore a quality of life that differs from both a nomistic and a libertine lifestyle. The present tense of the imperative *peripateite*, which denotes an exhortation to action in progress, implies that the Galatians were to continue doing what they were already doing, that is, experiencing the presence of the Spirit's working in their lives (cf. 3:3-5) and living by faith (cf. 5:5). So the exhortation to believers of Galatia is for them to continue to live their lives in the new reality of "the Spirit," as they had experienced that reality at their conversion and before listening to the Judaizers, and not in the old existence of "the flesh," which has to do with laws and self-indulgent license (Longenecke 1990: 244).

Jesus said that when the Spirit comes "… He will convict the world of sin, and of righteousness, and of judgment" (John 16:8). This means that wherever the Spirit dwells, He will always convict His host of sin when one is violating commands and principles of Scriptures. The prophet Amos asked this rhetorical question: "Can two walk together, unless they are agreed?" (Amos 3:3).

Anyone who walks with Christ will become increasingly conscious of his sinfulness. This will provoke a humble, broken, repentant or contrite spirit that agrees with the convicting work of the Spirit, then clings to the promise of perpetual cleansing of all sin, continually making us acceptable for His fellowship (1 John 1:9).

Anyone who is practicing secret or open sin, ignoring or quenching the conviction of the Spirit or violating the mandates and principles of Scripture is only faking a spiritual walk with God. If a person delights in sinning without a consciousness of guilt, he may not have the Holy Spirit present in his life at all.

On the other hand, when yielding one's personal rights of a selfish, self-centered lifestyle to the Spirit's control, sin loses its attraction, and the joy of walking with the Spirit replaces the desire of the flesh. Victory over sin, then, is not only a discipline, but is highly motivated by the undeserved graciousness of a Holy God willing to cover our sins and accept our repentant spirit that delights in His convicting presence. The Spirit, then, gives a superior satisfaction. There is nothing like walking in harmony with God.

(4) The manifestation of the gifts of the Spirit

All true Christians are given spiritual gifts, or special capacities to serve others and the Lord being uniquely motivated by the Spirit. These gifts are mentioned in 1 Corinthians 12:4-31, Ephesians 4:11 and Romans 12:6-8. The text of 1 Peter 4:11 categorizes the spiritual gifts into two realms: serving and speaking gifts.

The person who is filled with the Spirit, who testifies of the Lord and is victorious over the flesh, will have a desire and enablement to serve the Lord and others in specific and beneficial ways. He will feel a certain affinity or motivation toward an area of service to meet the needs of others that his gift or a cluster of gifts indicate. For this reason, it is difficult for the believer to discover his spiritual gifts if he is not filled with the Spirit and is not committed to serving the Lord. The gifts will remain dormant until he begins to serve others; in the same way that the filling of the Spirit is useless until the initiative is taken to be obedient to the commands.

When baptism and the filling of the Spirit are confused, this results in the teaching that the baptism of the Spirit is a prerequisite for receiving the spiritual gifts. "Upon receiving the baptism of the Holy Spirit and showing adequate evidence [namely tongues], the individual is immediately prepared to receive any and all of the nine gifts of the Spirit enumerated in 1 Corinthians 12:8-10." (Dalton, 1945, p. 106) Thus according to the Charismatic teaching, anyone who has not had the baptism of the Spirit (and the evidence of speaking in tongues) is not able or "prepared" to receive the other spiritual gifts for service to others. The Scriptures teach quite the contrary. Is everyone else who has not had this experience serving the Lord in the flesh?

On the contrary, the Bible promises that all believers have at least one gift: "To each person the manifestation of the Spirit is given for the benefit of all." (1 Corinthians 12:7 NET; See also 12:11). One of the evidences of the presence of the Spirit is the manifestation of His gifts and desire to serve to others.

(5) Direction in the will of God

The Bible promises special direction for those who have the Spirit. Romans 8:14 says, "For as many as are led by the Spirit of God, they are the sons of God." Being filled with the Spirit allows one to have control of his desires and ambitions and direction in life. The confidence that God has control of our lives and is going to guide us allows us to rest in His guidance. Those who are walking in the Spirit have an inner desire to obey His Word and fulfill His purpose for their lives. Paul wrote, "For it is God who works in you to will and to act according to his good purpose" (Philippians 2:13 NIV). If the Spirit is quenched through selfish disobedience there is a loss in our sense of direction for our lives.

As we have seen, one of the chief ministries of the Spirit is to "convict" us of sin. John wrote, "When he comes, he will convict [*elegcho*: "expose, reprove, show fault"] the world of guilt in regard to sin and righteousness and judgment" (NIV John 16:8). He leads us or guides us chiefly by bringing conviction in our conscience when we plan to deviate from His direction in the revealed Word of God, called the Moral will of God. This means we have to learn His commands that He expects us to practice. There are more than 365 NT commands we are to live by (See www.walkinghisway.com for a daily study of these commands). Jesus said, "if you love Me, keep My commandments" (John 14:15). Most Christians do not know even the Ten Commandments, much less any of the other commands in the NT. Most do not think it important enough to take the Bible seriously.

The sin of unwillingness to trust Christ (John 16:9) and all that He tells us in His Word is met with an inner conviction, a sense of wrongdoing or awareness of having deviated from what we know from Scripture how He wants us to live. This, too, can be quenched and ignored, leaving us to make foolish decisions.

By convicting us of selfish thinking, self-centered ambitions, egotistical desires for acceptance, approval from others, appreciation, and recognition, as well as secret desires to sin in a multitude of ways extending from self-righteous pride to lustful passions, the Holy Spirit seeks to mold us into the likeness of Christ with a mission to share His amazing salvation story with the whole world.

Every decision to obey His commands in Scripture is a step toward spiritual maturity, Spirit empowerment and Christ likeness. This is neither legalistic, nor mystical. It is just simple, practical Christian living led by the Spirit.

(6) Effective prayer life

The result of maintaining an intimate relationship with the Spirit is a meaningful and effective prayer life. According to Romans 8:26-27, "the Spirit helps us in our weakness. We do not know what we ought to pray for, but the Spirit himself intercedes for us..." Our sin causes us to be weak, self-centered and unable to perceive what God wants as we pray. Life is a constant quest to overcome our selfish focus, denial of our reality, and unwillingness to see life as a passing phase to be poured out for others rather than for ourselves.

Evidence of our weakness is seen in our self-centeredness and low priority for others in our prayers. For example, do we pray more for our personal needs of health, things, finances, success, and personal problem solving, than we do our personal maturity, insight into our foolishness that may be responsible for our problems, or how to be focused on others rather than ourselves? When we pray for others, however seldom this may be, do we pray for their physical condition or their spiritual maturity and effectiveness in their ministry? Do we pray for the peoples of the world as Jesus did or do we even know who they are?

Through Him, however, we have the promise of help in our prayers. Perhaps we do not know what we should ask, but the Spirit will illuminate our minds with His concepts and purposes, if we listen.

James 4:3 asserts that the reason why some do not receive what they desire is that they ask in error, "that ye may consume it upon your own lusts." Such persons do not ask according to the guidance of the Spirit, evidently having already quenched His conviction prompting by their greed and selfish interest in what they want for themselves, so they seek to use God to satisfy their own

Chapter 4: *The four aspects of the baptism of the Spirit* 61

selfish desires. The filling of the Spirit permits us to have a sense of what is selfish and contrary to His desires and the Word, thus guiding us to ask for the right things as we desire His will.

The power of God in our lives

The filling of the Spirit is that which produces the power of God in the life of a believer. There are 107 to 140 references in the NT to the power of God, depending on which translation is used in English. The vast majority of these references are focused on the transforming power working in every believer as Paul prays for the believers in Ephesus.

> "…what is the incomparable greatness of his power toward us who believe, as displayed in the exercise of his immense strength. This power he exercised in Christ when he raised him from the dead and seated him at his right hand in the heavenly realms" (Ephesians 1:19-20 NET).

The primary focus of His power is to enable the regeneration of sinners to live godly lives that reflect the character of Jesus. It is not for bragging rights or personal satisfaction. The quest to obtain the power of God has led many to desire an experience that will give them confidence that God is with them and that He is as real today as He was in the day of the apostles. This is like buying a car with a 300 hp engine and wanting to floorboard it every time it is started, just to see if you really have 300 hp. It is there when you need it, but not for showing off.

Without a doubt, the believer has the potential to demonstrate a life filled with the power of God, thereby glorifying Him through manifesting His reality today. Each one can find that power through the understanding of the Word of God interpreted in light of the context of its historical grammatical and cultural setting, then committing his life to practicing daily what is understood. Every step of obedience will require the power of God to obey.

When the work of the Holy Spirit is mentioned in the Scriptures (as in Acts), the filling is mentioned, but not the baptism. In Acts 2 the filling and the baptism occurred simultaneously to these Jewish believers in the Messiah and the author decided to speak only of the filling of the Spirit, which would be the characteristic of the new life of all believers. We know the initial baptism in the Spirit occurred because Jesus told the disciples just before His ascension, "For John baptized with water, but you will be baptized with the Holy Spirit not many days from now" (Acts 1:5 NET).

It should also be noted that the filling of the Spirit is not an end in itself, but a means to an end. The filling of the Spirit is not an experience to be enjoyed, but an empowerment that enables a special service rendered to others. It does not precede the act of service, but accompanies it. The focus is never on the filling, but on the resulting effective service that the Spirit used to change lives. The person who was filled may or may not have had any special emotional sensation within him, but usually has a perception that God is working in the lives of those who are listening.

The baptism in the Spirit is an important part of the doctrine of salvation, but the filling is vital in the practical life of the believer. Any believer who is sensitive to not grieve nor quench the Spirit will live a life filled with the Spirit. There may be disagreements with some doctrinal details, but when there is an inner willingness to walk with the Spirit, His love, joy and peace will fill any believer.

Terms

The filling of the Spirit was essential to empower the Church to be a testimony and fulfill its ministry in the world. The book of Acts emphasizes the power that produced the works of the early Church, but the baptism of the Spirit refers to the position of the believer in Christ. The purpose of the biblical author was to show the power of God manifested through His fillings. This "power" is necessary and available for every believer today since each of us has been baptized in the Spirit. By faith and understanding we can translate our position in Christ into a dynamic experience as we permit Him to guide and empower us through obedience to His Word.

Two Synonymous phrases

There are two phrases that have the same meaning.

(1) The first is "endued with power from on high" (Luke 24:49). It is the promise that the Spirit will indwell the bodies of believers, filling them with the power of His presence. Jesus reiterated the fulfillment of this promise in Acts 1:5, which assures that the baptism of the Spirit, was soon to begin. To be "endued" [*enduo*, "to sink into (cloths), to be clothed in"] with this power is to have the Holy Spirit in our lives, so as to be fully dressed in the Spirit. Each believer has been baptized in the Spirit and, as a result, has been endued with power. He does not have to wait a certain number of days any longer to receive this promise; when he receives Christ as his Savior, the Spirit indwells him immediately and brings His power along with Him. Therefore it is impossible to receive Christ and not receive the Holy Spirit. And likewise it is impossible to have the Spirit and not have the fullness of His power indwelling every true believer. They are inseparable.

If one does pray and ask for power, it is not correct to ask that God pour out more of His Spirit. Instead, he should ask that (1) he may believe and trust that he has all of the Spirit (Colossians 2:9-10 declares "in Him you have been made complete") and (2) that God take away any obstacle that impedes the Spirit's control in him. Since we can trust in His promised power, we can take steps toward godliness as Paul wrote in 2 Corinthians 7:1, "Since we have these promises, dear friends, let us purify ourselves from everything that contaminates body and spirit, perfecting holiness out of reverence for God". God is honored

Chapter 4: *The four aspects of the baptism of the Spirit*

when we step out to be obedient and to server others, depending on His Spirit to flow through us to help those we seek to serve.

Instead of the believer waiting for the Spirit, He is waiting on us! He wants to manifest himself to the world, but unbelief and carnality can block His work in us. To adjust oneself to the Spirit frequently requires waiting in prayer in order to get rid of sin, rebellion and egotism in our hearts. The good news is that every believer now has the indwelling and the power of the Spirit in him. We are clothed [endued] in His Spirit. We must simply allow Him to liberate us from our sin in order that the Spirit's power can enable us to continue to be obedient.

(2) The second much-used phrase is: "The pouring out of the Spirit" (Acts 2:16, 17; 10:45). The word that is used is *ekcheo*, "bestow, to give oneself in total commitment." This phrase always is related to the initial imparting of the Spirit to the Jews, Samaritans and Gentiles. In our days, the Spirit is poured out in each person at the moment of belief in Christ.

The New Testament makes it very clear in Titus 3:5b-6, "by the …renewing of the Holy Ghost; which he shed on us abundantly through Jesus Christ our Savior." The word used for "renewing" is *anakainosis*, which means, "to make new," a reference to the regeneration of a soul (BDAG Lexicon). This word modifies the verb "to save," which refers to a single action at the moment of our salvation. That is to say, as we receive Christ as Savior, the Holy Spirit regenerates us and is simultaneously shed [poured out] abundantly on us. If this has occurred, there is no reason to continue asking for it in prayer. The Bible says that if a person has Christ, he has the Holy Spirit in abundance and, therefore, all His power. The Spirit does not come in parts, but as a whole Person.

If that is true, and the Scriptures say it is, we are expected to believe this truth, trust that He is real and alive within our being, and step out in faith believing that His power is sufficient for us to obey any command or purpose He providentially presents us. How, then, can we manifest His power in our lives?

The Bible indicates that there are four necessary steps to enjoying the fullness of the Spirit in our lives.

Four Steps to Liberate the Power of the Spirit in Our Lives

The factors that limit the operation of the Spirit in our lives are always human, not divine. The radio waves of a short wave radio may have thousands of watts of power in the transmitter, but if the antenna is not correctly cut to the right length to match the precise frequency of the transmitter, there is little or no signal being emitted. The connections are all right, but all the parts must be in harmony (the bandwidth of the transmitting frequency must match the length of the antennae). This can happen in the lives of believers as well.

Step 1: Understand our position in Christ

The most important factor for the believer is to understand who we are in

Christ. In Ephesians 1:17-23, Paul prayed that the believers would receive "... the spirit of wisdom and revelation in the knowledge of him." He is not praying for another "spirit" or the "Holy Spirit," since he had just described their being "sealed with the Spirit" (1:13). He was asking that their inner spirit be so filled with the revealed wisdom and knowledge in Scriptures that they would understand the meaning and implications of being in Christ.

This should fill each one with "hope" because of the "riches" of our "inheritance." Paul also prayed that they would know the "greatness of His power," which resurrected Christ. This is the power that resides in the believer! A weak believer is one who is ignorant of these truths or does not understand what they mean (the "wisdom") which is revealed in the Scriptures.

If we do not understand what we have in Christ by believing in Him (verse 19), we will never be able to take advantage of the power He affords us. It is in vain to seek something that does not exist or something that we already have. It would be like someone who has millions of dollars in his bank account but does not know it. Who is at fault? We can appropriate these spiritual riches simply by knowing about them and acting upon that knowledge.

Step 2: Exercise faith to live according to our position

Knowledge is not enough; we must do something about what is believed. Beliefs must be changed into values and convictions that will motivate us to act. It is necessary to work out the power that is within us. James 1:22 says, "But be ye doers of the word, and not hearers only." Jesus warned us in the same way saying, ""If you know these things, blessed are you if you do them." (John 13:17). When we understand the promises and commands of the Word, we must put them into practice.

We put the Word into practice through obedience. It is when we practice the biblical teachings of testifying, serving, pardoning, giving, etc. that we discover that we have an internal strength that fortifies us. This strength is the Holy Spirit who enables us to obey His Word. He will fill us with His power if we are faithful to the Spirit through responding to His Word, and it will be evident that God is working in our lives.

This is not to say that it will always be easy to initiate such obedience, or that health, wealth and happiness will always result. On the contrary, the lightening of the load (Matthew 11:30) occurs after the yoke is accepted and the effort is initiated. Our commitment to obey or to accept difficult tasks for His kingdom is not contingent upon some previous manifestation of Christ's power. We are committed to build His Church even if we start alone, though we are never really alone (Matthew 28:20). God always blesses our initiatives undertaken for His glory, honor and His purpose.

The filling of the Spirit should not be a rare experience in the life of a believer, nor should it be an event in the past that is remembered with nostalgia. It should be always present as we sense God working through us. We should experience a perpetual filling of the Spirit.

Chapter 4: *The four aspects of the baptism of the Spirit*

Step 3: Commit totally to the will of God and to the obedience of the Scriptures.

The filling of the Spirit is not a quick or passing experience, as taught in the "second work of grace." It is not a question of a deeper life or higher level of the mystics, but learning how to be more obedient and Christ-like in daily relationships and situations, then doing it consistently.

Maybe in a crisis of decision to commit completely to Christ, one might feel emotions or have "goose bumps," but emotions depend on many things. Positively they can be the reaffirmation of actions, thoughts or intents that coincide with truths believed, or the response to a fulfilling hope. Often a negative emotion results from the struggle to retain control over one's life instead of yielding to the Lord. Upon resolving this interior conflict, suddenly one's life is filled with joy and peace. Even these emotions are the beginning of the manifestation of His power; they are part of His fruit (Galatians 5:22-23).

Paul prayed for the Colossians, asking God, "...that ye might be filled with the knowledge of his will in all wisdom and spiritual understanding: that ye might walk worthy of the Lord unto all pleasing...strengthened with all might..." (Colossians 1:9-11). It is obvious that there is a direct relationship between the knowledge of His will, the determination to put it into practice and the flowing of His power in the life.

The Spirit always guides the believer to the Word, to study and know it with assurance, to meditate on it and obey it in order to transform his mind (Romans 12:2), to become the same mind of Christ (Philippians 2:3-5), and to permit the power of God to enable the obedience. It is impossible to be filled with the Spirit without obeying the Word.

It could be possible to imitate some of the aspects of the power of the Spirit (a good moral life, even preaching or teaching), but the trials that the Lord will permit will show that these actions are not controlled by the Spirit, but by the pride of the flesh.

There are three laws for maintaining the filling of the Spirit. They are: (1) Obedience to the clear commands in the Scriptures already known in the form of personal convictions to honor the Lord. (2) Obedience to the Word interpreted in the human heart by the Holy Spirit for direct application daily; these are acts of the heart directed by the Holy Spirit. (3) Daily time alone with the Word in meditation seeking to understand more of His Word to apply to one's life.

Step 4: Persistent prayer

The experience of the filling of the Spirit is like a sign that activates the opposition of Satan. The power of God always stimulates the Devil to work through temptation and attacks against the children of God. Paul calls the Christian life "the good fight" (2 Timothy 4:7). This fight is not a war against other brothers, but against the forces of Satan. In Ephesians 6:10-20, the command "be strong in the Lord, and in the power of his might..." is in the imperative present progressive tense in the Greek. It means that we should be continually strengthening ourselves in the power of the Lord.

Just as in a football game there is a huddle before every play. We need a holy huddle with God who calls the plays from His Word. When we accept the play He calls, His power fills us to do it. With each such action we gather spiritual strength, wisdom and spiritual maturity into an increasing Christ-likeness

Since the nature of our enemy is spiritual (6:12), we must also take on spiritual armor. Through prayer we appropriate that armor for the spiritual battle. IT IS NOT AN ASPECT OF THE CONFLICT: IT IS THE PLACE OF THE CONFLICT! In prayer we struggle directly against Satan. Preaching and teaching are areas of indirect combat.

The goal of Satan's attacks is for the believer to abandon his armor, so that the "darts of the wicked" are more easily able to penetrate his life. If we live in disobedience doing it "our way," following the desires of the flesh instead of those of the Spirit, living by sight or feeling and not by faith, we remain exposed to the attacks of Satan.

As we are filled with the Spirit, we are fueled by the power of God; Satan cannot be victorious over us. Only in this way can we be prepared to serve God and have an effective ministry bringing blessing to other men and glorifying God.

There are no shortcuts, and we cannot rest on past experiences. We do not have the right to disobey the laws or commands of the Scriptures. By prayer we put on the armor of God as we become sensitive to His voice and obey His Word. We can then live in the power of the Spirit and confront the enemy. Because Satan does not rest from this war and will never stop until Jesus returns, we do not have the right to rest from the battle and satisfy our selfishness. We must continue obeying, depending on His power, desiring to reflect His image and accomplish His purpose of world evangelism until He comes.

MacArthur gives a great analogy that sums it up.

> "Once there was a dog that was crossing the bridge with a bone in his mouth. He looked over the edge and saw his reflection in the clear stream. The bone in the water looked better than the one in his mouth; so he gave up the reality for the reflection. My great fear is that there are many Christians who, with great zeal lacking knowledge, are doing the very same thing." (MacArthur 1978: 198)

CHAPTER 5

How can you know if you have been baptized by the Spirit?

Chapter 5: *Gifts for Today*

A major theme of the New Testament deals with the security of salvation and the evidence of intimacy with God that are established by the baptism in the Spirit. In fact, the whole purpose of 1 John is to present to us the evidences of an intimate, genuine relationship with God. "These things have I written unto you that believe on the name of the Son of God, that ye may know that ye have eternal life…" (1 John 5:13). These proofs are not miraculous evidences, but moral ones; they are not ecstatic experiences, but ethical and practical. That is to say, that which shows that one has received both the baptism and the filling of the Spirit in his new life is a transformed life. For example, "If we say we have fellowship with him and yet keep on walking in the darkness, we are lying and not practicing the truth" (1 John 1:6 NET). The focus of 1 John is to show the symptoms of a transformed life that can only be attributed to the presence of the Holy Spirit.

It is amazing how some are deceived into thinking they have "participation" (the real meaning of "fellowship") in Christ, yet their lives are not changed. Then in 1 John 1:7 John writes, "But if we walk in the light as he himself is in the light, we have fellowship with one another and the blood of Jesus his Son cleanses us from all sin." The key to knowing whether we have the Holy Spirit is our honesty and transparency before the Lord as we openly admit and confess our sinfulness (1:9) as the Spirit's presence convicts us (John 16:8).

Evidences of the reality of the baptism in the Spirit are very important to the Charismatic. "An experience so great and so important as the Baptism with the Holy Spirit undoubtedly will be accompanied by unmistakable evidences, so that the recipient will have no doubts whatsoever that he has indeed received the Promise of the Father." (Duffield 1987: 319) This quest for a tangible sign or physical manifestation to be assured of what God has promised seems to be a lack of willingness to take God at His word.

> Sometimes the baptism with the Holy Spirit occurs spontaneously, sometimes through prayer and the laying on of hands. Sometimes it occurs after water baptism, sometimes before. Sometimes it occurs virtually simultaneously with conversion, sometimes after an interval of time.... But one thing is constant in the Scripture, and it is most important: It is never merely assumed that a person has been baptized with the Holy Spirit. When he has been baptized with the Holy Spirit the person knows it. It is a definite experience (Christenson 1968: 38).

It is not "presumption" if we trust in the promise of the Word of God. Paul described the guarantee of the Spirit in every believer as an unconditional promise to be counted on: "In Him you also trusted, after you heard the word of truth, the gospel of your salvation; in whom also, having believed, you were sealed with the Holy Spirit of promise, who is the guarantee of our inheritance until the redemption of the purchased possession, to the praise of His glory" (NKJ Ephesians 1:13-14). The guarantee of our salvation is the Holy Spirit Himself residing within us.

Chapter 5: *How can you know if you have been baptized by the Spirit*

As one studies the Scriptures, he discovers that the following six major evidences of the presence of the Spirit apply to all believers who have been transformed by the new life of the Spirit:

Evidence #1: The awareness of our sin and disobedience from the conviction of the Spirit

Jesus promised, "... when He [the Spirit] has come, He will convict the world of sin, and of righteousness, and of judgment" (John 16:8). This is a characteristic of the Spirit's work in the world and represents the key to the power of the gospel message: when proclaimed the Spirit works through Word to bring a sense of guilt and lostness, especially through the exposure to the Law. When the Spirit is working in conviction "...every mouth may be stopped" (Rom 3:19). Although it primarily applies to the unsaved, the convicting work remains the key for the believer to learn how to walk in the Spirit.

The word for "convict" (*elegcho*) means to "bring to light, expose, point out, correct" (Gingrich). Thus in 1 John 1:7 a key sign to determine a genuine possessor of the Spirit in salvation is: "But if we walk in the light as He is in the light, we have fellowship with one another, and the blood of Jesus Christ His Son cleanses us from all sin" (1 John 1:7). By "walking in the light" means perceiving the convicting work of the Spirit who reveals our sinfulness and obeying what He commands in the Scripture.

The unsaved always think they are a pretty good people, or at least "good enough." It is only the believer indwelt by the Spirit who has had all his sins exposed him who quickly confesses his sinfulness. The unbeliever has no such conviction: "If we say that we have no sin, we deceive ourselves, and the truth is not in us" (1 John 1:8). He has no conviction of the Spirit yet.

As true believers we are constantly confessing "our sins, he is faithful and just to forgive us our sins and to cleanse us from all unrighteousness" (1:9). The effective work of the Spirit in a believer is to constantly convict or show him when he violates God's Word.

The believer can know he has the Spirit within him when he has an internal sense of wrongdoing that he may have never had before. When he disobeys a command in Scriptures the Spirit brings it to light through a sense of guilt.

> ..the conscience and the Spirit play similar roles, both performing the task of internal conviction. The conscience convicts us about the values that we recognize and apply. The Spirit convicts us about what Scripture teaches and the values we derive from it. It is impossible to know whether our internal sense of conviction comes from conscience or Spirit in most cases. The key issue is that we have to test all our feelings of conviction by an objective analysis of the Bible's teachings and our own application of its values. If an internal sense of conviction contradicts the Scriptures, we can be assured that it is not a conviction of the Spirit. If our feeling of conviction is in accord with the Bible and our values, then we must respond (Meadors 2003: 184).

We are exhorted to expect this convicting and correcting work of the Lord in our lives and to gain wisdom and maturity by responding to it. The author of Hebrews wrote, " And you have forgotten the exhortation which speaks to you as to sons: "My son, do not despise the chastening of the LORD, nor be discouraged when you are rebuked by Him" (Hebrews 12:5). The word "rebuked" is the same original word "convict." We cannot sin and get away with it internally.

Once again the word is used to encourage believers to recognize the genuineness of their relation to Christ in that "As many as I love, I rebuke and chasten. Therefore be zealous and repent" (Revelation 3:19). This is an abiding reality of anyone indwelt by the Spirit. The rebuking-convicting work of the Spirit is a very present reality for the believer and not to be ignored.

Evidence #2: The capacity to pray to God as our Father

The apostle John declared in John 1:12 that becoming a "child of God" occurs when we personally receive Christ into our lives. We don't need an external sign to give us assurance of this fact. We accept the promise of His Word as sufficient evidence. In Galatians 4:6 Paul says, "And because you are sons, God has sent forth the Spirit of His Son into your hearts, crying out, "Abba, Father!." The result of being made sons is that God gives us His Spirit. This is not separated from salvation, but is intricately associated with it. It is the Spirit who gives us the sense of having an intimate relationship with God like that of a family member. The word "*abba*" means "Father" in Aramaic. This word is the diminutive form used by little children in speaking to their fathers. Therefore, no matter the language, race or nationality, we are all equal; everyone who receives Christ has an innate sense that he is a child of God by the Holy Spirit.

Having security of salvation would be impossible without the presence of the Holy Spirit in our lives. Paul said, "…For as many as are led by the Spirit of God, these are sons of God. For you did not receive the spirit of bondage again to fear, but you received the Spirit of adoption by whom we cry out, 'Abba, Father.' The Spirit Himself bears witness with our spirit that we are children of God," (Romans 8:15-16).

This security is not the result of visions, signs, spectacular revelations or mystic experiences, but is simply the Spirit who gives us peace and tranquility because of our confidence in His Word. He listens to our prayers as a father listens to his children, and our confidence is that we may draw near to Him as our Father as He promised. This confidence grows as we discover that He, from His perspective, adopts us as sons and "having predestined us to adoption as sons by Jesus Christ to Himself, according to the good pleasure of His will, to the praise of the glory of His grace, by which He has made us accepted in the Beloved." (Ephesians 1:5-6).

The evidence Paul gave for this wonderful assurance is not that through the Spirit we are empowered to do miraculous works, receive ecstatic visions,

Chapter 5: *How can you know if you have been baptized by the Spirit*

speak in tongues, or any other kind of sensational phenomena. Rather, the first, most basic indication of our adoption is that we have a new form of address for God. The Spirit invites us to join in his invocation, crying "Abba, Father." (George 1994: 307)

After receiving Christ as our Savior, we were adopted as His sons and He gave us His Spirit to make us feel that we are children of God. If our hearts confirm this, and we are willing to trust the promises in the Word, it is because we have received the baptism in the Spirit.

We over sentimentalize this word when we refer to it as mere baby talk and translate it into English as "daddy." The word Abba appears in certain legal texts of the Mishna as a designation used by grown children in claiming the inheritance of their deceased father. (G. Kittle, "abba," TDNT 1.5-6). As a word of address Abba is not so much associated with infancy as it is with intimacy (*Ibid.*, 307).

There was a sense of intimate privilege granted to these formerly superstitious pagans who have been welcomed into the very heart of God: they were children of God and heirs of the promise, having received the fullness of God in the person of the Spirit (Col 2:9, "For in Him dwells all the fullness of the Godhead bodily"). There is nothing lacking, nothing more to acquire of God. A child has all rights of full intimacy with God, even an adopted son, just because he is a son.

Evidence #3: Understand the grace of God

When the Spirit enters into a life, one of the first things that He does is communicate the reality of the undeserved favor He has bestowed upon us at salvation. Paul explained it this way, "Now we have received, not the spirit of the world, but the Spirit which is of God, that we might know the things that are freely given to us of God" (1 Corinthians 2:12). The Spirit helps us to recognize the things we have received without having deserved them; He helps us to understand the grace of God. Those who do not have the Spirit continue thinking that they must earn or deserve the benefits of God.

The Epistle of 1 John was written both to show us how to have assurance of salvation and to indicate those who might think they have salvation but are deceived. As John elaborates on what it means to "walk in the light" (where nothing is hid, that is, we understand God's perspective of who we are). He gives a basic universal difference between the lost and the saved: the lost always think they are pretty good people, but the saved are always admitting their sinfulness and sense of not deserving the acceptance of God. 1 John 1:8, "If we say that we have no sin, we deceive ourselves, and the truth is not in us." That is, we are not in the light yet where we will see our sinfulness before a holy God according to the truth of God's Word. As a result of the convicting work of the presence of the Spirit, a person is left with the awareness of sin and being unworthy, being forced to depend upon and cling to His promise of cleansing and forgiveness (See Gal 3:24).

In 1 Cor 2:11, Paul declared that the only way to understand "the things of God" is to have the Spirit living within us. One of the principle purposes of the baptism of the Spirit is to make us aware of the blessing of the grace of God. He illuminates our minds so that we can understand His Word and appropriate more of His promises in our lives.

In the life of a believer, the Spirit develops and augments our appreciation for the grace of God, especially as it was expressed on the cross. This work of God provokes in our lives an attitude of humility and consuming gratefulness because of what we have received as a result of His mercy. Without the Spirit, we could not comprehend this grace. The unsaved have no perception of this sense of unworthiness yet gracious acceptance by God. They continue to attempt to prove their goodness to God, thus confirming their lostness! It is the work of the Holy Spirit that makes the difference, by showing our wickedness, then simultaneously, confirming through the Word, unconditional acceptance because of His grace.

Evidence #4: The consciousness of the love of God

When a person receives the Spirit, there are certain changes that occur in his heart. One of those changes is his attitude toward others. In Romans 5:5 we read, "...the love of God has been poured out in our hearts by the Holy Spirit who was given to us.." He made known to us His love in a personal way, in spite of all our faults, sins and weaknesses. This is not a romantic dream in which someone is content with the human race, but an intimate security that God loves us personally.

The verb in the phrase "the Holy Spirit who has been poured out," is in the indicative perfect passive tense. This verb means that the action occurred at one time to us by the Spirit and its effect or consequence continues on until the present. The love of God was poured out in our inner man and still affects the hearts and affection of those who have the Spirit.

The verb "was given" is in the aorist passive participle in the Greek, which indicates a single action completed in the past [at our conversion], done to us once and for all time. Therefore, the Spirit is given one time (not in two steps or a second work of grace, much less multiple times) in the life of a believer and reproduces His love in the believer's heart. We do not receive part of Him at salvation, then more of Him later. That is absurd. When we receive Christ into our life, we receive all the Holy Spirit in His fullness (Col 1:19; 2:9). This is evident by the inner assurance of God's unfailing love for us because His Spirit confirms to us through His Word that He is trustworthy and never fails to fulfill His promise of an unconditional love for anyone who repents and believes.

Chapter 5: *How can you know if you have been baptized by the Spirit* 73

Evidence #6: Security of salvation

The confidence that we are saved does not come from within us, by our intuition or imagination, but from God's presence in our inner man. In 2 Corinthians 1:21b-22 Paul wrote, "Now He who establishes us with you in Christ and has anointed us is God, who also has sealed us and given us the Spirit in our hearts as a guarantee..." The "guarantee" is the "down payment, the earnest payment" that assures a person will pay the rest. This was used to confirm a contract. Therefore, the presence of the Spirit in our lives is the guarantee that He will fulfill all the rest of our salvation: that is, our ultimate sanctification and glorification.

Biblical security of salvation never emphasizes an experience, but the presence of the Spirit. 1 John 3:24 says, "And by this we know that He abides in us, by the Spirit whom He has given us." Also in 1 John 4:13 we find, "By this we know that we abide in Him, and He in us, because He has given us of His Spirit." The presence of the Spirit in the life of the believer gives him the assurance and confidence of eternal life.

Some believers' assurance has been weakened or totally lost because of Satan's accusations, guilt, faulty understanding of the Bible promises or psychological problems; however, for those who have learned to "walk in the Spirit," that is to say, to know the Word and obey it in the power of the Spirit, their lives are marked by a security of salvation nothing can shake.

Evidence #7: Love for other believers

Perhaps the most notable evidence that we have received through the baptism of the Spirit is our love for our brethren in Christ. In 1 John 4:12-13, it says, "...If we love one another, God abides in us, and His love has been perfected in us. By this we know that we abide in Him, and He in us, because He has given us of His Spirit."

John uses this idea to write against the principles of Gnosticism, a heresy which emphasized the spirit over the flesh. Introspection, with a focus on mystical encounters and hidden truths only revealed in higher levels of intimacy, was its hallmark. John says here that the genuine evidence of the Spirit is neither interior nor mystical, but rather an external practical manifestation of love and concern for others. The more control the Spirit has over a believer, the more the believer's love will be manifested among the other believers. This is why true believers love the church, the gathering of the other believers for whom the Spirit gives a sincere love and commitment to serve.

The teaching that new believers have not yet received the Holy Spirit or only have a limited part of His powerful presence condemns them to lives without power, the lack of assurance of their salvation, little understanding of His love and limited understanding of the Word until they submit to some experience. The Bible teaches us, however, that our salvation is complete when we receive Christ (Colossians 2:10, "And you are complete in Him, who is the head of all principality and power"). It is not necessary to do anything more, or receive anything more, because He has given us all we need; in fact, all of Him that there is! Now we are to love and care for the brethren because they all belong to the Savior. The bond among the believers is deeper than the flesh, because it will last forever.

Essentially, the New Testament shows that the evidences of having received the baptism of the Spirit are moral, practical and ethical in nature. Though simple and not very sensational, they are spiritual and real.

Charismatic requirements

Are certain conditions necessary in order to receive the baptism of the Spirit? Charismatic believers say "yes," and within the Charismatic Movement. There are a variety of teachings about the requirements. "The various advocates have suggested such requirements as acts of obedience, prayer, repentance, humility, sinlessness, self-purification, yielding, emptying, 'leaving all,' being fully consecrated, 'going all the way,' abandoning, tarrying, and faith." (MacArthur 1978: 119)

There are two basic ideas most commonly mentioned: obedience and faith. If a person obeys to a certain extent and has special faith, then he can receive the baptism of the Spirit; it follows by implication, then, that those who have not yet received the baptism are lacking either in obedience or in faith.

The First Proposed Requirement for the Baptism of the Spirit: OBEDIENCE

Students of the Bible should immediately deduce that receiving the baptism of the Spirit as a result of obedience insinuates that it is not by grace, but by some level of merit. If it requires any work of obedience, then it is not by grace. Some teach that upon salvation we receive only the "down payment" of the Spirit, as if it were a reduced part; others say that we receive only the "Spirit of Christ" upon salvation and that later, by the baptism of the Spirit, we receive the Spirit in all His fullness. This is true, they say, only when the requirements of obedience and faith are met. At the beginning of the movement, many Pentecostals had already left the Holiness Movement because of the strict legalistic emphasis in the area of obedience. Duffield describes the Pentecostal process:

> By a full yieldedness of [one's] entire being, in order that the Holy Spirit might have His own way. This is often the most difficult condition to fulfill. After one realizes his need of the Baptism with the Spirit, and comes to the Lord for this Blessing, there is still the matter of the yieldedness of his various faculties to the control of the Spirit (Duffield 1987: 316).

When is a person yielded enough? Is this quest for sufficient yieldedness to continue until something happens? Dalton explains the requirements in order to receive this necessary baptism: "This experience is not for a select few, but

Chapter 5: How can you know if you have been baptized by the Spirit

for all who desire it and are willing to pay the price." (Dalton, 1945, p. 70) As pious as this may sound, it generates a vast uncertainty and introspection that often becomes unhealthy. There are three common aspects in the search for the baptism of the Spirit.

Aspect #1: Separation from all known sin.

One author says, "It is the Pentecostal conviction that when believers quit all their known sin, the Holy Spirit can live in their hearts although there are still some unconscious or unknown sins (therefore, apparently excusable)." In Pillars of Pentecost, another author writes, "We can receive the Holy Spirit, but not with sin in our hearts…The Holy Spirit and sin cannot live in the same heart." (Conn 1979) It is typical to hear that the Spirit cannot enter in a person who is contaminated with known sins. This emphasis defines sin in two categories: known and unknown (or unconscious). We should ask ourselves, if I am not conscious of the pride in my life, then am I innocent of this sin? No! If God accepted ignorance as an excuse, then it would be better not to preach the Gospel at all, because God would not condemn the world if it continued to be ignorant of its sin of unbelief.

To distinguish between known sin and unknown sin is to make a distinction that does not appear in the Scriptures. John Wesley upheld this doctrine, but Paul did not. He says in Ephesians 2:1-3:

"And you He made alive, who were dead in trespasses and sins, in which you once walked according to the course of this world, according to the prince of the power of the air, the spirit who now works in the sons of disobedience, among whom also we all once conducted ourselves in the lusts of our flesh, fulfilling the desires of the flesh and of the mind, and were by nature children of wrath, just as the others.."

Christ died for all sins (1 Peter 2:24 "who Himself bore our sins in His own body on the tree, that we, having died to sins, might live for righteousness"), not just for our known sins.

The concept that the Spirit cannot live in a body with known sin is false! The Spirit can live in a body with sin; otherwise there would be no hope for anyone of us. In Romans 7:23-25, Paul testifies of his struggle against sin in his life. "But I see another law in my members, warring against the law of my mind, and bringing me into captivity to the law of sin which is in my members. In spite of being a sinner who had not reached perfection (Philippians 3:12-13, "Not that I have already attained, or am already perfected; but I press on, that I may lay hold of that for which Christ Jesus has also laid hold of me. Brothers and sisters, I do not consider myself to have attained this…"), the apostle continued depending on the Spirit of God that lived in him (Romans 8:9). It would be impossible to have any victory over the flesh if it were not for the power and presence of the Spirit in the life of the believer.

To say that one must be completely victorious over sin before receiving the baptism of the Spirit is contradictory, since it is the Spirit who gives the victory over sin! One author says, "If we live a submissive life which is pure and holy in intimate communion with Him, the experience of the powerful baptism must come…The possibility of living a pure and holy life in intimate communion with God, even before the coming of the Spirit, is implicit in the Pentecostal conditions."

If a person does not have the power of the Spirit, however, it would be impossible to have victory over sin. How can we be victorious over sin through mere determination and discipline of the flesh? In the New Testament, it is not the pure, obedient and bold man who receives the Spirit, but the sinner who is void of strength.

The sinner receives the Spirit by confiding in Christ's righteousness, not in his own: "and be found in Him, not having my own righteousness, which is from the law, but that which is through faith in Christ, the righteousness which is from God by faith;" (Philippians 3:9). Through receiving the righteousness of God by faith, the sinner simultaneously receives the Spirit, who now gives the power to be victorious over sin, and begins a new life with the power of the Spirit.

The Charismatic need to be victorious over sin before qualifying to receive the power of God in Spirit baptism thus requires works instead of grace. If it is by grace that we have received the Spirit, then it is impossible that conditions of obedience are necessary; if it is by works that we receive the Spirit, then it is necessary that there be conditions of obedience. Which declaration is biblical? This is very like the problem that Paul confronted in Galatians 3:2. "This only I want to learn from you: Did you receive the Spirit by the works of the law, or by the hearing of faith?" The Bible teaches that the reason we are victorious over sin is that we have received the Spirit's power by grace, at the moment we exercised faith by trusting His promises for salvation, even while sinners! .

Aspect #2: Prayer

The teaching that it is necessary to pray to receive the Spirit comes from Luke 11:13, which says, "If you then, being evil, know how to give good gifts to your children, how much more will your heavenly Father give the Holy Spirit to those who ask Him!" Later, in Luke 24:49, Jesus commands His disciples to remain in the city of Jerusalem until they are invested with power from on high. Charismatic believers often use these verses to teach that they must wait in prayer, pleading with God to receive His power. Yet when we read the passages that describe the waiting period (Acts 1:12-14; 2:1), there is no insinuation that they were even praying! It is a mere presumption that they waited in prayer during the seven days before the Spirit appeared. In fact, there is not one passage in the entire Bible in which someone actually prayed asking for the Spirit.

Even in Luke 11:13, Jesus is not speaking of the conditions for receiving the Spirit, but rather He is illustrating the desire of the Father to give gifts to believers in response to their prayers, in the same way a father gives gifts to his children. This is like a hyperbole: God is so generous He would give the

Chapter 5: *How can you know if you have been baptized by the Spirit*   77

greatest gift of all, His Spirit, to any who asked, and thus, how much more would He respond to lesser requests. These gifts are neither deserved nor earned; they are simply gifts.

In addition, Luke 11 speaks of the conditions before Pentecost, when believers had not yet received the permanent and universal indwelling of the Spirit that Jesus was going to give them (John 14:16, 17). Prior to Pentecost, the Spirit still was promised to come; it had not happened yet. For this reason, praying to ask God to fulfill His promise to give His Spirit could have been legitimate during that period. Today, however, in the new era or dispensation, those prayers are not necessary because the Spirit has been given to all believers.

Even if praying for the Spirit were a valid prayer prior to Pentecost, the only requirement for the disciples to receive the baptism of the Spirit was, "that they should not depart from Jerusalem, but wait for the promise of the Father" (Acts 1:4-5). There was nothing mystical, selective or conditional except that they were in Jerusalem when the Spirit came. There is no suggestion in the text that they were praying for the Spirit. The disciples only had to remain in Jerusalem awaiting the time predetermined by the Father, which was to be on the feast day when the maximum number of Jews would be present for this inaugural event on the Feast of Pentecost.

Since that day, no believer has had to wait even an instant to receive the Spirit. In John 7:38-39, Jesus gives the only condition for receiving the Spirit, saying, "Jesus stood up and shouted out, 'If anyone is thirsty, let him come to me, and let the one who believes in me drink. Just as the scripture says, 'From within him will flow rivers of living water.'" (Now he said this about the Spirit, whom those who believed in him were going to receive, for the Spirit had not yet been given, because Jesus was not yet glorified.)" Here Jesus was referring to the baptism of the Spirit that all believers in Him would receive instantaneously.

Aspect #3: Total submission.

The first two aspects of the requirement of obedience are actions; the third has to do with the condition of the mind or heart. Pentecostal writer, Duffield states,

> "By a full yieldedness of the entire being, in order that the Holy Spirit might have His own way. This is often the most difficult condition to fulfill. After one realizes his need of the Baptism with the Spirit, and comes to the Lord for this Blessing, there is still the matter of the yieldedness of his various faculties to the control of the Spirit." (Duffield 1987: 316)

Some say that it is necessary to develop a passive state or to become empty of personal will in order to be submissive to the baptism of the Spirit. This is dangerous, however, because it can cause a person to be open to any spirit or influence. The application of this submission is usually an exhortation to ignore inhibitions and to accept whatever impression comes to your mind. It is precisely this emphasis that often produces inappropriate or extreme actions in Pentecostal meetings.

Total submission frequently causes a lack of self-control. Paul taught that the prophet controlled by the Spirit always had control of his own spirit (1 Cor 14:32) and is never out of control. Thus he was able to always obey the restrictions placed on the prophets and tongues-speakers in the early church. The fullness of the Spirit as evidenced by the fruit of the Spirit produces "self-control" (Gal 5:22).

When Paul prayed in 1 Corinthians 14:15, it was always with complete understanding, never in a state of a trance that would cause him to be unaware of what he said or what was happening around him. Therefore, biblical submission is not giving in to one's own impulses or a state of unconsciousness, but rather it is being willing to obey the clear revealed will of God as stated in His Word.

Total submission should be viewed as the result of the baptism of the Spirit, not as a means of receiving it. Submission to Christ is certainly the objective of the Christian life, but it would be impossible without the power and presence of the Spirit. In addition, instead of teaching we must force ourselves to achieve complete obedience while in the flesh (without the Spirit's power) in order to receive the baptism of the Spirit, the New Testament teaches we immediately receive the baptism of the Spirit with all His power upon believing. This power enables the believer to be obedient to the commands for the Christian life without forcing himself to do it. In this way total submission can become a reality. It is a practical, not mystical, obedience to the Word of God and the fulfillment of His purpose in our lives (Ephesians 2:10).

The Second Proposed Requirement for the Baptism of the Spirit: FAITH

Charismatic believers not only teach total submission, but they also insist that faith is also necessary to receive the baptism. Their literature usually outlines three aspects of this faith. Again, we observe the difficulty of insisting on meeting requirements before having the power to fulfill them. In spite of ample evidence from Scripture to confirm the powerful presence of the Spirit in every believer the insistence on the additional experience of the Baptism of the Spirit is insisted upon.

> Beyond conversion, beyond the assurance of salvation, beyond having the Holy Spirit, there is a baptism with the Holy Spirit. It might not make sense to our human understanding any more than it made sense for Jesus to be baptized by John.... We are not called to understand it, or justify it, or explain it, but simply to enter into it in humble obedience and with expectant faith (Christenson 1968: 37).

Christenson is right that "it might not make sense" because how could a person have the Holy Spirit without having been baptized in the Spirit? That is

Chapter 5: *How can you know if you have been baptized by the Spirit* 79

how one receives the Spirit! Are we expected to seek for some kind of experience even though it cannot be understood or explained from Scripture? These requirements complicate the definition of a "gift," because a gift given by grace cannot have prerequisites.

Aspect #1: Faith should be directed to the Spirit.

Myer Pearlman said, "Just as there is faith toward Christ for salvation, there is also a faith toward the Spirit for power and consecration." The problem with this concept of a second level of faith is that it is not found in the Bible! The Spirit, with all His power, comes "through Jesus Christ" as an inseparable part of salvation. A similar incorrect belief about directing faith toward the Spirit surfaces in Dennis Bennett's book The Holy Spirit and You, in which he says, "The baptism of the Holy Spirit depends exclusively on us, whether we will believe or not." (Dennis Bennett 1975) According to this logic, if a person doubts the baptism, he is committing the sin of unbelief and should feel guilt because of it.

Beliefs are valid only when they are in accord with what is written in the Word. If it is not found in the Word, then we should not believe it, no matter who says so. In Galatians 3:13-14, Paul describes an inseparable relationship between the faith of salvation and the coming of the Spirit. "Christ has redeemed us from the curse of the law, having become a curse for us (for it is written, "Cursed is everyone who hangs on a tree"), that the blessing of Abraham might come upon the Gentiles in Christ Jesus, that we might receive the promise of the Spirit through faith." Our faith in Jesus Christ opens the door to the gift of the Spirit; examining the Scriptures we find no suggestion of a second kind of faith.

Perhaps it would be good to ask, why had the disciples of Jesus not received the baptism of the Spirit? In John 14:16-17, the answer is clear: before Pentecost, the Spirit was "with" them, but later, He would be "in" them. From the Day of Pentecost, those who believe in Christ immediately receive the indwelling of the Spirit. It is not a second act of faith that has to be directed at the Spirit. When one receives the Savior, he receives the Spirit, since they are one Person.

Aspect #2: It should be total faith.

It is sometimes taught that our faith in Christ for salvation is inadequate to receive the gift of the baptism of the Holy Spirit. Now, it is true that our "faith" at the moment of salvation is minimal and needs to mature, but the Scriptures teach that it is sufficient. To make this distinction between the two types of "faith" is to suggest that the second is superior to the first. The end result of this is almost a depreciation of salvation faith and exaltation of the "faith" to receive the baptism of the Spirit.

Having understood this teaching of Charismatic believers, we can see why they are willing to accept as believers groups from marginal orthodoxy (i.e. Catholics and other religious groups). If they have been "baptized by the Spirit" and have spoken in "tongues," then they are true believers. The logic is this: speaking in tongues is a sign that the person has experienced the baptism of the Spirit and, as a matter of course, he should have previously received salvation faith. Therefore, as long as they have spoken in tongues, Catholics, Anglicans, Modernists, etc. are often accepted as brothers, no matter their doctrinal position on the Bible or salvation.

Total faith is essential in Charismatic teachings. The believer has to yield himself in all points, giving up all his inhibitions and his self-control. This total dedication is necessary before he is worthy of receiving the baptism of the Spirit obligating him to fulfill this dedication in his own strength. Joseph Dillow, in his book *Speaking in Tongues*, says,

> "These devotional absolutes call a believer not to grace in Christ but to an anguished search within his heart to find what is not there: absolute yieldedness. This leads to all kinds of introspection and worry as to whether he has "really yielded everything" and so on. Since no believer could ever say yes to that without claiming sinlessness (1 John 1:7-10), guilt complexes and bondage and self-absorption inevitably result (Dillow 1975: 79)

Therefore, when the person finally achieves the experience of speaking in tongues, he may feel great relief, but it is not biblical, rather a false psychological relief.

In other words, total obedience plus total faith equals the baptism of the Spirit. In this view, baptism is the result of a consecrated life. The Bible, however, teaches just the opposite! Baptism is not the result, but rather the initial cause and means of a consecrated life. It is like a fruit tree: What occurs first, the production of fruit or the planting of a tree? Just as the tree must be planted first, so the baptism of the Spirit must occur before the fruits of obedience and faith can be possible.

Aspect #3: Baptism comes only by faith.

In spite of what we have already mentioned, Charismatic believers insist that the baptism of the Spirit comes only by faith. What a paradox! After insisting on total faith and obedience, they finally say that it is a free gift.

> "Seekers ... after the Baptism in the Spirit should always remember that this experience is also called, 'The Gift of the Holy Ghost.' Gifts are not earned or won by choice or merit. Gifts cannot be forced from the giver...The Holy Spirit is a gracious ... God-sent Gift, and we receive Him by faith and by faith alone." (Riggs 1949: 105-106)

Chapter 5: *How can you know if you have been baptized by the Spirit*

Faith is completely without works

If there were conditions for receiving it, then the gift would not be received by grace but by merit. If faith is not simple confidence in what God said and did, then it is not faith. If we must achieve complete yieldedness before having faith, then faith is not faith alone but mixed with works. Romans 3:28 shows clearly that faith cannot be mixed with good works: "Therefore we conclude that a man is justified by faith without the deeds of the law." Admittedly the verse applies to justification, but the same principle applies to receiving the Spirit in Galatians 3:2: "Received ye the Spirit by the works of the law, or by the hearing of faith?" The two cannot be mixed; it is either by faith or by works, but not by both.

Faith is the conviction that Christ will fulfill His Word, without need of more external proof or signs.

Mixing works and faith results in an "intellectual or feeling-based faith." This kind of faith comes when someone has convinced himself of something based on evidence found outside the Bible. For example, Dennis Bennett said in The Holy Spirit and You:

To speak in tongues is an act of child-like faith…in the same way that a child begins to babble his first words, to open his mouth and make sounds… With whatever sounds one makes, offering his tongue to God in simple faith, he can begin to speak in tongues… If we do not accept the experience as real (the sounds of babbling), we will not be conscious of the reality, that is to say, any sound should be accepted by faith as the gift of tongues (Dennis Bennett 1971)

True faith, on the other hand, is conviction based on the revealed Word with respect to spiritual things. Bennett asks us to exercise intellectual, or worse, a blind faith, not biblical faith, since there is no insinuation in the Bible that babbling is anything like the initial gift of tongues.

There are two characteristics of faith that Charismatic believers ignore in this issue of the baptism in the Spirit: (1) biblical faith stands alone, without works, and (2) biblical faith is a profound conviction that Christ will fulfill His Word, without necessity of signs or external proofs to convince us that His promise is true.

In Ephesians 2:8 we read, "For by grace are ye saved through faith; and that not of yourselves: it is the gift of God." The reflexive pronoun "that" (neuter), does not refer to "faith" (which is feminine), but rather has an antecedent that refers to the completed work of salvation. Therefore, before we do any works, God gives us a complete salvation by grace simply through our faith in Him. This faith has one requirement, "So then faith comes by hearing, and hearing by the word of God." (Romans 10:17). To have faith, a person must merely hear with an implied meaning to understand and trust in God's Word; this is the only basis for faith. Personal experience is never a basis for faith.

If faith for salvation comes by understanding and confiding in what the Word says, then it is the same for faith that powers the Christian life. Paul said, "For we walk by faith, not by sight" (2 Corinthians 5:7). Faith for the Christian life does not come by trusting in our experience, but only by understanding and trusting more of God's Word. The more we are willing to obey what we come to understand, the more understanding God will give us, augmenting our trust; this is true Christian growth. In other words, true faith is never generated in our own minds from our experiences. If we must convince ourselves to believe, then that belief is not from God.

Just as we do not need works to help our faith, we also do not need miracles to convince us. One of the dangers of basing our belief on miraculous experience is that the miracle can take the place of the Word of God as the basis or authority for our faith. This is also a disingenuous intellectual faith. Jesus had this problem with his followers. John 2:23-24 says, "Many believed in his name, when they saw the miracles which he did. But Jesus did not commit himself unto them, because he knew all men." Many believed intellectually because of His signs, but not because they knew He was fulfilling his Word. They wanted a Liberator, not a Messiah who would fulfill Psalm 22 and Isaiah 53.

Convictions become deeper only through the study and application of the Word in our lives. Signs and phenomena never augment our faith; they only call attention to the Word, the true basis of faith. The phenomena of today that are touted as miracles only stimulate curiosity—in other words, intellectual faith—which may or may not be genuine. The evidence of true faith is the willingness to accept what the Bible says without the need for more proof.

CHAPTER 6

The gift of the Spirit: By works, mystical experience or by grace?

Every false religion in the world has two characteristics in common: a rigid legalistic system to deceive its followers into believing that they can become good enough for whatever happens in the next life and secondly, a mystical way to experience an encounter with whatever deity their religion proposes. These two false notions invaded Christianity from the beginning of its history corrupting the gospel message and deceiving those who do not understand the Scriptures into believing that they are acceptable and surely will go to heaven because they feel something.

In his letters to the churches, Paul pointed out some problems that have continued to appear time after time throughout the history of the Church. The main problem is works or experience versus grace. Without a proper understanding of justification by faith there has always been a tendency among Christians to think legalistically and/or mystically; to believe that we can improve upon our standing before God by our behavior, mystical devotion, or worship rituals whereby we seek an inner experience that assures us we must be saved. In this chapter we will examine the teaching in Galatians and Colossians and find attitudes that the believer should develop from his understanding of how God designed our relationship with Him.

The basic foundation of the Bible teaches us we can only receive God's free gift of salvation by faith (Eph 2:8-9) in His Word. The Legalists are asking us to perform certain tasks or to meditate enough in order to receive the Spirit or the fullness of the Spirit; in other words, they put the believer again under a system of rules or disciplines in order to acquire the blessing of the Spirit.

COMPARISON WITH THE PROBLEM IN GALATIANS

Paul found two problems of this category in his day as he described in his epistles to the churches of Galatia and Colossi. In both instances, false teachers tried to establish a system of works or disciplines in order to take their relationship with Christ to a higher level. They scorned the idea of a simple salvation and exalted a more profound or mystical experience so that the believers would experience more profound depths of God. As a result, many of the Galatians were deceived by the promise of a richer experience and began seeking more than just being satisfied with a comprehensive and complete salvation.

In one of Paul's earliest epistles Paul established the purpose of the law and the abuse of the law. Jesus said that He did not come to destroy the law or the prophets, but to fulfill them (Matt 5:17), then to make it clearer, He stated that the law will "accomplish its purpose" until "heaven and earth disappear" (Matt 5:18). Jesus told the strictest followers of the law, "Did not Moses give you the law, yet none of you keeps the law?" (John 7:19) Instead of getting defensive, they should have been honest and recognized that He spoke the truth: they were all guilty. However, they had no way in themselves of dealing with their guilt.

The purpose of the law was to teach us that we cannot ever measure up to God's standards. Paul wrote, "...the law was our tutor to bring us to Christ, that we might be justified by faith" (Gal 3:24). The word "tutor" is the Greek

Chapter 6: *The Gift of the Spirit: by works mystical experience or by grace?*

word *paidagogos*, from which we get the English word, "pedagogy" or teaching technique. God wrote the law with His finger in stone (Ex 31:18; Deut 9:10) to show all mankind that no one can measure up to His standards.

Paul wrote, "Now we know that whatever the law says, it says to those who are under the law, that every mouth may be stopped [or silenced], and all the world may become guilty before God" (Rom 3:19). There is no hope for salvation in trying to obey the law, "for through the law comes the knowledge of sin" (3:20). It is a teaching tool from God to show us how guilty we are before a holy God, and that our only hope is faith in a merciful God.

Once a person puts his faith in Jesus Christ as his Savior, the condemnation of the law is paid for: "For Christ is the end of the law, with the result that there is righteousness for everyone who believes" (Rom 10:4NET).

When this truth is not understood and someone makes a profession of faith continuing to believe that he is a pretty good person, he really has not been saved at all (1 John 1:8, 10 NET, "If we say we do not bear the guilt of sin, we are deceiving ourselves and the truth is not in us."), that is, we don't understand that the purpose of the law was to condemn us as guilty sinners desperately needing a Savior. Until a person understands this truth he cannot be saved.

Notice that these are people who say they "have fellowship with him" (1:6). they are professing Christians, but not possessing Christians. However, when such persons with false professions come inside the church they need a form of legalism to justify their goodness and false mystical experience to feel blessed by God. Their typical symptoms are a lack of brokenness, pride and unrepentant spirit, and a desire to feel good about themselves and be entertained instead of taught in the Scriptures. Ray Comfort describes it this way:

> "People who make a commitment to Christ without the Law may do so because they are seeking true inner peace and lasting fulfillment. They come to fill a "God-shaped vacuum" in their lives. There is no trembling. There is no fleeing from wrath. There is no fear. To them, God is a benevolent, fatherly figure, not a holy God of wrath. Without the Law, they haven't been stripped of self-righteousness. They don't truly believe that their just reward is eternal damnation. Therefore, even as professing Christians, they think they are basically good.
> Because of this faulty foundation, these converts are likely to think that they are pleasing God by reading the Bible, praying, fasting, and doing good works. They are susceptible to being deceived into thinking that somehow their good works commend them to God, and they are therefore liable to stray into legalistic standards such as "do not touch, do not taste, do not handle" (Col 2:21)" (Comfort 2006:55)

A group of false teachers from among the Galatian churches taught that through special obedience everyone would receive the fulfillment of their salvation through the Holy Spirit. Paul addresses this problem in Galatians 3:1-3. The phrase "now made perfect by the flesh" shows that they thought they were made perfect or complete and by their own works they wanted to reach sanctification. They admitted that faith was the first step, but they also believed that faith was only the beginning; only by adding sincere efforts through total devotion in order to attain perfection, would they be able to accomplish the consummation of the blessing of God. Wiersbe simplifies the issue:

> The Holy Spirit is mentioned eighteen times in this epistle and plays an important part in Paul's defense of the Gospel of the grace of God. The only real evidence of conversion is the presence of the Holy Spirit in the life of the believer (see Rom. 8:9). Paul asks an important question: did they receive the Spirit by faith in the Word of God, or by doing the works of the Law? Of course, there could be but one answer: the Spirit came into their lives because they trusted Jesus Christ (Wiersbe 1989: Gal 3:1).

Paul, however, highlighted a difference between receiving the Spirit by faith (trusting and believing in that which they had heard and nothing more) and receiving Him or His special approval by that which we do, that is, good works. In Galatians 3:4-15, he declared that by faith we receive "the promise of the Spirit." This means the baptism of the Holy Spirit, and all the fullness or completeness of the entire Godhead (Col 2:9) now resides in the believer. It is impossible to add to, improve or invalidate this relationship.

Evidently, these false teachers seemed so sincere and persuasive that the Galatians did not understand how they could not be from God. But Paul spoke emphatically: faith does not include any human effort or discipline. There is much more to this problem than merely obligating certain rituals or lifestyle changes.

The emphasis of Paul on appreciating the fullness of God in the believer by faith without any additional works seems to indicate in Galatians and later in Colossians that an additional mystical union was being pursued. This problem would continue to plague the Church, especially in the different forms of legalistic mysticism. Morrison writes that it was the mystic's doctrine of "perfection," which laid the foundation for Wesley's own teaching in this area. In an article on "Perfectibilists" in Blunt's Dictionary of Sects, Heresies, Ecclesiastical Parties and Schools of Thought, the writer states:

> Many mystical divines have believed that a life of profound devotional contemplation leads one to such a union with God that all which is base and sinful in the Christian's soul becomes annihilated, and there ensues a superhuman degree of participation in the Divine perfection. Such a doctrine was held by the great mystic whose works pass under the name of Dionysius, and from him was handed down to the Quietist Hesychasts, the strict Franciscans, the Molinists, the Jansenists, and the German Mystics [Dominicans such as Eckhart and Tauler], from whom it passed on to the English Methodists, among whom it has always been a special tenet that sanctification may, and ought to, go on to perfection. (Blunt 1990: 422)

Chapter 6: *The Gift of the Spirit: by works mystical experience or by grace?*

No matter if the teachers were very sincere in wanting to add works to faith in order to gain a special experience or a more profound relationship in their salvation; it is impossible to add anything more than what we have in the Spirit. It is an error to place such emphasis on seeking more of God's promised presence through obedience or special devotion since we have received already all the full blessing of the Spirit by faith. There is a human tendency to seek a more intimate and profound relationship with deity, but this is not seeking more of God or receiving something that we are lacking in our salvation.

COMPARISON WITH THE PROBLEMS IN COLOSSI

The second problem was with the Colossians, whose problems mirror those of the Galatians. False teachers wanted to introduce something supplementary to salvation, a more profound and mystical relationship with God.

First, they taught that we are still lacking something after having received Christ.

False teachers always want to introduce something more to salvation, making the mere salvation experience seem insufficient or inferior. They diminish the salvation experience, considering it as a beginning point from which the believer can reach more profound experiences and deeper truths by discipline and faith. In Colossi, these teachers said that believers needed something in addition to Christ in order to be satisfied; in this case, that additional element was the Holy Spirit.

In Colossians 2, Paul addressed these false teachers and their message. His insistence on "being complete in Him" (verse 10), suggests that some believed they needed more than just having Christ in their lives. Paul wanted to assure the believers that it is absolutely impossible to improve on our salvation in Christ, that we are complete in Him. Also, in verse 9, we see that "For in Him dwells all the fullness of the Godhead bodily." That is to say, if we have Christ, we have all the fullness of God dwelling within us; there is no more of God that can be added. It is nonsense and does not make sense to beg God for more of Him when we already have all He is and all He has to give us. Evidently Paul had good reason for giving these instructions, because someone was teaching the opposite.

Essentially, there is no greater spiritual blessing than finding Christ. Ephesians 1:3 says, "Blessed be the God and Father of our Lord Jesus Christ, who hath blessed us with all spiritual blessings in heavenly places in Christ." In other words, in Christ we have all the spiritual blessings God can give us now. It is our responsibility to discover what these blessings are from their revelations in the Word of God. We cannot add more to them, nor can we discover them from mystical encounters in prayer, or unconscious trances. There is no relationship more profound than when Christ lives within us by faith.

When we are told that we lack the true joy and peace brought by a secondary baptism of the Spirit, the experiencing of special spiritual gifts and the promises of extraordinary and exhilarating power of the Holy Spirit, we are being taught the same false doctrine that was taught in Colossi.

This kind of teaching always has a tendency toward mysticism, which is defined in Wikipedia as…

> "the pursuit of achieving communion with or conscious awareness of ultimate reality, the divine, spiritual truth, or God through direct, personal experience (intuition or insight) rather than rational thought; the belief in the existence of realities beyond perceptual or intellectual apprehension that are central to being and directly accessible through personal experience; or the belief that such experience is a genuine and important source of knowledge. In the Hellenistic world, "mystical" referred to secret religious rituals." ("Mysticism": 1)

The perception of having had a genuine and personal encounter with God or a sense of speaking in a mystical language that only God could understand replicates the ancient Greek mystics. A real experience or sense of God speaking to them personally can be very convincing. MacDonald writes:

> The Gnostics professed to have deep, secret mysteries, and in order to learn what these mysteries were, a person had to be initiated. Perhaps the secrets included many so-called visions. Supposed visions are an important element in such present-day heresies as Mormonism, Spiritism, Catholicism, and Swedenborgianism. Those who were members of the inner circle were naturally proud of their secret knowledge (MacDonald 1995: 2:23).

In Colossians 2:18-23, the following four false doctrines appeared: (1) Their false humility was enticing and impressive; (2) They were preoccupied by angels or supernatural beings, who apparently appeared to them in visions or dreams. They used these experiences to appear to be more spiritual, especially more so than the apostle Paul (2:18); (3) they did not emphasize that Christ is the Head of the Church, as the Bible clearly states. The "revelations" they received from angels or from the "Spirit" were more important to them than the study of the already revealed Word of God (2:19); and (4) They insisted on conformity to their decrees of ethics and rules about things they could not touch, taste or handle (2:20-21), insinuating that these dietary, fasting and self-disciplinary practices made one more spiritual. Paul declared that such teachings were heresies and should be combated with the Word before they destroyed the church.

When we compare those false teachers with the different movements of today, we find many parallels. Normally such persons are very persuasive and can convince the unprepared of anything. Unfortunately, the majority of believers are not prepared biblically to refute, discern or resist the intimidation of their accusations or declarations.

Chapter 6: *The Gift of the Spirit: by works mystical experience or by grace?*

Two Dangerous Consequences of Mystical Teachings

Christian mysticism has long been a practice of the Roman Catholic Church and various sects to create a sense of direct contact with God as opposed to the "indirect" contact with God merely through Scriptures. In the Catholic Church, where the Bible has been prohibited for centuries, mystics created a devotional religion.

> In the sixteenth century, we find mystics such as Ignatius Loyola, Teresa of Avila and John of the Cross developing a systematized mysticism in their writings, laying out the steps by which one may achieve personal union with the divine, as if it was an ascent up a ladder or mountain, or down into the labyrinthine depths of the soul.
> These writings have been popularized throughout the Christian scene for many years, especially in Charismatic and neo-evangelical circles today where they are recommended as wholesome reading matter. For example, in Power Evangelism by John Wimber, we find that Ignatius Loyola and Teresa of Avila are commended (Morrison 2007: 7).

Paul gave various warnings about Christians guarding against a "different gospel" (Gal. 1:6). The major "difference" in that gospel consisted of mixing grace with works, or it may not include either one! All that is needed is an experience supposedly with God. Morrison added,

> Recently, I read an interview in the 'Jesus Army' magazine with John Arnott, Senior Pastor in the Airport church in Toronto. He was asked by Noel Stanton: "Do you see [the Toronto Blessing] as breaking out into evangelism and mission?" Arnott replied: "Absolutely. Unbelievers are being converted just through going out under the power of the Spirit." So evangelicals believe today that conversion is a mystical experience. (Incidentally, this is very much like the ancient pagan practice of "Incubation," whereby one goes into a special sleep in a sacred place where the gods allegedly work on you while you're out. (*Ibid.*, 13)

If someone preaches the gospel, but announces blessings are to be received in pieces or that there is a series of later experiences, then it is not the same gospel as the Bible teaches. There are also many scholars who, although plainly discerning enough to know the difference between religious mysticism and biblical spirituality, fail to alert their readers to it. For example, the well-known book Great Leaders of the Christian Church published by Moody Press has, refers to one of those great leaders, the Spanish Counter-Reformation mystic, Teresa of Avila. She is literally sandwiched between John Knox, Blaise Pascal and John Owen! (Woodbridge 1988:iii)

There are two dangerous consequences of believing mystical teachings.

First consequence: A special focus on a wrong teaching frequently becomes a substitute for the truth.

In the history of the Church, when the emphasis shifted from the grace of God or the exposition of the Word to some other experience or truth, this new emphasis became a substitute for truth. In Galatians 6:14 ("But God forbid that I should boast except in the cross of our Lord Jesus Christ, by whom the world has been crucified to me, and I to the world") Paul shows that focus should be on the cross and the person and sacrifice of Jesus. Looking at the Bible, it is easy to see that the ministry of the Spirit is not to glorify or exalt Himself. Compared to those that talk about Christ, there are few verses that talk of the Spirit. The Spirit, who inspired the Bible, gave us enough information to be able to know Him, but He also made it obvious that He is not the one who should be magnified.

In Colossians 3:1-3 we see where the center of our attention should be: Christ, sitting at the right hand of God. Likewise, John 16:13-14 says, "Howbeit when he, the Spirit of truth, is come, he will guide you into all truth: for he shall not speak of himself; but whatsoever he shall hear, that shall he speak: and he will show you things to come. He shall glorify me: for he shall receive of mine and shall show it unto you." Therefore, the Spirit came to speak only of Christ and to communicate His glory, not His own.

Today, in the author's opinion, some emphasize the miraculous signs and the gift of tongues instead of introducing the unbeliever to the grace of God. Thus such a focus diminishes the gospel in its essence, or confuses the gospel with so many experiences. Supernatural phenomena can be so exaggerated that any gospel offered is given almost in passing; Christ is mentioned only in relation to the Spirit, because the Spirit is the center of the messages and their beliefs. The emphasis is what we can experience today, not on what occurred on the cross and how the cross should affect us still.

Therefore, this special focus on personal experiences can become a substitute for fundamental truth. An example of this is seen in the Christian mystic and Dominican priest Johannes Tauler's sermons (1300-1361). Some evangelicals elevate his writings as the beginnings of the Reformation. Admittedly, he was not a promoter of the Roman Catholic Church, but neither did most of the mystics who generally despised any form of the organized church, which stands in the way of the mystics' spiritual quest of being "one with God."

An examination of his sermons shows that Tauler speaks of the three stages in the mystical life: 1) a life of spirituality and virtue, bringing us close to God's presence; 2) Spiritual poverty, when God withdraws himself from the soul, leaving it "anguished and denuded;" 3) the transition into a "divinized life," into what he describes as "a union of our created spirit with God's uncreated one." (Tauler, 1985, on 1 Pet. 3:8). This is an example of the mystic language. The search for a spiritual reality or a deeper sense of God's presence may be from a lack of understanding the amazing truths in God's Word we should be resting in them instead of pursuing deeper levels of mystical encounters.

Chapter 6: *The Gift of the Spirit: by works mystical experience or by grace?*

Many books show the clear linkage between Pentecostalism and Catholic Mysticism such as Edward O'Connor's book The Pentecostal Movement in the Catholic Church. In a chapter entitled "Pentecost and Traditional Spirituality" (by which he means Mystical Spirituality), he looks first at the Spanish Carmelite, John of the Cross's mystical teachings, especially in his Ascent of Mount Carmel. After referring to the experiences involved in one particular stage in the mystical process, he writes: "These experiences can serve as points of comparison for the 'Baptism in the Spirit' that figures so prominently in the Pentecostal Movement." (O'Connor 1971: 22)

Without a doubt there are many sincere people in these movements, but abuses can easily predominate. Morrison's research into mysticism in world religions sees a remarkable similarity among mystics of the world religions.

> We find that what mysticism is all about - as it has manifested throughout the world over the centuries, whether it is Eastern mysticism or so called Christian mysticism - can be reduced to two heads: 1) The seeking out of a direct experience with God, without any mediator; 2) The setting up of the individual's subjective experience as the sole arbiter of religious truth. (Morrison: 5).

In his investigations into different movements he discovered that the Lutheran Pietists were not exempt from this tendency to want to substitute truth for experience.

> "It is highly significant that one of the principal reforms demanded by the German Pietists, according to Routledge's Encyclopaedia of Religions, was 'that the theological schools should be reformed by the abolition of all systematic theology, and that morals and not doctrine should form the staple of all preaching.' And what would you suspect to be the result of that reform? In their eagerness to eschew systematic theology, the mystics and Pietists embraced a systematized devotionalism. Systematic theology devoid of heart religion is bad enough. But a heart religion which is devoid of systematic theology is a scourge." (Morrison:16)

The Roman Catholic Charismatic Renewal continues to grow at a rapid pace. All around the world, Roman Catholics are experiencing the Charismatic's second baptism known as the "baptism of the Holy Spirit." Statistics show that at least half the Charismatics in the world are also Roman Catholic. Many Roman Catholics are being "slain in the spirit" and are "speaking in tongues." Much of the Roman Catholic priesthood has embraced the "charismatic experience," which, incidentally, has received the Pope's official blessing.

The Second-Blessing "spirit-baptism" experience, visions and inner voices, raptures and ecstasies, alleged prophesying's, falling under "the power," speaking in gibberish-style tongues. All these mainstays of the Charismatic and Pentecostal Movements are entirely in accord with Roman Catholic mysticism. Because Pentecostals and Charismatics now make up the bulk of those who profess to be evangelicals today, we see that Catholicism and neo-evangelicalism are unashamedly moving in the same compromised direction. (Morrison: 22)

O'Connor writes in *The Pentecostal Movement in the Catholic Church*,

"Although they derive from Protestant backgrounds, the Pentecostal churches are not typically Protestant in their belief, attitudes or practices. Many historians, as well as many of their own members, regard them as a 'third force' in the Christian world, between Protestantism and (Roman) Catholicism." (O'Connor, 1971: 23)

Another reason that so many Protestant Christians have been attracted to mysticism is because they have been so poorly taught. This is a result of low standards in both the pulpit and publications. We have already seen the acceptance of mysticism in purportedly evangelical books.

The same is true of many evangelical newspapers and journals. For example, Morrison reports that in a widely read neo-evangelical newspaper recently there appeared a full-page article about the French mystical, ecumenical haven "Taizé" (which uses practices which border on interfaith religious experience), without any critical comment. People were simply left to "make up their own minds". But that is not what Christian teaching should be about — especially in relation to the training of the young, who are very susceptible to the ill effects of "fudge." What is needed today is clear, unambiguous exposition of Biblical principles (Morrison: 30).

Praise songs and prayers of Taizé are available on Amazon.com. A typical statement that attracts the uninformed is, "If there are times you feel the Divine Presence, then you're half way to becoming a mystic. And if you want to unite with that Presence, then you're an aspiring mystic." (Meister Eckhart 2007:1)

Mystical meditation techniques are being promoted by various Charismatic and non-charismatic authors including New Age techniques, visualization, meditation and other metaphysical techniques to gain whatever they want. Programs in universities such as Spiritual Formation Programs or Interspirituality that focus on contemplative techniques and programs is often drawing from New Age and medieval mystic sources. These are usually couched in spiritual and seeming biblical terms that the undiscerning does not recognize. The walk in obedience to the Word of God, the authority of the Word of God in personal lives, and the task of sharing the clear gospel of Christ with the world is lost in the shuffle of mystical experiences.

Chapter 6: *The Gift of the Spirit: by works mystical experience or by grace?*

Second consequence: A system of law or mystical obedience produces false guilt and preoccupation.

The Charismatics speak of super-devotion as a requirement for receiving the Spirit. They put the responsibility on the believer, using phrases such as "submission in every area," "total trust in Christ," and "Do you have enough faith?" Another intimidating question that is common is, "Do you have the whole Gospel?" Passing the responsibility for receiving the Spirit to the response of the believer was never intended as a teaching of the New Testament.

In Philippians 2:13 (" for it is God who works in you both to will and to do for His good pleasure"), God has the responsibility of producing the change in our lives; it is not something that we do to gain the prize of the Spirit. Certainly we must diligently add to our faith certain attitudes (2 Peter 1:3-8) in order to mature spiritually, but this does not apply to the completion of our relationship with the Spirit.

Submission to God, prayer and separation from sin, or whatever other action of the believer, are not legalistic requirements for experiencing the consummation of salvation. On the contrary, they are privileges that God's grace produces in us and are the evidence of all that we are in Christ.

When the charismatic believers speak of the "complete gospel," they are not talking about what we have in Christ because of our belief in Him, but they are referring to what we could have as a result of our submission, fasting, prayer, or separation, etc. If this were the case, we should be concerned that we may never know just when we have arrived at enough sanctification to be awarded the experience of intimacy with God.

It is true that the believer should examine himself, but not in order to receive more of God; he already has all of God's presence abiding within him. The motivation should be from a heart filled with gratitude motivating us to a more obedient and surrendered walk with God by the power of the Holy Spirit to apply His Word and fulfill His purpose for our lives.

Charismatics teach that the gospel brings the Holy Spirit initially, but not totally in His fulness; they believe that grace and faith alone are not enough to experience the profound, complete, victorious, abundant and full life of the Spirit. They believe that it is necessary to have a special encounter with God, to have certain attitudes and to take certain steps to arrive at the kind of life that the Spirit will accept.

The logical conclusion for many of those who seek such an experience and do not find it, is: "It is all my fault!" People can live feeling this constant frustration and guilt, and they constantly examine themselves to try to arrive at the level of spirituality where they can experience the promised peace and fullness of the Spirit. They fast for days, pray for personal holiness that will be enough for a God-encounter and power-baptism for a satisfying relationship with God and service.

The truth is that, the more they worry, the more doubt they generate about whether they are completely yielded to God. This kind of introspection keeps them from thinking they are at a level of spirituality to deserve the baptism of the Spirit, much less be useful to God in the ministry or able to advance His kingdom. They simply find themselves more and more sinful, frustrated and doubtful. This often leads to irresponsibility in other areas, which brings the pressure of other authorities in their lives.

Some are able to convince themselves that their sins are not so bad, or that they are only faults instead of sins in order to achieve the mystical total dedication. But fulfillment, many times, does not come. Since they have determined that the cause is not their sin, they put the blame on their personality. One Charismatic believer said, "After praying, asking for the baptism and confessing all known sin, the only impediment can be a person's inhibitions." So, if the person does not have the mystical experience, one or both of two things are at fault: some secret sin or his personal inhibitions.

To make matters worse, the temptation arises to fake the experience. If that is yielded to, the internal guilt only magnifies until a breaking point occurs.

Charismatics carry subtle or conscious guilt until at last they achieve their goal of speaking in tongues. Probably a part of their joy in finally speaking in tongues, consciously or unconsciously, is relief from a self-induced or false guilt. It is common to find much joy and enthusiasm in these churches when one of their own speaks in tongues, because the greater part of the preaching emphasizes the necessity of speaking in tongues and/or experiencing miracles.

Those who do not reach this goal continue to live under the pressure of false guilt. Could it be that they emphasize this experiential aspect of their belief as the only way to find joy and power in their lives because they must find relief from the guilt that they themselves have induced? This may be an unfair question, but is worth considering.

The following story illustrates the frustration of many of our Charismatic friends:

> There was a man who spent his life looking for silver in the mountains of California. He was so obsessed with his quest that his wife and children felt compelled to abandon him. When he died, few people attended his funeral. They found a letter he had written saying that his last desire was that he be buried beneath his cabin. They dutifully began to dig a grave under this humble miner's shack and, there, they discovered a shiny gray substance. It was pure silver! The place came to be known as the famous "Comstock Silver Vein," the richest silver mine in the history of California. The miner had been a multimillionaire all his life, but he never was able to take advantage of his riches! The believer is also rich in Christ. The poor miner had no idea that he was living on top of the riches he was looking for, and in the same way, many believers do not know the spiritual riches they have within themselves through the Holy Spirit. We need not look anywhere else! (MacArthur: 1978)

Chapter 6: *The Gift of the Spirit: by works mystical experience or by grace?*

Two Key Passages (2 Peter 1:3-4 and Colossians 2:9-10)

> "I can pray this because his divine power has bestowed on us everything necessary for life and godliness through the rich knowledge of the one who called us by his own glory and excellence. Through these things he has bestowed on us his precious and most magnificent promises, so that by means of what was promised you may become partakers of the divine nature, after escaping the worldly corruption that is produced by evil desire" (2 Peter 1:3-4 NET).

As II Peter says, we have all we need to live a victorious Christian life. We simply need to learn to obey and take advantage of the instruction and promises. All the "things" (promises of God, Word of God, Holy Spirit) have been given to us, that is, we have no need to acquire them. Everything necessary for life or living and godliness, how to please God, has been given to us in the knowledge of Christ, as revealed in His Word. As we focus on knowing correctly and applying practically to our lives this knowledge and promises we are transformed into Christ's image. Peter goes on to talk about a seven-step process of how to apply these principles. There is nothing mystical about this formula for the Christian life, but rather it is intensely practical and applicable to everyone.

Paul warned his readers about the invading mystical tendencies that would later grow into a Gnostic sect that would corrupt Christianity for centuries. In Colossians 2:18 these teachings and practices were already infiltrating the Early Church as Paul wrote,

> "Let no one who delights in humility and the worship of angels pass judgment on you. That person goes on at great lengths about what he has supposedly seen, but he is puffed up with empty notions by his fleshly mind."

The introducing negative, *medeis*, means to "absolutely have nothing to do with, or the thing is forbidden" (Thayer's Greek Lexicon). The negative with the present imperative verb, "beguile or pass judgment" demands that the reader stop this action already in progress, that is, "stop letting people disqualify you or intimidate you by saying you do not qualify for genuine spirituality." This refers to delighting in the pretense of false humility, angelic worship encounters, dreams and visions that supposedly were experienced and stay away from people with inflated egos of their own importance and mystical experiences.

The delighting in humility seems positive, but it is a characteristic of false teachers. Humility is never the focus, but is the result of godly actions. It is defined in Phil 2:3-4 as making the needs of others the highest priority in one's life. This is similar to the author who supposedly wrote the book, "Humility and how I obtained it." One author said, "When one delights in humility it ceases to be genuine humility and becomes pride!"

The word for "humility," *tapeinophrosune*, often referred to fasting and several Jewish Christian writings specify that the consequence of this ascetic practice is entrance into the heavenly realm. This self-effacement or humiliation of one's mind is always a negative connotation in classical Greek. When someone "delights" in humility, it becomes pride and manipulation to gain praise from others.

Humility is an admirable characteristic that gives the impression that a person must be walking with God since he is so humble. However, when someone continually "delights" [or "chooses on purpose"] to appear in "humility" as a means of "passing judgment on you" [*katabrabeuo*, "beguile" or using charm and persuasion to deceive]. His false humility gives him a mask of spiritual superiority, by which he exploits the unsuspecting believer.

> "The Gnostic prided himself upon special visions of secret things which were not open to the eyes of ordinary men and women. No one will deny the visions of the mystics, but there is always danger when a man begins to think that he has attained a height of holiness which enables him to see what common men - as he calls them - cannot see; and the danger is that men will so often see, not what God sends them, but what they want to see." (Barclay 1959: 181)

They took great pride, though covered in the pretense of humility, to create the impression that they had real spirituality, and therefore a sense of fulfillment, that could only be attained through entering into these deep secrets or attaining deeper levels of intimacy with God.

The word for "supposedly seen," or intruding," *embateoo*, is used in the Mystery religions of Paul's day. When a person "intruded" into the spiritual realm where God dwells, this meant he had paid the price of being initiated so that now he was considered to be "spiritual" in that mystery religion. The false teachers were telling the Colossians that they are not qualified to be initiated into the deeper levels of intimacy or enter into the heavens spiritually and thus were unable to communicate with heavenly beings on their level. This accusation intimidated them into yielding to false mystic teachings of encounters with spiritual beings, visions and dreams, or directly with angels.

> The Gnostic prided himself upon special visions of secret things, which were not open to the eyes of ordinary men and women. No one will deny the visions of the mystics, but there is always danger when a man begins to think that he has attained a height of holiness which enables him to see what common men-as he calls them-cannot see; and the danger is that men will so often see, not what God sends them, but what they want to see. (*Ibid.*,182)

These are all symptoms that take many different forms through the ages, but the bottom line is a focus away from the Word of God, its serious study and application and the mission of the church, world evangelism. Rather the focus is all on us and "worship" instead of service to the kingdom.

True worship humbles one because he gains a glimpse of the holiness of

Chapter 6: *The Gift of the Spirit: by works mystical experience or by grace?*

God as revealed in His Word (Isaiah 6:1-5) and overwhelming gratitude that because of the blood of Christ we find ourselves acceptable in His sight (Eph 1:6). What is gained in such worship is fresh insight into how He wants us to live (conviction of the Holy Spirit) and how He wants us to serve others for His glory (Isa 6:8-9).

Mysticism is very different from a genuine worship and from legalism. It is based on subjective experiences, which are suppose to make one more "spiritual" than anyone who has not had such experiences. Mysticism is so subjective that it cannot be proved or disproved, but the symptoms are inevitable. These mystics supposedly saw angels between God and man as intermediaries or protectors of believers who could be called upon in need. Was this an early form of spiritual warfare?

Paul's main point in Colossians 2 is that all you need is Christ as He is portrayed in Scriptures, not in dreams or visions. This is not to say that believers will not have legitimate supernatural experiences serving Christ, but they should not become the focus of one's spiritual life, nor should anyone depend upon temporary experiences for a sense of intimate walking in His Spirit (Gal 5:16).

Beware of anyone who will judge you or intimidate you by making you think that you will not get the "reward" or God's approval unless you have a specific "experience" or subjective encounter like they did. Beware of anyone who holds up certain "standards" which must be obeyed if you are to be "spiritual" or to enter into the "deeper" truths or higher levels of your relationship with God. Either of these will lead you into bondage and away from a high value on the Word of God. If God gives you a wonderful experience in communion with Him, prize it and keep it to yourself. Pride is a subtle enemy. Not only does it corrupt the speaker, it provokes envy in the hearer – a double sin to avoid.

Chapter 6: Gifts for Today

CHAPTER 7

The transition of the work of the Spirit

Chapter 7: Gifts for Today

A student of mine asked me the other day, "Is Jesus Christ the same yesterday, and today and forever?" This was not the real question, but rather he was asking me that if Jesus did miracles when He walked on earth does He do miracles today?

He was nearly quoting Hebrews 13:8. I answered him, "Yes, Jesus is the same Person that He was before the foundation of the earth, but He does change the approach He takes to reach out to man. He is no longer the Creator, though He could be; He is no longer the 'angel of the Lord' though He could be; He is no longer the dying Savior, but is the living Savior; He no longer walks on earth, but lives in heaven interceding for us day and night. Though He is doing different things, He is still the same Person."

This verse is telling these Hebrew Christians as precious and faithful as He was to the leaders before you (13:7), so he will be with you as well. This verse is often quoted to prove that the miracle gifts of the apostles in the Early Church are just as valid today as then. However, there is no hint of this application in the context.

This "miracle" interpretation has a number of problems. In the context (always the first place to look to understand a passage) the previous verse deals with the former leaders of the early Christian churches who were examples to these believers, but now were deceased. They were to remember their lifestyles and "imitate their faith" (v. 7). Just as Jesus was with them and gave them victories, so He is with us today. Jesus will always be the same, always be there and always be the best Model and Companion.

Do things change? Thankfully, yes! No longer does God kill anyone who lies in church (Acts 5), or do they get eaten up with worms immediately as a judgment for being proud (Acts 12:23) nor does He rain down fire and destroy a city like Sodom and Gomorrah for immorality (Jude 7), etc. To use this verse (Heb 13:7) to teach that Jesus gave tongues in the Early Church so He must give them now, is like saying to everyone that they have to sell everything they have to follow Jesus, because He said it once to a rich young man (Matt 19:21; Luke 18:22). Verses have to be understood in their cultural, historical and grammatical contexts or they can be twisted to mean many strange things.

In order to grasp the scriptural perspective on the work of the Holy Spirit, we must analyze the biblical references one by one and understand the author's language in its linguistic-historical context. One of the distinctions that must be made is between the actions that are normative, and those that are unique to a singular historical event.

"Normative" refers to the normal operating procedure of the Holy Spirit. That is, actions that take place in the life of every believer are "normative." We will see a transition from the dealings of the Spirit in the Old Testament to that of the New Testament, which are related by the Gospels and the book of Acts.

The transition from the Old Testament religious life to the New Testament life required years of gradual change. The sacrificial system, Temple-centered religion, hereditary priesthood, and geographical Israel-centered religion transitioned into a single sacrifice system (the death of Christ), a believer's-body-temple religion, a universal priesthood and a global Church united by the Holy

Spirit held in common by all believers. The Israel of the OT did not mutate into the Church of the NT, rather the Church is an entirely new entity born out of the early Jewish converts. Israel as a nation remained in unbelief until a future day when she shall be restored by faith in her Messiah at His second coming.

In the context of referring to Gentiles and Jews, Paul gives this description of the Church, "For he [Christ] is our peace, the one who made both groups [Jews and Gentiles] into one and who destroyed the middle wall of partition, the hostility, when he nullified in his flesh the law of commandments in decrees. He did this to create in himself one new man out of two [Jew and Gentile], thus making peace" (Ephesians 2: 14-15 NET).

To begin, we have to realize that the revelation of the Holy Spirit in the Old Testament, especially the unique manifestation of Yahweh, is very scarce. The revelation of the New Testament gives an abundance of references to the Spirit as a distinct Person, yet united in the godhead, with the fullness of God. All this new revelation was introduced gradually, beginning in the Gospels and progressing to the Epistles, where the Spirit is more clearly explained. It is essential that we see the totality of the revelation about the Spirit in the New Testament and not form premature conclusions from isolated texts and events early in the progressive revelation of the NT as it transitions from the OT.

Evidence of this transition period is seen in the reluctance of the early Church to preach to Gentiles. It was ten years before the first gentile is converted (Acts 10) and that required extraordinary double revelations (on the part of the gentile Cornelius and on the part of the Apostle Peter). This reluctance of the early Jewish Christians to engage with the gentiles is further seen in Acts 11:19, "Now those who were scattered after the persecution that arose over Stephen traveled as far as Phoenicia, Cyprus, and Antioch, preaching the word to no one but the Jews only." It would be nineteen years after the resurrection of Christ (AD 49) until the church at Jerusalem would formally accept the conversion of Gentiles!

The transition was not only evident in the maturing of the early Church's vision to reach the world, but also in how God engineered this transition to assure the unity of the Body of Christ and the establishment of the new Church with a consistent and unified working of the Spirit among the Gentiles and Jewish believers. Three or four times unique events took place during this transition that made this time period unusual, never repeated, and served a particular purpose in the transition to the NT church. This will be discussed in the next chapter when the Holy Spirit introduced a new age of how God was going to henceforth relate to all mankind. The paradigm shift in the NT is particularly evident in the dramatic transition from the OT working of the Spirit to the new and unique functions of the Spirit in the NT.

The Transition from the Old Testament to the New Testament

Jesus made the first suggestion to His disciples of a transition toward a new relationship with the Holy Spirit when he said in NET John 14:17, "The Spirit of truth, whom the world cannot accept, because it does not see him or know him.

But you know him, because he resides with you and will be in you."

This is the first of five verses dealing with the new instructions for the Holy Spirit, called the *Paraklete* passages (John 14:26; 15:26; 16:7-11, 12-15), from the English title given, the "Comfortor" which translates *paraklemenos*, "one called alongside" (TDNT 5:803). We know two things from this verse: (1) They did not have the Spirit living in them at that time, and (2) there was an anticipated transition toward a new relationship with the Spirit, in which He would dwell in the disciples. Christ gave them this revelation on the night before His crucifixion to prepare them for the great change that would occur, altering forever the disciples' relationship with the Holy Spirit.

These disciples were a unique group that cannot be compared to any believers in modern day. They were essentially OT saints who discovered their Messiah. An example of their unique situation can be seen in John's testimony. John would actually not "believe" until he saw the bed clothes in the wrapped position but with no body inside: John 20:8 "Then the other disciple [John], who came to the tomb first, went in also; and he saw and believed." They were saved in the OT sense, but the indwelling Holy Spirit was not yet "in" them.

> A careful consideration, however, will show that the baptism with the Spirit is not regeneration. This operation places the believer "in Christ" (Rom 6:3, 4; Gal 3:27; 1 Cor 12:13; Col 2:12), whereas regeneration results in Christ in the believer (John 17:23; Col 1:27; Rev 3:20). Regeneration imparts life. The baptism with the Spirit unites the life-possessing one to Christ and to those who possess life in Him. Did not the Lord Jesus, in His great Upper Room Discourse, when uttering words prophetic of the Spirit's Advent into the world at Pentecost, and His ministry during this present age, refer to a distinction between these two operations of the Spirit as "ye in Me" (baptism with the Spirit) and "I in you" (regeneration) (John 14:20)? The baptism with the Holy Spirit and regeneration are thus two complementary, and yet distinct, works of God, simultaneously and eternally wrought in the believer the moment he exercises saving faith in Christ. By regeneration the soul is quickened from death into life (Eph 2:1-4). By the baptism with the Spirit the quickened soul is vitally united to Christ as Head (Eph 1:22, 23) and to all other believers as members of the one Body (1 Cor 12:12-27) (Unger 1944: 233-234)

As Jesus began His discourse on the revelation of the work of the Spirit He made a distinction between how they were currently related to the Spirit ("with you") and what they would eventually have by the Baptism in the Spirit ("will be in you"). This marked a dramatic change in relationship between God and believer. There would be a period of time until every group of people would be united in their relationship with the Spirit and the Church would become normalized. After this, more revelations from God would reveal a number of other works of the Spirit that occur simultaneously at salvation to make up the foundation for the newly formed Body of Christ, the Church. A transitional period is understandable.

Chapter 7: *The transition of the work of the Spirit*

This study will break the transition period into two segments: (1) Initial revelation in the Gospels thru Pentecost (chapter 7), and (2) the historical revelations of the transition through the Book of Acts (chapter 8), especially as it is related to the unique initial manifestations. There were five steps of instructions given with respect to the Spirit through the Gospels in the form of new revelations for this transition from the Old Testament to the New Testament.

(1) In the Old Testament, the Spirit came upon those He wanted.

References to the Spirit in the Old Testament are almost always in connection with special people like judges (Jdg. 3:10), civil administrators (Num 11:25), builders (Ex 35:31, 35) and prophets (2 Chron 24:20). Some were spiritual and others were not. Some were Jews and others were not. In other words, it seems as if a person's spiritual condition did not affect the activity of the Spirit as much as God's purpose for that person. Some gained the capacity to receive and proclaim the Word of God; others received wisdom to guide the nation of Israel. Some had the power to perform occasional miracles and others had the capacity to build the beautiful Temple, but all of them received these abilities from the Spirit when He came upon them.

All of these instances had to do with the direction, provision and protection of Israel. From Joshua to David there were few godly men, but the Spirit came over them anyway, using them in a powerful way to guide or protect the nation of Israel. Later God raised up the prophets to call the nation to repentance.

It may be possible to argue that all believers of that period had the Spirit as we have him today; however, the Old Testament Scriptures are silent on the matter. The men and women who belonged to these special groups, however, are the only ones that the Old Testament refers to as possessors of the Spirit. There may have been more, but that is an argument from silence. The text does not say so. If they were believers they had the regeneration of the Spirit, and the gift of God's righteousness (Gen 15:6), thus a spiritual life, but not the special empowerment of the Spirit for special service.

Thirty-two references describe the Holy Spirit coming upon men in the Old Testament, but there are no references in the New Testament Epistles that describe the Spirit coming upon men. Something changed between the Old Testament and the New Testament.

(2) John the Baptist announced that One would come baptizing in the Spirit.

John announced that the baptism in the Spirit would begin soon, but the lack of interest in the theme suggests that no one understood. There is no evidence of questions, no sign of curiosity about the baptism of the Spirit. John's announcement is found in all four Gospels (Matt 3:11; Mk 1:8; Luke 3:16; John 1:33). In spite of this dramatic and emphatic announcement there is no further reference to this Spirit's baptism until after the resurrection when this same announcement is repeated in Acts 1:5 just before the ascension, but on this occasion with a more specific time as to when it would begin: "not many days from now."

When Jesus mentioned that His followers would have to forgive offenders seven times a day (Luke 17:4). That seemed like a hard command to obligate them to obey, since rabbis taught only four times was sufficient. Peter later asked Jesus for clarification (Matt 18:21) and got the shocking answer that four hundred and ninety times a day His followers would have to forgive offenders! On the other hand, their curiosity was not even aroused about the baptism in the Spirit to ask for further clarification (Luke 11:13).

Even so, the new revelation about the promise of sending Holy Spirit (or "Comforter" in John 14:16, 26; 15:26; 16:7) marked a clear line between the former OT relationship that would follow Christ's baptism in the Spirit. This new relationship with the Spirit would mark the beginning of a new way that God would henceforth relate to mankind.

The fact that the promise of the Spirit was fulfilled at Pentecost seven days later indicated a new beginning had occurred. The Spirit was never again a future promise, nor did any believer ever have to wait again to receive the Spirit, but rather immediately upon believing in Christ the Spirit would be granted. The single exception to this transition was the first believers in a non-Jewish context in Samaria. There is a transition in process in Acts, which will be discussed in the next chapter.

> "In Acts we go form the synagogue to the church, from law to grace, from Old Testament saints to New Testament saints, from a body of Jewish believers to the body of the church made up of Jews and Gentiles, who are all one in Christ." (MacArthur 1978: 85)

There can be no doubt that the Day of the Feast of Pentecost A.D. 30 marked a new way that believers would forever relate to God.

(3) Jesus insinuated that the Father would eagerly give the Spirit.

The next reference to the Spirit is in Luke 11:13, where Jesus said the Father was so gracious that He would be willing to give the Holy Spirit to whomever asked for Him. It is evident in the Gospels that there was little to no interest in the Holy Spirit; they did not even know what He was talking about.

Years later, when some of John's disciples were confronted with the gospel, they declared their ignorance about the Spirit saying, "We have not so much as heard whether there is a Holy Spirit" (Acts 19:2) That ignorance was probably typical of the Jews in the Old Testament and at the beginning of the New Testament period. Or perhaps the disciples, who knew about the promise of John the Baptist, but were not particularly interested because, like so many other new concepts, teachings and promises of Jesus, the meanings and importance was likewise, not understand.

The context in Luke 11:13 is part of a teaching parable. The context follows the narrative on how to pray using the Lord's Prayer as a model then Jesus

Chapter 7: *The transition of the work of the Spirit* 105

gave several illustrations that even a friend will not always awaken in the night to respond to your knocking, but Jesus declares (11:9) that we are to ask and knock on the Heavenly Father's door and we will "receive" our needs, "find" what we are seeking and a "door" will be open. The main idea is the vast difference between the responsiveness of a "friend" and God who is much more eager to answer our needs.

Then another analogy of the parable is given of a son (not just a friend as earlier) asking for necessary "bread" or an "egg" that would not be denied by his earthly father, much less would the seeker be given in response a serpent for a fish, or a scorpion instead of an egg (Luke 11:10-11). The objective is to demonstrate that an earthly father would always give the son what he needs, yet how much more would God meet the needs of His children.

We know that the Spirit would be given as a gift (Luke 11:13), not something earned or deserved. Just as parents want to give good gifts to their children, so also the Father wanted to freely give the Spirit to whomever would ask Him. There can be no comparison between earthly father in the parable and our heavenly Father, because our heavenly Father has a much greater desire to give gifts, even the greatest gift in creation, the divine Holy Spirit, to those who want Him.

"The goal of each parable is to point up an analogy between the story and the intended lesson or appeal." (Bailey 1998: 36) In this context the parable follows a lesson on prayer in which Jesus is teaching that God is trustworthy, immensely more willing to listen and respond to our prayers and grant us anything that is needed, even up to the Holy Spirit. It is a lesson in contrast, not a specific instruction to pray for the Spirit. It is a lesson of encouragement to pray to the heavenly Father and to depend on Him more than on any earthly father.

Neither is the point of the parable to show the necessary of importunity or perseverance in the prayer, as some have suggested. Remember the parable is a contrast. Pleading is only necessary with a "friend," but not with our God who is immediately ready to respond, even granting the greatest prize in the universe, the Holy Spirit. The parable is about God's attitude toward the praying believer, not the granting of the Holy Spirit.

Having said this, Jesus is certainly attempting once again to awaken their curiosity and interest in the topic of the Holy Spirit. He had earlier stated that "He who believes in Me, as the Scripture has said, out of his heart will flow rivers of living water" (John 7:38). They did not understand this until later after the Holy Spirit was given to all believers at Pentecost.

Whatever the intent was at this point in time in the Gospels, the idea of praying for the Holy Spirit to be given to a believer was never taught or practiced anywhere else the New Testament. Had that been the lesson of this parable surely someone would have prayed for or requested the Holy Spirit. The only exception to this evidence was Simon, the sorcerer, who said, "Give me also this power, that on whomsoever I lay hands, he may receive the Holy Spirit" (Acts 8:19). He only wanted the Spirit for his selfish benefit and profit.

(4) Christ breathed on the disciples that they might receive the Spirit.

In the conclusion of the Gospel narratives, there was another experience that marked a transition in the relationship with the Holy Spirit. In John 20:22, after the resurrection, Jesus appeared in the midst of the disciples that were found gathered that Sunday. After greeting them, He gave them visible evidence that He was indeed the same Jesus who had been crucified (20:20).

Later, He commissioned them as His special envoys, "As the Father has sent me, so I send you" (20:21). This was the fourth reference to the Great Commission in his post-resurrection ministry. Then "He breathed on them, and said to them, "Receive the Holy Spirit..." He had promised that He would send them "another Comforter" using the word *allos*, meaning something that is "different, but exactly like the former." Jesus had promised the disciples that He would be with them always. His presence in the Holy Spirit would be indispensable to fulfill the Great Commission. Harris writes in *A Biblical Theology of the New Testament*:

> "It is common for this statement to be understood as John's version of Pentecost, the fulfillment of Jesus' promise in the Farewell Discourse (16:7) to send the Holy Spirit after His return to the Father. It is better, however, to view Jesus' action in breathing on the disciples as symbolic of the outpouring of the Spirit at Pentecost rather than as an actual bestowal of the Spirit at the time of this post-resurrection appearance to the disciples. The disciples' behavior in the remainder of the gospel of John does not reflect the confident and powerful behavior they exhibited following the day of Pentecost according to Acts 2. In fact, if John 20:22 represents an actual bestowal of the Holy Spirit in some sense, one of the Twelve, Thomas, was not even there to receive the Spirit at the time (v. 24). Jesus had already made other proleptic statements in the gospel of John, notably with regard to His glorification that followed His death, resurrection, and return to the Father (17:1-5). It should not be surprising to find Him doing the same in relation to the giving of the Spirit." (Harris 1994: 201)

Some have suggested that breathing the Spirit onto the disciples was necessary because none of them had asked the Father for the Spirit (Luke 11:13). Whether or not this is true, at this moment it seems that they did not yet have the Spirit in their lives and were going to need the Spirit in a special way until Pentecost. Even though He breathed on them the Spirit, they would still have to wait for the coming of the Spirit on Pentecost, so the two are not the same. This was a transitional step toward full and permanent indwelling of the Spirit, which would begin shortly.

Jesus was going to leave them in just a few days to ascend to the Father, and he promised them that he would not leave them "orphans;" that is to say, He would not leave them without His presence to guide and teach them (John

Chapter 7: *The transition of the work of the Spirit*

14:18). Seven days would pass after His ascension before the Comforter came to live in all believers and this would never be necessary again. Therefore, the belief is that Jesus breathed on His disciples so that they would have the Spirit in the sense of being "on" them in power while they waited the fulfillment of the promise when the Spirit would thereafter always be "in" them.

These conditions could never exist after the Day of Pentecost, nor could anyone have the authority to breathe the breath of the Holy Spirit on pre-Spirit-baptized believers (a description that is impossible today). During this transition period a few rare events such as this occurred and were accurately recorded, but not as examples to be repeated, because the conditions cannot be duplicated, only as a record of the transition.

(5) The Comforter came to dwell permanently in believers, without needing to be asked.

The last step was given as a promise in the Gospels, but it was not fulfilled until the Day of Pentecost in approximately 30 A.D. Jesus said in John 14:16-17, "And I will pray the Father, and he shall give you another Comforter, that he may abide with you for ever; Even the Spirit of truth." Essentially, He was telling them that it was not necessary for them to ask in prayer for the Spirit. He would ensure that they, and all believers thereafter, would receive the Spirit through His own prayer.

Later, in John 16:7 on the evening before His crucifixion, Jesus gave a clearer indication about the time of the fulfillment of His promise. "Nevertheless I tell you the truth. It is to your advantage that I go away; for if I do not go away, the Helper will not come to you; but if I depart, I will send Him to you..." In other words, Jesus had to be absent in order to send the Spirit. Therefore, the disciples on the road to Emmaus did not receive the Spirit in the same sense (because Jesus was still there); instead, the Spirit came over them in the Old Testament sense until the Day of Pentecost when He entered into them, as He has done with all the other believers since. Jesus was promising a new relationship with the Spirit that began on the Day of Pentecost.

Before that date no one evidently had this kind of relationship with Christ. The Spirit empowerment in the Old Testament period was task specific and did not include all the ministries and functions that the Spirit would have in His post-resurrection relationship with believers.

Pentecost and the Five Works of the Spirit Henceforth

Scriptures indicate that the Day of Pentecost was significant with respect to the Holy Spirit. Exactly what He did on that day was not revealed at the moment it occurred, but some years later Jesus gave us the understanding of what that day meant through the Apostle Paul. The Day of Pentecost marked the last stage in the transition between the Old and New Testaments.

Christ ascended to heaven seven days before the Feast of Pentecost.

There were fifty days between the Day of Atonement and Feast of Pentecost ("Pentecost" means fifty days). If Christ was in the grave three days and later walked with the disciples for 40 days more (Acts 1:3), then according to the Jewish calendar there was one week between the Ascension and the Feast of Pentecost. As commanded in Luke, the 120 disciples were waiting in Jerusalem for the promise of the "Comforter" (Luke 24:49 "Behold, I send the Promise of My Father upon you; but tarry in the city of Jerusalem until you are endued with power from on high."). They needed to be in Jerusalem for the Feast day anyway, but they did not know how long they would have to remain there as they waited for the promise to be fulfilled.

When the day came, something happened that changed forever the nature of believers: a real corporate relationship was established between Christ and each of them through the Spirit. The 120 disciples were the only ones who have ever had to wait; none of the first 3,000 converts had to wait. No believer today has to wait for the blessings that the Spirit brings at the moment of salvation. The original disciples had to wait until the Spirit became accessible on the Day of Pentecost.

The Consequence #1: The coming and indwelling of the Spirit in the new people of God

In John 14:17, Jesus promised that the Spirit would live in the believer ("... for he dwells with you and will be in you"). This change would be such a benefit for us that Jesus said, "It is expedient for you that I go away" (John 16:7). The word "expedient" (*sumphero*) means "to bring together, bear along with or together, to bear jointly," then secondarily, "to confer a benefit, be useful or profitable"—Liddell and Scott's Greek-English Lexicon). He was saying that there would be much more advantage for them, because His Spirit would be with each one of them in a permanent and empowering relationship, if He left so that the Spirit could come. He would establish an intimate relationship with each believer, a task that would be impossible for Jesus in His human body.

In 1 Corinthians 6:19, our bodies are called the "... the temple of the Holy Spirit who is in you, whom you have from God, and you are not your own?"(1 Corinthians 6:1 NET). In 1 Kings 7, we see that the presence of God was in the Temple in Jerusalem, but since the Day of Pentecost, the Spirit of God indwells the bodies of believers and does not inhabit temples made by men.

There were two conditions for the fulfillment of Jesus' promise to the disciples: (1) Jesus had to ascend to heaven (John 16:7), and (2) the disciples had to stay in Jerusalem—neither Bethany nor Bethlehem would do (Luke 24:49).

From written evidence about the Day of Pentecost, we know that the Spirit came and now lives in the bodies of believers. In Acts 2:38-39NET, "Peter said to them, "Repent, and each one of you be baptized in the name of Jesus Christ for the forgiveness of your sins, and you will receive the gift of the Holy Spirit. 39 For the promise is for you and your children, and for all ...."

Chapter 7: *The transition of the work of the Spirit*

The promise mentioned in verse 39 refers to two things from verse 38: (1) the remission of sins, and (2) the gift of the Spirit. For the first converts on the Day of Pentecost, the reception of the Spirit was an integral part of their salvation, which, with the remission of sins, was a major part of the promise.

Since then it is impossible to belong to Christ, that is, to be saved, unless we have received the Holy Spirit: "Now if anyone does not have the Spirit of Christ, this person does not belong to him" (Rom 8:9). The indwelling of the Spirit marked the difference between the people of God in the Old Testament (the Jews) and the people of God in the New Testament (the Church) formed by all believers.

Consequence #2: Pentecost represents an event that has never been repeated and cannot be repeated again

Certain events like the Creation, the incarnation, and the death, burial and resurrection of Christ, as well as the pouring out of the Spirit on the Day of Pentecost are events that never can be repeated. God gave the Spirit only once, and the Spirit never has left the Church since then. Jesus promised, "I will not leave you comfortless: I will come to you." (John 14:18), and He came in the Person of the Spirit. The Spirit still is here and, since on the Day of Pentecost the Spirit came to stay, how can something that is still occurring be re-initiated?

In one sense, the Day of Pentecost can be compared with the day of the inauguration of a new president. There is a time of ceremony and great celebration, but no one thinks that the events of that day will characterize the duration of his term being repeated day after day. In the same way, the Day of Pentecost inaugurated the coming of the Spirit with a "sound of thunder as of a strong wind," the appearance of "tongues as of fire sitting over each one" of the disciples and miraculous tongues of foreign languages; but it is not necessary these special aspects continue forever. Just as our presidential inaugurations are not repeated, neither has the Day of Pentecost been repeated. To beg God for the re-inauguration of this singular event when the Spirit began to indwell all believers is unnecessary and illogical. The Comforter is still fulfilling his purpose here. All those who believe in Christ anywhere in the world are baptized immediately in the Spirit, just as were the 3,000 who believed on that day.

Consequence #3: Pentecost marked the beginning of the work of the Spirit in this era

Since the special work of the Spirit could not begin until after the Ascension (John 16:7), it is apparent that the work of the Spirit after Pentecost would be different to the work of the Spirit in the Old Testament. There were various changes that began that day, forever altering the Church. The more important ones include regeneration, the Baptism of the Spirit, the Indwelling of the Spirit, the Sealing of the Spirit and the Filling of the Spirit. The Baptism, the Indwelling and the Sealing have no antecedents of any kind in the Old Testament. The other two, the regeneration and the filling, are insinuated in certain texts but never in the sense that we have in the New Testament. All five works of the Spirit, however, have occurred in every believer since the Day of Pentecost.

1. Regeneration of the Spirit

The Scriptures say that we were once dead in our sins, and that later, "And you He made alive, who were dead in trespasses and sins,… [God] made us alive together with Christ (by grace you have been saved)," (Ephesians 2:1,5). In other words, that which was dead within us received life. In addition, John 5:24 says, "Most assuredly, I say to you, he who hears My word and believes in Him who sent Me has everlasting life, and shall not come into judgment, but has passed from death into life…" At the moment that one receives Christ, the work of regeneration occurs by the Holy Spirit. "Not by works of righteousness which we have done, but according to His mercy He saved us, through the washing of regeneration and renewing of the Holy Spirit" (Titus 3:5). Regeneration occurs at the moment of our salvation.

2. Baptism in the Spirit

The second work of the Holy Spirit is the union of the believer with Christ through the baptism in the Spirit. In 1 Corinthians 12:13 we read, "For by [en] one Spirit are we all baptized into [eis] one body…and have been all made to drink into [en] one Spirit." The Day of Pentecost was the first time in history that this kind of baptism occurred. The function of the body of believers after that moment is to be the "temple of God" (1 Corinthians 6:19), because through the baptism in the Spirit we receive the Spirit in our bodies. That is to say, the Spirit enters by the baptism and becomes a permanent part of our lives from the moment of our salvation.

3. Indwelling of the Spirit

Once the Spirit has entered into the believer, he resides there permanently. Jesus said of the Spirit, "for He dwells with you and will be in you. I will not leave you orphans; I will come to you." (John 14:17, 18). His promises are all in the future tense, suggesting that He never will abandon those in whom He dwells.

The presence of the Spirit means that the believer is "endued with power from on high" (Luke 24:49). The verb "endued", *enduo*, means "to sink into (clothing), envelop in, to hide in or cloth oneself." In the same verse Jesus had just told them to stay in Jerusalem until this enduement occurred, so this refers to what occurred on the Day of Pentecost, thus to be "endued" with power is to be clothed or enveloped in the Spirit. The term is metaphorical of power that is inseparably linked to the powerful presence of the Holy Spirit indwelling and enveloping the believer. We are literally wrapped up in the powerful presence of the Spirit. How absurd it is to say that we have the Holy Spirit at salvation, but do not have His power, thus we need a second work of God! How could we be clothed in the Holy Spirit and not have His power?

This indwelling and enduing of the Spirit is the experience of every believer, without exception. In Romans 8:9 Paul said, "But ye are not in the flesh, but in the Spirit, if so be that the Spirit of God dwell in you. Now if anyone does not have the Spirit of Christ, he is not His" or the NET Bible says, "...this person does not belong to him." It is absolutely impossible for a saved person not to have the powerful indwelling of the Spirit. It is the direct result of the baptism of the Spirit and happens immediately after the regeneration of the Spirit at the moment of our salvation.

4. Sealing of the Spirit

Just like a fulfilled, irrevocable, guaranteed contract is finalized with an unbreakable seal, so is the "contract" of our salvation. We know that the indwelling Spirit is permanent in the life of a true believer and that the new life of regeneration is eternal because we have the promise of the seal of the Spirit until eternity with Christ begins.

According to Ephesians 1:13, "In Him you also trusted, after you heard the word of truth, the gospel of your salvation; in whom also, having believed, you were sealed with the Holy Spirit of promise." The beginning of His sealing occurred the moment they believed. The duration of the seal is mentioned in Ephesians 4:30, "And grieve not the Holy Spirit of God, whereby ye are sealed unto the day of redemption."

The powerful indwelling Spirit sealed up in our body is a "guarantee" that ultimately we will be united with Christ, "who also has sealed us and given us the Spirit in our hearts as a guarantee" ["down payment"] (2 Corinthians 1:22). No one dared to break the seal of the emperor, how much less the seal of God?

> All these activities are what marks believers as God's people and are indispensable to ongoing Christian existence. The seal of the Spirit is not some second blessing. "Having believed" (13b) means effectively 'when you believed,' i.e. 'once you had put your trust in [the gospel]' (NJB). These activities of the Spirit foreshadow in type and quality what he will do more fully in the new creation, and so the Spirit with whom God marks us with his stamp of ownership is also appropriately called the 'pledge', 'guarantee', even 'first installment' of our inheritance (cf. Rom. 8:23; 2 Cor. 1:22; 5:5). But the blessings we receive now are just a foreshadowing: according to Paul we still await our inheritance in the final and total redemption of the world by God at the end of time. 4:30 re-emphasizes this, reminding us that we are sealed with the Spirit 'for the day of redemption' to come. Then God's purpose, begun in Christ, will be brought to consummation, and seeing it from beginning to end will evoke the creation's praise of the Creator (Carson 1994: 1:13).

Chapter 7: *Gifts for Today*

The purpose of being sealed by the Spirit, then, is the protection and guarantees that all who believe in Christ will be saved until the day of redemption. We belong to Him forever because of the seal. The permanent powerful indwelling of the Spirit assures the seal of the Spirit. We do not have to feel this to make it a reality; rather we discover this truth in the Scriptures, believe it and rejoice in its reality. This great fact occurred also at the moment of our salvation

5. Filling of the Spirit

When the Spirit makes his residence in a life, He wants to manifest himself in every believer by His filling, His fruit or His character. The filling should be the normal experience of the believer. Just as anger can fill a person and make him act irrationally (Luke 4:28, "filled with wrath" they wanted to kill Jesus), so being filled with the Spirit makes a person want to submit to obey God's Word and do His will. The ways in which the filling of the Spirit is manifested are: the fruit of the Spirit, power in testifying, victory over the flesh, evidence of a spiritual gift and effectiveness in prayer. The filling of the Spirit empowers our initiative to obey His Word. All this begins on the day of our salvation encounter with Christ, but this work of the Spirit is contingent on our willingness to be obedient to His Word (not quenching or grieving His Spirit) and aggressive in sharing His Word as witnesses.

Consequence #4: Pentecost was the first occasion in which the baptism in the Spirit occurred, and through it the Church was formed

The baptism in the Spirit puts the believer into the body of Christ (1 Corinthians 12:13, see chapter 3). In Ephesians 1:23 NET, "Now the church is his body, the fullness of him who fills all in all." If we were put into His Body by baptism in the Spirit, then there was not a Body of Christ before the beginning of this operation. If the Church is His Body, as we have seen, then it must have begun simultaneously with the Spirit baptism on the Day of Pentecost, AD 30.

We could say that the church existed before Pentecost as an assembly or maybe as a primitive organization, but the true essence of the Church is not just an external organization but also an organism. This organism is possible only through a corporal or bodily union with Christ and that union is only made possible by the baptism in the Spirit.

Just as the birth of Christ was the incarnation of the Son of God (John 1:14), so Pentecost was the introduction of the Holy Spirit in every believer. It is like a second incarnation where God continues to manifest His "grace and truth" through the individual members of His Body in the church.

It is called the "body" of Christ by the nature of this union. In Ephesians 5:29b-30, the union with Christ is describes with terms related to a body: "for we are members of his body, of his flesh and of his bones." We are as much a part of Christ as is His own flesh and bones. The resulting relationship of the Church is that all are "partakers of the divine nature" (2 Peter 1:4). This is the

Chapter 7: *The transition of the work of the Spirit*

consequence of the Day of Pentecost.

Pentecost is as unrepeatable as the creation of the world or of man; as once-for-all, as the incarnation and the death, resurrection, and ascension of Christ. This appears from the following simple facts: (1) The Spirit of God could only come, arrive and take up His residence in the church once, which He did at Pentecost. (2) The Spirit of God could only be given, received, and deposited in the church once, which occurred at Pentecost. (3) The event occurred at a specific time (Acts 2:1), in fulfillment of a specific Old Testament type (Lev. 23:15-22), in a specific place (Jerusalem; cf. Luke 24:49), upon a specific few (Acts 1:13, 14), for a specific purpose (cf. 1 Cor 12:12-20), to introduce a new order. The event did not constitute the continuing and recurring features of the new order once it was introduced. (Unger 1971: 17-18)

Consequence #5: The prophecy of Joel will be universal, in contrast with Pentecost, which was local

The Day of Pentecost was a marvelous experience, but even more marvelous will be the fulfillment of the Joel's prophecy that speaks of the pouring out of the Spirit "upon all flesh" (Joel 2:28), at the beginning of the millennium. When the three signs occurred on the Day of Pentecost (tornado-like wind, tongues as of fire, and unknown tongues), marking the coming of the Spirit, the multitude of Jews rushed to the source of the noisy wind (Acts 2:2) and some understood the tongues being spoken (probably the Hellenistic Jews from their homeland in the Roman colonies) while others accused the disciples of being inebriated (probably the Jerusalem Hebrews). In defense of the events of that day, Peter cited the prophecy of Joel 2 as a reason for not thinking that these events were strange. Peter was not declaring that the events of Pentecost fulfilled the prophecy of Joel, because there was much more in Joel 2 that was not fulfilled, but that they were the same thing—God pouring out His Spirit—only on a reduced scale at Pentecost. The following are two reasons make it evident that Peter did not mean to say that the Day of Pentecost fulfilled the prophecy of Joel 2:

(a) *Much of the prophecy still is future*

The time of the fulfillment of the prophecy is mentioned in the same text. In Joel 2:28 the prophet says, "And it shall come to pass afterward, that I will pour out my spirit upon all flesh." We should ask ourselves, "After what?" This chronological reference refers to the fulfillment of various prophecies mentioned in verses 12-27 that must precede this outpouring of the Spirit.

The following seven prophecies must happen before the complete fulfillment of Joel chapter 2: (1) Repentance of the nation of Israel (vs. 15-18); (2) The miraculous provision of corn, wine and oil until they are satiated in the land of

Israel (v. 19); (3) The enemy of the north (Russia? Syria?) will be destroyed (v. 20); (4) The fear of exterior dangers will be taken away forever (vs. 21-22); (5) Israel will produce an abundance of food as never before (vs. 22, 24); (6) The dry areas in Israel will be converted into fruitful areas because of abundant rain (v. 23); After years of being under foreign armies that will destroy the earth, God will restore it in an unbelievable way so that they will never again be ashamed (vs. 24-25, 27); and (7) God himself will be permanently "in the midst of Israel" so that all will know Him (v. 27).

These are literal prophecies that will literally be fulfilled. It only does harm to the Scriptures to allegorize these prophecies into some imaginary spiritual blessings in order to make Joel 2 be fulfilled in Acts 2.

In addition to these seven prophecies that have to be fulfilled before the pouring out of the Spirit, there will also be "wonders in the heavens and in the earth" (Joel 2:30). For example, there will be columns of smoke, the sun will be darkened and the moon will become red (2:30-31). Immediately after the fulfillment of these things, God will pour out His Spirit over "all flesh" (2:28). That day will be marked by prophecies, dreams, and visions (2:28) as the norm for all those who receive the Spirit at the beginning of the millennium. The "servants" of 2:29 refer to the nation of Israel. "The servants of Jehovah" is a common term in Isaiah that refers not to certain individual within the nation but rather to Israel as a whole.

If we take Joel's prophecies to be literal, then we can easily observe that none of the prophecies, which he said would occur before the Spirit pours over all flesh, occurred prior to Pentecost, and they have still not taken place. Those prophecies will be fulfilled at the end of the Great Tribulation and the beginning of the millennium.

Allegorizing this whole passage to make it fulfilled at Pentecost could make numerous passages meaningless. We have to remain consistent in our hermeneutics. We cannot switch back and forth from allegorical to a literal interpretation. If the majority of these prophecies have not yet occurred, then why did Peter refer to Joel's prophecy in his response in Acts 2?

(b) Pentecost is only an illustration of the day of Joel

In Acts 2:16 Peter says, "But this is that which was spoken by the prophet Joel." The phrase "this is that" could mean two things: (1) It is the same thing, the literal fulfillment; or (2) It is the same thing, in the sense of being essentially the same experience, but obviously it was not the total fulfillment of the prophecy. Peter cited the entire context, including the prophecies not yet realized, so that by the way he used the phrase he was showing that he knew that the Day of Pentecost was not the fulfillment of Joel 2. For example, neither the sun nor the moon had changed. None of the prophecies that were to precede the promised pouring out of the Spirit had happened, so Peter was saying that it was like this prophesied event, but distinct. He used the prophecy of Joel as an illustration to demonstrate that God would establish something new with Israel and later with the Gentiles; Pentecost was just the beginning. Joel was speaking of a worldwide transformation and especially of the whole nation of Israel; on the other hand, Peter was speaking of an individual transformation. The scale is different, but the results are similar. Evidently 3,000 people accepted his explanation, because later they accepted the Messiah, were saved and immediately received the Holy Spirit without the dramatic events of first group of 120 disciples.

Summary

The importance of recognizing the nature of the transition through out the historical portion of the New Testament is the unique and sometimes inconsistent events that occurred. Should we only preach the gospel to the Jews (as in Acts 11:19)? Do we have to wait for an Apostle to lay hands on us before we can receive the Holy Spirit (Acts 8:17)? Does everyone who is baptized in the Spirit get "tongues of fire" on their heads (Acts 2:3)? These and other unusual events did actually occur in the opening days and early years of the Church, but most of them were never repeated nor referred to as a normal experience for all believers. "The only teachings in the Book of Acts that can be called normative (absolute) for the church are those that are doctrinally confirmed elsewhere in Scriptures." (MacArthur, 1978, p. 85) This is one of the main areas where confusion, misunderstanding and erroneous teaching have caused many to change their focus from the Scriptures to their subjective experiences.

Chapter 7: *Gifts for Today*

CHAPTER 8

The Gift of the Spirit: By works or by grace?

Chapter 8: Gifts for Today

Every false religion in the world has two characteristics in common: a rigid legalistic system to deceive its followers into believing that they can become good enough for whatever happens in the next life and secondly, a mystical manner to experience an encounter with whatever deity their religion proposes. These two false notions invaded Christianity from the beginning of its history corrupting the gospel message and deceiving those who do not understand the Scriptures into believing that they are acceptable and surely will go to heaven because they feel something.

In his letters to the churches, Paul pointed out some problems that have continued to appear time after time throughout the history of the Church. The main problem is works or experience versus grace. Without a proper understanding of justification by faith there has always been a tendency among Christians to think legalistically and/or mystically, that is, to believe that we can improve upon our standing before God by our behavior, mystical devotion, or worship rituals whereby we seek an inner experience that assures us we must be saved. In this chapter we will examine the teaching in Galatians and Colossians for the attitudes that the believer should develop as a result of understanding how God designed our relationship with Him.

The basic foundation of the Bible is we can only receive God's free gift of salvation by faith (Eph 2:8-9) in His Word. The Legalists are asking us to perform certain tasks or to meditate enough in order to receive the Spirit or the fullness of the Spirit; in other words, they put the believer again under a system of rules or disciplines in order to acquire the blessing of the Spirit.

COMPARISON WITH THE PROBLEM IN GALATIANS

Paul found two problems of this category in his day as he described in his epistles to the churches of Galatia and Colossi. In both instances, false teachers tried to establish a system of works or disciplines in order to take their relationship with Christ to a higher level. They scorned the idea of a simple salvation and exalted a more profound or mystical experience so that the believers would experience more profound depths of God. As a result, many of the Galatians were deceived by the promise of a richer experience and began seeking more than just being satisfied with a comprehensive and complete salvation.

In one of Paul's earliest epistles Paul established the purpose of the law and the abuse of the law. Jesus said that He did not come to destroy the law or the prophets, but to fulfill them (Matt 5:17), then to make it clearer, He stated that the law will "accomplish its purpose" until "heaven and earth disappear" (Matt 5:18). Jesus told the strictest followers of the law, "Did not Moses give you the law, yet none of you keeps the law?" (John 7:19) Instead of getting defensive, they should have been honest before the law and recognized that He spoke the truth: they were all guilty. However, they had no way in themselves of dealing with their guilt.

The purpose of the law was to teach us that we cannot ever measure up to God's standards. Paul wrote, "...the law was our tutor to bring us to Christ,

Chapter 8: *The Gift of the Spirit: By Works or by Grace?*

that we might be justified by faith" (Gal 3:24). The word "tutor" is the word *paidagogos*, from which we get the English word, "pedagogy" or teaching technique. God wrote the law with His finger in stone (Ex 31:18; Deut 9:10) to show all mankind that no one can measure up to His standards.

Paul wrote, "Now we know that whatever the law says, it says to those who are under the law, that every mouth may be stopped [or silenced], and all the world may become guilty before God" (Rom 3:19). There is no hope for salvation in trying to obey the law, "for through the law comes the knowledge of sin" (3:20). It is a teaching tool from God to show us how guilty we are before a holy God, and that our only hope is faith in a merciful God.

Once a person puts his faith in Jesus Christ as his Savior then the condemnation of the law is paid for: "For Christ is the end of the law, with the result that there is righteousness for everyone who believes" (Rom 10:4NET).

When this truth is not understood and someone makes a profession of faith continuing to believe that they are a pretty good person they really have not been saved at all (1 John 1:8, 10 NET, "If we say we do not bear the guilt of sin, we are deceiving ourselves and the truth is not in us."), that is, we don't understand that the purpose of the law was to condemn us as guilty sinners desperately needing a Savior. Until a person understands this truth he cannot be saved.

Notice that these are people who say they "have fellowship with him" (1:6), that is, are professing Christians, but not possessing Christians. However, when such persons with false professions come inside the church they need a form of legalism to justify their goodness and false mystical experience to feel the blessed by God. Their typical symptoms are a lack of brokenness, pride and unrepentant spirit, and a desire to feel good about themselves and be entertained instead of taught in the Scriptures. Ray Comfort describes it this way:

> "People who make a commitment to Christ without the Law may do so because they are seeking true inner peace and lasting fulfillment. They come to fill a "God-shaped vacuum" in their lives. There is not trembling. There is no fleeing from wrath. There is no fear. To them, God is a benevolent, fatherly figure, not a holy God of wrath. Without the Law, they haven't been stripped of self-righteousness. They don't truly believe that their just reward is eternal damnation. Therefore, even as professing Christians, they think they are basically good.
> Because of this faulty foundation, these converts are likely to think that they are pleasing God by reading the Bible, praying, fasting, and doing good works. They are susceptible to being deceived into thinking that somehow their good works commend them to God, and they are therefore liable to stray into legalistic standards such as "do not touch, do not taste, do not handle" (Col 2:21)" (Comfort, 2006, p. 55)

A group of false teachers from among the Galatians churches taught that through special obedience everyone would receive the fulfillment of their salvation through the Holy Spirit. Paul addresses this problem in Galatians 3:1-3. The phrase "now made perfect by the flesh" shows that they thought they were made perfect or complete and by their own works they wanted to reach sanctification. They admitted that faith was the first step, but they also believed that faith was only the beginning; only by adding sincere efforts in total devotion in order to attain perfection, would they be able to accomplish the consummation of the blessing of God. Wiersbe simplifies the issue:

> The Holy Spirit is mentioned eighteen times in this epistle and plays an important part in Paul's defense of the Gospel of the grace of God. The only real evidence of conversion is the presence of the Holy Spirit in the life of the believer (see Rom. 8:9). Paul asks an important question: did they receive the Spirit by faith in the Word of God, or by doing the works of the Law? Of course, there could be but one answer: the Spirit came into their lives because they trusted Jesus Christ (Wiersbe, 1989, p. Gal 3:1).

Paul, however, highlighted a difference between receiving the Spirit by faith (trusting and believing in that which they had heard and nothing more) and receiving Him or His special approval by that which we do, that is, good works. In Galatians 3:4-15, he declared that by faith we receive "the promise of the Spirit." This means the baptism of the Holy Spirit, and all the fullness or completeness of the entire Godhead (Col 2:9) now resides in the believer. It is impossible to add to, improve or invalidate this relationship.

Evidently, these false teachers seemed so sincere and persuasive the Galatians did not understand how they could not be from God. But Paul spoke emphatically: faith does not include any human effort or discipline. There is much more to this problem than merely obligating certain rituals or lifestyle changes.

The emphasis of Paul on appreciating the fullness of God in the believer by faith without any additional works seems to indicate in Galatians and later in Colossians that an additional mystical union was being pursued. This problem would continue to plague the Church, especially in the different forms of legalistic mysticism. Morrison writes that it was the mystic's doctrine of "perfection," which laid the ground for Wesley's own teaching in this area. In an article on "Perfectibilists" in Blunt's Dictionary of Sects, Heresies, Ecclesiastical Parties and Schools of Thought, the writer states:

> Many mystical divines have believed that a life of profound devotional contemplation leads on to such a union with God that all which is base and sinful in the Christian's soul becomes annihilated, and there ensues a superhuman degree of participation in the Divine perfection. Such a doctrine was held by the great mystic whose works pass under the name of Dionysius, and from him was handed down to the Quietist Hesychasts, the strict Franciscans, the Molinists, the Jansenists, and the German Mystics [Dominicans such as Eckhart and Tauler], from whom it passed on to the English Methodists,

Chapter 8: *The Gift of the Spirit: By Works or by Grace?*

among whom it has always been a special tenet that sanctification may, and ought to, go on to perfection. (Blunt, 1990, p. 422)

No matter if the teachers were very sincere in wanting to add works to faith in order to gain a special experience or a more profound relationship in their salvation; it is impossible to add anything more than what we have in the Spirit. It is an error to place such emphasis on seeking more of God's promised presence through obedience or special devotion when we have received already all the full blessing of the Spirit by faith. There is a human tendency to seek a more intimate and profound relationship with deity, but this is not seeking more of God or receiving something that we are lacking in our salvation.

COMPARISON WITH THE PROBLEMS IN COLOSSI

The second problem was with the Colossians, whose problems mirror those of the Galatians. False teachers wanted to introduce something supplementary to salvation, a more profound and mystical relationship with God.

First, they taught that we are still lacking something after having received Christ.

False teachers always want to introduce something more to salvation, making the mere salvation experience seem insufficient or inferior. They diminish the salvation experience, considering it as a beginning point from which the believer can reach more profound experiences and deeper truths by discipline and faith. In Colossi, these teachers said that believers needed something in addition to Christ in order to be satisfied; in this case, that additional element was the Holy Spirit.

In Colossians 2, Paul addressed these false teachers and their message. His insistence on "being complete in Him" (verse 10), suggests that some believed they needed more than just having Christ in their lives. Paul wanted to assure the believers that it is absolutely impossible to improve on our salvation in Christ, that we are complete in Him. Also, in verse 9, we see that "For in Him dwells all the fullness of the Godhead bodily." That is to say, if we have Christ, we have all the fullness of God dwelling within us; there is no more of God that can be added. It is nonsense and does not make sense to beg God for more of Him when we already have all He is and all He has to give us. Evidently Paul had good reason for giving these instructions, because someone was teaching the opposite.

Essentially, there is no greater spiritual blessing than finding Christ. Ephesians 1:3 says, "Blessed be the God and Father of our Lord Jesus Christ, who hath blessed us with all spiritual blessings in heavenly places in Christ." In other words, in Christ we have all the spiritual blessings God can give us now. It is our responsibility to discover what these blessings are from their revelations in the Word of God. We cannot add more to them, nor can we discover them from mystical encounters in prayer, or unconscious trances. There is no relationship more profound than when Christ lives within us by faith.

When we are told that we lack the true joy and peace brought by a secondary baptism of the Spirit, the experiencing of special spiritual gifts and the promises of extraordinary and exhilarating power of the Holy Spirit, we are being taught the same false doctrine that was taught in Colossi.

This kind of teaching always has a tendency toward mysticism, which is defined in Wikipedia as...

> "the pursuit of achieving communion with or conscious awareness of ultimate reality, the divine, spiritual truth, or God through direct, personal experience (intuition or insight) rather than rational thought; the belief in the existence of realities beyond perceptual or intellectual apprehension that are central to being and directly accessible through personal experience; or the belief that such experience is a genuine and important source of knowledge. In the Hellenistic world, "mystical" referred to secret religious rituals." ("Mysticism," 1)

The perception of having had a genuine and personal encounter with God or a sense of speaking in a mystical language that only God could understand replicates the ancient Greek mystics. A real experience or sense of God speaking to them personally can be very convincing. MacDonald writes:

> The Gnostics professed to have deep, secret mysteries, and in order to learn what these mysteries were, a person had to be initiated. Perhaps the secrets included many so-called visions. Supposed visions are an important element in such present-day heresies as Mormonism, Spiritism, Catholicism, and Swedenborgianism. Those who were members of the inner circle were naturally proud of their secret knowledge (MacDonald, p. 2:23).

In Colossians 2:18-23, the following four false doctrines appeared: (1) Their false humility was enticing and impressive; (2) They were preoccupied by angels or supernatural beings, who apparently appeared to them in visions or dreams. They used these experiences to appear to be more spiritual, especially more so than the apostle Paul (2:18); (3) they did not emphasize that Christ is the Head of the Church, as the Bible clearly states. The "revelations" they received from angels or from the "Spirit" were more important to them than the study of the already revealed Word of God (2:19); and (4) They insisted on conformity to their decrees of ethics and rules about things they could not touch, taste or handle (2:20-21), insinuating that these dietary, fasting and self-disciplinary practices made one more spiritual. Paul declared that such teachings were heresies and should be combated with the Word before they destroyed the church.

When we compare those false teachers with the different movements of today, we find many parallels. Normally such persons are very persuasive and can convince the unprepared of anything. Unfortunately, the majority of believers are not prepared biblically to refute, discern or resist the intimidation of their

Chapter 8: *The Gift of the Spirit: By Works or by Grace?*

accusations or declarations.

Two Dangerous Consequences of Mystical Teachings

Christian mysticism has long been a practice of the Roman Catholic Church and various sects to create a sense of direct contact with God as opposed to the "indirect" contact with God merely through Scriptures. In the Catholic Church, where the Bible has been prohibited for centuries, mystics created a devotional religion.

> In the sixteenth century, we find mystics such as Ignatius Loyola, Teresa of Avila and John of the Cross developing a systematized mysticism in their writings, laying out the steps by which one may achieve personal union with the divine, as if it was an ascent up a ladder or mountain, or down into the labyrinthine depths of the soul.
> These writings have been popularized throughout the Christian scene for many years, especially in Charismatic and neo-evangelical circles today where they are recommended as wholesome reading matter. For example, in Power Evangelism by John Wimber, we find that Ignatius Loyola and Teresa of Avila are commended (Morrison n.a.:7).

Paul gave various warnings about Christians guarding against a "different gospel" (Gal. 1:6). The major "difference" in that gospel consisted of mixing grace with works, or it may not include either one! All that is needed is an experience supposedly with God. Morrison added,

> Recently, I read an interview in the 'Jesus Army' magazine with John Arnott, Senior Pastor in the Airport church in Toronto. He was asked by Noel Stanton: "Do you see [the Toronto Blessing] as breaking out into evangelism and mission?" Arnott replied: "Absolutely. Unbelievers are being converted just through going out under the power of the Spirit." So evangelicals believe today that conversion is a mystical experience. (Incidentally, this is very much like the ancient pagan practice of "Incubation," whereby one goes into a special sleep in a sacred place where the gods allegedly work on you while you're out. (*Ibid.*, 13)

If someone preaches the gospel, but announces blessings are to be received in pieces or that there is a series of later experiences, then it is not the same gospel as the Bible teaches. There are also many scholars who, although plainly discerning enough to know the difference between religious mysticism and biblical spirituality, fail to alert their readers to it. For example, the well-known book Great Leaders of the Christian Church published by Moody Press has, refers to one of those great leaders, the Spanish Counter-Reformation mystic, Teresa of Avila. She is literally sandwiched between John Knox, Blaise Pascal and John Owen! (Woodbridge, 1988)

There are two dangerous consequences of believing mystical teachings.

First consequence: A special focus on a wrong teaching frequently becomes a substitute for the truth.

In the history of the Church, when the emphasis shifted from the grace of God or the exposition of the Word to some other experience or truth, this new emphasis became a substitute for truth. In Galatians 6:14 ("But God forbid that I should boast except in the cross of our Lord Jesus Christ, by whom the world has been crucified to me, and I to the world") Paul shows that focus should be on the cross and the person and sacrifice of Jesus. Looking at the Bible, it is easy to see that the ministry of the Spirit is not to glorify or exalt Himself. Compared to those that talk about Christ, there are few verses that talk of the Spirit. The Spirit, who inspired the Bible, gave us enough information to be able to know Him, but He also made it obvious that He is not the one who should be magnified.

In Colossians 3:1-3 we see where the center of our attention should be: Christ, sitting at the right hand of God. Likewise, John 16:13-14 says, "Howbeit when he, the Spirit of truth, is come, he will guide you into all truth: for he shall not speak of himself; but whatsoever he shall hear, that shall he speak: and he will show you things to come. He shall glorify me: for he shall receive of mine and shall show it unto you." Therefore, the Spirit came to speak only of Christ and to communicate His glory, not His own.

Today, in the author's opinion, some emphasize the miraculous signs and the gift of tongues instead of introducing the unbeliever to the grace of God. Thus such a focus diminishes the gospel in its essence, or confuses the gospel with so many experiences. Supernatural phenomena can be so exaggerated that any gospel offered is given almost in passing; Christ is mentioned only in relation to the Spirit, because the Spirit is the center of the messages and their beliefs. The emphasis is what we can experience today, not on what occurred on the cross and how the cross should affect us still.

Therefore, this special focus on personal experiences can become a substitute for fundamental truth. An example of this is seen in the Christian mystic and Dominican priest Johannes Tauler's sermons (1300-1361). Some evangelicals elevate his writings as the beginnings of the Reformation. Admittedly, he was not a promoter of the Roman Catholics Church, but neither did most of the mystics who generally despised any form of the organized church, which stands in the way of the mystics' spiritual quest of being "one with God."

An examination of his sermons shows that Tauler speaks of the three stages in the mystical life: 1) a life of spirituality and virtue, bringing us close to God's presence; 2) Spiritual poverty, when God withdraws himself from the soul, leaving it "anguished and denuded;" 3) the transition into a "divinized life," into what he describes as "a union of our created spirit with God's uncreated one." (Tauler, 1985, on 1 Pet. 3:8). This is an example of the mystic language The search for a spiritual reality or a deeper sense of God's presence may be from a lack of understanding the amazing truths in God's Word and resting in them

Chapter 8: *The Gift of the Spirit: By Works or by Grace?*

instead of pursuing deeper levels of mystical encounters.

> Many books show the clear linkage between Pentecostalism and Catholic Mysticism such as Edward O'Connor's book The Pentecostal Movement in the Catholic Church. In a chapter entitled "Pentecost and Traditional Spirituality" (by which he means Mystical Spirituality), he looks first at the Spanish Carmelite, John of the Cross's mystical teachings, especially in his Ascent of Mount Carmel. After referring to the experiences involved in one particular stage in the mystical process, he writes: "These experiences can serve as points of comparison for the 'Baptism in the Spirit' that figures so prominently in the Pentecostal Movement." (O'Connor, 1971)

Without a doubt there are many sincere people in these movements, but abuses can easily predominate. Morrison's research into mysticism in world religions sees a remarkable similarity among mystics of the world religions.

> We find that what mysticism is all about - as it has manifested throughout the world over the centuries, whether it is Eastern mysticism or so called Christian mysticism - can be reduced to two heads: 1) The seeking out of a direct experience of God, without any mediator; 2) The setting up of the individual's subjective experience as the sole arbiter of religious truth. (Morrison, p. 5).

In his investigations into different movements he discovered that the Lutheran Pietists were not exempt from this tendency to want to substitute truth for experience.

> "It is highly significant that one of the principal reforms demanded by the German Pietists, according to Routledge's Encyclopaedia of Religions, was 'that the theological schools should be reformed by the abolition of all systematic theology, and that morals and not doctrine should form the staple of all preaching.' And what would you suspect to be the result of that reform? In their eagerness to eschew systematic theology, the mystics and Pietists embraced a systematized devotionalism. Systematic theology devoid of heart religion is bad enough. But a heart religion which is devoid of systematic theology is a scourge." (Morrison n.a.:16)

The Roman Catholic Charismatic Renewal continues to grow at a rapid pace. All around the world, Roman Catholics are experiencing the Charismatic's second baptism known as the "baptism of the Holy Spirit." Statistics show that at least half the Charismatics in the world are also Roman Catholic. Many Roman Catholics are being "slain in the spirit" and are "speaking in tongues." Much of the Roman Catholic priesthood has embraced the "charismatic experience," which, incidentally, has received the Pope's official blessing.

The Second-Blessing "spirit-baptism" experience, visions and inner voices, raptures and ecstasies, alleged prophesying's, falling under "the power," speaking in gibberish-style tongues. All these mainstays of the Charismatic and Pentecostal Movements are entirely in accord with Roman Catholic mysticism. Because Pentecostals and Charismatics now make up the bulk of those who profess to be evangelicals today, we see that Catholicism and neo-evangelicalism are unashamedly moving in the same compromised direction. (*Ibid.*,. 22)

O'Connor writes in The Pentecostal Movement in the Catholic Church,

"Although they derive from Protestant backgrounds, the Pentecostal churches are not typically Protestant in their belief, attitudes or practices. Many historians, as well as many of their own members, regard them as a 'third force' in the Christian world, between Protestantism and (Roman) Catholicism." (O'Connor, 1971, p. 23)

Another reason that so many Protestant Christians have been attracted to mysticism is because they have been so poorly taught. This is a result of low standards in both the pulpit and publications. We have already seen the acceptance of mysticism in purportedly evangelical books.

The same is true of many evangelical newspapers and journals. For example, Morrison reports that in a widely read neo-evangelical newspaper recently there appeared a full-page article about the French mystical, ecumenical haven "Taizé" (which uses practices which border on interfaith religious experience), without any critical comment. People were simply left to "make up their own minds". But that is not what Christian teaching should be about — especially in relation to the training of the young, who are very susceptible to the ill effects of "fudge." What is needed today is clear, unambiguous exposition of Biblical principles (Morrison n.a.:30).

Praise songs and prayers of Taizé are available on Amazon.com. A typical statement that attracts the uninformed is, "If there are times you feel the Divine Presence, then you're half way to becoming a mystic. And if you want to unite with that Presence, then you're an aspiring mystic." (Meister Eckhart, p.1)

Mystical meditation techniques are being promoted by various Charismatic and non-charismatic authors including New Age techniques, visualization, meditation and other metaphysical techniques to gain whatever they want. Programs in universities such as Spiritual Formation Programs or Interspirituality that focus on contemplative techniques and programs is often drawing from New Age and medieval mystic sources. These are usually couched in spiritual and seeming biblical terms that the undiscerning does not recognize. The walk in obedience to the Word of God, the authority of the Word of God in personal lives, and the task of sharing the clear gospel of Christ with the world is lost in the shuffle of mystical experiences.

Chapter 8: *The Gift of the Spirit: By Works or by Grace?*

Second consequence: A system of law or mystical obedience produces false guilt and preoccupation.

The Charismatics speak of super-devotion as a requirement for receiving the Spirit. They put the responsibility on the believer, using phrases such as "submission in every area," "total trust in Christ," and "Do you have enough faith?" Another intimidating question that is common is, "Do you have the whole Gospel?" Passing the responsibility for receiving the Spirit to the response of the believer was never intended as a teaching of the New Testament.

In Philippians 2:13 (" for it is God who works in you both to will and to do for His good pleasure"), God has the responsibility of producing the change in our lives; it is not something that we do to gain the prize of the Spirit. Certainly we must diligently add to our faith certain attitudes (2 Peter 1:3-8) in order to mature spiritually, but this does not apply to the completion of our relationship with the Spirit.

Submission to God, prayer and separation from sin, or whatever other action of the believer, are not legalistic requirements for experiencing the consummation of salvation. On the contrary, they are privileges that God's grace produces in us and are the evidence of all that we are in Christ.

When the charismatic believers speak of the "complete gospel," they are not talking about what we have in Christ because of our belief in Him, but they are referring to what we could have as a result of our submission, fasting, prayer, or separation, etc. If this were the case, we should be concerned that we may never know just when we have arrived at enough sanctification to be awarded the experience of intimacy with God.

It is true that the believer should examine himself, but not in order to receive more of God; he already has all of God presence abiding within him. The motivation should be from a heart filled with gratitude motivating us to a more obedient and surrendered walk with God by the power of the Holy Spirit to apply His Word and fulfill His purpose for our lives.

Charismatics teach that the gospel brings the Holy Spirit initially, but not totally in His fullness; they believe that grace and faith alone are not enough to experience the profound, complete, victorious, abundant and full life of the Spirit. They believe that it is necessary to have a special encounter with God, to have certain attitudes and to take certain steps to arrive at the kind of life that the Spirit will accept.

The logical conclusion for many of those who seek such an experience and do not find it, is: "It is all my fault!" People can live feeling this constant frustration and guilt, and they constantly examine themselves to try to arrive at the level of spirituality where they can experience the promised peace and fullness of the Spirit. They fast for days, pray for personal holiness that will be enough for a God-encounter and power-baptism for a satisfying relationship with God and service.

The truth is that, the more they worry, the more doubt they have that they have completely yielded to God. This kind of introspection keeps them from arriving at a level of spirituality that would allow them to deserve the baptism of the Spirit, much less be useful to God in ministry and advancing His kingdom. They simply find themselves more and more sinful, frustrated and doubtful. This often leads to irresponsibility in other areas, which bring the pressure of other authorities in their lives.

Some are able to convince themselves that their sins are not so bad, or that they are only faults instead of sins in order to achieve the mystical total dedication. But the fulfillment, many times, does not come. Since they have determined that the cause is not their sin, they put the blame on their personality. One Charismatic believer said, "After praying, asking for the baptism and confessing all known sin, the only impediment can be a person's inhibitions." So, if the person does not have the mystical experience, one or both of two things are at fault: some secret sin or his personal inhibitions.

To make matters worse, the temptation arises to fake the experience. If that is yielded to, the internal guilt only magnifies until a breaking point occurs.

Charismatics carry subtle or conscious guilt until at last they achieve their goal of speaking in tongues. Probably a part of their joy in finally speaking in tongues, consciously or unconsciously, is the relief from a self-induced or false guilt. It is common to find much joy and enthusiasm in these churches when one of their own speaks in tongues, because the greater part of the preaching emphasizes the necessity of speaking in tongues and/or experiencing miracles.

Those who do not reach this goal continue to live under the pressure of false guilt. Could it be why they emphasize this experiential aspect of their belief as the only way to find joy and power in their lives is because they must find relief from the guilt that they themselves have induced? Admittedly this is an unfair question, but maybe worth considering.

The following story illustrates the frustration of many of our Charismatic friends. There was a man who spent his life looking for silver in the mountains of California. He was so obsessed with his quest that his wife and children felt compelled to abandon him. When he died, few people attended his funeral. They found a letter he had written saying that his last desire was that he be buried beneath his cabin. They dutifully began to dig a grave under his humble miner's shack and, there, they discovered a shiny gray substance. It was pure silver! The place came to be known as the famous "Comstock Silver Vein," the richest silver mine in the history of California. The miner had been a multimillionaire all his life, but he never was able to take of advantage of his riches! The believer is also rich in Christ. The poor miner had no idea that he was living on top of the riches he was looking for, and in the same way, many believers do not know the spiritual riches they have within themselves through the Holy Spirit. We need not look anywhere else!

Two Key Passages (2 Peter 1:3-4 and Colossians 2:9-10)

"I can pray this because his divine power has bestowed on us everything

Chapter 8: *The Gift of the Spirit: By Works or by Grace?*

necessary for life and godliness through the rich knowledge of the one who called us by his own glory and excellence. Through these things he has bestowed on us his precious and most magnificent promises, so that by means of what was promised you may become partakers of the divine nature, after escaping the worldly corruption that is produced by evil desire" (2 Peter 1:3-4 NET).

As II Peter says, we have all we need to live a victorious Christian life. We simply need to learn to obey and take advantage of what we have been instructed and promised. All the "things" (promises of God, Word of God, Holy Spirit) have been given to us, that is, we have no need to acquire them. Everything necessary for life or living and godliness, how to please God, has been given to us in the knowledge of Christ, as revealed in His Word. As we focus on knowing correctly and applying practically to our lives this knowledge and promises we are transformed into Christ's image. Peter goes on to talk about a seven-step process of how to apply these principles. There is nothing mystical about this formula for the Christian life, but rather it is intensely practical and applicable to everyone.

Paul warned his readers about the invading mystical tendencies that would later grow into a Gnostic sect that would corrupt Christianity for centuries. In Colossians 2:18 these teachings and practices were already infiltrating the Early Church as Paul wrote,

"Let no one who delights in humility and the worship of angels pass judgment on you. That person goes on at great lengths about what he has supposedly seen, but he is puffed up with empty notions by his fleshly mind."

The introducing negative, *medeis*, means to "absolutely have nothing to do with, or the thing is forbidden" (Thayer's Greek Lexicon). The negative with the present imperative verb, "beguile or pass judgment" demands that the reader stop this action already in progress, that is, "stop letting people disqualify you or intimidate you by saying you do not qualify for genuine spirituality." This refers to delighting in the pretense of false humility, angelic worship encounters, dreams and visions that supposedly were experienced and stay away from people with inflated egos of their own importance and mystical experiences.

The delighting in humility seems positive, but it is a characteristic of false teachers. Humility is never the focus, but the result of godly actions. It is defined in Phil 2:3-4 as making the needs of others the highest priority in one's life. This is similar to the author who supposedly wrote the book, "Humility and how I obtained it." One author said, "When one delights in humility it ceases to be genuine humility and becomes pride!"

The word for "humility," *tapeinophrosune*, often referred to fasting and several Jewish Christian writings specify that the consequence of this ascetic practice is entrance into the heavenly realm. This self-effacement or humiliation of one's mind is always a negative connotation in classical Greek. When someone "delights" in humility, it becomes pride and manipulation to gain praise from others.

Humility is an admirable characteristic that gives the impression that a person must be walking with God since they are so humble. However, when someone continually "delights" [or "chooses on purpose"] to appear in "humility" as a means of "passing judgment on you" [*katabrabeuo*, "beguile" or using charm and persuasion to deceive]. Their false humility gives them a mask of spiritual superiority, which they exploit the unsuspecting believer.

> "The Gnostic prided himself upon special visions of secret things which were not open to the eyes of ordinary men and women. No one will deny the visions of the mystics, but there is always danger when a man begins to think that he has attained a height of holiness which enables him to see what common men - as he calls them - cannot see; and the danger is that men will so often see, not what God sends them, but what they want to see." (Barclay, 1959, p. 181)

They took great pride, though covered in the pretense of humility, to create the impression that they had real spirituality, and therefore a sense of fulfillment, that could only be attained through entering into these deep secrets or attaining deeper levels of intimacy with God.

The word for "supposedly seen," or intruding," *embateoo*, is used in the Mystery religions of Paul's day. When a person "intruded" into the spiritual realm where God dwells, this meant he had paid the price of being initiated so that now he was considered to be "spiritual" in that mystery religion. The false teachers were telling the Colossians that they are not qualified to be initiated into the deeper levels of intimacy or enter into the heavens spiritually and thus were unable to communicate with heavenly beings on their level. This accusation intimidated them into yielding to their false mystic teachings of encounters with spiritual beings, visions and dreams, or directly with angels.

> The Gnostic prided himself upon special visions of secret things, which were not open to the eyes of ordinary men and women. No one will deny the visions of the mystics, but there is always danger when a man begins to think that he has attained a height of holiness which enables him to see what common men-as he calls them-cannot see; and the danger is that men will so often see, not what God sends them, but what they want to see. (Barclay, 1959, p. 182)

These are all symptoms that take many different forms through the ages, but the bottom line is a focus away from the Word of God, its serious study and application and the mission of the church, world evangelism. Rather the focus is all on us and "worship" instead of service to the kingdom.

True worship humbles one because he gains a glimpse of the holiness of God as revealed in His Word (Isaiah 6:1-5) and overwhelming gratitude that

Chapter 8: *The Gift of the Spirit: By Works or by Grace?*

because of the blood of Christ we find ourselves acceptable in His sight (Eph 1:6). What is gained in such worship is fresh insight into how He wants us to live (conviction of the Holy Spirit) and how He wants us to serve others for His glory (Isa 6:8-9).

Mysticism is very different from a genuine worship and from legalism. It is based on subjective experiences, which are suppose to make one more "spiritual" than anyone who has not had such experiences. Mysticism is so subjective that it cannot be proven or disproved, but the symptoms are inevitable. These mystics supposedly saw angels between God and man as intermediaries or protectors of believers who could be called upon in need. Was this an early form of spiritual warfare?

Paul's main point in Colossians 2 is that all you need is Christ as He is portrayed in Scriptures, not in dreams or visions. This is not to say that believers will not have legitimate supernatural experiences serving Christ, but they should not become the focus of one's spiritual life, nor should anyone depend upon temporary experiences for a sense of intimate walking in His Spirit (Gal 5:16).

Beware of anyone who will judge you or intimidate you by making you think that you will not get the "reward" or God's approval unless you have a specific "experience" or subjective encounter like they did. Beware of anyone who holds up certain "standards" which must be obeyed if you are to be "spiritual" or to enter into the "deeper" truths or higher levels of your relationship with God. Either of these will lead you into bondage and away from a high value on the Word of God. If God gives you a wonderful experience in communion with Him, prize it and keep it to yourself. Pride is a subtle enemy. Not only does it corrupt the speaker, it provokes envy in the hearer – a double sin to avoid.

Chapter 8: *Gifts for Today*

CHAPTER 9

Seeking the Miraculous

Chapter 9: *Gifts for Today*

Christianity has undergone major changes in the past hundred years, and especially in the past thirty years around the globe. The numbers of Christ followers have increased in staggering proportions. The major factor for this growth appears to be the declared miraculous nature of the ministries in the churches. It is stated that experiencing or witnessing a miracle has influenced the majority of conversions around the globe. Some have questioned the validity of some of these miracles, but how do you argue with the amazing statistics?

The question that is hard to focus on is, what does the Scripture say? Is everything that is big and amazing always a God-thing? For the purpose of this study we are focusing on the biblical texts used to defend the different doctrines of the movements. Fewer and fewer authors are raising questions about the foundations of the Charismatic movement today.

> "Christianity is undergoing a paradigm shift of major proportions—a shift from faith to feelings, from fact to fantasy, and from reason to esoteric revelation. This paradigm shift is what I call the Counterfeit revival. . . . Some of the most recognizable names in the Christian community are endorsing this paradigm shift with little or no reservation. The appeal is so staggering that churches on every continent are now inviting their people to 'experience' God in a brand-new way" (Hanegraaff 1997: 9).

Does God do miracles today as He did in era of the Bible? Many people have written and declared that they desire to experience today the power of the early Church as in the book of Acts. They are discouraged with the lack of apparent power in the contemporary Church and want to return to the time of the apostles where supposedly miracles were abundant.

Bixler ridicules anyone who denies the apostolic-type miracles today as having a "faith, which gives no room for a Jesus Christ who is the same yesterday, today, and forever. They are quite comfortable with a distant God who hasn't done anything significant in 2,000 years." (Bixler 1970:59)

However, the desire to be like one of the New Testament churches has some problems. With all of the churches that are highlighted in the New Testament, one wonders which of these churches they would want to imitate. Anyone who understands all the problems that existed in the church of Corinth would never want to imitate it. They were actually in worse spiritual condition than most churches today. In addition, though Paul showed his approval of the churches in Thessalonica and Philippi, there is no indication that any of these ancient churches, with the exception of the church of Jerusalem because of the presence of the apostles, possessed more powers or experienced more miracles than modern churches. In other words, there is no indication that all of the early churches were consistently experiencing miracles.

If we limit our study to an examination of the churches and not of the apostles, then we will see that they were very similar to contemporary biblical churches. They had problems such as adultery, theft, divisions, respecting of persons, gossip, divorce and doctrinal deviations. There is no evidence that the early churches "turned the world up side down" (Acts 17:6), as it was said with respect to the apostle Paul and his colleagues. In fact, only a few churches were commended for their evangelism. As we have seen, it took almost twenty years before the church at Jerusalem would approve the evangelism of Gentiles. The analysis of the seven churches in Revelation 2 and 3, however, can be considered a realistic evaluation of the early Church. Only two of these churches were basically "spiritual," and none were characterized by miraculous powers.

Conversely, many writers appear to claim that if miracles are not experienced in a church, then church is not spiritual. They base this claim on certain verses that, in their opinion, insinuate that miracles should continue in spiritual churches. The sense of intimidation can become very powerful, and this can cause overcompensation, exaggeration or worse.

One author says: "There is probably not a time in church history when there were not some who knew the fullness of the Holy Spirit and spoke in tongues." (Bennett 1971: 61) Speaking about contemporary times, he said: "Many Christian leaders today speak in tongues but do not admit to it because they fear prejudice," and also, "There are a number of people who have spoken in tongues, but don't know it!"(*Ibid.*: 61)

So great is the necessity of having miracles that they invent the evidence! Bennett goes on to claim that Martin Luther, Charles Finney and D.L. Moody spoke in tongues; however, there is no evidence of such. These declarations are exaggerated and impossible to prove, yet some churches teach them as evidence of the universality of the gift of tongues.

Three key (controversial) passages

If no gift of the Spirit can be manifested without the baptism of the Spirit and this baptism does not occur without speaking in tongues (according to the Charismatic teaching), then there is a grave problem in the history of the Church. Charismatics have to presume that each gifted person in history had received the baptism of the Spirit and had spoken in tongues, even if unconsciously.

Looking at the Scriptures, we can see that part of their error in understanding miracles, especially with respect to tongues, comes from the misinterpretation of three particular passages. For this reason it is very important that all believers have a good and clear understanding of the following: Mark 16:17-18, 1 Corinthians 12:31 and 1 Corinthians 14:5. For each passage we will look at a number of different problems of interpretation that have arisen to obscure the true meaning of the verses.

(1) Mark 16:17-18 Signs should follow.

"And these signs will follow those who believe: In My name they will cast out demons; they will speak with new tongues; "they will take up serpents; and if they drink anything deadly, it will by no means hurt them; they will lay hands on the sick, and they will recover."

This is the most common passage in defense of miracles and speaking in tongues. We should note that some ancient manuscripts do not contain the last verses of the chapter; for our study we will accept them as valid and part of the original Scriptures, because the great majority of the manuscripts do contain the complete passage. Burgon shows that only two manuscripts out of 620 that contain the Gospel of Mark omit the verses Mark 16:9-20. (Burgon 1871: 60-61)

Five Signs

Upon reading the passage, the first notable thing is that the promise includes the following five signs that would follow those who believed: (1) Casting out of demons, (2) Speaking in new tongues, (3) Taking up serpents without being harmed, (4) Drinking poison without being harmed, and (5) Healing the sick.

Naturally, this brings up questions: If Charismatic churches believe that these are valid for today, then why are not all five signs practiced and that by everyone that believes? They have chosen the gift of tongues, the casting out of demons and healing as the miracles that would follow believers. Not all "those who believe" have practiced even these three manifestations. What happened with the other two signs? Taking up serpents and drinking poison are not common signs though there might be occasions in history when they have occurred. Most of the practical manifestations of these sign gifts would be dependent upon a circumstance when they would be needed or beneficial.

In the biblical text, one of the miracles is that "they will speak new tongues" (Mark 16:17). In the Greek, the adjective "new" is translated as *kainos*, which refers to something "new in quality." Some say that the use of *kainos* instead of *neos* (a synonym for "new") implies ecstatic speaking instead of speaking an earthly tongue, because a heavenly tongue (1 Cor 13:1) could be described as something "new in quality." The word *neos*, however, means "new in time or origin" while the word *kainos* denotes something "new in experience;" in other words, *kainos* is something "different from the norm, impressive, better than the old, superior in value or attraction." Behm compares all the passages where the two words appear and comes to the conclusion that, "The distinction becomes less strict with study." (Belm, *kainos*, TDNT 1974: 449). This means that ecstatic speaking is in no way the meaning here, but rather, refers to a genuine speaking in tongues that was new in the sense of being previously unknown or strange to the speaker.

Verb Tense

The aspect most frequently ignored in this passage is the tense of the verb in Greek. The translator unfortunately translated it in the present tense: "These signs will follow those who believe" (16:17). If this were the case, then it would be necessary for us to have seen these signs following all believers throughout the entire history of the Church, or else they would not be true believers. As worded, the verse does not permit any condition or exception. A more detailed examination reveals that the verse actually says something different. In this verse the Greek verb "believe" is in the aorist tense, which is a past or completed tense meaning. A better translation is "those who have believed." It is an antecedent to the principal verb, "These signs will follow..." This phrase probably refers to the first believers, those who had believed when Jesus declared His promise.

In order to know if there is any fulfilling of this promise we need to see the entire context and the way the language operates within it. This fulfillment is described at the end of Mark 16. In verse 20, we see that "they went forth, and preached everywhere, the Lord working with them, and confirming the word with signs following." The pronoun, "they" is emphasized in the Greek text. It does not say that everyone did the confirming, but the grammatical emphasis is on only the "eleven" that Mark describes in 16:14. This is the same group referred to again in Acts 5:12, "And through the hands of the apostles many signs and wonders were done among the people."

It is also notable that the tense of the verbs in Mark 16:20 is past tense; in other words, when Mark wrote his gospel he referred to the confirmation ministry by the eleven as a past event. It should be noted that Mark was probably the first book of the New Testament to be written around A.D. 50-55.

The Ministry of "Confirmation"

Hebrews 2:3-4, "How shall we escape if we neglect so great a salvation, which at the first began to be spoken by the Lord, and was confirmed to us by those who heard Him, God also bearing witness both with signs and wonders, with various miracles, and gifts of the Holy Spirit, according to His own will?"

Hebrews identifies a unique group of Christ followers who had a special ministry of confirming the divine nature of Christ's message of salvation. Once confirmed and authenticated it would stand forever as true and trustworthy. The verb "to confirm" (*bebaioo*) in Mark 16:20 is the same one that appears in Hebrews 2:3-4 where the author refers to the ministry of "confirmation." It is important to note who had that special ministry in these verses. In the text there are three divisions of persons: (1) The Lord, who first announced the Gospel, (2) a group of "those who heard" the message directly from the Lord, who in turn "confirmed" that message, (3) to the third group—in which the author of Hebrews was included, as evident by the use of "us"—or those who observed their confirmation evidence, apparently without participating in the miraculous ministry. Here are a number of observations from this passage:

First, the tense of the verb in Heb 2:3 ("was confirmed" or *ebebaiothe*) is the past tense (passive aorist). The indication of the verb is that the "confirmation" was not occurring when the book of Hebrews was written during approximately 64 A.D, but rather was seen as a past-completed series of events, at least by the author.

This is a judicial term, which means "things guaranteed by fact" (Liddell, *Liddell-Scott-Jones Greek-English Lexicon*: art. 8122), thus the truth of Christ's message was proven as in a court of law once and for all time to be true.

The present tense gerund, "bearing witness," is a participle in Greek and is related to the verb "was confirmed," explaining how God confirmed His message as being valid. In other words, it is a description of something that happened some time before the writing of Hebrews, which places the period of confirmation between the years of 30-60 A.D.

Second, the passage put emphasis on this particular group. Literally Heb 2:3 should read, "by those who heard Him to us it was confirmed." The arrangement seeks to prioritize this particular group who did the confirmation. It should be noted that the author's choice of words shows that he excluded himself from that group. The confirmation ministry was never something for everyone. In 2:4 the verb "bearing witness," *sunepimartureo*, has a prepositional prefix –*sun* meaning "with," thus the verb means "testifying together with…", which implies that God was bearing this witness "with" someone referred to in the context, that is, the specific group that heard Jesus personally. Many translations add the pronoun to clarify the meaning, "God also bearing witness with them at the same time…" There is no indication that this was ever meant to be a normal practice through out the church age by every believer.

Third, the manner in which God testified through them was with "signs and wonders and diverse miracles." These are the same terms used in Acts to describe the specific work and ministry of the apostles and as well as the ministry of Paul in Romans 15:19 "in mighty signs and wonders, by the power of the Spirit of God, so that from Jerusalem and round about to Illyricum I have fully preached the gospel of Christ." Also is seen in 2 Corinthians 12:12 "Truly the signs of an apostle were accomplished among you with all perseverance, in signs and wonders and mighty deeds." [Italics mine] The uniqueness (not commonness) of the apostolic ministry gave the miraculous foundation for the church to follow the apostolic teaching with total confidence as to being genuine. Thomas Edgar explains why this was not to be a continuing experience:

> The New Testament sets standards for an apostle that preclude the continuance of this gift. Not only must an apostle be able to perform miracles (2 Cor 12:12), not only was the early church very careful about granting anyone, even Paul, the title of "apostle" (Gal 2:1–10), but also an apostle must have seen the resurrected Lord (1 Cor 9:1–2; Acts 1:22–26). Paul

explicitly stated that he was the last one to see the resurrected Lord (1 Cor 15:8), and he specifically connected this fact with his apostleship (Edgar, *Miraculous Gifts*, pp. 60-62). This requirement for apostleship refers to genuine appearances of the resurrected Christ and not to "visions." There have been no resurrection appearances since the apostolic age. Paul clearly stated that the last appearance was to him. (Revelation 1:12–18 refers to a vision, and is not an appearance of the resurrected Lord in bodily form on earth.) Therefore apostles in the sense of the Twelve and Paul cannot occur today (Edgar 1988:145: 378)

Since speaking in tongues was a miraculous sign (1 Corinthians 14:22), it is very probable that tongues, healings and other miracles (as the five mentioned in Mark 16) would have been common in the ministry of these apostles. The only exceptions of believers who were not apostles, but still performed miracles in the NT, were Phillip, Stephen and Ananias. There is a high possibility that they had heard the message directly from Jesus in His earthly ministry; though this is speculation, it is a reasonable conclusion. A number had followed Jesus from his baptism to his resurrection from which two were chosen to replace Judas (Acts 1:21-22), of whom we have no other record. According to Hebrews 2, no one else had the ministry of the confirmation of Jesus' message by signs and miracles. Our confirmation today is the recording of those miracles from the first century.

Once a confirmation of a truth has been made in science or in a court of law, it is never necessary to prove it again; the evidence has already been declared sufficient. It is unnecessary to try to prove again something that has already been proven.

In the same way, the "faith" of the New Testament is based on the evidence offered by the historic text, indisputable through the centuries. Our theme is "we walk by faith, not by sight" (2 Corinthians 5:7). Genuine faith is always based on biblical or textual evidence that is accepted as true and trustworthy (Rom 10:17) and it follows that we put our trust in the biblical evidence by faith, without the need of additional proofs.

This is not blind and irrational faith, but faith that presupposes a valid, undisputed, historical evidence. The preaching of the Gospel demands that the confirmed biblical evidence be accepted just as it is written, requiring no further evidence or proof.

(2) 1 Corinthians 12:31 The "best" gifts
"But earnestly desire the best gifts. And yet I show you a more excellent way."

Some authors argued that all the gifts in the New Testament existed in the Old Testament, with the exception of the gift of tongues. So the "best gifts," or at least the gifts that are the newest in the NT revelation, the believer should seek, especially the gift of tongues. The verse is used to prove that the believer should seek certain specific gifts and that any believer can acquire the desired gift (especially the miraculous gift of tongues) if he seeks them with diligence.

1 Corinthians 12:28 Categories of gifts

"And God has appointed these in the church: first apostles, second prophets, third teachers, after that miracles, then gifts of healings, helps, administrations, varieties of tongues."

In the immediate context, we see how the apostle categorized by priority the gifts using the words, "first..., second..., third..., after that..., then..." (12:28). These categories do not refer to time or a chronological order, which would be foreign to the context. Rather the terminology refers to priority, value or importance. It should be noted that tongues is listed in the final or fifth category.

The "better gifts" refer to those gifts that directly produce edification for all other Christians to benefit them in their spiritual lives. The word "better" (*kreitton*) means "more useful, more serviceable" in a practical sense to others. It is probable this exhortation was necessary because some gifts placed in the final list in categories of lesser priority were being made more notable, such as miracles, healing and speaking in tongues. The exhortations directed to the church demanded a kind of action that prioritized the gifts that edify, rather than the sensational gifts.

The Word "earnestly desire or seek"

The word "earnestly desire" in 1 Corinthians 12:31 does not refer to seeking something or getting a gift, but rather it emphasizes being continually careful to give value and priority to the "better" gifts with great zeal or priority.

The verb *zeloo* is the Greek word translated "seek." The Greek form of the verb can be either imperative ("seek" as a command) or indicative ("you are seeking"). The latter seems more appropriate to the immediate context, both before this verse and the context following this verse. Paul is stating what they were doing (i.e. seeking what they considered the greater gifts), then he adds, "and yet I show you a more excellent way." (12:31) The church is to focus on loving and caring for others, and thus to focus on the permanent and edifying gifts – chapter 13), which is the way of love.

The church of Corinth was prioritizing the lessor or fifth category of the gifts, thinking they were the "best" while ignoring the higher priority edifying the church. Paul's argument (chapter 14) will establish step-by-step why his higher categories of gifts were superior to the miraculous gifts they were seeking and those gifted teaching ministries should be more highly esteemed.

Rather than teaching directly against their worship practice in their assembly, Paul is establishing a statement that they will agree with, and then he builds principles for re-establishing their congregational priorities. This argumentation is noted by Chadwick:

Chapter 9: *Seeking the Miraculous* 141

The entire drift of the argument of 1 Cor. xii-xiv is such as to pour a douche of ice-cold water over the whole practice. But Paul could hardly have denied that the gift of tongues was a genuine supernatural charisma without putting a fatal barrier between himself and the Corinthian enthusiasts.... [for] the touchstone of soundness in the eyes of those claiming to be possessed by the Spirit was whether their gift was recognized to be a genuine work of God. To deny this recognition was to prove oneself to be altogether lacking in the Spirit. ... a masterly sentence which has the effect of brilliantly forestalling possible counter-attack at the most dangerous point, and indeed carries the war into the enemy camp. To have refused to recognize the practice as truly supernatural would have been catastrophic. Paul must fully admit that glossolalia is indeed a divine gift; but, he urges, it is the most inferior of all gifts... No stronger assertion of his belief in the validity of this gift of the Spirit could be made; and in the context it is a master touch which leaves the enthusiasts completely outclassed and outmaneuvered on their own ground (Robinson, 1972: 49-50).

The broader context of chapter 12 has been teaching that the Corinthians were to stop seeking spectacular gifts for personal benefits (discussed later), rather they were to discover how God had already gifted each one of them to prepare them for ministry in His kingdom (Eph 2:10). They have all been fit for service (1 Cor 12:7). Seeking gifts out of personal preferences motivates a self-centered interest and destroys the interdependent plan of God for the church (1 Cor 12:14).

The meaning of the word "seek" in the eleven instances where it appears in the NT means "to be jealous of, or deeply concerned about" something. The idea is to be jealous or protective of anything that upstages or usurps the priority of the "best gifts" (12:31).

This verb is in the plural so it is directed to the entire church as a group, not to individuals. The church leadership must restrict the manner in which its congregation can exercise the gifts in the assembly (1 Cor 14:26-38). The context emphasizes the priority of the edification gifts—apostle, prophet, and teacher—over the spectacular gift of tongues, healings and miracles, which, apparently, had received too much importance in the Corinthian church.

The Greek language has other words that mean "to seek" (*zeteo, orego*) and "desire" (**thelo**, *epithumeo and boulomai*), but they are never used to refer to seeking a gift of the Spirit.

Paul used these verbs frequently in other verses. The verb *zeteo* is used 19 times, even in the same context, but not in the sense of seeking a gift. He used *orego* to describe seeking or desiring to be a bishop as a ministry (1 Timothy 3:1), but it was never in relation to desiring spiritual gifts. Paul used *thelo* 60 times, *boulomai* 8 times and *epithumeo* 5 times to communicate that which we should "seek or desire," but he did not use them anywhere to exhort believers to seek any particular spiritual gift.

All the passages with zeloo are better translated "be jealous for, enthusiastic about, or envious of" instead of "seek" or "desire."

The same word is used in 12:31, 14:1 and 14:39 with the same meaning. After a parenthesis in Chapter 13, Paul returned to the theme of the major controversy in the church. Paul will give ten reasons why the gifts of edification are superior and of higher value that the gift of tongues (14:2-20). The argument that continued until verse 25 has nothing to do with an individual seeking a gift, but rather it is talking about the priority or preference that the church should give to the edification ministries in the assembly. Similarly, in 14:39, Paul says that the whole church should be jealous for or enthusiastic about prophecy, not that each person should seek (*zeloo*) the gift of prophecy, but it should be held in higher esteem and given priority.

Paul had already proven that it is useless for everyone to seek to acquire any one specific gift, since our wanting to acquire a gift has nothing to do with how God has distributed the gifts to each believer (chapter 12).

In 14:12, "since you are zealous for spiritual gifts, let it be for the edification of the church that you seek to excel," [Italics mine]. They were zealous, but for the wrong thing.

Paul used the noun *zelotai* (jealousy, Zealot, burning with zeal and the verb seek (*zeteo*). Since the Corinthians were jealous (*zeleo*) or protective of the spiritual gifts, they should have sought (*zeteo*) for the congregation the gifts to edify the church, that is for the benefit of others, which is the meaning of love in 13:1-7.

Using the two words (*zeloo* and *zeteo*) in the same verse (14:12), Paul wanted to mark the difference between the two. To paraphrase, Paul says, "Since you are zealots (*zelotai*) for spiritual things, seek (*zeteo*) to edify." This is not commanding everyone to seek the sensational gifts, but to prioritize and emphasize the teaching, edifying and instructing gift manifestations.

1 Corinthians 14:1 Focus on edification gifts

"Pursue love, and desire spiritual gifts, but especially that you may prophesy."

In 1 Corinthians 14:1, the verb form "desire or be enthusiastic about" (*zeloo*) is the same verb in the same form as 12:31. The verb form is the same for the present indicative and present imperative, so the context must determine which is to be understood. Here the context would demand the imperative form, i.e., they were to "be continually desiring the spiritual gifts, especially that you may prophecy (plural tense)" [author's added nuance or sense of the Greek verb]. From the context it is evident that they were not doing this (so it is not descriptive), but needed to be commanded to start changing their priorities.

The context indicates that the priority of the activity in the assembly, not principally of individuals, should be "spiritual gifts" (the same word is in 12:1). We should be enthusiastic about the spiritual gifts, but "rather that ye may prophesy."

The last phrase definitely refers to an attitude on the part of the entire church, not to a literal possibility. In the context of chapters 12 and 14, the apostle has clarified the impossibility of everyone prophesying (see 14:5, 24, 31); he had just finished saying that all are not prophets (12:29). If Paul were to say that all should prophesy, then he would be invalidating the entire argument of chapter 12, which taught that no single gift would ever characterize the church. Paul is not speaking to individuals, but to the corporate church. There are no instructions for individuals seeking these gifts for personal benefit.

Paul had just demonstrated how that the Corinthians should be pursuing "love," which is the sacrifice of selfish interests for the benefit of others. The lack of love in the believer generates all kinds of selfish sins. Their desire for the phenomenal, attention-getting gifts for their own benefit and approval by others was the root cause of the myriad of carnal conflicts in the church.

However, priority of the edifying gift of prophecy is not to the exclusion of the serving gifts, nor to minimize the value of the other gifts. Paul is seeking to secure a shift in values in the church. The pursuit of "love" demands a serving mentality that benefits everyone in the congregation building up their understanding of the revealed Word of God through the ministry of the gifts.

The necessity of being content with the gift that God has given

The emphasis on individuals seeking gifts, especially miraculous ones, is contrary to the context. In 12:11, Paul had said that God gives gifts as He "wills" or "determines." In verse 18, the point is reiterated, "just as He pleased." Seeking gifts in addition to those God has given us expresses dissatisfaction with His will for our lives. The believer must accept the spiritual gifts that God has assigned to him and not envy those who have other gifts, especially sensational gifts. God has engineered us such that our deepest fulfillment will come as we serve others by how He has made us and gifted us by His Spirit.

Upon examining the context we see five categories of gifts and a contrast between three perspectives, one of which is discouraged. One perspective focuses on the sensational or miraculous gifts of tongues, a second prioritizes the "best gifts," while the third employs all the gifts or any action in a ministry of love in which the believers serve one another. The actions of love [selflessly benefiting others] are superior to any of the gifts. This was the message of 1 Corinthians 13:1-7. The lifestyle of love and that of the gifts should coexist; however, one does not and cannot exclude the other. The text is speaking of the focus, not the exclusion of some gifts. The higher priority gifts should be emphasized, protected, and used with the right motivation in the spirit of love, making each other's needs the priority (Philippians 2:2-4) while encouraging all the gifts to be exercised correctly (1 Cor 14).

Thus, we see that there is nothing in the Bible to indicate that a person should seek any gift for personal benefit or sense of spiritual experience. There is also no indication that a person will be able to acquire any additional gift he may want, especially for selfish gratification. On the contrary, in 1 Corinthians 12 we see that the gifts are given out as God ordains (1 Cor 12:11), and each believer should be content with the gift or gifts he has received. Finally, spiritual gifts that edify the entire Church, not an individual, should be emphasized with jealousy.

(3) 1 Corinthians 14:5 The wish that all spoke in tongues

"I wish you all spoke with tongues, but even more that you prophesied; for he who prophesies is greater than he who speaks with tongues, unless indeed he interprets, that the church may receive edification."

The Charismatics want to use 14:5 to say that all believers should speak in tongues because Paul said: "I wish you all spoke with tongues..." Paul had been warning them about the abuse of tongues and is about to explain the inferiority of tongues. Why would he exacerbate the problem by wanting everyone to be involved?

The Contradictory Interpretation

Once again Paul used an exaggerated statement or impossible extreme in his teaching for the purpose of emphasis (13:1-3). Such hyperboles are not to be taken literally (12:16-17), much less to be the basis of a teaching. Furthermore, if it were possible for everyone to speak in tongues, it would be contrary to what Paul had just taught in 12:4-31, where he declared that everyone has different spiritual gifts, and he just said so emphatically in 12:30 that not all could speak in tongues.

However, using this verse as a false basis, many Charismatics encourage all believers to speak in tongues in prayer, in praise and in devotional times. They think that this private use of tongues is necessary if one wants to grow in personal edification.

Such a means of "edification" is not only contradictory to the teaching that no gift is common to all (12:17, 19), but also, it contradicts the same verse in which Paul said, "...*but rather that ye may prophesy.*" If it were possible, the priority should be that everyone prophesizes, but that is just as impossible.

The two declarations (that everyone spoke in tongues or everyone prophesied) are hyperboles or exaggerations contrary to reality; it is just as impossible that everyone speak in tongues as it is that everyone prophesies. What would Paul say? Given the hypothetical case that all could have only one or the other gift, he says it would be much better for it to be prophecy rather than speaking in tongues.

Verb Tense

In the statement, "I would that ye all spoke in tongues," (14:5) the verb "would" (*thelo*) is not an imperative. Paul is not giving a command to all Christians. The verb is in the present indicative active tense, making it an expression of personal desire, but it is not a command. Once again we have an exaggerated statement to demonstrate his argument.

The second part of the sentence is introduced with "but even more" or "to an even greater degree" he would desire them to prophecy. The whole idea is hypothetical, but is used to express the preferred option or preference of the Apostle: prophecy over tongues. This is the thrust of the passage in its context and should not be made to say something that it never intended to say.

The Importance of Paul's Desire

This kind of exaggerated expression is common in Paul's writings. This is called reduction ad absurdum, or an argument to absurdity to demonstrate that a "false, untenable, or absurd result follows from its acceptance (Rescher, Retrieved 21 July 09).

Romans 9:3 says, "For I *could wish* that myself were accursed from Christ for my brethren." Paul expressed a desire contrary to reality to demonstrate his burden to win Israel for Christ. However, no matter how much he talked, his standing before Christ was not changed.

In 1 Corinthians 7:7, Paul used the same verb (*thelo*) to express another desire: "For I would that all men were even as I myself;" that is, a bachelor! Again, we see that *thelo* was an expression of desire, but not a command. Paul used such rhetorical expressions to illustrate an exaggerated point for the sake of his argument, although he knew his statements were not possible, nor should ever be taken to be possible.

Paul is insinuating that having everyone speak in tongues would not be as advantageous as having everyone prophesy; at the same time, neither of the two is actually feasible. The whole context is proving that the exhortation gifts like prophesying are far superior to the miracle gifts like speaking in tongues. It would be out of place in the context if Paul taught that all should have a miracle gift.

Chapter 9: *Gifts for Today*

CHAPTER 10

Categories and times of miracles

Chapter 10: *Gifts for Today*

There are various questions that we should ask about miracles. What is a miracle? Did miracles exist during all the historical epochs? Are the miracles in the Bible common? Many times we call happenings and events "miracles" when they are simply providential. What is the difference? We must form our own realistic opinions and concepts through a careful study of the biblical evidence. Before analyzing the gifts that are valid in our times, it is necessary to understand certain concepts about miracles.

Miracles are not always a sign of what God is doing. Great discernment is necessary so that false miracles do not deceive even believers. God has allowed Satan to attract people into error, especially by performing miracles (Ex 7:11; Acts 8:9-24; 13:8; and 2 Thes 2:9; Rev 16:14) and deceive believers (2 Cor 11:3, 14; Eph 6:11). Even more subtle is the fact that Satan can cause people to pay "attention to deceitful spirits and doctrines of demons" (1 Tim 4:1). Satan can empower false miracles, signs and wonders to deceive people and deviate attention from God's Word to his delusion. The ones who are susceptible to his "deluding influence" are those who "did not receive the love of the truth" (2 Thes 2:10). How can we discern what is a divine miracle?

> The effecting of miracles also was a temporary sign gift. A miracle is a supernatural intrusion into the natural world and its natural laws, explainable only by divine intervention. God often leads us, helps us, or warns us by working through other Christians, through ordinary circumstances, or through natural laws. Those are supernatural workings of providence by God, but they are not miracles. A miracle is an act of God that is contrary to the ordinary working and laws of nature, an act that only He could accomplish by overruling nature and that could not otherwise occur through any circumstances. (MacArthur 1984: 301.)

Jesus alone performed miracles that were related to nature such as changed water to wine, took a coin from the mouth of a fish, walked on water, and ascended into a cloud. No disciple or apostle is ever recorded as doing a miracle with regard to nature.

The word that is used to describe the miracles of the disciples is *dunamis*, "power," which is often associated with casting out demons (Luke 4:36; 6:18; 9:42). This was the power the Lord gave to the apostles and the seventy (Luke 9:1; 10:17-19). There is no indication that it has been granted to all believers, since it was a special sign to authenticate His specially selected disciples. Philip and Stephen demonstrated the gift of miracles (Acts 6:8; 8:7).

One of the most comical stories in the Bible occurred when some Jews attempted to cast out demons without the true gift of miracles. The result was that the demon possessed man beating them up and tore off their clothes, chasing them out of town (Acts 19:14-16).

B. B. Warfield demonstrated from Scripture how these miracles only accompanied the early disciples as long as they were revealing the Word of God. When the revelations stopped, the signs likewise stopped:

"These miraculous gifts were part of the credentials of the apostles, as authoritative agents of God in founding the church. Their function confined them distinctly to the apostolic church, and they necessarily passed away with it." (Warfield 1918: 21)

Gary Derickson's analysis of the NT record suggests that Paul was unable to accomplish healing miracles near the end of his ministry, but non-miraculous gifts continued to be given to believers by the Spirit.

Some accuse cessationists of being antisupernatural, of denying all miracles. Yet this is only rarely the case. Almost all evangelicals affirm that God can and does intervene today in miraculous ways. The issue for them, however, is whether He does so through human agents, or whether He sometimes performs miracles in answer to prayer apart from so-called "healers" or miracle workers. (Derickson 1998: 300).

The Charismatic Bennett writes, "Paul's power in the Holy Spirit did not decrease as he grew older. We find him manifesting God's miraculous keeping and healing power more strongly, if anything, in the last chapter of Acts, than in the earlier times (Acts 27–28). Paul never slowed down even in his old age." (Bennett 1971: 131). However, the evidence indicates that Paul was unable to heal Epaphroditus during his first Roman imprisonment (approximately 62 AD), then he had to leave sick Trophimus behind and could only offer Timothy some medical advice (about 64 AD).

Proponents of the charismatic movement have managed to shift the burden of proof regarding the temporary nature of some gifts to their opponents. They have done this by assuming that all things are to be the same throughout the church age, and they have demanded proof otherwise.. ... Since the facts of church history reveal that the Holy Spirit has not been functioning in all the ways that He did in the book of Acts, then the basic assumption that all things remain the same is false. It is contrary to the facts; therefore the burden of proof properly falls upon those who claim that all gifts are for the entire duration of the church age. (Edgar, 2001: 267)

Miracles appeared to be of some impact, but were never a major emphasis in the apostolic ministry, nor were they ever the purpose of their ministries. They were occasional, that is they occurred when the need arose, but were not sought or performed as spectacle. The gospel was the priority always. Nothing distracted them for preaching the cross. It was not miracles that drew people to Christ; rather, it was the message of salvation. Paul never pointed people to miracles as the key to conversions, because "faith comes from hearing, and hearing by the word of Christ" (Rom 10:17). In Corinth the evidence of Paul's apostleship was not his miracle working powers, but the transformation of the

Corinthian believers themselves (1 Cor 9:1-2).

Even though this is an argument from silence, from AD 60 and later, the lack of evidence of the amazing miraculous beginning of the gospel become deafening. Any careful reading of the NT reveals that the Early Church was not characterized by power and miracles as some want to assume.

Rather it was characterized by problems, conflicts, false doctrines and heresies (Rev. 2 and 3 for six examples of the early churches). The apostles for the most part were only ones who performed miracles (Acts 2:43; 5:12). The charismatics assume that the entire church today should be able to perform all the miracles that the apostles did in the NT era.

Biblical evidence of some gifts being temporary

The gifts of "apostle," is a term commonly referring to "representative" of local churches, but when referring to the NT leadership, it is used of the Twelve and Paul, all of whom clearly possessed the miraculous gift of an apostle (2 Cor 12:12). Most denominations, including most Pentecostals, have held that the NT sense of authoritarian miracle working apostles has not continued throughout the church. The dependence on the English Bible and imprecise use of Scripture is a common failing according to Ken L. Sarles (Sarles 1988: 70).

The NT set standards for an apostle that limited the continuance of apostleship. To be identified as an apostle he must demonstrate the ability to perform miracles (2 Cor 12:12). The early church was very reluctant to put the title "apostle" on anyone, even Paul (Gal 2:1-10), and he also must have been an eyewitness to the resurrected Lord (1 Cor 9:1-2; Acts 1:22-26). Furthermore, Paul stated that he was the last one to have seen the resurrected Lord (1 Cor 15:8), which gave him credential to be called an apostle (Edgar 2001: 60-62). This had to be a genuine personal appearance in bodily form of the resurrected Lord, not seeing Him in a vision.

> Since the ones who performed the miracles were only in the beginning church, it is logical that the miracles themselves were only for the apostolic age. Since the ability to perform such miracles was evidence of apostleship (2 Cor 12:12), then with rare exceptions others could not have performed such signs and wonders, and they would not continue when the apostles ceased. In addition to this implication the temporary nature of miracles is directly supported by Scripture. (Edgar 1988: 382).

Similarities and dissimilarities

The differences or dissimilarities between the nature of the miracles described in the Gospels and Acts and the contemporary declared miracles are obvious. Biblical miracles were observable, instantaneous, and creative (that is, new physical flesh was created instantaneously as lepers received new skin as a baby).

Having observed many phenomena overseas in different contexts, the author has seen some alarming similarities between common practices in Pentecostal-type meetings and shamanism and spiritism.

Entering into trances, going unconscious for long periods, then returning to consciousness with supposed insights or communication with another world or spirits, the ability to heal many physical illnesses and command the evil spirits of possessed persons to leave, the ability to read what another person is thinking, speaking to the spirit world (called the "excluded middle") in a language unknown to the shaman and perform other miracles that defy explanation (i.e., transmigration into a jaguar), even levitating are all practices in both pagan rituals and Pentecostal meetings, yet none are similar to the biblical descriptions of miracles. The chanting, entering into a frenzy, shaking, jerking and entering unconscious states have little similarity to the NT expressions of faith and worship, but a lot of similarities with pagan religions.

Certainly this should not be brushed off as satanic imitations of the Spirit's work. The lack of clear Scriptural models should be sufficient warning to anyone familiar with the texts.

Three Basic Concepts about Miracles

(1) A specific declaration is not always necessary to prove a doctrine.

Several cardinal doctrines do not have specific proof verses. These doctrines are established inductively through the study of a collection of verses. There is not a more cardinal doctrine than that of the Trinity, and while there is not a single passage that teaches about it in its entirety, there is much evidence for the validity of this doctrine. It is true that there is not a passage that declares that Jesus is the God-Man, but there are many that declare that He is God and many others that declare that he is Man. There are passages that put the name Jesus and God in apposition, making them the same grammatically. The totality of the Scriptures must be in accord in order to consider accepting a doctrine. The method of comparing various verses and gathering evidence to form a doctrine in agreement with the Scriptures is called Inductive Study.

This is the method we will use to study the scriptural evidence about miracles. The conclusion will not come from only one passage, but rather from all of the scriptural evidence taken together. These compiled Scriptures are just as valid as a single verse, especially when no one passage is conclusive. In the chapters following, each passage will be added to the collection of evidence, even if no passage alone will necessarily prove a certain doctrine.

(2) There are categories of miracles.

In the Bible we find categories of miracles. Some brethren say that if we do not believe that God can still produce the miracle of speaking in tongues today, then we do not believe in God's capacity to perform other miracles. If we say that God is not giving the gift of tongues, does this also mean that God does not do miracles today? No! God does do miracles today. He performs miracles of protection, provision, and direction about His will, and He also answers prayers. However, we must understand that there are two kinds of miracles in the Scriptures.

First Kind: God works through natural laws.

This kind of miracle requires the explanation, "I know that God did it." This is what happened to Job in Job 1:16, when a flash of lightening from a storm destroyed his stables and his animals. In Acts 27:21-26, Paul was traveling to Rome, but a storm caused his ship to change course to the island of Malta so that Paul could fulfill a ministry according to God's will. This first classification of miracles is when God intervenes by controlling events or nature not always for our benefit. This can also be called "providence" as God uses natural laws to provide for our necessities.

God promised us in Proverbs 3:5-6 that He will guide us. He often uses circumstances, counselors or the Word to clarify His direction for us. God does not use the mystical, such as voices heard in the night, but rather He uses practical circumstances to show us His will. In Romans 8:28, Paul says, "… all things work together for good to them that love God." In other words, all circumstances that happen in our lives have a purpose. There are no accidents, because the power of God controls the circumstances in our lives.

We classify such events as miracles because God is evidently manifested. At least, it is evident to the receiver when God intervenes by protecting, providing necessities, or giving special direction. It is too "lucky" to say, "What a coincidence!" When our money is diminished, the food in the kitchen is scarce or we are at the point of desperation over some other disaster, we call it a miracle when the person, who we have long forgotten he owed us some money, suddenly appears to return the loan just when we needed it.

There are no coincidences in the life of the believer. Perhaps a terminally ill person suddenly receives the news that doctors have found a new cure for his sickness, and he gets well with the new treatment. Can that be a coincidence? No! God intervened. He arranges events in order to meet us at a strategic point in our lives.

"Providence" is definitely God's intervention, but it is still distinct from a "miracle" that is undeniably supernatural.

Second kind: God can override the laws of nature.

If someone were to fall from an airplane and "by luck" survive as he falls

Chapter 10: *Categories and Times of Miracles*   153

into some soft substance, or through thick trees that slow his descent, then no law of nature would have been overridden; there would be no genuine miracle. The providence of God protected him, and it could be possible for this to occur. This actually happened to a young girl over the Peruvian jungle in 1973. She survived when a plane broke in two in a storm and she fell from the DC-6 to the ground still strapped in her seat, then walked out.

The second classification of miracles is what could not be explained by any natural laws, coincidence or, in human terms, what has no possibility of happening. The following are some examples of this kind of miracle in the Bible: the dividing of the Red Sea; the survival of the three men in the fiery furnace; the floating ax of Elisha, instantaneous healings of Jesus; the changing of water into wine; the sun standing still for Joshua; etc. There is no natural explanation for any of these miracles.

As we read the Bible, we note that this kind of miracle did not occur all the time. It was not a common occurrence, nor was there a constant need for a miracle. There were certain periods that were characterized by these special miracles and always for a good reason.

(3) There are characteristics of the periods when biblical miracles occurred.

Miracles were not commonplace in the Bible. One would think that the people of God would experience a continual series of miracles, since the need for miracles is almost ever present. Since the NT age there have been very few, if any, miracles in any way comparable to what was evident in the NT. One has to ask, why such miracles would be absence for nearly two millennia? Chrysostom, a fourth-century theologian, testified that they had ceased so long before his time that no one was certain of their characteristics. (Chrysostom, *Homily XXIX*, 12:168)

The record shows that very few of the prophets manifested a miracle, unless you count divine revelation. Obviously their prophecies were miraculous, but a supernatural sign might have convinced some of their contemporaries of their genuineness, instead many of the prophets suffered horrible persecution (Heb 11:32-40). The evidence points towards a few specific periods when miracles occurred and long periods when few if any miracles occurred.

To argue that the gifts merely declined rather than ceased is contrary to the evidence and is an unrealistic exercise in semantics. (Mallone 1983: 22). Dayton willingly admits that many charismatics prefer to admit that certain miraculous gifts ceased, because they see the modern day phenomena as the Latter-Rains pouring out of the Spirit from the allegorical view of Joel 2:23. (Dayton 1987: 26-28) In other words, to have a "former" rain (considered the Early Church's miracles), then a break with no miracles, followed by the present period called the "Latter Day Rains" when miracles were restored.

The only problem is that there is no evidence from Scripture that there will be a reoccurrence in the church of the sign gifts or that Christians will be able to manifest apostolic miracles in the end of the age. The Latter Rains theory is derived from an allegorical imagination and distortion of the clear meaning of Joel 2 to make the passage say whatever they want it to say.

The fact that a few individuals in Bible history did perform miracles, but others did not continue them, demonstrates that miracles were not a permanent characteristic of the people of God. If this trend is characteristic of Bible times, then we should expect a similar response in the NT. History demonstrates that the NT miracles ceased in the Early Church period.

In the Bible we observe the following three divisions of the second kind of miracles:

Division 1: Miracles in periods of special revelation

No Bible believer doubts that Moses performed a series of miracles providing for the liberation of Israel from Egypt; however, these miracles did not continue throughout the OT, nor was anyone, or Israel as a whole, expected to perform those miracles.

There are three periods of special revelation when miracles were the norm: the time of Moses and Joshua, the time of Elijah and Elisha, and the time of Christ and the apostles. History reveals that these were definite periods, and during these periods of special revelation, God used miracles to attract attention to His message and to His messenger. Miracles were so common during these times that no one appeared to be surprised when they occurred. This is not to say that everyone was performing miracles; rather, God used a few people as special instruments, giving them special miraculous abilities to confirm His message.

Division 2: Miracles in extraordinary periods

These extraordinary periods occurred while the nation of Israel was under direction and while the Church was being founded (e.g. in the period of the plagues in Egypt, during Elijah's debate with the prophets of Baal and when early miracles marked the founding of the Church). History reveals that these periods were temporary, and the vast majority of the miracles have never been repeated. No one has ever been able to imitate the way Moses willed the ten plagues into being; or the way Elijah stopped the rain and announced its return; or how the apostles declared death to liars and revived the dead, etc. Never in the Bible do we see miracles continuing in this way, and it is also never revealed as God's plan for them to continue.

Division 3: Miracles in periods of exception

During these periods, miracles were the exception and not the norm. Some examples include the unusual strength of Samson, Gideon's fleece of wool, Daniel's dreams and the three Israelites in the fiery furnace in Babylon. Miracles in these times were rare in comparison with the times of the prophets and special revelation. It is likely that these were not the only miracles that occurred, but still they were uncommon.

Currently we are in a period of exceptions. Without a doubt God continues doing miracles, but they are not the norm. In God's plan, the great majority of history has been marked by periods of exception, that is to say, periods of few miracles.

Three Periods of Special Revelation

Some people think that there is a continual series of miracles from the beginning of the Scriptures to end, but miracles have always been the exception, related always to the fulfillment of God's promises to the Jews. In fact, many of the miracles related to biblical promises have not happened yet and are reserved for the time of the second coming of Christ. For example: "I will pour upon the house of David and upon the inhabitants of Jerusalem, the spirit of grace and of supplications" (Zechariah 12:10). This has nothing to do with Pentecost; verse 9 tells us that it will happen when Jehovah destroys the nations that come against Jerusalem, and the destruction will be concentrated in the Valley of Megiddo during Armageddon (verse 11). According to Revelations 19, this prophecy speaks of Christ's return. Israel will see Jesus, "whom they have pierced, and they shall mourn for him" (Zechariah 12:10).

Today we can be confident in His miraculous direction, His consolation in our lives and His providential care. We can expect God to intervene miraculously in answer to our prayers. We know that there will be another period of miracles at the Second Coming of Christ, but thus far in biblical history there were only three epochs of miracles, between which there were centuries when miracles were scarce. These three periods are as follows:

Moses and Joshua (1441 to 1370 B.C.)

All the miracles experienced in this period were related to the redemption of Israel from Egypt and their supervision in the desert for 40 years. It is important to note that the miracles did not continue perpetually, because they were no longer necessary. For example, Joshua 5:11-12 explains why manna ceased to appear as a daily provision for Israel: they had "the fruit of the land of Canaan" and did not need it any more. This is a very important principle: God provides what His children truly need and nothing more.

After Joshua, 500 years passed until God intervened with miraculous signs again. In the interval some miracles and providential interventions occurred from time to time, but not to the extent as those experienced during an epoch of miracles.

Elijah and Elisha (870 to 785 B.C.)

In a time of apostasy in the history of Israel, God raised up two prophets to counsel and exhort the nation. In the middle of so much false religion, they needed miracles to demonstrate that they were truly from God and to identify themselves with Moses. However, after they preached their messages, the miracles ceased. Many prophets came after them, but none of them had such miraculous gifts as Elijah or Elisha had.

In the introduction of new epochs, it is not rare to see God using miracles to announce that He is bringing a new era and allowing the old one to pass. Elijah and Elisha heralded the era of the prophets, and afterward many prophets followed their examples and preaching. They even established schools of prophets, but there is no evidence that any of the students had the capacity to do miracles as they did.

After Elisha, more than 800 years lapsed before God began to manifest miraculous signs to Israel again. Again, there were exceptions to this generalization when God did intervene, i.e. Daniel in the lion's den or the three friends of Daniel in the fiery furnace, but these were the exception rather than the rule.

Christ and the Apostles (28 to 90 A.D.)

The third era of miracles occurred during the lives of Christ and the apostles. In John 20:30-31, we see the purpose of the signs: "And many other signs truly did Jesus in the presence of his disciples... But these are written, that ye might believe that Jesus is the Christ, the Son of God; and that believing ye might have life through his name." The purpose of the miracles was to prove His divinity. Once it was clear that Christ was God in human form, the Messiah and Emmanuel (God with us), it was unnecessary for the miracles to continue.

The apostles, for a time, continued doing miracles as a sign of their authority. In 2 Corinthians 12:12, such miracles are called "signs of the apostles;" in other words, the authority of an apostle was evident through the divine ability to demonstrate at will "signs, wonders and miracles." After their authority was generally accepted, miracles ceased. The fulfilled their purpose.

The epochs of miracles always had two purposes: (1) authenticate the new revelation and (2 to verify the men who would present the new revelation.

In Exodus 4:1-5, God declared His purpose in giving to Moses the gift of changing the rod into a snake so that Israel would believed that God had truly appeared to Moses. The miracle was performed once in the presence of Israel and did not have to be done again. It proved his authenticity and did not need to prove it again.

Moses did not have to repeat the miracle of the leprous hand each time his authority was doubted. These miracles occurred only one time; the oral repetition of history was sufficient for the people to have confidence in his

Chapter 10: *Categories and Times of Miracles*

leadership and his message. It would be absurd to ask Moses, "Would it be possible to do your miracles once more just to confirm our confidence in you?" The evidence was given once, and those who wanted to accept it did so. Those who doubted his leadership and the authority of his signs perished in the desert.

In Hebrews 2:3-4, God gave those who heard Him personally the authority to do "signs and wonders and diverse miracles and gifts of the Holy Ghost, according to his own will" with the purpose of confirming the message of salvation through Christ. These miracles occurred so that the authority of the apostles would be verified, and as a result the early Church was convinced that the message of the apostles had the same authority as that of Jesus. Because of this, "they continued steadfastly in the apostles' doctrine" (Acts 2:42). In each one of the three eras of miracles, signs fulfilled these two purposes of confirming the message and the messenger. In each occasion the signs ceased when the miracles had confirmed God's message. Thereafter the message would be accepted by faith in the validity of the miraculous confirmation previously manifested.

We should note a very important point: Miracles appeared at the moment the messenger arrived with his revelation, never before! In the Bible, miracles always appeared in relation to a crisis or a change that God wanted to make, and they ceased at the end of the lives of the leaders involved. For this reason, we should expect the re-establishment of an era of miracles after the coming of Christ, not before!

In the following diagram, note the contrast between the length of the periods of miracles and that of periods of silence or absence of them:

Moses and Joshua Lasted ±70 yrs 1441-1370 B.C.	500 years Silence	Elijah and Elisha Lasted ±70 yrs. 870-785 B.C.	814 years Silence	Christ and apostles Lasted ±70 yrs. 28-95 A.D.	1,900 yrs Silence

In each case, miracles ceased with the death of the principle leaders of each period. The past tense of the verb "was confirmed," in Hebrews 2:3-4 indicates the acceptance that the period of confirmation had already past when Hebrews was written in 66 A.D. The authority of both the message and the apostolic messengers was not in doubt: they had already been confirmed. Today we accept the same evidence as the Early Church for the basis of our faith.

There is no doubt that God performs miracles in answer to our prayers. In addition to this, however, Charismatics believe that miracles should be as much the norm of operations today as they were in the special epochs. The Bible does not agree, however; God does not have to reconfirm that which he has already established.

Chapter 10: Gifts for Today

CHAPTER 11

*Ten Principles from
1 Corinthians 12–14*

Chapter 11: *Gifts for Today*

Before analyzing the gift of tongues, it is important to establish the biblical principles for gifts in general. In all of the texts that treat the theme of gifts, very few give many details or descriptions of the gifts. In this section we will focus on 1 Corinthians 12-14, where Paul corrects the abuse of gifts in the Corinthian church. The gift of tongues comprises the major portion of biblical treatment on the subject because the Corinthians needed much correction in their beliefs and practices concerning the gifts; however, while Paul is writing about tongues he also establishes general principles that govern the use of the rest of the gifts. Because of this letter, we can conclude that, like some churches today, the church of Corinth was violating many of the principles, especially with the practice of the gift of tongues.

Inserting his apostolic authority into his argument in 1 Corinthians, Paul concludes his exposition in 14:37 as follows: "If any man think himself to be a prophet, or spiritual, let him acknowledge that the things that I write unto you are the commandments of the Lord."

In other words, these teachings are not merely Paul's opinions or options for the believer to either obey or ignore; as we will see, these are principles that the Lord established for the practice of the spiritual gifts and guides for recognizing false manifestations.

The church at Corinth had major problems of carnality and syncretism with pagan practices of the Graeco-Roman religions of Paul's day. Such pagan practices as drinking and dancing themselves into hyper frenzies, even going into a trance or unconsciousness, they considered to be the highest form of communion with their gods. MacArthur describes the irony of the church at Corinth thinking they were so spiritually superior because of their experiences:

> In the church at Corinth much of the tongues–speaking had taken on the form and flavor of those pagan ecstasies. Emotionalism all but neutralized their rational senses, and selfish exhibitionism was common, with everyone wanting to do and say his own thing at the same time (v. 26). Services were bedlam and chaos, with little worship and little edification taking place.
>
> Because of the extreme carnality in the church at Corinth, we can be sure that much of the tongues–speaking there was counterfeit. Believers were in no spiritual condition to properly use true spiritual gifts or properly manifest true spiritual fruit. How could a congregation so worldly, opinionated, selfish, cliquish, envious, jealous, divisive, argumentative, arrogant, disorderly, defrauding, inconsiderate, gluttonous, immoral, and desecrative of the Lord's Supper exercise the gifts of the Spirit? For them to have done so would have defied every biblical principle of spirituality. You cannot walk in the Spirit while exercising the flesh. (MacArthur 1984: 370–371).

Paul's argument has three major divisions with several sub-points. In 1 Corinthians 12-13, there are ten principles in understanding the purpose of spiritual gifts. Later in 1 Corinthians 14, there are ten arguments showing the

Chapter 11: *Ten Principles from 1 Corinthians 12-13* 161

inferiority of the gift of tongues, followed by ten rules that apply specifically to this gift. Why the emphasis on the general principles and rules? The only way to distinguish a genuine gift from a false one is to compare them to biblical teaching about the gifts.

If a "gift" does not act in accord with the biblical principles, then logically we must conclude that it is not genuine. For this reason, we will examine the teaching that practicing the gift of tongues supposedly gives power and effectiveness in ministry to every believer. If the biblical principles found in 1 Corinthians contradict anyone's teachings on the exercise of the gifts, then those teachings should be corrected.

Ten Principles of Spiritual Gifts

1. Each believer has his own gift(s) (1 Corinthians 12:8-11).

"For to one is given the word of wisdom through the Spirit, to another the word of knowledge through the same Spirit, 9 to another faith by the same Spirit, to another gifts of healings by the same Spirit, 10 to another the working of miracles, to another prophecy, to another discerning of spirits, to another different kinds of tongues, to another the interpretation of tongues. 11 But one and the same Spirit works all these things, distributing to each one individually as He wills."

The first principle is found in 1 Corinthians 12:7 and 11. It says that the manifestation of the Spirit has been given to "each one" (v.7) and "distributing to each one individually" (v. 11). The latter phrase can be translated to "each one separately." In other words, each believer has his gift—man or woman, spiritual or carnal. There are no conditions or exclusions: new believers in Christ all have a spiritual gift without exception and from the moment of the indwelling of the Spirit. It is declared in clear terms that each believer receives a gift when he is placed into the Body of Christ (12:13) where the "members" are uniquely gifted believers.

"God, through his Spirit, gives to every person in the community of believers exactly the right gifts for him or her to provide the needed services for the church and for God's kingdom." (Barton and Osborne 1999:174)

In Ephesians 4:16 this principle is reiterated: "From whom the whole body fitly joined together and compacted by that which every joint supplies, according to the effectual working in the measure of every part." The expressions: "every joint" and "every part," indicates that each believer has a unique function or gift that becomes a composite whole in the interactions of the body of Christ, the church. Since the declaration includes all believers, this implies that the gifts are received at the moment of salvation when the Holy Spirit takes up residence in a new believer; even those recently converted as members of the Body have gifts or ministries to be discovered.

According to these verses, it is impossible for a believer to be without at least one gift. Peter made this idea even clearer: "As each one has received a gift, minister it to one another, as good stewards of the manifold grace of God. (1Pe 4:10 NKJ)." God distributed the gifts to each believer so that he would be motivated and enabled to minister to others. When the Spirit is received, He brings with Him all His gifts, manifesting the ones He chooses in every believer's life. The important thing to remember is that every believer has his spiritual gift for service, from the moment when the Spirit indwells him. Each one is different, unique and special. Since all believers have at least one gift, they are all useful and necessary in the function of the body of Christ. The "call" of God on every believer's life is to discover his/her spiritual gift and serve the body of Christ in the area of his giftedness.

Therefore, the idea that the believer should seek and choose his gift is not biblical. It is clear that he has already received his gift upon salvation. We are given our gift before we know anything about any of the gifts of the Spirit. How the gifts are distributed are evidence of God's wisdom to balance and harmonize complimenting the variety of ministries in the church.

2. The purpose of the gifts is to benefit others (1 Corinthians 12:7 and 25).

12:7 "But the manifestation of the Spirit is given to each one for the profit of all."

12:25 "That there should be no schism in the body, but that the members should have the same care for one another."

In the next chapter Paul is going to explain how the love motive should govern the functioning of all the spiritual gifts, saying that love "does not seek its own" (13:5). Our fallen nature wants everything to be for our benefit and we want it our way. R. C. H. Lenski, the well-known Bible commentator, wrote, "Cure selfishness and you have just replanted the garden of Eden" (quoted by MacArthur 1984: 344-345).

1 Corinthians 12:7 says, "the Spirit is given to every man for the profit of all" (NKJ). The word "profit" is *sumferon* in the Greek, which means, "carry together, contribute mutually." In New Living Bible it says, "so we can help each other." Our gifts, therefore, are given to us so we can benefit others, particularly in a local church.

Paul emphasizes this ministry of the gifts in verse 25: "but that the members should have the same care one for another." Similarly, in 1 Corinthians 13:5 we see that the gift exercised by love "is not self-seeking" (NIV), or "is not self-serving" (NET). Therefore, when the use of a gift is motivated by love, the user will not benefit directly. The whole concept behind the use of the gifts from a motive of love indicates that the real beneficiary of our gifts is always primarily someone else.

In chapter 14, the emphasis is on the need to edify others (see 14:3, 6, 12, 26), and in 1 Peter 4:10, we are supposed to "minister it to one another" as the

Chapter 11: *Ten Principles from 1 Corinthians 12-13*   163

main reason why we were given our respective gift. Note that it does not tell us to minister it to ourselves. Can you imagine any of the gifts like teaching, giving, mercy and evangelism being used for the benefit of the possessor? Ministering to others with our gifts is the only way to be a good administrator of what God has given us. There is no verse that teaches that God gave the gifts for personal benefit. On the contrary, His purpose is to create an interdependence of the ministries, where we need to minister one to another.

The gifts are the power of God for the members of the Body so that they have the strength, motivation, inner capability to supply specific needs of others. Some gifts can be oriented toward unbelievers, but the majority is oriented toward other believers.

3 The believer does not determine which are his gifts; God is the one who decides (1 Corinthians 12:11).

"But one and the same Spirit works all these things, distributing to each one individually as He wills."

Another fundamental principle for the use of all the gifts is that they are given according to the sovereign will of God, not according to the desires of the believers. In 1 Corinthians 12:11, we read that He who decides which gifts each believer receives is described as, "distributing to each one individually *as He wills* (1Co 12:11 NKJ)." The New Living Translation states, "He alone decides which gift each person *should have*." (1Co 12:11 NLT) The same concept is repeated in 12:18, "But as a matter of fact, God has placed each of the members in the body *just as he decided*." (1Co 12:18 NET) The distribution of gifts to each believer upon salvation occurred without consulting the individual. God fulfilled His will in each person as He thought best.

The whole purpose of 1 Corinthians 12:12-20 is to demonstrate that all the gifts are necessary and that a person should not consider his own gift as insignificant simply because another has a more notable or spectacular gift. This is implied in 12:15, "If the foot shall say; Because I am not the hand, I am not of the body; is it therefore not of the body?" In 12:16 we read, "And if the ear shall say, Because I am not the eye, I am not of the body; is it therefore not of the body?"

In other words, Paul is saying that no one should feel insignificant because he does not have certain gifts and, at the same time, no one should think that he is more important than another because he has a particular or more spectacular gift. The entirety of this passage is based on the fact that the individual does not choose his gift, and he cannot change it for one he prefers. The foot cannot become a hand, so it must be satisfied to be a foot.

Romans 12:3-8 emphasizes humble service, saying, "according as God hath dealt to every man the measure of faith" (verse 3). We should think "soberly" (*sophroneo*, or "reasonable, sensible," instead of selfishly. The word "For" in verse 4 connects this sentence with the earlier thought, demonstrating our tendency to exalt our own importance and to compare our gifts to those of others. Paul's argument would have been invalid if the believers could actually obtain specific gifts by seeking them.

There is no passage in the Bible that speaks of anyone who has received a gift by seeking it. Simon the magician tried it in Acts 8:18-24, when he sought the power to give the Holy Spirit by the laying on of hands; although this is not a gift mentioned in the lists, Peter called it a "gift from God" (verse 20). We do not know exactly what the magician's motivation was, but Peter's reaction indicates that there was evil in his selfish desire and that his heart was not right before God. The condemnation is against the idea of obtaining a "gift of God" through human efforts for personal benefit.

What about the passages that seem to suggest that we should seek the best gifts? In the Greek, the plural verb, "covet, desire" (*zeloo*) in 1 Corinthians 12:31 and 14:1, 39 implies that together (meaning of plural tense) we should "be zealous or emphasize" certain gifts. It is an attitude (i.e. being jealous for something, protective or emphasize something) instead of an action of seeking to possess something. The passage is directed to the entire congregation, asking that they restrict the actions of some activities during the assembly and help each other to put their interest on the more important gifts for edification. The emphasis in the context is to motivate the local church to adopt as a priority the edification of understanding through the exercise of the important gifts such as apostle, prophet or teacher (1 Corinthians 12:28).

Other related verbs (*zeteo*, or *orego*, both mean to "seek;" *thelo*, *epithumeo* and *boulomai* means to "desire") are never used in reference to the spiritual gifts, but they are used in many other contexts. In 1 Timothy 3:1, when Paul wanted someone to seek the position of bishop, he used two verbs, *orego* and *epithumeo*, for desiring to acquire something, but not *zeloo*. The "bishop" is not seeking a gift, but rather an area of ministry or service. The attitude of desiring or seeking more gifts apart from those that God has given us is not found in the Bible. It would be like seeking to mutate existing cells in a physical body with inevitable strange results: not advisable!

4. There is unity in diversity (1 Corinthians 12:24-25).

"But our presentable parts have no need. But God composed the body, having given greater honor to that part which lacks it, 25 that there should be no schism in the body, but that the members should have the same care for one another."

God's plan is to create unity in diversity. The metaphor in 1 Corinthians 12 is a "body" that represents the bond of all believers, especially in a congregation; the members within that body represent the different spiritual gifts. We should note that the "members" are not persons in the context, but rather gifts. Obviously people possess gifts, but here the emphasis is on the gift, not on the person. Therefore, "the body is one and has many members (gifts)" (12:12). At least 20 gifts are named in the New Testament. If we accept that God can make combinations of gifts, we can see almost an infinite number of

Chapter 11: *Ten Principles from 1 Corinthians 12-13*   165

possible varieties, especially if we see God's gifting of believers even beyond the revealed spiritual gifts.

Unity in the midst of such diversity is possible when all the members are "likeminded" (Philippians 2:2), that is to say, when "the members...have the same care one for another" (1 Corinthians 12:25). Any self-centered interest or motivation detracts from the unity that God desires of the church. No true gift motivates the person to worry about or focus on himself, but rather to be concerned for others.

Paul wrote, "God composed the body" (1Co 12:24). Here we find the very interesting verb *sunekerao*, which means "mix together, cause the several parts to combine into an organic structure." (Strong 4786). The verb is in the aorist tense meaning a one-time action and not a repeating action. It is used to describe a painter who mixes his colors before painting. The reason that the body is so beautiful is that God is painting an image of the Body of Christ with the various gifts of the Spirit. Each gift is as a distinct color to enhance the image. To change the distribution of those gifts would be like changing the color the artist intended to use thus ruining the picture of the body that God is painting.

Ephesians 4:16 reads, "the whole body, joined and knit together by what every joint supplies, according to the effective working by which every part does its share." The word "joined" is the word that we find in 2:21 meaning, "frame together," like parts of a building. The root of the word describes joints that have been fixed in unity. It is like a symphony with many different instruments functioning in harmony, each one contributing something unique to the overall purpose of providing everything necessary for good music. When we hear an individual instrument play its score or musical part, it often doesn't make sense or sound pretty, but when everyone together contributes their parts, it becomes beautiful. The body of Christ is similar. If everyone played the same instrument, there would be no harmony and the sound would not be pleasant. With diversity of gifts and commitment to one another, we have a beautiful picture of the body of Christ in action.

5. The possessor of a gift should not envy or desire the gift of another (1 Corinthians 12:7, 11, 18).

"But the manifestation of the Spirit is given to each one for the profit of all:"
"But one and the same Spirit works all these things, distributing to each one individually as He wills."
"But now God has set the members, each one of them, in the body just as He pleased."

Since God distributes gifts as He wills (1 Corinthians 12:7, 11, 18) with the purpose of enabling the believer to fulfill His will, the believer should not underestimate what he has, nor should he desire greater powers. Normally, we would aspire to the gifts that bring more recognition, but in 1 Corinthians 12:16 Paul combats the temptation to change the placement of a member in the body. He says, "If the ear shall say, because I am not the eye, I am not of the body; is it therefore not of the body?" Paul was motivated to write this verse as a result of the unreasonable emphasis that the Corinthians had put on certain gifts, especially tongues, to the point that some felt excluded because they did not have that gift. This type of thinking is not biblical.

The passage in Romans 12:3-8 emphasizes humility regarding the use of the gifts God gave them them. The word "for" in verse 4 connects the two verses and communicates the tendency of the believer to exalt his own importance with respect to the gift he has, comparing it with those of other brethren.

Looking again at Acts 8:18-24, we see that Simon sought the power to impart the Holy Spirit by the laying on of hands. We do not know why he wanted it, but it may have something to do with the fact that this power was related to the authority of being an apostle (Acts 2:4). As a result of Simon's actions, Peter condemned him for desiring a gift he did not have. "Repent of your wickedness and pray to the Lord. Perhaps he will forgive your evil thoughts," (Act 8:22 NLT). This is the only time in the New Testament when someone sought a gift that he had not been given, and as we can see, this desire is totally contrary to the teaching of the New Testament.

The passages of 1 Corinthians 12:31 and 14:1, 12, 39 may seem to be in conflict with this principle, but this is because they not interpreted correctly. The whole emphasis of the New Testament with respect to the believer's service to God is on developing his ministry around the gift(s) that God has already bestowed upon him. This service is for the benefit of others and is motivated by the Holy Spirit. This is the purpose of life (Eph 2:10).

The purpose of 1 Corinthians 12:19-27 is to show the importance of each gift. No gift should be preferred over another because of the high value of each one. The following two factors must be understood:

(1) It is God who "has set" (1 Cor 12:18) the members of the body precisely where He wanted. In other words, God distributed the gifts according to His will and purpose, as He formed His body (12:18). To desire another gift is to show disapproval of His plan and will for one's life and ministry. All of this implies that the possession of a gift is not the consequence of our prayers or desires. God strategically places the gifts to fulfill His purposes in the body.

(2) God promised that He would give "greater honor to that part which lacks it," (1Co 12:24) or as the NLT translates it, "extra honor and care are given to those parts that have less dignity."

This suggests that God will one day prove to everyone the *equality and importance of all the gifts*. Perhaps those who currently possess the gifts of presiding, leading, exhortation and teaching will receive no more honor than those with gifts of service, helps, or giving; in fact, those who have the "invisible" gifts will receive "greater honor."

We can leave that aspect in the hands of our loving Lord. No one will lack recompense if he has exercised his gift(s) faithfully and he has given the honor and glory to the Lord Jesus. If, on the other hand, he uses his gift to be recognized here or to appear important on earth, then he already has his recompense (Matthew 6:1-4). The point is that no gift is more valuable than another before God. If gifts are used according to the Word of God and for His glory and purpose, then there will be equal rewards.

6. The gifts are categorized according to priority (1 Corinthians 12:28).
"And God has appointed these in the church: first apostles, second prophets, third teachers, after that miracles, then gifts of healings, helps, administrations, varieties of tongues."

Although there is no difference in the value of the gifts before God (or the rewards to be given), in day-to-day ministry it is necessary for someone to lead. It must be someone who is apt to teach, preside or exhort. As we have shown, to give honor to those who have priority now does not mean that the other gifts are inferior or less significant; they are just different. Some gifts are not as evident in the congregation because they do not contribute directly to the direct edification of others.

The priority in numeric order is specifically declared in 1 Corinthians 12:28, "And God hath set some in the church, **first** apostles, **secondarily** prophets, **thirdly** teachers, **after that** miracles, **then** gifts of healings, helps, governments, diversities of tongues."

Evidently, in the church of Corinth, there was an inappropriate emphasis on some of the gifts, especially on the gift of tongues, to which they gave a high priority. According to the Scriptures, in reality the gift of tongues belongs in the fifth category. This gift is mentioned primarily in 1 Corinthians 12-14, where the purpose is to put it in its proper place of importance and priority.

There is no evidence that any other church in the first century, besides that of Corinth, attempted to practice speaking in tongues. There are also no insinuations that the believer should seek the gift of tongues. On the contrary, all the emphasis of the context (1 Cor 12-14) is to discourage its emphasis. Paul thought perhaps that his lessening of the value of tongues and limiting its exercise (chapter 14) would discourage a functional gift so he added, "forbid not to speak in tongues" (14:39). The rules and principles for the use of the gifts would control their practice and demonstrate the presence of false gifts (1 Corinthians 14).

The five-fold sequence does not refer to the time in which they were given, but to their **priority** in practice. The ministry of the apostles was to be given the highest priority; the early Christians were "devoting themselves to the apostles' teaching" (Act 2:42 NET). After that came the prophets who proclaimed new revelations, and then the teachers clarified the meanings of the apostles and prophets.

Obviously Paul did not include all the gifts in the list, since we can easily recognize the absence of exhortation, giving, service, mercy, leading, and evangelists and pastors. He did include those necessary to communicate that the gift of tongues had an inferior place of importance in comparison to the other gifts in the Bible, however; it is not a coincidence that the gift of tongues is in last place. We notice that tongues as well as even healings and miracles have less priority than the gift of teaching. We should ask ourselves: How important is the teaching ministry in the priorities of the local church today?

When Paul exhorted the believers in Corinth saying "covet earnestly the best gifts" (12:31), he was ordering them to be zealous in emphasizing the gifts of greater priority in the list. For example, the basis of the argument in 1 Corinthians 14 is that the gift of prophecy is more important than the gift of tongues because what it announces is better for edification, and the chapter ends with the same theme, "desire earnestly to prophesy" (1 Cor 14:39).

Paul had put such low value on speaking in tongues, saying that it had virtually no value if it were not properly interpreted, that the Corinthians might have concluded that the gift of tongues was to be eliminated. For this reason, Paul ended the chapter saying: "forbid not to speak with tongues" (14:39). Paul's meaning is clear, however; tongues without interpretation did not have practical value and, therefore, should be of much less priority. Paul wrote to correct the abuse of the gift of tongues, and we can say with certainty that any individual, group or church that abuses this gift is equally in error. Even if the gift of tongues were genuine, overemphasizing it would not be helpful to the church and would be contrary to the priorities in the Bible.

In the New Testament, different gifts are used for different purposes in the Church and in the will of God. As we study the Scriptures we find the following three main purposes of the spiritual gifts:

(a) The purpose of confirming the message. In Mark 16:20, God worked through the apostles to "confirm" their message of salvation through Jesus Christ. In Romans 15:19, Paul says: "Through mighty signs and wonders, by the power of the Spirit of God; ... I have fully preached the gospel of Christ." In 2 Corinthians 12:12, it becomes evident that confirming the message was an integral part of the gift of an apostle: "Truly the signs of an apostle were wrought among you in all patience, in signs, and wonders, and mighty deeds." Similarly, in the book of Acts, doing miracles and producing signs is almost exclusive to the apostles: "And by the hands of the apostles were many signs and wonders wrought among the people" (5:12).

(b) The purpose of training and perfecting the saints. In Ephesians 4:11-14, men are given special gifts (4:8) to play different roles in the overall ministry to train others in the areas of ministry, spiritual maturity, unity, stability in doctrine, knowledge of the Son of God and the development of the potential for serving God, always with the focus on others.

(c) The purpose of serving others. Gifts are important because they give the person the ability and motivation to serve others. The NKJV translates 1 Corinthians 12:7, "But the manifestation of the Spirit is given to each one for the profit **of all**." This means that He gives energy and motivation to

Chapter 11: *Ten Principles from 1 Corinthians 12-13*   169

contribute to and benefit others in different ways. In the Bible, those who benefit directly from the gifts are not those who have the gifts; rather the gifts enable believers to fulfill God's purpose of ministering to others. The gift of tongues is no exception, but its only benefit will be when interpreted.

7. It is impossible that all believers possess the same gift (1 Corinthians 12:29-30).

"Are all apostles? Are all prophets? Are all teachers? Are all workers of miracles? 30 Do all have gifts of healings? Do all speak with tongues? Do all interpret?"

In 1 Corinthians 12:29-30, again it is clear that no one gift is for all believers. The obligatory answer for each question is "No!" In the Greek when the negative me is introduced into question, the obligatory answer has to be "no." All these rhetorical questions contain me, so they could be translated: "All are not apostles, right? All are not prophets, right?" Then Paul concludes, "All do not speak in tongues, right?" This is a straight forward statement that all believers do not speak in tongues, nor are expected to do so.

This is not a denouncement of those who speak in tongues or heal, but rather it is an emphatic declaration that it is not God's plan that all have the same gift, whether it is tongues, healing or any other gift. God did not intend that all prophesy, that all be teachers, that all do miracles or that all speak in tongues.

It would be contrary to the context to say that all should have the same gift: 1 Corinthians 12:17 says, "If the whole body were an eye, where were the hearing?" and in 12:19, "If all were one member, where were the body?" The concept of the body would be destroyed if everyone had the same gift, and making exceptions for the gift of tongues is not biblical. In fact, Paul declared in Romans 12:4-6 that it is actually impossible that all believers have the same gift: "For as we have many members in one body, and all members have not the same office: so we, being many, are one body in Christ, and every one members one of another." The body is made up of many different members with different capacities.

The purpose of 1 Corinthians 12 is to explain that different gifts are given to each believer. Note the following phrases: "there are diversities of gifts" (verse 4); "for to one is given by the Spirit the word of wisdom; to another the word of knowledge by the same Spirit" (verse 8). In verses 17-22, Paul declared that everyone cannot have the same gift, saying, "If the whole body were an eye, where would be the hearing? If the whole were hearing, where would be the smelling?"

Paul emphasized again and again that all believers will never have the same gift and that each gift is important and vital. It is apparent that he was correcting a similar problem to that of the present day, in which some teach that all believers can and should beg the Father for one gift, especially the gift of tongues. Since they commonly say, "All believers should speak daily in tongues during their prayers," it seems that they have not read verse 30.

Therefore the Greek grammar and the context are in accord that it is impossible for a gift be universal among believers. Those who genuinely spoke in tongues were a small minority of the congregation according to God's plan.

8. No gift is valid without love (1 Corinthians 13:1-3).

"Though I speak with the tongues of men and of angels, but have not love, I have become sounding brass or a clanging cymbal. 2 And though I have the gift of prophecy, and understand all mysteries and all knowledge, and though I have all faith, so that I could remove mountains, but have not love, I am nothing. 3 And though I bestow all my goods to feed the poor, and though I give my body to be burned, but have not love, it profits me nothing."

After establishing the order of priorities with respect to the gifts, Paul demonstrates that no gift is effective in the service of others if it is not exercised in love. In 1 Corinthians 13:1-3, speaking in and exaggerated style or hyperbole Paul affirmed that if any gift—whether it is speaking in tongues of angels, understanding all prophecy (which no one had, according to 13:9), having all knowledge, having all faith so as to move mountains (which no one possessed), or having the gift of giving to the point of being without, including giving one's body to be burned (something that Paul had not done)—is not done from a basis of love, then they do not accomplish the purpose of the gifts.

In the general context Paul is speaking of spiritual gifts; specifically, prophecy, faith, giving and tongues are mentioned in reference to the corresponding gifts. All are in parallel. In the Bible, when the majority of a series or list is found in parallel, we can suspect that all the other parts are in parallel as well.

Paul is using a figure of speech called hyperbole to demonstrate that love is greater than the possession of any gift, even though the gift's manifestation may be astonishing and extreme. In the following graph, we will see a gift and, in each case, its respective exaggeration—in other words, something impossible or not even experienced by Paul.

Possible gift/experienced by Paul	Impossible gift/not experienced by Paul (an exaggeration to show its uselessness without love)
If…human tongues	Speak in angelic tongues
If…prophecy	Understand all mysteries and all knowledge
If…faith	Ability to move mountains
If…giving	Give body to be burnt

Chapter 11: *Ten Principles from 1 Corinthians 12-13*   171

If someone possesses even the exaggerated expression of any gift and its use is not motivated by love, then that gift lacks value. Love is not an emotion in the New Testament, (i.e., we have to "love our enemies" is not a feeling), but rather it is a motivation toward sacrificial actions for the benefit of someone else. Love shows concern for someone else (12:25) and not for one's self. If love is concern for others, then the opposite, "I do not have love," indicates that the person is concerned for himself or selfish interests, instead of others. The concept that a gift is for ministering to oneself is totally contrary to the principle of love in 1 Corinthians 13.

9. Gifts exercised in love seek the benefit of others (1 Corinthians 13:4-7).
"Love suffers long and is kind; love does not envy; love does not parade itself, is not puffed up; 5 does not behave rudely, does not seek its own, is not provoked, thinks no evil; 6 does not rejoice in iniquity, but rejoices in the truth; 7 bears all things, believes all things, hopes all things, endures all things."

The manifestation of the gifts motivated by love is very personal, not ambiguous or intangible. As we have said, the motivation should always be the benefit of the other person. In 1 Corinthians 13:4-7, Paul specified how the gifts should function when motivated by love. The passage was not written for lovers but for believers who desire to serve others through their gifts.

We must consider each aspect of the description of love in relation to the use of the spiritual gifts in our commitment to each other. This is what love does. Love ... :

Is patient—It is patient with persons who do not have the same gift. It can wait its turn. It accepts wounds and offenses without the desire to seek revenge.
Is kind—It desires to help and benefit others, especially when they do not deserve it.
Does not envy—It is never jealous of others for their spiritual gifts. Jealousy indicates a selfish passion, desiring something someone else has for one's own benefit. It has the same root as the word "covet" (12:31 and 14:1). It does not flaunt its qualities; it is not ostentatious, as were the believers in Corinth (14:26).
Is not boastful—It does not exaggerate reality, and it does not worry about what others think nor seek to manipulate their approval or praise.
Is not vain—It is not infatuated with its own self-worth; it is not proud, thinking itself spiritual because of its gifts. Paul had accused the Corinthians of the sin of arrogance (4:18; 5:2; 8:1; 4:6, 19).
Does not behave itself unseemly—It does not act unscrupulously, but rather always with courtesy; it never loses self control. It always acts decently and in order, causing no upheaval. Rude conduct or lack of good manners indicates the absence of love. In Corinth there were problems in the conduct of the

women (11:2-16) and abuses in the Lord's Supper (11:17-22).

Is not selfish—It is not motivated by its own edification, but it seeks to benefit others. The Corinthians had to learn to limit their liberty to that which would contribute to the edification of others (10:23, 24, 33).

Does not become irritated—It is not easily upset or easily offended upon being criticized, or if its efforts are not recognized. It does not permit resentment to begin. Paul and Barnabas suffered similar situations in Acts 15:39. The word "discord" has the same root as "irritable."

It thinks no evil—It does not remember past offenses even though the offender does not recognize them. Love does not make a list of offenses in order to save them for a future reproach (Romans 12:19) to get even. Love always pardons and does not permit the past to affect the future.

Does not rejoice in iniquity—It is not happy over a moral fall, even if it happens to an enemy. It does not enjoy "kicking a person when he is down."

Rejoices in the truth—It always wants to know what the Bible has to say about gifts and is quick to obey.

Bears all things—This is a hyperbole. It literally means "to cover" (1 Peter 4:8), protecting others. This characteristic highlights the positive in others, especially in the area of their gifts or ministries. It is capable of tolerating others (Colossians 3:13) in the midst of irritations brought on by personality conflicts, lack of gratitude, etc. It is compatible with the most difficult person.

Believes all things—It is willing to risk itself for the benefit of others. It sees the best in others instead of suspecting that they are not spiritual. It prefers to err on the side of confidence in others instead of judging them or having a critical spirit.

Hopes all things—It always sees the positive in others, never accepting failure as final. It recognizes that God has not finished transforming us.

Endures all things—It is persistent even in the face of rejection. This is a military term conveying the ability to face suffering and persecution as well as complaints and offenses. It perseveres through opposition, having in mind the coming of Christ (1 Thessalonians 1:3; 1 Peter 1:2-7; Revelations 3:10-11).

In each case above, love does something to benefit another person. It is very active. In the New Testament, the commands for serving one another are expressions of love through the use of the gifts. The gifts are designed to cover all the necessities of the body, if they are exercised without self-interest and egotism.

10. Some gifts are not permanent, but love never ends (1 Corinthians 13:13).

"And now abide faith, hope, love, these three; but the greatest of these is love."

It is vital to have a correct perspective on spiritual gifts. They are very important, but they are not the key to the Christian life. In 1 Corinthians

Chapter 11: *Ten Principles from 1 Corinthians 12-13*

13:8-13, Paul indicates that certain gifts are temporary, but faith, hope and love are more enduring. Love will endure even longer than faith and hope.

In verse 8, Paul said that prophecy and knowledge "will cease" or literally, "they will be put away." The tense of the verb *katargeo* is future passive. It means "to make inactive, inoperative or invalid; to repeal; to abolish." The main point is not to focus so much on the more dramatic gifts, especially prophecy, knowledge and tongues, because they are not permanent. This principle fits the general argument of 1 Corinthians 12-14, that faith, hope and love are more important and more beneficial to each other than the sensational gifts.

This trio appears frequently in the instructions to the New Testament churches (Romans 5:2-6; Galatians 5:5-6; Colossians 1:4-5; 1 Thessalonians 1:3; 5:8; Hebrews 6:10-12; 10:22-24; 1 Peter 1:21-22).

The priority in the church, then, should be the expression of love. This is the "most excellent way," that is to say, even better than emphasizing the "better" gifts, and much better than emphasizing the miraculous gift of tongues.

The citizens of Corinth could have exaggerated his meaning in 1 Corinthians 13, so that the gifts would have been underestimated, but Paul wanted the church to maintain a balance. So that the Corinthians would not go to extremes, after finishing the discussion on love Paul wrote, "Pursue love (ardently) and be eager for the spiritual gifts, especially that you may prophesy." (1Co 14:1 NET).

At the same time, the New Testament does not indicate that spiritual gifts bring much benefit the possessor. In none of the exhortations about the walk of the believer do we find any reference to the gifts as a means of personal growth. No one is actually urged to seek or depend on spiritual gifts.

When we analyze the requirements for the Christian life, it is evident that no gift helps us to be obedient. In Romans 12:9-15, there is a series of exhortations to love "without dissimulation" as follows:

> "Don't just pretend to love others. Really love them. Hate what is wrong. Hold tightly to what is good. Love each other with genuine affection, and take delight in honoring each other. Never be lazy, but work hard and serve the Lord enthusiastically. Rejoice in our confident hope. Be patient in trouble, and keep on praying. When God's people are in need, be ready to help them. Always be eager to practice hospitality. Bless those who persecute you. Don't curse them; pray that God will bless them. Be happy with those who are happy, and weep with those who weep." (Rom 12:9-15 NLT)

These exhortations are the same for all believers. All believers have the capacity to live the Christian life, and their gifts have nothing to do with their obedience or their spirituality. Therefore, our spiritual gifts do not make us spiritual.

In addition, spiritual gifts are not part of the spiritual armor set forth in Ephesians 6:10-18. The things that make up the armor of God are truth, justice, the Gospel, faith, salvation, the Word of God and Prayer, but no reference to the spiritual gifts. Likewise, the lack of reference to the gifts in the books of Philippians and Colossians, where there are long lists of exhortations for the Christian life, indicates the minimal importance of the gifts in daily life (See Col. 3:12-17.).

Finally, Christian maturity is not related to spiritual gifts or mystical experiences. Maturity is the result of knowing the Word of God and making decisions before the Lord for putting its principles into practice (Heb. 5:13-14). It is the knowledge and the practice of the Word that helps the believer escape the corruption of the world (2 Peter 1:4).

The believer is exhorted to diligently add to his faith virtue, knowledge, self-control, patience, goodness, piety, brotherly affection and love, but never is the believer exhorted to add a gift. Peter promises us that if these things are in us, then they will make us fruitful and occupied in service. Although a believer has gifts, if he lacks these fruits then he will be blind and unspiritual (verse 9).

The goals for the Christian life are Christ-likeness, spiritual and emotional maturity, and helping others produce spiritual fruit in their lives. Scripture does not say that a believer's gifts could improve his own life, but rather, they should always be used for the benefit of others [meaning of "love"].

Our perspective should be that spiritual gifts are important, but only when they are exercised in the love that will outlast the gifts themselves.

CHAPTER 12

Ten Arguments for the Inferiority of Tongues

Chapter 12: *Gifts for Today*

As we have seen, the main problem in the church of Corinth was the practice of tongues. As a congregation, we can deduce from the nature of the commands given to the church that they spoke in a disorderly way and without interpreters, thinking that tongues were spiritual whatever and whenever the manifestation. For this reason, Paul took the first 19 verses of chapter 14 to demonstrate that tongues are inferior to other gifts, but also that they are of little value in the church.

By his use of the original language Paul made a distinction between the gift of tongues that comes from the Spirit and speaking in tongues as the pagans did, especially in Corinth. The repetition of the verb "to speak" (*lalein*) twenty-four times in chapter 14, demonstrates that Paul is primarily referring to two types of gifted speech: tongues (*glossolalia*) and prophecy. Because the Corinthians had not asked Paul which of the two are to be preferred, he is gracious and develops his case step-by-step, with the apparent objective of quenching the overwhelming enthusiasm for tongues in the assembly and seeking to get them to pay more attention to the Word of God delivered through prophecy at this time. Before the written Scriptures God enabled the churches to know God's will through prophets in the local churches.

David Garland in his book on 1 Corinthians in the Baker Evangelical Commentary series gives the following paragraph describing the concept of prophecy in the church:

> Prophecy is to predominate in worship. "To prophesy" means to proclaim a divine revelation (see further the comments on 12:8–10) or, more simply, "to speak on behalf of God" (R. Collins 1999: 491). Thiselton (2000: 1084) labels it even more simply as "healthy preaching" (cf. D. Hill 1979: 123, "pastoral preaching"). Prophecy is not individualistic in focus (Friedrich, TDNT 6:854) but is meant to communicate to others in rational, intelligible language. It builds up the community (14:4, 5) through exhortation and consolation (14:3, 31) and its didactic function (14:19, 31). It convicts unbelievers and leads them to repentance and worship of the one true God (14:25). The prophet is inspired by revelation but is not regarded as infallible, since the word spoken is to be weighed and sifted (14:29). Since Paul encourages all the addressees to desire eagerly to prophesy, he does not envision it as a spiritual activity limited only to persons holding a particular office. In principle, any person might be gifted by God to prophesy (Grudem 1982: 231–39; Schrage 1999: 384; so also Wolff 1996: 328; Lindemann 2000: 297). Implicit in this exhortation is the conviction that the Spirit is free "to choose any Christian through whom to speak" (Forbes 1995: 258). In 14:24, Paul does not think it out of the question that all could prophesy so that an unbeliever is convicted "by all." In 14:31, he again emphasizes the "all" by asserting that they all are able to prophesy in turn so that all may learn and all be instructed. If he were referring only to a limited circle of prophets, there would be no need to retain the "all" (Forbes 1995: 259). Some may have the gift of prophecy in greater

Chapter 12: *Ten Arguments for Inferiority of Tongues*

measure, but Paul believes that all the Lord's people can be prophets (cf. Num. 11:29). (Garland, 2003:632–633).

As we have seen, Paul wanted the churches to follow certain general principles in their use of spiritual gifts, and he also explained why certain gifts (prophecy, knowledge and tongues—along with their related gifts) were temporary. Although both of these gifts are included in the temporary list, the principles, values and priorities of this chapter remain ever present in the churches. In 1 Corinthians 14:1-20 he introduces the following ten arguments for the inferiority of tongues:

Argument 1: Any speaking gift if used in love, speaks to other men for their edification, exhortation and consolation (14:2-3)

"For he who speaks in a tongue does not speak to men but to God, for no one understands him; however, in the spirit he speaks mysteries. 3 But he who prophesies speaks edification and exhortation and comfort to men."

Paul preferred prophecy to tongues because it had better results in lives of the hearers. It is not saying that speaking to God is inferior, but assuming it is a genuine communication, it still is not beneficial for the church. He said, "… but rather that ye may prophecy" (verse 1), because its result is "edification, exhortation and consolation" (verse 3) for others. The gift of tongues does not produce any of these results of itself, rendering it less valuable to anyone in the congregation.

Paul is going to argue that the church is built up and confirmed by the communicating of God's Word and its implications, promises and directives.

The carnality of the Corinthians was evident by their interest in speaking "mysteries" that no one could "understand" (*akouo*, literally, what "no one hears" in verse 2.) Since none of the Hebrew Jews from Jerusalem knew the tongues spoken in Acts 2:1-3 in the Hellenistic Jews' languages, they may have assumed that only God could understand the tongues that were spoken. The Corinthians were interested in the emotion and the self-gratification of speaking what was a "supernatural" language, not in the meaning or the message of the words.

The "mysteries" were associated with pagan religions, which the believers had evidently practiced before they put their faith in Christ. In the Greek pagan religions, the "mysteries" (14:2) —as their name indicates—were mystical, mysterious or occult "truths" that only those who belonged to the initiated or elite had the privilege of knowing.

The mysteries of the Bible, however, are truths that were hidden, therefore unknown, from the foundation of the world but were given to us now by divine revelation. If a tongue were given to reveal a "mystery" or truth about God or His will that had been hidden for a time (Romans 11:25; 16:25; 1 Corinthians 2:17; 13:2; 15:51; Ephesians 3:3, 4, 9; 5:32; Colossians 1:26), then it is imperative that the tongue be interpreted and the message revealed!

The speaker who is more fascinated with the tongue itself than with God's message has an obvious flaw in his values and perspective. Therefore, exalting the gift of speaking a language that no one can possibly understand is pagan and unbiblical. The purpose of the gifts of speaking is always to edify the church through sharing understanding and meaning from the Word (edification), the application of that illumination (exhortation) and the effect of the communicated truths (consolation). All of these depend upon the communication of the meaning of the message.

> It is an interpretive key to this chapter to note that in verses 2 and 4 tongue is singular (cf. vv. 13, 14, 19, 27), whereas in verse 5 Paul uses the plural tongues (cf. vv. 6, 18, 22, 23, 39). Apparently the apostle used the singular form to indicate the counterfeited gift and the plural to indicate the true. Recognizing that distinction may be the reason the King James translators supplied unknown before the singular. The singular is used of the false because gibberish is singular; it cannot be gibberishes. There are no kinds of pagan ecstatic speech; there are, however, kinds of languages in the true gift, for which the plural tongues is used. The only exception is in v. 27, where the singular is used to refer to a single man speaking a single genuine language. (MacArthur Jr.1984:373.)

Why would God inspire the message of a language if it were not for the purpose of communicating a message to the congregation? Otherwise, the speaker just returns the communication to God without passing the revelation on to the church; it's like a short circuit. It does not make sense that God would send a message in an unknown tongue only to have it return to Him again from a person who never understood the message! The only way it would have value would be if it were interpreted to the church, otherwise, prophecy is much more beneficial to understanding the will of God, which is the best definition of edification.

Argument 2. It is better to prophesy if there is no one to interpret the language (14:4).

"He who speaks in a tongue edifies himself, but he who prophesies edifies the church."

Any gift of speaking must be for the benefit of others (if love is the motivation), not necessarily for the speaker himself; genuine tongues can have this result only when they are interpreted. The model is given by Judas and Silas in Acts 15:32, "Now Judas and Silas, themselves being prophets also, exhorted and strengthened the brethren with many words." (Act 15:32). Tongues by themselves can never do this.

Paul is arguing that by itself, the gift of speaking in tongues is useless to minister to others. Attempting to edify one's self contradicts the definition of using the gifts from a love motive (love "does not seek its own"- 13:5). Spiritual gifts are given in order to be spiritually and practically useful in lives of the hearers, whether they are believers or not.

The gift of tongues was so useless that Paul later prohibited its practice in the church unless an interpreter was present (verse 28), so that the church could potentially be edified by the message. If an experience does not produce more understanding of God's will and subsequently more obedience, it does not benefit or edify anyone.

The word edify (*oikodomeo*, "to build a house") has a positive and a negative connotation. It is used negatively in 1 Corinthians 8:10 to describe the person who "edifies" his conscience in order to violate his conscience and eat certain places or foods that he had thought were sinful. This edification becomes sinful because he convinces himself he is strong or spiritual and ignores his conscience. His "edified" or puffed up conscience ends up destroying him, because now he can ignore it in other areas and fake his spirituality in other areas, especially if this generated a special status or respect as a "tongue speaker" in a church.

Some speculate that this self-edification means:

It affords access to the unconscious dimensions of the soul and allows repressed impulses access to the consciousness. It enters into an inner space dissociated from the everyday realities surrounding them and it may result in a feeling of peace and even euphoria (Garland 2003: 634).

One has to ask the discerning question, "Where does anything like this definition find root in any NT concept of spiritual growth or maturity?" It sounds totally foreign to the NT, yet remarkably familiar in pagan settings.

From the major conflicts and chaos this practice was creating in the church at Corinth, it seem more likely that this self-edification was using the experience to "meet one's own ego needs rather that the needs of the church" (Ibid.).

Conversely, he who prophesies edifies others who are motivated by love to apply the Word in practical obedience; he does not try to destroy them by his superior knowledge. The idea of "edify himself," without regard to the benefit of others, falls into the category of a negative application. Paul is showing how self centered these tongues speakers were not recommending that they genuinely were "edified" in a positive biblical sense.

Argument 3. There is no benefit if someone speaks in an unknown tongue (14:6).

"But now, brethren, if I come to you speaking with tongues, what shall I profit you unless I speak to you either by revelation, by knowledge, by prophesying, or by teaching?"

Paul had stated emphatically the purpose of the manifestation of the Spirit was "profit" or benefit to others (12:7). In 14:6, in stead of accusing one of them, he hypothetically states that "if" he were to come talking in "tongues" that no one understood it would be useless. He declared categorically that tongues do not accomplish any beneficial purpose, saying, "If I come to you speaking with tongues, what shall I profit you…?" The implied answer to the question is "in no way will tongues benefit anyone." No matter what the perceived benefit to tongues might be to an individual, it is considered inferior and useless to benefit anyone else.

The Corinthians appreciated the gift of tongues even without the benefit of edification. Not even an apostle could edify through a tongue that no one understood; however, all of the possible spiritual benefits of a tongue depend on another gift, that of interpretation. This dependency on another gift for spiritual benefit is additional evidence of its weakness.

The only manifestations of the Spirit that edifies the congregation are "revelation, or … knowledge, or … prophecy, or … doctrine." These gifts are divided in two categories: (1) internal reception: revelation and knowledge, and (2) external communication: prophecy and doctrine (teaching). When these messages were communicated to the church, the message was comprehended and they gained greater understanding of the will of God, His plan, purpose and promises. If there is no benefit like this in the gift of tongues or any speaking gift, then it should not have importance among the believers.

It is interesting, while on the subject of "revelation," how Paul treated his own incredible "revelation" in 2 Cor 12:1, "It is doubtless not profitable for me to boast. I will come to visions and revelations of the Lord:" He concludes this discussion without telling the reader what the vision was stating, "But I refrain, lest anyone should think of me above what he sees me to be or hears from me. And lest I should be exalted above measure by the abundance of the revelations" (12:6b-7a). Paul was extremely careful not to let people think of him as special because of his supernatural gifts as an Apostle. His authority came from their transformed lives as he built them up in their understanding of the faith.

Argument 4. *Just like musical instruments that only make noises or sounds, tongues are useless when they are not understood. It is also deceiving for believers to depend on them (14:7-9).*

"Even things without life, whether flute or harp, when they make a sound, unless they make a distinction in the sounds, how will it be known what is piped or played? 8 For if the trumpet makes an uncertain sound, who will prepare himself for battle? 9 So likewise you, unless you utter by the tongue words easy to understand, how will it be known what is spoken? For you will be speaking into the air."

Music has rhythm, harmony, and melody in an ordered structure, all of which distinguish it from simple meaningless noises made with the same instruments. In order for music to be music, it must conform to musical rules in order to communicate a tune.

The "distinction of the sounds" (*diastole*) refers to the variation and order of notes as they communicate their purpose of joy, sadness, seriousness,

Chapter 12: Ten Arguments for Inferiority of Tongues

excitement or adoration. The sounds are arranged distinctly or an order which is pleasant and communicates a distinct melody. The Corinthians could appreciate this illustration because the city contained a great musical theater that held 20,000 people.

Can you imagine how they would have responded if a harpist had plucked the strings at random? Similarly, in the ancient armies trumpet players made different sounds to communicate different orders to the soldiers. A soldier who did not know how to play the trumpet could not communicate the orders he was given by only making unintelligible noises.

In the same way it is impossible to communicate biblical truths by making sounds that have no meaning. The phrase "So likewise ye…" in verse 9 indicates that they were only making noises with their "tongues" as someone making noise (not music) with musical instruments, because (1) they were speaking random syllables, not actual languages, and (2) there were no interpreters, thus making their speech useless.

> The implication from this description of tongues as indistinct sounds is that the Corinthian tongues are not xenoglossolalia—speaking an unlearned foreign language—but the utterance of inarticulate noises and syllables (Schrage 1999: 394–96). No earthly lexicon could decipher their meaning… The glossolalists probably imagined themselves as glowing with a certain spiritual aura and probably relished basking in the admiration of others. He puts their performance in a completely different light with the implication that the indistinct sounds made on the flute, harp, and bugle are made by inexpert players—mere novices. Perhaps to some extraterrestrial creature it may be music, but to the human ear it is only screeches and squawks. The same is true of tongues, which communicate nothing to others. Garbled speech is the stuff of comedy. (Garland 2003: 636-637).

Paul concluded this argument by saying that they must "utter by the tongue words easy to be understood" (verse 9). He also declared that he who speaks in tongues (without an interpreter) is speaking as if "into the air" (verse 9). It is as useless and unproductive as a boxer who only "beats the air" (1 Cor 9:26). There is no value here, thus inferior to what produces genuine edification, teaching in a language understandable.

The Corinthians were so carnal that they did not think it was important to communicate any truth; they only wanted to impress others or themselves (self-edification?), rather than to communicate a message to people or to edify them with God's Word. Therefore this attitude is not derived by *love* by definition, and consequently, it cannot be led by the Holy Spirit. He does not contradict Himself.

Chapter 12: *Gifts for Today*

Argument 5. All languages or idioms in the world are distinct, and all communicate intelligible, sensible ideas (14:10).
"There are, it may be, so many kinds of languages in the world, and none of them is without significance."

Paul reiterated the uniqueness of a true language implying a comparison of genuine language "in the world" with tongues, which are always one of these languages. True languages (*phone*, "language or dialect" – Gen 11:1, 7 in LXX) have the purpose of communicating understandable messages; false tongues do not communicate anything more than noise or babble. The genuine gift of tongues is the capacity of speaking in a true language (Acts 2, 10, 19).

Likewise, the science of linguistics, which analyzes languages to discover their grammar, phonetics and morphology, agrees that each language sound conveys a meaning and has a structure in order to constitute a language. If "tongues" sounds do not have structure or meaning, then they are only random noises, babble that is not a language at all. Many of the more "primitive" tribal languages rival the most sophisticated languages on earth in grammar complexity and the ability to communicate ideas and meaning.

It should be noted that each language has a distinct set of phonics or sounds unique to that language. When you hear foreigners try to speak English and pronounce the words with the phonics of their mother tongue, they are almost unintelligible. To speak a new language someone must use a different set of phonic sounds. Numerous linguistic studies have been made with the following conclusions:

- What the research does show is that free vocalization is not an intrinsically miraculous and therefore infallible sign of the working of the Holy Spirit.
- Formal linguistic analysis has concluded that there is no difference between phonetics of the "tongue" and the speaker's mother language indicating that it is not supernatural nor a different language, rather free vocalization in the speaker's mother language.
- No study has concluded that contemporary tongue speaking does not have any characteristic of a natural language, or phonological structure, morphological order typical of any natural language. (Poythress, 1986, 469-489)

Another study done by the Hartford Seminary Foundation posted this: "The Linguisticality of *Glossolalia*," that analyzed thousands of glossic utterances came to this linguistic definition of *glossolalia*: "A meaningless but phonologically structured human utterance believed by the speaker to be a real language but bearing no systematic resemblance to any natural language, living or dead" (Samarin, Summer 1968:69). He likewise investigated the correlation between a glossic utterance and the interpretations that occasionally followed, only to find, "Interpretations do in fact take place, but they are usually pious exhortations in the language of the group where the glossic

Chapter 12: Ten Arguments for Inferiority of Tongues

utterance are made. They are often strikingly longer or shorter than the glossic utterance and show no correlation." (*Ibid.*)

Paul declared that a genuine tongue always communicates "meaning" or understanding. The last word refers to something "dumb," (*aphonos*) that is, it does not communicate anything. It has no phonetic structure as a language. Any supposed speech that does not "say anything" is not a language at all, only so much noise.

Argument 6. If the hearer does not know the meaning of the words, then he will feel as if he were a foreigner (14:11).

"Therefore, if I do not know the meaning of the language, I shall be a foreigner to him who speaks, and he who speaks will be a foreigner to me."

It is not only necessary for a language to communicate meaning, but it is also important for the hearer to understand it; otherwise, there is no communication. The word barbarian or "foreigner" comes from the Greek word *barbaros*. It refers to a person who did not understand Greek and spoke a language the Greeks did not understand. Using onomatopoeia to create the term, the Greeks called them barbarians because they made sounds like "bar-bar," signifying the stuttering, repetitive sounds of a foreign language that has no meaning to the listener. Multiple speakers of different languages in the congregation alienate believers making non-speakers feel outside the inner-circle of the fellowship creating divisions.

We should note that they did not seem to mistake these sounds for ecstatic speech or an unintelligible language; although the Greeks could not understand the language, they presumed that it still could be understood. They classified the speakers of other languages as foreigners, and these foreigners, in turn, also classified the Greeks as foreigners.

This logic is relevant to the study of tongues as well; the Greek notion of foreignness applies if Paul is speaking of a genuine language, but it makes no sense in the case of an ecstatic speech. Regardless of his native language, no one can understand an ecstatic speech, and the speaker cannot expect to be understood apart from the help of a miraculous interpretation. Therefore, it is likely that those who do not understand ecstatic speech would consider the speaker a "foreigner," because the only thing that makes a person a "foreigner" is his inability to be understood in the language he is speaking.

In the case of ecstatic speech in the church, the hearer will inevitably feel like a foreigner since he does not understand this strange speech, thus alienating him further from the united worship in the church. Ecstatic speech would make ministry impossible since edification would be impossible.

Argument 7. The emphasis on edification excludes the use of the gift of tongues (14:12).

"Even so you, since you are zealous for spiritual gifts, let it be for the edification of the church that you seek to excel."

Paul did not want to reject any spiritual gift, but he did assert that any gift that did not produce edification should not deserve priority in the church. The phrase, "Even so you," ties verse 12 with the three previous verses, that is, just as foreign language speakers make it impossible for people to understand what is going on, so their eagerness for some spiritual experience is just as absurd. Paul is saying they should "reorder their priorities" (Meyer 2009: 2:11–12).

Here Paul is restating their enthusiasm for "spiritual gifts" (*pneuma*, plural, "spirits"; this is a different word from 14:1 where Paul says they were seeking *pneumatikos*, "spiritual things" or gifts) that is, in 14:12 they were seeking a plurality of manifestations or phenomena of any kind. (Thiselton 2000: 1107). The New Jerusalem Bible translates *pneuma* as "powers of the Spirit."

> Where Paul diverges from the Corinthians is in his insistence that since the Spirit is also the Spirit of Christ, and since Christ gave himself for others, any claims about "spirituality" or powers of the Spirit become problematic if they have more to do with self-enhancement than with the welfare and benefit of others. Hence all this burning concern about powers of the Spirit must be redirected into a more Christlike eagerness for the building up …of the church community as a corporate whole. (*Ibid.*)

Paul emphasized gifts that directly edify the congregation through the communication of truths and understanding rather than through a tongue that no one understands. As we have shown, the benefit of the gift of tongues is possible only through interpretation (14:13); otherwise, the speakers will be like strangers, unable to communicate. The reasoning is simple: edification is impossible without communicating understanding and meaning.

The definition of "edification," *oikodome*, is "amplification, building up, or construction." It is pictured as building a block or stone building one block at a time. Isaiah used the phrase "precept upon precept" (Isa 28:10) to answer the question "Whom will He teach knowledge?" (28:9). God is all about transforming lives by building principles from His Word into the lives of His followers.

If there is no growth or increase in understanding, then edification has not occurred, nor have lives been changed. Edification demands greater understanding of the will of God and His Word; neither emotional experiences nor witnessing miracles increase understanding.

The gift of tongues (even if genuine) cannot produce edification for anyone, not for the speaker or for the hearer; therefore, the gift of tongues by itself is inferior and not useful.

Zeal for "spiritual things" or manifestations of the Spirit is not bad; however, the Corinthians lacked the proper desire for edification, the very purpose of spiritual gifts. Rather than focusing on their own self-centered edification, Paul was trying to steer them toward prioritizing the edification of the church as a whole.

When we take our eyes off ourselves to attend to the church body and

Chapter 12: *Ten Arguments for Inferiority of Tongues*   185

dedicate ourselves to supply its needs, the unsaved will be converted and believers will be fortified.

Argument 8. If a person prays in an unknown tongue, then his understanding is unfruitful; it is not edified (14:14).

"For if I pray in a tongue, my spirit prays, but my understanding is unfruitful."

Paul had just concluded his argument that the only benefit of speaking in a tongue would be the interpretation of what was said. Paul then commanded that the speaker continually pray (present tense imperative) "that he may interpret" (14:13) so there could be some benefit. Now he describes another hypothetical situation to clarify a misconception.

Paul has proven that not everyone has the gift of tongues (chapter 12), but given the assumption the Paul does have the gift, he writes, "For if I pray in a tongue..." He is not saying that he does or has, but hypothetically if he did. His shift from third person to first person narrative is to identify with his audience to demonstrate a truth.

Our human spirit is the vehicle by which men understand men (1 Cor 2:11) and in a similar fashion when we receive the Holy Spirit we can understand God (2:12).

Some wanted to make a dichotomy of spirit and mind ("understanding"), allowing an isolated communication with God through the spirit of man without input, awareness or understanding by the conscious mind. Hypothetically, Paul is saying that IF he prayed in a tongue, it would only be his spirit that would be praying something. Somehow Paul was left out of the circle of communication. It was as if a separate being were inside Paul talking to God.

When a person spoke in an unknown tongue, his mind or understanding would remain "unfruitful," *akarpos*, "barren, and unproductive of what it should produce" (Thayer, 181), or "useless" (Friberg, 845). In other words, the tongue could not produce any edification or beneficial results for Paul. This verse negates the possibility that any biblical edification could occur through speaking through the gift of tongues, no matter what the emotional response may be by the orator, because without fruit of meaningful communication of God's will to the heart and mind there is no edification.

This forces a direct contradiction to the positive view of possible self-edification of tongues mentioned in 14:4. Either Paul is saying that his spirit can be edified without his mind/understanding being edified or he is categorically stating that there is no benefit to the speaker when speaking in a tongue. The latter seems to fit the context the best as the next verse implies.

The illustration Paul gave in verse 14 is hypothetical and negative. To pray in "spirit" is not very clear: is this speaking of a spiritual gift of tongues or of the "inward man?" The desire of God for the inward man is not some secret communication that no one understands, thus rendering no benefit whatsoever, but rather "You desire integrity in the inner man; you want me to possess wisdom." (Psa 51:6 NET). If God communicates anything it will be His wisdom and understanding to help us live with integrity.

The "spirit" is different from "the mind," the conscious and rational part where understanding occurs. Nothing happens in the heart or in the spirit of a person until the mind analyzes, accepts and chooses to trust and assimilate the revelation of God. The spirit is molded by what the mind perceives as truths resulting in attitudes and reactions from what is believed and valued. This is the process of being transformed into His image (2 Cor 3:18). Without understanding this edification process is impossible.

The man who prays using tongues does not understand what his own mouth is saying, not because he is in a trance or is unconscious, but because in his mind he simply does not understand the language. Having an interpreter is the only solution that can produce real fruit from speaking in tongues (verse 13), even to the speaker. This is why Paul commanded that the tongues-speaker pray for the interpretation, that he might be edified as well. The lack of fruit has nothing to do with the state of the speaker, but rather with the inability to understand the language.

Some have tried to interpret this verse to say that speaking in tongues does not produce fruit in others, but in verses 15 and 19 it is evident that the mind (*nous*) is not involved in any way when someone speaks in an unknown tongue. The bottom line is that if it does not increase the understanding of the speaker, thereby producing fruit, then neither can it communicate fruit to others, thus tongues is inferior to speaking gifts that can be understood.

Argument 9. Paul never spoke in the churches or in private through the gift of tongues (14:15-19).

"What is the conclusion then? I will pray with the spirit, and I will also pray with the understanding. I will sing with the spirit, and I will also sing with the understanding. 16 Otherwise, if you bless with the spirit, how will he who occupies the place of the uninformed say "Amen" at your giving of thanks, since he does not understand what you say? 17 For you indeed give thanks well, but the other is not edified. 18 I thank my God I speak with tongues more than you all; 19 yet in the church I would rather speak five words with my understanding, that I may teach others also, than ten thousand words in a tongue."

Paul mentioned three areas where the Corinthians apparently practiced tongues inappropriately. The first area was prayer: to pray without understanding (in an unknown tongue) is a negative action that does not produce fruit or edification of any kind. Obviously those who prayed this way had some kind of positive sensation or approval by others, that motivated their continuance, but praying for an emotional experience is not the same as prayers resulting in edification. If it were possible for the speaker to be edified apart from his own understanding, then we would have to ask, "If someone is spiritually stimulated simply by uttering and hearing sounds that he cannot understand, then why are not others also stimulated by the same sounds?" In

Chapter 12: Ten Arguments for Inferiority of Tongues

the text, it seems impossible for the speaker to be edified if the hearers cannot receive any benefit.

Paul declared that he prayed "with his spirit" (in sincerity of feelings and emotions from his inner man) and "with understanding" or his conscious mind (14:15). Therefore we can deduce from this passage that Paul did not pray in an unknown tongue, because there is no understanding in an unknown tongue.

Paul said that he preferred to speak and pray audibly in the church in a known language (verse 19), because his priority was the benefit or edification of the hearer, not his own emotions. Praying for a supposed personal benefit seems out of character with the nature of prayer (James 4:3).

Praying in tongues is also useless in the church because no one else can agree in prayer along with the person praying aloud. The practice in the early church, as presented in verse 16, is that one prayed and the others accompanied his prayer saying, "Amen" (meaning "so be it," or "I am in agreement"). If someone "blesses" or prays in an unknown tongue, then no one else can pray with him, thereby destroying the sense of biblical corporate prayer. They never practiced all praying different prayers audibly at the same time with no one understanding what the others were saying.

In the same fashion, Paul wrote against singing in unknown tongues whether in church or in private, though it is apparent that some were practicing this in the church in Corinth. Singing personal thoughts to God (usually very privately) is a wonderful expression of worship. But Paul chose to not sing in tongues, because he wanted to express to the Lord his sincere adoration with his mind and understanding. Essentially, meaningless, blind and emotional worship in an ecstasy of unknown tongue, or any language, has no meaning to the speaker and was contrary to God's objective for the meetings and was contrary to the will of God revealed in His Word. Why would God want worship from a worshiper that did not know what he was saying?

Yet Paul did not want to alienate his readers, so he adds, "I speak with tongues more than you all." His own experience argues that tongues are practically no benefit to the public worship as well. If Paul used tongues as another apostolic sign (2 Cor 12:12) especially to unbelievers where they were designed to be exercised (Acts 2; 1 Cor 14:22), then it makes sense because everywhere Paul traveled were multitudes of different languages. The Roman Empire was made up of hundreds of people groups that spoke multiple languages, Greek often being their second language. Could this be a practical usage of the apostolic use of tongues? Though we have no description of such a usage it would make sense and fit within the scope of the description of purpose of tongues.

The hyperbole of speaking ten thousand (*murioi*, "innumerable;" the largest number in Greek) words in a tongue further illustrates that mindless, incomprehensible jabber helps no one. If we are not motivated by a love for benefiting others in the exercise of our gifts, then we are "sounding brass or a clanging cymbal" (1 Cor 13:1). Paul is setting himself up as an example by "renouncing spiritual glory and status" and "rights and privileges" to benefit

Argument 10. It is childish immaturity to speak in a meaningless language in order to impress others (14:20).

"Brethren, do not be children in understanding; however, in malice be babes, but in understanding be mature."

The Corinthians' infatuation with tongues was another indication of their immaturity and worldliness, which was referred to in 3:1-3 where Paul could not write to them as "spiritual," rather as "babes (*nepioi*, "infant, little child; metaph. childish, untaught") in Christ." Earlier in 13:11 he used the imagery of "childishness" to describe their speaking, thinking, and reckoning as a child (*nepios*) to illustrate their need to stop acting selfishly, self-centered, calling attention to themselves and enamored by the showy gifts of apparent miracles.

The commandment "do not be children" (*me paidia ginesthe*) is in the present imperative tense and, since it is in a negative form, it signifies to "stop being children." Specifically, the Corinthians were acting like children in their attitude toward tongues. Instead of wanting to be useful to others, they wanted to entertain or to feel important, as a false spiritual acceptance. They wanted the spectacular instead of the practical.

They needed to change their manner of thinking by conforming to the teachings that God was giving through Paul (14:37). If they had emphasized prophecy in the church, which would have resulted in edification, exhortation and consolation, then they would have put aside the things that did not edify. Maturity is marked by an attitude of benefiting others instead of seeking to enjoy personal emotional experiences.

They were to remain innocent regarding evil, instead of engaging in immorality (5:8) or self-serving attitudes that created divisions in the church. The church in Corinth had almost all the manifestations of the flesh and practically none of the evidences of the Spirit (Galatians 5:19-23). They were like "children, tossed to and fro, and carried about with every wind of doctrine, by the sleight of men, and cunning craftiness, whereby they lie in wait to deceive" (Ephesians 4:14).

Because of their egotism, they abused the gift of tongues while they ignored the rest of the family of God. They could not correct those who spoke in tongues, because teaching was not important to them; their personal experience or the prestige of being the speaker of a mystical revelation was their priority. They wanted to interrupt the meeting to speak in tongues (verses 23, 27, 30). They were preoccupied with using spiritual activities and even other brothers for their own interests. They were not seeking the truth, but were seeking experiences; they did not want good doctrine, but rather good feelings. They were not interested in benefiting anyone but themselves. They were not like the Bereans who "with all readiness of mind, and searched the scriptures daily, whether those things were so" (Acts 17:11), and they did not bother to examine what they were hearing through the light of the Scriptures.

Chapter 12: Ten Arguments for Inferiority of Tongues

They did not bother with trying "the spirits whether they are of God" (1 John 4:1), but rather they accepted anything that seemed phenomenal, mystical or supernatural to them as though it came from the Spirit. Experiences took precedence over the revealed will of God.

Paul always teaches about a theme before giving the commands or exhortations related to it; for example, the doctrine of salvation appears in Romans 1-11, and the exhortations for the Christian life follow in Romans 12-16. In keeping with this model, upon finishing the arguments against the exaggerated value of tongues in the church of Corinth, Paul now gives the rules for the use of this gift in the congregation.

CHAPTER 13

Ten rules governing the gift of tongues

Chapter 13: *Gifts for Today*

Paul was motivated to write rules and guidelines for the use of gifts because he saw the ways that the church of Corinth abused them. The majority of these rules appear in 1 Corinthians 14 and are important because (1) they are commands of the Lord (14:37), and (2) they provide a way to evaluate whether or not a person is a genuine prophet and/or spiritual (14:37). A sincere and godly believer will respond positively to Paul's commands instead of trying to avoid the implications of chapter 14.

We have a commandment to not accept just any doctrine, spirit or person simply because he claims to be from God. In 1 John 4:1 we read, "Beloved, believe not every spirit, but try the spirits whether they are of God, because many false prophets are gone out into the world." Is it any different in the 21st century?

The early churches that practiced these verses had to reject many people who said they were spiritual. To the church at Ephesus where the Apostle John ministered, Jesus said: ""I know your works, your labor, your patience, and that you cannot bear those who are evil. And you have tested those who say they are apostles and are not, and have found them liars" (Rev 2:2 NKJ) In other words, not only were there many false prophets, but also there were many false apostles.

It is interesting to note that the very gifts that were used as signs for confirmation and for apostles and prophets (Mark 16:17-18, Hebrews 2:3-4) were the ones that were most often imitated.

Based on 1 Corinthians 14:37, we see that the way the churches tested individuals was to observe their response to the Scriptures or their manifestation of the gift of discernment. As a result, today we can deduce that a person should be rejected if he pretends to be spiritual or manifest a sign, but does not show any interest in following biblical instructions for the use of gifts. Proverbs should warn us: "The wise are glad to be instructed, but babbling fools fall flat on their faces." (Pro 10:8 NLT)

The rules in chapter 14 serve to help the church function "decently and in order" (14:40); false gifts could not operate according to these rules. Therefore, it seems evident that if the Corinthians' use of tongues had been genuine, they would not have had a problem following the rules that Paul imposed over the manifestation of the gift.

The following rules are a synopsis of the second half of 1 Corinthians 14. Below each rule there will be a discussion of the evidence in the chapter and, in some cases, other verses that contribute to the discussion.

1. A gift must be a judicial sign to the unbelieving Jews (14:21-25).
"In the law it is written: "With men of other tongues and other lips I will speak to this people; And yet, for all that, they will not hear Me," says the Lord. 22 Therefore tongues are for a sign, not to those who believe but to unbelievers; but prophesying is not for unbelievers but for those who believe. 23 Therefore if the whole church comes together in one place, and all speak with tongues, and there come in those who are uninformed or unbelievers, will they not say that you are out of your mind? 24 But if all prophesy, and an unbeliever or an uninformed person comes in, he is

Chapter 13: Ten rules governing the gift of tongues

convinced by all, he is convicted by all. 25 And thus the secrets of his heart are revealed; and so, falling down on his face, he will worship God and report that God is truly among you."

In 14:21 Paul cites Isaiah 28:11, which refers to the destruction of Israel where the prophet is announcing a judgment against Israel. Since Israel had refused to listen to God through the understandable language of a prophet He would now speak to them through a foreign language of the conquering Assyrian Army.

Paul alters the Hebrew text from Isaiah 28:11 as an interpretive paraphrase with full rights as an apostle writing under inspiration to apply to the Corinthian situation. The Hebrew text talks of the enemy's characteristics: "For with stammering lips and another tongue He will speak to this people" (Isa 28:11 NKJ) The word "stammering" (*la'ag*) means "scorn, ridicule, make fun of." This does not refer to his way of speaking, but rather to the content of what he says. The context describes God's impending judgment over Israel when they heard a nation speaking to them in a tongue strange to their ears. The prophecy was completed when the Assyrians, who spoke in a different language from the Israelites, carried them away into captivity.

In Isaiah 28:11, the expression "strange tongue" refers to a language that was "another, different, foreign." The word "tongue" always refers to a human language or to the physical organ. The two expressions, "stammering tongue" and "*strange* tongue" (*'acher*, "the tongue of a stranger, foreign language, different"), are parallel concepts that refer to the spoken language of the imminent invader Assyria.

Jeremiah made the same prophecy to Judah concerning Babylon, "Behold, I will bring a nation against you from afar, O house of Israel," says the LORD. "It is a mighty nation, It is an ancient nation, A nation whose language you do not know, Nor can you understand what they say." (Jer 5:15 NKJ). In other words, the sign of the judgment of God would be a language they did not understand. Because Israel had rejected the clear word of the prophets (Isaiah 28:9-10), saying that they were not children who require simple teaching, God sent them a complex message in another language through foreigners (28:1-12). When God speaks through unintelligible languages, it is to judge.

> In the Corinthian context, speaking in "other tongues" will fail to convey any meaningful message or bring repentance, just as it failed to do in Isaiah's day. The citation from Isaiah makes clear that tongues are not a saving sign but a sign of retribution. They do not stimulate belief but instead seal unbelief. In jeering at the simple message of the cross, the unbelievers in the Corinthian setting are like Isaiah's nemeses. They find the message of Christ crucified to be utter foolishness. Nevertheless, this simple message is the only message that will bring about their repentance. (In the Corinthian context, speaking in "other tongues" will fail to convey any meaningful message or bring repentance, just as it failed to do in

Isaiah's day. The citation from Isaiah makes clear that tongues are not a saving sign but a sign of retribution. They do not stimulate belief but instead seal unbelief. In jeering at the simple message of the cross, the unbelievers in the Corinthian setting are like Isaiah's nemeses. They find the message of Christ crucified to be utter foolishness. Nevertheless, this simple message is the only message that will bring about their repentance. (Garland 2003: 648.)

The word "therefore" in 1 Corinthians 14:22, ("Therefore tongues are for a sign, not to those who believe but to unbelievers; but prophesying is not for unbelievers but for those who believe") introduces a conclusion based on previous information. Since verse 21 referred to a human language, verse 22 also is speaking of a human language. The connecting word in verse 23, "if therefore..." indicates that the same theme continues.

The purpose of the gift of tongues is defined as follows: "tongues are for a sign...to them that believe not" (14:22). Likewise, in Acts 2:4-11 tongues were a sign for unbelievers, and it is irrefutable that tongues were human languages or dialects here. Unbelievers who heard in their own languages, with their respective accents, phonology, grammar and vocabulary, could not help but recognize it as a miraculous sign.

Conversely, an ecstatic language would not have been a miraculous sign to unbelievers, because this was a common practice among pagans. Only crazy people, feigners, drunkards, and pagan prophets spoke that way. For this reason, the pilgrims in Jerusalem accused the disciples of acting like pagans at first, until some recognized their own languages.

Those who recognized that the tongues were a sign began to ask, "What does this mean?" (Acts 2:12). The Jews knew that a miraculous language indicated a sign from God, particularly one of judgment, and they wondered how God was going to judge them. About 37 years later, in 70 A.D., the Romans destroyed the Temple and the nation. The few Jews who were left in Israel rebelled again in 135 A.D. when the Romans massacred the remnant. The nation of Israel did not exist for 1,878 years. The sign of this judgment was an unknown tongue, as in the days of Isaiah in 722 B.C.(Assyrian invasion) and Jeremiah in 586 B.C. (Babylonian invasion) (See Isaiah 28:11-12)

Those who announced judgment over Israel were the apostles and prophets, whose authority was manifested by miraculous gifts and signs (2 Corinthians 12:12; Romans 15:19; Hebrews 2:3-4). Evidently one of those signs was the gift of tongues, which Paul told the Corinthians he had spoken "more than all of them" (14:18).

Paul had just made clear in the context that he did not speak in tongues in prayers, in songs or in the churches. Where, then, did Paul speak "more than all" in tongues? If speaking in tongues is a sign to the Jews, then perhaps Paul spoke in tongues to the Jews in the synagogues or other meeting places as the apostles did on the Day of Pentecost. Paul always went to the Jews first, probably because they would understand the implications of his signs and OT applications. However, we do not have any evidence of this supposition, but it could be a logical conclusion since tongues were a sign to the Jews and not to the churches. The only ones in the first century who would understand the implications of the sign of tongues would have been knowledgeable Jews in the audiences.

What happened with the sign of judgment (tongues) when the judgment occurred? Israel was judged in 70 A.D., and the nation dispersed and ceased to exist. Therefore, the sign of the judgment had no purpose after the judgment occurred. For this reason the gift of tongues disappeared before the end of the first century. There was no longer a reason for its existence. Israel had ceased to exist as a nation.

In the church of Corinth, the purpose of the gift of tongues had been perverted and used in the congregation of believers to prove their miraculous powers. Paul declared that tongues "are for a sign, not to believers" (14:22), that is, it was not necessary to confirm the divine origin of the message.

Therefore, the gift of tongues cannot be the sign of the "baptism of the Spirit," because that would make it a sign to believers, which Paul clearly denied. A "sign," *semeion*, indicates a miracle with an ethical purpose. It is an authentication (Romans 4:11; 2 Thessalonians 3:17). The mature mentality (14:20, "do not be children in understanding") understands that the place of tongues was not the church, but rather among unbelievers.

Even in the time of it's use, the gift of tongues was, at times, an impediment to worship and evangelism. Paul exaggerates this possibility and says in 14:23, "if...all speak with tongues and come in those that are unlearned, or unbelievers, will they not say that ye are mad?" Therefore, if tongues turn unbelievers away, they are useless as an instrument of evangelism in the Gentile church.

The "unlearned" (*idiotes*) are the ignorant or uninstructed; Gentiles will not understand the nature and purpose of the sign because they were not instructed in the OT implications. The phrase "you are out of your mind" (*mainomai*) means a "rage, delirium, frenetic behavior, or lose judgment." A Gentile visitor in a hypothetical meeting of this kind would leave thinking he had witnessed a frenetic meeting of the pagan religions. With their unrestrained use of tongues, the Corinthians were a discredit to Christianity and would have justly been called "crazy" because no one could understand them. Garland shows how uncontrolled frenzies were part of some mystery religions:

> Livy (History of Rome 39.8–19) records the crackdown on Bacchic rites in Italy in 186 B.C. and describes them as a cacophony of noise resounding with shrieks, chanting, cymbals clashing, drums beating, and cries. He contends that the worshipers thought that they hit the height of religious achievement when they could regard nothing as forbidden: "Men, apparently out of their wits, would utter prophecies with frenzied bodily convulsions, matrons, attired as Bacchantes, with their hair disheveled... ." (*Ibid.*: 652).

On the other hand, taking another hypothetical or exaggerated case, if all prophesied—something equally as impossible because of 12:29, but given the case—then the unbeliever would be "convinced by all, he is convicted by all. And thus the secrets of his heart are revealed" (1Co 14:24-25 NKJ) as God's standards are taught revealing man's desperate need for cleansing and forgiveness. This is the convicting work of the Holy Spirit through His Word (John 16:28) which is the "power of the gospel" (Rom 1:16). In the same manner, the proclamation of the Word of God has the power to produce conviction in hearts (Hebrews 4:12). Therefore, the most powerful weapon of the church is not ecstasies, but it is the preaching of the Word with clarity and courage.

When the gift of tongues is wrongly used, the result is confusion, frustration and misunderstandings. Unbelievers reject the church services and believers are not edified. Paul had just said that he did not see any reason to demonstrate the sign of tongues in the congregation (14:19), because the sign of tongues is not for the church or for individuals, but rather for the unbelieving nation of Israel.

The results of prophecy occur in the following three stages in the unbeliever: (1) conviction of sin (1 Corinthians 14:24); (2) the "call to accountability" (1 Corinthians 2:14-15), which describes his state in light of Scripture. Theoretically if everyone is a prophet then the unbeliever is challenged to deal with his sins from everyone delivering God's Word; and (3) his guilty standing before God weighs on his own conscience (verse 25) as his secret sins are declared. This is not a miraculous revelation to the prophet of some individual, rather the truthful application of the biblical description of sinners that fits everyone. It might be perceived by the individual as being a personal exposure.

The "secrets of the heart" is a generic phrase as a result of being forced to face the application of the Ten Commandments, which condemn everyone. At this stage he will be "falling down on his face," meaning he will be repentant and broken for his own sins. This is a beautiful picture of how the law brings us to Christ: "Therefore the Law has become our tutor to lead us to Christ, that we may be justified by faith." (Gal 3:24 NAS)

Repentance is the rejection of any dependence on one's personal merit or goodness; it is humility before a holy God asking for mercy. This is the way that people should come to Christ for reconciliation (Luke 17:16; 18:13) with the God they have offended by their sins. They will be prepared to believe through what they understand in the Word and by the order in the gatherings (14:40) and love (13:1-7) they observe in the behavior of the congregation, which brings the conviction that God is certainly among them (14:25). Thus the prophetic Word is far superior to speaking in tongues because it results in illumination, conviction, confession, conversions and worship.

2. A gift must edify, not cause confusion (14:26).

"How is it then, brethren? Whenever you come together, each of you has a psalm, has a teaching, has a tongue, has a revelation, has an interpretation. Let all things be done for edification"

Chapter 13: Ten rules governing the gift of tongues

According to 1 Corinthians 14:26, everyone in the congregation wanted to share a "psalm...doctrine...tongue...revelation...interpretation" (14:26). The command that follows seems to indicate that these were almost in competition with each other, which voided their purpose.

The phrase "each one" does not mean every single person, but those that do were of four categories. Thiselton sees this as another hypothetical description (Thiselton 2000: 1133). A "psalm" was a reading, possibly a song from the Old Testament Psalms, and the doctrine probably refers to their favorite teaching. Believers used the psalms to exhort and encourage each other (Eph 5:19-20; 1 Cor 14:26).

Some spoke in tongues, either genuine or false, while others may or may not have interpreted. Because of Paul's exhortation that follows, we suppose that although there were many people with the gift of interpretation, not all tongues were interpreted.

Others claimed to have received revelations from God like those given by the prophets or apostles. The exhortation in verse 29 obliges the congregation to judge those who spoke as prophets, presumably with revelation. In other words, no one with a "revelation" was to be accepted easily. This may refer to the "word of knowledge" (12:8; 13:8) or prophecy. Even when a person shared a revelation, they had to be evaluated or analyzed to make sure that what they spoke aligned with the rest of God's revelation through the apostles.

This listing should not be considered absolute or complete nor an order of service, but rather illustrative for the command that follows.

The problem in Corinth seems to be that everyone came to the meeting with the desire to participate in the glory of communicating something miraculous, and many wanted to do it simultaneously. No one listened to anybody else except for a few visitors who were perplexed by the confusion and disorder (14:33). It was impossible that anyone could be edified in the midst of such chaos. No one was interested in serving, learning, evangelizing or edifying others, must less being edified by the Word, but rather they wanted to express themselves and glorify themselves. Everyone wanted attention, preeminence, and importance. Thus, the value of the gifts was annulled by their improper practice (1 Corinthians 13:1-3).

Paul left an order: "Let all things be done for edification." This should be the universal goal. The word edification (*oikodome*) literally means "construction of a house." Therefore, the translation means to "grow, improve, mature, augment learning." The test of value and focus in the church is what best "builds up" others with the Word of God. Edification is the watershed issue in the chapter (14:3, 4, 5, 12, 17; earlier 8:1; 10:23). "The thrust of this chapter makes clear that he wishes to thwart those expressions of spiritual gifts that build up only the individual (14:4) and to encourage those gifts that edify the entire community." (Garland 2003: 658).

The edification of the believers is the principle responsibility of the leaders in the church (Ephesians 4:12), but it is equally the responsibility of each believer in the body (Ephesians 4:16). "Wherefore comfort yourselves together, and edify one another, even as also ye do" (1 Thessalonians 5:11).

Likewise, "Let every one of us please his neighbor for his good to edification. For even Christ pleased not himself: but, as it is written, the reproaches of them that reproached thee fell on me" (Romans 15:2-3). He never sought what could have been beneficial for him, but he sought what would benefit others.

The main evidence of immaturity and lack of love in the church of Corinth was the believers' egotism, or their interest in self-satisfaction instead of edification of others (see verses 3-5, 12, 17, 26, 31). They did not obey the Word, which says, "Let us…follow after the things which make for peace, and things wherewith one may edify another" (Romans 14:19). That which edifies others also produces harmony, just as egotism and self-seeking produce disorder, confusion and division.

We are edified by only one thing: the Word of God. 2 Timothy 3:16-17 says, "All Scripture is given by inspiration of God, and is profitable for doctrine, for reproof, for correction, for instruction in righteousness, that the man of God may be complete, thoroughly equipped for every good work." In other words, edification must produce more understanding and personal application of the Word in the life of the believer, so that it can be applied to other lives in the "work of the ministry" (Eph 4:12, as 2 Tim 2:2).

The emphasis on prophecy had the objective "that all may learn, and all may be comforted" (14:31), but likewise in this context prophecy incorporates *kerygma* or gospel proclamation/clarification for a mixed audience. This is true edification. If there is no learning and no practical application of learning to one's personal life, then there is no edification.

3. Meetings should have a limit of two or three speakers at any one time (14:27).

"If anyone speaks in a tongue, let there be two or at the most three, each in turn, and let one interpret."

The text suggests that the Corinthian believers were losing self-control, acting the same as the pagans, seeking mystical and ecstatic experiences. The Spirit does not produce the loss of control, but conversely His filling produces "temperance" (Galatians 5:23) or self-control.

To restore order in the meetings of the church in Corinth, Paul ordered that there be only two speakers, or three if necessary, who might speak in a tongue. This divinely imposed limitation was to limit the possible tongues being spoken and to keep a balance with the prophetic preaching. It appears that everyone wanted to demonstrate his charismatic powers resulting in bedlam as pictured in 14:23 should "all speak with tongues" thus dominating the meeting.

It seems that the church thought that there was blessing in hearing someone speak in a tongue, no matter what he said. They must have thought, "The more the better!" The church's main errors were mistaking the phenomenal for the miraculous and thinking that to merely see or hear a miracle was to be

Chapter 13: *Ten rules governing the gift of tongues*

edified. Paul's rules were written with the purpose of correcting these errors.

Teaching what edifies another person is not a phenomenon. Edification, as we have said, is the result of clarifying the understanding the Word. The Holy Spirit can bring conviction to a person only when he hears and understands the Word. The understanding empowered by the Spirit brings conviction and clarity of how to apply God's Word personally to his life. Paul's restriction prevented speaking in tongues from dominating the meetings and also maintained equilibrium between the gift of tongues and the other speaking gifts.

Paul does not deny the validity of the gift of tongues here, but he does limit its manifestation in the public meeting. In any one meeting there would only be allowed "two or at the most three" to speak in a tongue, and only then if beforehand they confirm that there is a known interpreter present. He could be saying that the one who is speaking should do the miraculous interpretation as well (14:13), but Paul's question in 12:30 implies differently.

With the apparent enthusiasm in the meetings enforcing this command would demand the grace of the fruit of the Spirit of "self-control" (Gal 5:23). If tongues are genuinely of the Spirit then the Spirit's filling will enable the obedience to God's Word as surely as produce a gift of the Spirit.

It seems that even the gift of prophecy could have been subject to abuse as well, since the same rule of allowing only two or three to exercise their gift in each meeting was also applied to the prophets (14:29), with the additional responsibility of "judging" (*diakrino*: "discern, or evaluate") what was said by each prophet.

Other prophets had to compare any new revelation to those that had already been given, knowing for certain that the Holy Spirit does not contradict himself. Those whose prophecy strayed from the established revelation were to be rejected (1 John 4:1; 1 Thessalonians 5:20-22). These rules of evaluation were critical in the beginning, because the prophets were helping in the formation of the Church (Ephesians 2:20) and had not recorded their revelations for all the churches.

4. These gifts must be exercised in turn, one person at a time (14:27).
"If anyone speaks in a tongue, let there be two or at the most three, each in turn, and let one interpret."

The two or three permitted to speak in a tongue were not to speak simultaneously or to interrupt the meeting by speaking whenever they pleased. They had to speak "each in turn" or "taking turns." Therefore, order, understanding and courtesy were required in the proceedings. Having two people speaking at the same time would cause confusion, but if they happened to be speaking in different languages then the confusion would turn to chaos.

For this reason, competition among the speakers was never permitted. One of the most evident errors of contemporary Charismatics is that they permit many people to speak, pray or sing different songs simultaneously while no one pays attention to what any one particular person is saying. Each one speaks to himself and ignores the others, violating the command to speak in turn and to speak always for edification.

Even though the passage does not specifically speak to the prophets, they should also speak in turn, "one by one" (verse 31). This is implicit because the others had to judge their prophecies, and that would be difficult if all were speaking at the same time. Manners, courtesy and order had to control the meetings (verse 40). The objective of the gifts of speaking is learning and exhortation toward edification.

5. There must be interpretation (14:27).
"If anyone speaks in a tongue, let there be two or at the most three, each in turn, and let one interpret."

Anything said in an unknown tongue had to be interpreted. Paul says, "...let one interpret." In the Greek, "one" (*eis*) is in the emphatic position, to indicate that only one person does the interpretations. If that is the case, then only three can speak in tongues and only one can interpret. If this is the command, then it is a transgression to violate this obligated procedure.

As the gift of tongues is plural, that is one can speak in various languages, it would not be unusual that the gift of interpretation be enabled to miraculously interpret multiple languages. It is possible that the interpreter could be one of the two or three who spoke in tongues (14:13), or someone else with the gift of interpretation, but the practice was always to allow only one at a time. Having two or more interpreters in a meeting was never permitted.

This implies the following two things: (1) Each unknown tongue has only one interpretation. In our day, sometimes we find manifestations of tongues in which three or more interpretations are given to one tongue presentation, evidently indicating that the tongue is false. (2) The person with the gift of interpretation can interpret any tongue, at any time, under any circumstance. It is not necessary for him to be caught up in a special emotion or sentiment; the interpretation should be made logically and phrase-by-phrase to assure an accurate translation.

If the "interpretation" were another complete revelation, then the tongue presentation would not have been necessary and the interpreter would be in essence a prophet. The gift is to understand what was said, not receive a different revelation. If no such gifted interpreter were present at any church meeting then speaking in tongues was not to be permitted. This presupposes a general awareness of who has the gift of interpretation within the congregation.

An implied procedure would be necessary to follow the command. Evidently, someone must appeal to the leadership to present a gift of tongues, followed by a search for a gifted interpreter, and should no interpreter be found, the tongues speaker would not be allowed to speak in public.

In 14:29, Paul ordered the congregation to "judge" the speakers. The basis of their judgment was conformity to the inspired already revealed Word. Before the canon of the New Testament was established, however, there was a dependence on the gift of discernment to "judge" the prophetic manifestations. The pronoun "others" in verse 29 has its antecedent in the prophets, suggesting that those who had the gift of prophecy also manifested the gift of discernment; in other words, the prophets "judged" the prophets.

Though the text does not restrict the prophets except in number, if the parallel command to the prophet were applied they should not even have permitted prophecy in the meetings unless someone with the gift of discernment were present. If someone ignored the Word and treated Paul's commands negligently, then they were indicating that their "tongue" was false, and the church was commanded to pay no attention to that person (14:38).

6. The speaker must remain quiet if there is no interpreter (14:28).

"But if there is no interpreter, let him keep silent in church, and let him speak to himself and to God."

Although the gifts of tongues and interpretation are different, they should not be exercised apart from one another. The person with the gift of interpreting would have nothing to interpret if someone with the gift of speaking in tongues were not present. There is no indication that the gift of interpretation was used outside the context of interpreting the miraculous gift tongues. Similarly, Paul argued that the person with the gift of tongues was prohibited to speak if no one in the meeting was known to have the gift of interpretation. The two gifts had to go hand-in-hand.

This implies that the congregation in Corinth had to know who had the gift of interpretation before any tongue would be permitted. If that person were not present, then it was not permitted for anyone to speak publicly in an unknown tongue. If no interpreter is present, then the tongues speaker is not to be allowed to speak, rather if he has to speak then he must keep it between himself and God.

Paul also implied that the preparations for the meetings should be made beforehand rather than improvised, so that interruptions and disorder could be avoided. If everything is supposed to be done in order, then someone must have the responsibility of organizing the meeting so that each person can speak in turn. Before the meeting, then, it is the job of the leaders of the church to organize the participants. Even prophets had to give up the platform if another prophet received a message, however; no prophet could dominate the meetings, and sometimes they also had to remain quiet.

It is incorrect to believe that a person under the impulse of the Spirit cannot control himself. The loss of self-control is a symptom of carnality. When someone is under the impulse of anger, passion, rage or fear, he cannot control himself and the instincts of the flesh will dominate; when someone is under the control of the Spirit, he should have more self-control, not less (Gal 5:23). The filling of the Spirit never obliges us to ignore or disobey the commands of His Word.

7. The gift of tongues must be under the control of the speaker (14:32-33).
"And the spirits of the prophets are subject to the prophets. 33 For God is not the author of confusion but of peace, as in all the churches of the saints."

The instructions to the prophets are similar to those given to those who spoke in tongues (verse 28). The "spirits" refer to the interior part of the prophets that motivates their actions. The context says that the gift does not control the gifted person, but rather that the person's spirit controls the gift (12:1; 14:12) and likewise his behavior. The urge to speak is "subject" (*hupotassetai*, present progressive tense, "continually subordinate to or yielded to…") to the prophets or speakers. The impulse to speak can be sensed, but the higher priority of order and courtesy to other speakers encourages him to yield his urges and wait his turn or another opportunity. The gifts of tongues and prophecy, or any speaking gifts, are limited and controlled by the speaker; therefore, speaking on impulse is not biblical.

The Bible does not indicate that people who were filled with the Spirit lost control of themselves or were unaware of what they were doing. This concept stems from a wrong interpretation of the filling of the Spirit (Eph 4:18). Typically a pagan would use liquor to get into an uncontrollable state, so Paul sought to make a vast distinction when he said, "Do not be drunk with wine, in which is dissipation…" (*asotia*, "abandoned, senseless deeds, reckless deeds") "but be filled with the Spirit." (*alla*, "an adversive conjunction indicating an emphatic contrast" – (*Low-Nida Lexicon*: 89.125). The whole notion of being "drunk in the Spirit" is fabricated from a false understanding of the meaning of the conjunction.

The idea of losing control of yourself in a trance or ecstasy has always been a characteristic of paganism, not of biblical Christianity (1 Corinthians 12:2). They were encouraged to continue speaking until the impulse left them, regardless of the disruption they might cause.

This verse gives a way to evaluate whether the person is speaking by the Holy Spirit or by some other spirit. 1 John 4:1 says, "Believe not every spirit, but try the spirits whether they are of God." Paul is saying that if someone cannot control himself, especially in observing the order of the service, then they are not prompted by the Spirit of God, but rather a different spirit, or the flesh, that is controlling him.

In verse 33, the word "for" (*gar*, "introduction of a reason") connects the two verses. God never produces "confusion" (*akatastasia*: "disorder, rebellion, insurrection," from which we have the word "catastrophe.") The whole service should have peace (Col 3:15) and order (14:40), reflecting the character of God (Romans 15:33; 2 Thessalonians 3:16; Hebrews 13:20), and those who are guided by the Spirit produce this result. The Spirit is not in control when there is confusion, disorder and chaos. "The disorder in Corinth is not attributable to the workings of the Holy Spirit but to narcissistic exhibitionism, disdain for others with "lesser" gifts, and disregard for the common good." (Garland 2003:

Chapter 13: *Ten rules governing the gift of tongues*

664) The leaders have the responsibility to quiet those who are not subject to the "commandments of the Lord."

If someone has the impulse to speak during the meeting while another is speaking, or if he speaks in tongues without first finding an interpreter, then he is not motivated or filled by the Spirit; it is the speaker's pride, his emotion or a seducing spirit that is prompting him to be disobedience to the Word.

There is no indication that the gifts of prophecy, tongues or any other gift are associated with convulsions, foaming at the mouth, unconsciousness, rolling eyes and head thrown back, changes in the voice, jerking, convulsions or falling to the floor, as is noted among some Pentecostal meetings. These characteristics do not promote peace and are not conducive to order. No wonder unbelievers think that Christians are "crazy" (14:23). There is also no evidence that trances or ecstasies are associated with the gifts of evangelism, teaching, giving, service, or administration, and there is no insinuation that the sacred writers wrote while under trances or while unconscious, since the Bible was inspired under the control of the Spirit.

When there is a command given by the Spirit, those who are controlled by Him will have the power and the desire to obey it (Philippians 2:13). If there is an uncontrollable impulse dominating a person and causing him to act in a way contrary to the teaching in the Word, then obviously it is not the Spirit who is motivating that person. In this way we should "judge" or discern if the spirit is of God or some other source (1 Corinthians 14:29, 37; 1 John 4:1).

8. Men, not women, should exercise the gift of tongues/prophecy in meetings (14:33b-36).

"... As in all the churches of the saints. 34 Let your women keep silent in the churches, for they are not permitted to speak; but they are to be submissive, as the law also says. 35 And if they want to learn something, let them ask their own husbands at home; for it is shameful for women to speak in church. 36 Or did the word of God come originally from you? Or was it you only that it reached?"

Just as Paul put certain limitations on those who spoke in tongues and prophesied, he also obligated that everyone else in the church be "silent" (*sigao*: "keep silent") while these are exercised (14:28). He also required that the women "keep silence in the churches" (14:34).

Paul dedicated three verses to the theme of women, who apparently were speaking in tongues and prophesying in the church at Corinth. He says that there is no reason and no place in the meeting for a woman to speak in tongues, to prophecy, nor apparently to speak in general. Women who contributed to the confusion in the church of Corinth only made the situation worse. Note again that all of these restrictions indicate that the people under the Spirit's influence can control themselves and submit to what the Spirit says to the churches. Conversely, those who are not controlled or filled by the Spirit are disruptive and impulsive and self-serving.

The phrase "as in all churches of the saints" (14:33b), indicates that this rule was not local, geographic or cultural, but rather was to be universally applied in all churches regardless of time or place. Arguments that try to limit this commandment to the first century distort the Scriptures in order to disobey the clear restriction of the Spirit of God (14:37).

Some commentators want to begin verse 34 with the pared-down phrase, "as in all the churches." We should remember that the original inspired writers did not include any punctuation. The divisions of the verses came later with translations of the Bible and when the Greek text was changed from capital letters to small letters to facilitate reading. Whether it should conclude the previous statement commanding order and peace in the meeting of the church or it introduces the section concerning women speakers, is irreverent, because it must apply to both, and, in fact, to all of Paul's teachings.

They typically were all read and taught (Acts 2:42) in all the churches (Col 4:16).

The limitations imposed on women came from the Old Testament, because Paul adds, "as the law also says" (14:34). It was not permitted for women to speak in the synagogues or Temple. Paul reiterates this in 1 Timothy 2:11-12, saying, "Let the woman learn in silence (*hesychia*: "quiet, no disorder") with all subjection. But I suffer not a woman to teach, nor to usurp authority over the man, but to be in silence." Paul is neither denying women the use of their gifts of speaking (Acts 21:9) nor denying the possibility for them to have those gifts in the first place, but rather he is saying that they should use them in circumstances that do not include the whole church body. Feminist J.M. Bassler questions:

> How can women like Euodia and Syntyche (Phil. 4:2–3), Prisca (Rom. 16:3; 1 Cor. 16:19), Mary (Rom. 16:6), Junia (Rom. 16:7) and Tryphaena and Tryphosa (Rom. 16:12) function as co-workers in the churches if they cannot speak in those churches? How can Phoebe fulfill her role of deacon (Rom. 16:1–2) if she cannot speak out in the assembly? How can a woman like Nympha, who is influential enough to host a house church (Col. 4:15), have been required to remain silent in her own home (cf. also Prisca, the wife of Aquila, 16:19)? (Bassler 1992:n.a.)

It seems as if 1 Cor 11:5-6 ("every woman who prays or prophesies...") is an exception for this severe rule as long as they have their head covered. Paul's argument in 1 Timothy comes from two historic facts: (1) Adam was created before Eve. (2) Adam was not deceived, but Eve was (2:13-14).

God's design is that men take the leadership by demonstrations of caring love for their wives, and the women are to respond with a loving, submissive attitude.

It is not a question of who is better or more intelligent, but of the biblical order. Women can be great teachers of the Word, but their gifts cannot be exercised over men in the congregation (1 Tim 2:12). In many cultures men cannot minister directly to women, so women must exercise their gifts to evangelize and disciple children and other women (especially that men are not allowed to minister to in many cultures). The order that God has established in the church, just as in His creation, is to have male leadership. When this order is ignored and disobeyed, God is not in control; on the contrary, it is another spirit that controls the situation in order to deceive.

Paul declared that it is "a shame for women to speak in the church" (14:35b). The word "shame" (*aischros*: "shame, disgrace") describes outsiders' opinions or a cultural attitude concerning the congregation and, more specifically, it refers to God's opinion about the congregation. It is shameful before God!

In the context the issue is dealing with prophecy and the reaction of the congregation (14:29). Women appear to have caused frustration because of their desire to learn in the congregation, which motivated them to ask questions in the meetings. This interrupted the services, implying their husbands' ignorance and the lack of leadership in their homes. Paul implied that the responsibility of the husband was to teach his wife. The women had the right to learn, but not to ask questions in the church, since they could ask their husbands at home (14:35).

Following the delivery of a prophecy or the Word of God the audience was to discern or judge what was said (14:29). In this context a question in the middle of the service can take authority away from the speaker. The Bible prohibits that a woman usurp authority over a man for any reason (1 Tim 2:12). God has guided many women to do work that men have refused to do or cannot do, but the Holy Spirit has never guided any woman to fill a role that He has restricted to men.

The restriction here and in 1 Timothy is especially directed toward married women. The word *gynaikes*, is "woman" in a general sense, but the context indicates whether she is single (1 Corinthians 7:34) or married (1 Corinthians 5:1; 9:5 and 14 times in chapter 7). There are two points that show that he is talking about married women here: (1) The phrase "be under obedience" (*hupotassesthosan*, verse 34) is always applied to a wife who is subject to her husband (Ephesians 5:22; Colossians 3:18; Titus 2:5; 1 Peter 3:1, 5); (2) The phrase "ask their husbands" (14:35) expresses to whom they should direct their questions.

Submission did not obligate silence at home (14:35), but rather at church. Nor did it imply the impossibility of learning, because "all" are to learn in the church (14:31). It would be difficult if they were unmarried or if they had unbelieving husbands (7:13). If the woman did not have a believing husband, she must learn from another man or from women who were authorized to teach other women (Titus 2:4). It seems as if other single women could participate in limited ways, if they did not take authority from or teach men. Additional instruction is given to the women concerning how they are to be fitly adorned (11:12-16).

Silence on the part of the women demonstrated their submission to their husbands. We should note that this never implied inferiority. The relationship between men and women is similar to that of the Father and the Son (1 Corinthians 11:3). The Son is constantly in submission to the Father (Matthew

26:39; Hebrews 10:7), but He has never stopped being equal with the Father in all things (John 5:17-18; 10:30; 14:9; Philippians 2:6). Therefore, God established the order of leadership, authority, accountability and submission without any insinuation of inferiority.

The reference to the "Law" is probably from Genesis 3:16 where the woman is told, "he shall rule over thee." This implies subordination with equality. Paul assumes this reference to the law gives credibility and authority to his argument. Some people presume to have more authority than the Bible and the apostle Paul thus placing themselves above the Scriptures by either ignoring them or interpreting them as they want.

Paul's sarcasm in 14:36 was very sharp but obviously merited, when he said, "Or did the word of God come originally from you? Or was it you only that it reached?" In effect, he was saying, "If you did not write the Word, then obey it." No believer ever has the right to ignore, alter or disobey the Word of God. Apparently the people of Corinth wanted to change all of the churches to conform not to the Scriptures, but to their ways, so that they could justify their own behavior.

9. God allows men who refuse to listen to be ignorant (14:38).
"But if anyone is ignorant, let him be ignorant."

Paul anticipated that there would be opposition to his instructions (11:15), but he said that those who opposed him were taking risks (4:18-21). The warning in 14:37 is followed by the consequence in 14:38. Those who treat Paul's words as merely his own opinions, which could be argued with or modified when convenient, are seriously mistaken. Paul was not teaching his own opinion or philosophy that could be debated or ignored; he was repeating what the Lord told him to write, because in 1 Corinthians 14:37 he says, "They are commandments of the Lord." As he said in 11:23, "I have received of the Lord that which also I delivered unto you." With this regard, Jesus told us to "teach [disciples] to obey all things that I commanded you" (Matt 28:20). All of Paul's commands come from the Lord Jesus and should be received as from His lips.

This indicated that the apostolic authority did not reside within Paul individually, but within his message; he was simply God's messenger, and he never said anything that did not originate in the inspiration of the Spirit of God with His full authority. Paul also did not pretend to be infallible in his person (Phil 3:12), but rather he declared that everything he taught about God, His Gospel and His church, was God's own teaching or the "commandments of the Lord."

From time to time he expressed his opinions without having heard exact instructions from Jesus, but on those rare occasions like in 1 Corinthians 7 he made it very clear that they were his opinions (1 Cor 7:6, where he recommended remaining single). Then in 7:10 he makes it clear that this is not his opinion, but a command directly from Jesus, "Now to the married I command, yet not I but the Lord." While under inspiration Paul's words had the same

Chapter 13: *Ten rules governing the gift of tongues*

weight and authority as those of Jesus. Therefore, regardless of his position, training, experience, talents or capacities, a person who rejects the teachings of the apostle Paul also has to be rejected as a teacher or leader in His church. No human authority can annul Paul's apostolic authority.

The verb "ignore" (*agnoeo*: "not to be recognized, or understood; discarded") is translated "must be ignored" and describes the attitude that others should have toward someone who rejects these principles. Perhaps this means that God would ignore him (Matthew 10:32-33), because his actions indicated that he had never known God (1 Corinthians 8:3; Matthew 7:22-23; 1 John 4:6). It is also possible that the verb indicates Paul's hope that the church would not recognize such persons. Essentially, it is a form of discipline on the part of the church to discard false teachers who refuse to conform to the teachings of Paul. This ostracism did not necessarily exclude the person from attending the church, but it did prohibit him from speaking out in the congregation.

10. It was necessary to do everything decently and in order (14:39-40).
"Therefore, brethren, desire earnestly to prophesy, and do not forbid to speak with tongues. 40 Let all things be done decently and in order."

God is not the author of confusion, but of peace (verse 33). His gifts, then, can be controlled. Those who interrupt the peace and order of a meeting by insubordination or uncontrolled activity creating chaos and interfering with other ministries are deceived and are also deceiving. God's nature had to be reflected in the meetings where peace and order predominated (Col 3:15). For this reason, the preferred emphasis in the congregation must be prophecy, the understandable revelation of God's words to man, because this is the gift that edifies and instructs the churches. Prophecy is important because edification is vital.

In the context, the restrictions against the abusive use of tongues were so severe that some have interpreted the chapter to mean that Paul wanted to completely eliminate the practice of speaking in tongues. As we have shown, however, if they obeyed the rules for the exercise of the gifts of tongues and prophecy, they could permit a genuine manifestation of tongues and other speaking gifts. It is apparent that the rules were put in place to impede the manifestation of false gifts and egotists.

The verb phrase "forbid not" is in the plural, directing it to the church as a whole rather than to individuals. Therefore, Paul was not encouraging anyone to seek the gift of tongues, since this was a very limited gift in purpose, function and duration. Paul says that the gift of tongues should not be scorned or refused in the church, but it always has to be practiced within the standards of 1 Corinthians 14, with the purpose of being interpreted for the edification of the church.

Paul was not saying that anyone at any time who wanted to speak in tongues should be allowed to participate in the meeting. We have the responsibility of obeying the entire chapter in its context and to correct the abuse of tongues in the church. We are exhorted to be sure that the two or three men who are permitted to speak with an interpreter do it in turn (14:27), that the church discern whether their messages are in accordance with the revealed Word of God (14:29), and that the others in the congregation are quiet and that women are forbidden to speak in the meetings (14:34-35).

The commandment to do "all decently" (*euschemonos*, "respectfully, beautifully, attractively;" "honorably" in 1 Thessalonians 4:12; "honestly" in Romans 13:13) describes the result of keeping the rules of order in this chapter. The word "decently" is a compound word that means "harmony and attraction" (*eu* = "well" plus *chemonos* = "formed.") When the commandments of God are kept, all is beautiful and harmonious. These rules were to restore the peace in the congregation, correcting the abuses of speaking in tongues without interpretation, of speaking simultaneously, and of women speaking in the congregation.

The word "order" (*taksi*: "fixed succession, proceeding, or precedent") means "by turns" or "one by one" (verse 27). It is a military term that refers to having each soldier in his place, doing his job correctly and on time. If something is done in an impulsive or uncontrolled way, then it does not come from God. Therefore, before God, it is the responsibility of the leaders of the church to assure that the activities and meetings are carried out according to the rules of the New Testament. God is a God of beauty and harmony, respect and order. Everything that His children do should reflect His character and virtues.

Was the church to continually have this conflict and restrictions in its meetings or was this primarily a temporary situation that was concerned with the beginning of the Early Church? The rules of order in 1 Corinthians 14 remain throughout the Church Age regardless of whether the specific gifts of prophecy or tongues are present.

Chapter 13: *Ten rules governing the gift of tongues*

Chapter 13: *Gifts for Today*

CHAPTER 14

Fourteen areas of evidence for the Cessation of the Gift of Tongues

Chapter 14 : *Gifts for Today*

At some point in time the Scripture states that the gifts of prophecy and tongues will cease: The question is, "When are these gifts to stop functioning?" In this chapter we will discuss the duration of certain gifts. Are they all permanent? Were some temporary? Have some ceased?

Some Christians believe that all gifts have had a permanent manifestation throughout Church history and will exist until Christ's return. Others believe that while the majority of the gifts have continued until today, certain gifts ceased with the apostles and prophets in the first century when they fulfilled their temporary function. Finally, a few take the position that none of the gifts exist today and that the members of Christ's body are to mutually serve and teach one another for edification.

We know that at least three gifts were not permanent because 1 Corinthians 13:8 says, "but whether there be prophecies, they shall fail; whether there be tongues, they shall cease; whether there be knowledge, it shall vanish away." The question is: Are there indications that Paul described under inspiration that indicated when these gifts would cease?

Some suppose that the Spirit is operating today in the same way as He did in the early first century. This popular theme comes from Hebrews 13:8, "Jesus Christ the same yesterday, and today, and forever." They reason that if Jesus healed in the first century, then he is still healing today. This argument has a fault, however; if Christ is God and is always the same, then why was He not healing in the centuries before His first coming? ("the first of his miraculous signs, Jesus performed at Cana in Galilee" John 2:11). By this criterion, if we can point to a time when Christ began healing, then He was not always the same. Even in His own life He did not always do miracles, since He began performing miracles only after John baptized Him.

There is also no evidence that Jesus performed healings after His resurrection. In other words, there is no biblical foundation to affirm that Christ has always done and will always do exactly what He did while He walked on earth.

In the context of Hebrews 13, the author contrasts Jesus with the great leaders of the early Church and who apparently no longer existed when Hebrews was written. The use of the past tense in verse 7, "Remember those who rule over you, who have spoken the word of God to you, whose faith follow, considering the outcome of their conduct," [author's italics] indicates that only the memory and the example of those leaders remained.

In contrast to them, Jesus said, "I will never leave thee, nor forsake you" (13:5), so that we can say, "The Lord is my helper" (13:6). The point is that men come and go, but Jesus is always with us. His presence, essence, character and virtue never change. The verse has nothing to do with the continuation of miracles in the churches.

The focus in this section will deal principally with the issue of cessation versus the continuation of the gifts of tongues and other sign gifts. Although they are not directly in focus here, the gifts of miracles and healings will also be examined through much of the evidence contained in this chapter.

The evidence will be divided into five areas with a total of fourteen

Factors. Some of the evidence is clearer and more conclusive than others; the conclusion does not exclusively depend on any one argument, but rather on the accumulated evidence. There is a principle of inductive hermeneutics that permits the formation of a doctrine by the accumulation of biblical evidence when one verse may not teach it comprehensively. The five categories of relationships for the gift of tongues are as follows:

1. The relationship of tongues with God and Israel
2. The relationship of tongues with the foundation of the Church
3. The relationship of tongues with the confirmation of the canon
4. The relationship of tongues with the authentication of the apostles
5. The relationship of tongues with Acts and primitive history

1. The Gift of Tongues in Relation to God and Israel

Before beginning our analysis, it is important to specify our hermeneutics. We interpret the Bible historically, grammatically, linguistically and culturally. This method of interpretation is in opposition to the method of allegorical interpretation, which spiritualizes a text according to the imagination of the interpreter seeking a "deeper" meaning.

There are certain passages that lend themselves to allegory in preaching, but not in the teaching of the text. It is the contention of this writer that a passage will have principally one interpretation with a variety of applications. A passage of Scripture gives a specific teaching in a historical context and in accordance with its grammatical and literary form. To interpret it in another way is a perversion of the text and can lead to error, as we will see.

To illustrate this point lets look at the meaning of the mystery of the Church. Paul says,

> "How that by revelation he made known unto me the mystery...Which in other ages was not made known unto the sons of men, as it is now revealed unto his holy apostles and prophets by the Spirit...And to make all men see what is the fellowship of the mystery, which from the beginning of the world hath been hid in God who created all things by Jesus Christ" (Ephesians 3:3, 5, 9).

These texts make it evident that before the apostle Paul, no one knew about the institution of the Church. When Jesus mentioned it in Matthew 16:18, "I will build My church," people did not understand because they were not anticipating anything different from Judaism. It was only by revelations given by Peter, and especially Paul, that men came to understand the existence and purpose of the Church. Therefore, in the Old Testament, there is no revelation or prophecy about the Church, but the OT prophets saw the period that follows the Church age, that is, the Millennium.

In the Old Testament there were many prophecies about a miraculous era, but if the Church were a mystery, not seen by the prophets —as the Scriptures declare— then those prophecies can be applied only to Israel in the Millennium, not to the Church. Since these prophecies refer historically, grammatically and literally to Israel, we should maintain the same interpretation. Those who teach the Scriptures allegorically want to apply the entire Bible to the Church, but it was not written with that intent, therefore should not be understood with a new perspective not intended. There are three factors in the relationships of miracles to the nation of Israel.

Factor 1: Miracles and signs will be the norm when Christ is on the earth.

When Isaiah wrote his prophecy on the coming of the Messiah, he described the epoch in the following way:

"It shall blossom abundantly and rejoice, Even with joy and singing. The glory of Lebanon shall be given to it, The excellence of Carmel and Sharon. They shall see the glory of the LORD, The excellency of our God. 3 Strengthen the weak hands, And make firm the feeble knees. 4 Say to those who are fearful-hearted, "Be strong, do not fear! Behold, your God will come with vengeance, With the recompense of God; He will come and save you." 5 Then the eyes of the blind shall be opened, And the ears of the deaf shall be unstopped. 6 Then the lame shall leap like a deer, And the tongue of the dumb sing. For waters shall burst forth in the wilderness, And streams in the desert.... No lion shall be there, nor any ravenous beast shall go up thereon" (Isaiah 35:2-6, 9).

The prophecy applies to the geographic area of Israel (Lebanon, Mt. Carmel and Sharon) in a time when God himself will come and healings will be in abundance. The three epochs of miracles that we have studied (Moses, Elias and Jesus) were small, local eruptions of miracles in comparison with the epoch of the Millennium when miracles will occur universally. Though these miracles were on a small scale, the apostles thought they were seeing the anticipated fulfillment of Isaiah 35.

When John's disciples came to Jesus asking if He were the Messiah, Jesus responded: "Go and tell John the things which you hear and see: 5 'The blind see and the lame walk; the lepers are cleansed and the deaf hear; the dead are raised up and the poor have the gospel preached to them.'" (Matthew 11:4-5). Jesus gave them the evidence of Isaiah 35 to prove that He was the Messiah.

Jesus fulfilled only a brief aspect of Isaiah's prophecy, however. His miracles were an introduction or a glimpse of what it will be like when all of Israel will "see the glory of the Lord" and "God will come with vengeance, with the recompense of God." Likewise it is promised to Israel that there will be springs of water bursting forth and new streams in the Negev or desert areas of Israel making them great agricultural farms.

Just as miracles were the norm when Jesus was on Earth, they will also be the norm during His millennial reign, even to a greater degree because it will be universal.

When Peter preached on the Day of Pentecost, he was so filled with expectation of the promises for Israel that he compared the experience of the day of the Feast of Pentecost with the prophecy of Joel 2:28 (Acts 2:16-21).

Those that seek to interpret the Acts passage to mean that Peter was saying that the prophecy of Joel 2 was fulfilled at Pentecost is to make Peter a false prophet. He was not claiming that the prophecy had been fulfilled, because it obviously was not fulfilled, as Luke knew. He was making a comparison and nothing more, because no part of the prophecy was fulfilled!

Joel 2

In the context preceding Joel 2:28-32, the following prophecies had to be fulfilled before the promised out pouring out of the Spirit would occur:

1. Israel will be satisfied with abundant corn, wine and oil produced in the new environment of abundant rain, and they will never again be reproached by the world (verse 19).
2. The enemy army to the north of Israel will be driven away (verse 20; see also Zechariah 14:2; Daniel 11:40; Joel 3:9, 12).
3. The entire earth, animals and fruit will blossom, especially in Israel.
4. There will be an abundance of rain in Israel (verse 23).
5. The chief crops of Israel, wheat, wine and oil, will be in abundance (verse 24).
6. Israel will be permanently restored in abundance and "never more will be ashamed" (verse 26)
7. God will be "in the midst of Israel" (verse 27)

Verse 28 begins with these words: "And it shall come to pass afterward, that I will pour out my spirit upon all flesh." After fulfilling the seven mentioned prophecies, God will pour out His Spirit as described in Joel 2. Before pouring out His Spirit, God will restore the nation of Israel to a position of world supremacy and will change the physical climate of Israel to greatly favor agriculture. None of these things occurred in Acts 2 or in the entire history of the Church. These events are still to come.

The pouring out of the Spirit and the other manifestations of Joel 2:28-32 must occur after these prophecies ("it shall come to pass afterward..."). There will be "wonders in the heavens and in the earth, blood, and fire, and pillars of smoke. The sun shall be turned into darkness, and the moon into blood, before the great and the terrible day of the Lord come" (Joel 2:30-31).

Besides the seven mentioned signs, these visible wonders must occur before the pouring out of the Spirit. This sounds like Revelation 6:12 and 8:12, which describe the days immediately before the Second Advent of Christ at the end of the Tribulation period. Therefore this prophecy will be fulfilled after the Second Coming of Christ, not after His First Coming, since Joel revealed prophecies concerning the beginning of the Millennium.

There is no age of promised miracles prior the Second Coming of Christ. After the Tribulation when Christ returns, all the surviving sons of Israel will become prophets; they will dream dreams and will see visions (Joel 2:28). There will be healings for all illness. It will be a millennium of miracles.

A literal translation of Acts 2:16 is: "But this is the thing that has been said by the prophet Joel." The Greek word translated "the thing" is neutral and refers in general to all the happenings of prophecy. It is natural to wonder why Peter mentioned Joel 2 in Acts 2 since the prophecy was not actually fulfilled. He obviously knew the prophecy because he spontaneously cited the text from memory. We should note that this statement was not included in his message, as it did not begin until Acts 2:22. The reference to Joel 2 was in response to the accusation of being drunk (2:13).

If we take the text to mean what it says, there are two possibilities which explain why Peter referred to Joel 2 on Pentecost are as follows:

(1) Peter may have anticipated the Kingdom to be established immediately. If Israel had repented during the first preaching of the Gospel, then it is possible that God would have established the Kingdom then. Peter's offer of "salvation" (Acts 2:21) is as millennial as it is spiritual (see 3:19-23); all the signs would have been fulfilled if Israel had repented. The concept of the Church was still a mystery at this point in time to the prophets and even to the twelve apostles until it was revealed to the apostle Paul some years later.

(2) Peter may have used the prophecy of Joel 2 to defend his actions against the accusation of being drunk. He is saying that the outpouring of the Spirit and speaking in a different language was not so absurd since the prophet had spoken of such things. Joel said that God would pour out His Spirit, and those who received him would prophesy; that was what happened on the Day of Pentecost. He cited almost the entire context of Joel's prophecy to show that the events in Acts 2 were not the fulfillment of it, but rather to use it to prove that their actions had biblical foundations.

Factor 2: If miracles and signs were for this time, the literal fulfillment of the prophecies would have to be spiritualized (Joel 2).

People tend to spiritualize or allegorize prophecy when, if they accepted certain elements of that prophecy as literal, it would undermine their theology or eschatology. The passage in Joel 2 has often been spiritualized because its literal fulfillment does not fit into the epoch of the Church.

Those who deny the existence of a millennium (amillennialists) have to explain the text in another way; they spiritualize the physical promises made to Israel (harvests, fruit, animals and national supremacy) with the purpose of transforming them into spiritual blessings for the Church (i.e., soul winning, changed lives, prosperity and national recognition). Each physical element

Chapter 14: Fourteen areas of evidence for cessation of Gift of tongues

has a corresponding spiritual element; it all depends on the imagination and creativity of the interpreter.

As an example of spiritualizing or making an allegory, the interpretation of the "early and latter rains" of Joel 2:23 is frequently mentioned in the preaching in Pentecostal churches. They interpret the verse to say that God poured out His Spirit on the Day of Pentecost (the early rains) and later, at the end of the church age, He pours out His Spirit as in the beginning (the latter rains). This interpretation is used to defend the contemporary Charismatic movement, seen as the "latter rains;" however, this teaching is a distortion of the text!

The Latter Rain interpretation began a late 19th century radical Holiness theology, which began in western North Carolina and eastern Tennessee that merged into modern Pentecostalism in the 1920's (Mayer 1961: 308). One of the earliest manifestations of speaking in tongues was in a Baptist revival meeting in 1892 led by Richard Spurling, Jr, in Liberty, Tennessee. Spurling was thrown out of the Baptist church along with 30 other members of the congregation and started meeting in the home of W. F. Bryant nearby (Clark 1949:100-101). They formed the Camp Creek Holiness Church in 1896 and attracted A. J. Tomlinson who became the pastor (Wacker 2003: 248) and changed the name to the Church of God in 1907.

Their influence nationwide motivated the small group of students in Topeka, Kansas under Charles F. Parham, then later the Azusa Street revival under William J. Seymour (Clark 1949: 101) to a similar experience called the "Outpouring of the Latter Rains" (Ibid.). Tomlinson became the General Overseer of the Church of God denomination, but was later expelled for division and strange doctrines (Ibid.).

The Latter Rains movement was revived after WWII by William Branham who led many revival meetings across the country spreading his Latter Rains theology for more than a decade before enthusiasm for these new doctrines began to decrease. The Pentecostal movement backed away from close association, but later the Charismatic movement would embrace much of his Latter Rains theology, which included Joel's Army of the Manifest Sons of God, Gideon's sword, Toronto and Kansas City prophets, Apostolic Reformation movement, the Kingdom Now Theology and Strategic Level Spiritual Warfare doctrines. The imagination and progressive\ revelations continue to feed the thirst for even more spectacular ideas to captivate the gullible public. (For more on this subject see http://www.letusreason.org/latradir.htm).

Meanwhile, the entire context in Joel is speaking of the physical promises for the Promised Land when God is "in the midst of Israel" (Joel 2:27), that is, when Christ, the Messiah, returns, so this has nothing to do with the church.

In addition to Joel, Isaiah (2:15; 44:3) and Ezekiel (11:19; 36:26) also speak of an era of the Spirit, but they speak of the future millennium. How can anyone take literally the part of prophecy that refers to the Spirit while spiritualizing the rest of the passage? We must interpret the Bible with a single hermeneutic methodology to be consistent.

Similarly, it is incorrect to teach something that does not have a biblical basis.

Where in the Bible is the evidence of an outpouring of the Spirit in the last days of the Church? How could Joel speak of an era of the Church age when Paul said that it was a mystery to all of the prophets of the Old Testament? (Eph 3:9NET, "...and to enlighten everyone about God's secret plan--a secret that has been hidden for ages in God who has created all things").

There is also no biblical evidence for the teaching that there will be more signs and wonders at the end of the Church age. The only thing that the Bible says that will occur in the end of the Church age is the increase of false miracles and false prophets (1 Tim 4:1).

The passage in Joel 2 speaks of literal rains in a literal land (Israel). The terms "early" and "latter" refer to the two periods of the rainy season in Israel. The rains begin in the fall ("early rains") and become strong again at the end of the growing season in the spring ("latter rains"). None of the other passages that refer to the latter rains are related to the pouring out of the Spirit or with spiritual gifts. Peter made it clear that Joel's prophecy does not speak about the beginning of the Church Age, but rather about the end of times of the Gentiles, the period after the Tribulation; he refers to it saying, "in the last days" (Acts 2:17).

To interpret these prophecies as applying directly to the Church is to admit other problems. If in Acts 2 Peter is saying—as the allegorists affirm—that the Church Age is "the last days," then there would be no distinction between "early" and "latter" rains; all Church history would be the "latter" rains. The passage does not lend itself to the interpretation that there will be a period of little or no manifestation sandwiched between times of gifts and miracles.

No other dream is mentioned in the New Testament except those given to Joseph in the very beginning of the New Testament, before the complete gospel had been completed on the cross; and to the wife of Pilate, a Gentile (Mt 1:20; 2:13; 27:19). It is never mentioned concerning believers in the churches.

Another problem is the prophecy that the Spirit will be poured out over "all flesh," but today this is seen only among Pentecostals and Charismatics. It is also inconsistent to say that the pouring out of the Spirit applies only to certain gifts, ignoring the gifts of evangelism, teaching, exhortation, mercy, etc. The Bible never says that God would give certain gifts in the first century then permit them to disappear for 1800 years, only to reinstate them again later. Such teachings are the inventions of men.

The equating language that Peter employs ("this is that") stresses an incipient fulfillment of the Joel passage without precluding or minimizing a yet future and more exhaustive fulfillment in events associated with the return of Christ.

Factor 3: If miracles and tongues were signs of judgment against Israel for its unbelief, then they no longer have purpose since Israel was destroyed in 70 A.D. (1 Corinthians 14:21-22).

In 1 Corinthians 14:21-22, "tongues" were a sign for "this people" (14:21), which according to context of the prophecy in Isaiah 28 was written historically

Chapter 14: *Fourteen areas of evidence for cessation of Gift of tongues*

as a judicial sign against Israel. In the same way that Isaiah used unfamiliar languages as the sign to Israel that its impenitence would bring its destruction, Paul also said tongues were a sign for unbelievers, especially unbelieving Jews who understood the meaning of the sign. Origen's testimony to an earlier form in Aquila should not be ignored: "unintelligible tongues will be ineffective in causing 'This people to listen to the Lord' " (Thiselton, 2000: 1124), which was a reference to Gentiles of the early third century.

Paul wrote 1 Corinthians in the year 54 A.D. God had been giving the sign of tongues since 33 A.D. and was going to continue giving it until the Romans destroyed Israel in 70 A.D., just 16 years after 1 Corinthians was written. At the point the nation ceased to exist. The judicial warning was not an idle threat to the nation of Israel.

We know from 1 Corinthians 13:8 that the gift of tongues would disappear at some point; if we also understand that tongues were a sign especially for unbelieving Jews as it was in the OT, then it makes sense that tongues would disappear after Israel's destruction. There would be no reason to continue a sign for an unbelieving nation that had ceased to exist.

Thiselton declares that the "glossolalia is indeed promoted in some circles today as a sign of God's 'power' ministry to reach outsiders as well as authenticate the tongue-speakers" (Thiselton 2000: 1125). One must consider whether the use of tongues as a sign, as described by Isaiah for a judgment warning, should be completely reversed without explanation by the author to mean a positive authentication of contemporary tongues speakers.

Throughout the Old Testament we find that God miraculously intervenes until the moment His intervention becomes unnecessary. For example, in Joshua 5:12 we read, "And the manna ceased on the morrow after they had eaten of the old corn of the land; neither had the children of Israel manna any more; but they did eat of the fruit of the land of Canaan that year." After forty years of providing the manna daily, God stopped providing it because it was no longer needed. God's acts change, and they are not always miraculous; His intervention varies based on the need and the purpose of the signs or wonders. When they have fulfilled their purposes, they cease to exist, never to be repeated. The same conditions occurred with just about every miracle in the OT. That is what happened with the gift of tongues; now it has no purpose since the destruction of Jerusalem in 70 A.D.

2. Tongues in Relation to the Foundation of the Church

In the second category of evidence with respect to the cessation of the gift of tongues, we will examine its relationship with the foundation of the church. In 1 Corinthians 13, the gift of tongues is related to the gifts of knowledge and prophecy, which were directly responsible for the foundation of the church. It seems there was also an association among the three gifts. The church of Corinth is the only church where the practice of speaking in tongues is recorded, but it is possible there were others. What was its purpose of tongues in the churches? Are there more indications the gift of tongues was temporary? The answers to these questions are found in 1 Corinthians 13 and 14.

Factor 4: The gift of tongues is related to the period of the infancy of the Church, and it ceased when the Church matured

In the text of 1 Corinthians 13:8-11, Paul is comparing several transitory gifts to the permanence of love. The gifts listed in this passage that were never meant to be permanent in the church were knowledge, tongues and prophecy. Paul wrote, "But if there are prophecies, they will be set aside; if there are tongues, they will cease; if there is knowledge, it will be set aside (1Co 13:8 NET)." The logical question to ask is, when? In the chapter, Paul used temporal relative pronouns ten times to convey some element of time, e.g. "when, now, then," Therefore, the passage was written to show some indicators of the time of the termination of the three gifts.

In 13:8-12 there are three illustrations, all of which indicate something about the time when certain gifts would disappear. Paul was looking toward the future when he wrote this chapter (forty years before John wrote the last verses of the NT), and we must put ourselves in Paul's place at that time in order to interpret the passage accurately.

When he wrote this letter, just three or four New Testament books had been written, which represent only a small portion of the total revelation in the New Testament. For this reason, Paul felt like a child, lacking full understanding. At the same time, Paul wanted to see the child (the infancy of the church) become a man (the maturity as the body of Christ).

In his argument, Paul compares the stages of his own childhood to the development of the church at that time. The illustration is of a child who became a man. To a Jew, this indicates the *bar mitzvah* ("son of the law"), which marks the change from childhood to adulthood. Though he does not become a fully mature adult in every sense, he is no longer considered a child and begins to carry the responsibilities of a man.

Paul's testimony of his transition to maturity is used to represent the functioning of the body of Christ. The development of the "child" is the development of the church from a state of immaturity and dependency to a relative and progressive maturity. Just as the transition from childhood to maturity occurred early in Paul's early life, the same happened in the life of the church. At twelve years old a Jewish child was considered to be a man, even though he had to learn and grown in many more ways. Essentially, for both a growing child and the growing church, maturity is not absolute but relative.

Paul uses the analogy of his own upbringing to picture the church growing from immaturity to adulthood. The word "child" (*nepios*, "infants, metaphorically, simple, immature, inexperienced"- Friberg Lexicon 2000: 18993) was used earlier, "I, brethren, could not speak to you as to spiritual people but as to carnal, as to babes in Christ." (1Co 3:1 NKJ) Now Paul makes a similar contrast to the goal of spiritual maturity of the whole church.

The verbs (speak, think and reason) used to describe the characteristics of the immature stage of the church age are all in the imperfect tenses meaning a continuous past action in a process of growing: "I used to talk like a child."

The second verb, to think, (*phroneo*) is not a reference to intelligence, but rather the idea "to form or hold an opinion or "set one's mind upon, which here would denote having childish interests and concerns. ... the most probably candidate seems to be 'I used to form opinions like a child.' (Thiselton 2000: 1066–1067).

The third characteristic, "I used to think as a child" (*logizomai*, "reckon or a thing is reckoned as or to be something," Strong 1988: 3049). Children consider their imagination to be real and are impressed with fantasies and myths. The conclusion of process, "when I became a man" uses the perfect active which means a completed action, "reached adulthood" with no going back.

The verb phrase "put away" in verse 11 ties this illustration of maturity with the rest of the context, because it is the same verb *katargeo* ("finish, leave") found in verses 8, 10 and 12. It means, "to render idle, inactive, inoperative, cause a thing to have no further efficiency, deprive of force, influence, power" (Thayer 1889: 2824).

When that goal is reached ("the perfect or completion" is reached) "I put away childish things," which translates *katargeo*, "to make ineffective, render inoperative, abolish, or wipe out" with the intensive *kata-* added to the verb, thus the perfect tense meaning is definitive and forceful.

Different translations try to capture this action: NRSV, "put an end to;" but Moffatt's version seems closer: "I am done with childish ways;" or Collins's, "I abandoned childish ways."

Therefore, the way the church spoke, thought, and judged would be changed for a more mature and complete way. It is possible that these three verbs are parallel to the three gifts in verse 8, since the same verb is used with the same emphasis: something immature or incomplete is changed for something mature and complete. Therefore, the church transitioned from childhood to maturity simultaneously when prophecy and knowledge made way for the fruits they produced.

Joseph Dillow marks certain steps of maturity that illuminate this passage. A child becomes a man when he is independent; he becomes mature when he leaves his home and can sustain himself without his parents' help (see Genesis 2:24; Matthew 19:5.)

In the same way, Christianity developed from Judaism; in a sense, Judaism was like the parent of the church in its infancy, since it was completely identified with Israel in the beginning (for the first 20 years at least). For a long time the church was practically Jewish; until Acts 11:19, evangelism was done exclusively by Jews reaching other Jews, with very few exceptions.

Between the years 32 and 70 A.D., the church was considered a sect or denomination of Judaism and did not gain complete independence from Israel until the Romans destroyed the nation in 70 AD. At that point the church continued growing independently, and the believers no longer met in the synagogues or depended on Jewish leadership. (Dillow 1975: n.a.).

Another characteristic of maturity is reached when one attains a certain level of understanding. A child becomes a man when he has understood the things necessary to function as an adult.

In 1 Corinthians 14:20, Paul calls the believers to be mature and stop being like children in their "understanding." The specific problem was they did not understand the purpose of the gift of tongues; they would become more mature if they could learn to understand all that Paul was revealing about the gift of tongues. The maturity that Paul desired for them was the knowledge of the Word of God, and he specifically desired that they understand that the gift of tongues was a sign to Israel before God destroyed their nation.

Essentially, when the church acquired its independence from Israel and apostolic leadership, acquiring the necessary understanding of God's will and Word, it passed from childhood to a relative maturity. After this time, it had to continue growing in its dependence on God and the application of the complete revelation of His instructions given in the Word.

The illustration in 13:11 indicates that the childish elements of communication (speaking, understanding, and thinking) were going to be changed by something so superior and complete that it would produce spiritual maturity, and the former elements would be eliminated for lack of use.

Factor 5: The gifts of tongues, prophecy and knowledge are associated with the foundation of the Church.

At the beginning of the Church, the gifts of knowledge and prophecy were the media for transmitting the Word of God. Once the divine revelation had been given, those media elements became unnecessary and were annulled (13:8), since there was nothing more of the Word of God to reveal. One of the last verses of the Bible even prohibits the addition of more prophecies. In Revelation 22:18 we read, "I warn everyone who hears the words of the prophecy of this book: If anyone adds anything to them, God will add to him the plagues described in this book."

The severe warning declared by the Lord Jesus against pretending to have received a revelation after the close of the Book of Revelation says that the person is deceiving himself and others, and bringing upon himself the plagues of the Book of Revelation. No one has claimed divine inspiration or inspired, infallible revelations from God since this day, except false prophets, false religions and cults (i.e. Montanists attempted continued revelations in the early church).

During the second awakening (1790-1840) a passion for the supernatural of the early church was eulogized and revelations were sought, while seeking to return to the primitive age of the childhood of the church. Spontaneous "revelations" were encouraged, prophetic enthusiasts gave seed for Joseph Smith, Mary Baker Eddy, Shakers and other false prophets who attempted to

Chapter 14: *Fourteen areas of evidence for cessation of Gift of tongues*

claim divine revelations and the prophetic gift. Most movements that seek to restore prophetic revelations to the church generally deviate from the truths of Scripture.

Since prophecies spring from the gift of prophecy, it will be difficult to prove from Scripture that the Spirit is continuing to give additional revelations after the warning of Rev 22:18 where any additional revelations are not coming from the Spirit. No one who respects God's Word would think of adding to the finality of Rev 22.

If there are no more revelations from God, then the gift of prophecy is null. Even though the gift of knowledge is not mentioned in the New Testament apart from Corinthians 12 and 13, by implication it is always tied to that of prophecy; so, when one terminated, the other did also.

In 1 Corinthians 13:8, the gift of tongues is associated with the gifts of knowledge and prophecy. It seems that the termination of one of the gifts should coincide with that of the others since they are all declared to cease in the same verse (13:8).

Apostles

Of the gifts associated with the prophets, the gift of apostleship has more evidence in the New Testament and defines the happenings in the early Church, since there are descriptions of the qualifications and procedures to become an Apostle (Acts 1). What applies to the apostles also applies to the prophets, and, by implication, whatever applies to the prophets also applies to those with the gift of tongues. The NT has a number of warnings about false prophets (Matt 7:15; 24:11,24; Luke 6:26; 2 Pet 2:1; 1 Jn 4:1) and false apostles (2 Cor 11:13). We must compare Scriptures with clearer meanings to those that are not as clear in order to understand their application.

In Ephesians 2:20-21 we read, "having been built on the foundation of the apostles and prophets, Jesus Christ Himself being the chief cornerstone; in whom the whole building, being joined together, grows into a holy temple in the Lord." Some interpret this passage to say that the apostles and prophets built the foundations of the Church and continue to amplify it through the missionary task by starting new churches in new regions.

The grammar of the phrase "foundation of the apostles and prophets," is in the genitive case in the Greek, thus indicates content, possession or relationship. Here it means apposition (two elements placed side by side, with one element serving to define the other). The literal translation would be something like, "the foundation that is the apostles and prophets." Just as Jesus Christ is the cornerstone, so the apostles and prophets are in apposition to the foundation, which means they are the same thing. The apostles and prophets did not found the Church; they are the foundation of the Church.

Paul describes the Church as a building made up of people. The cornerstone is Jesus Christ; it is evident that the building refers to other believers, that is, the Church. Paul uses the second person plural, "you are," when he refers to the building, as if he were part of a different aspect of the Church. This suggests further that the foundation is made up of the apostles and prophets. Since there is no need for more cornerstones, there is also no need for any other foundation for the Church. The Church is the beneficiary of the redemptive work of Jesus and of the inspired work of the apostles and prophets. The cornerstone and the foundation remain fixed and the only thing that continues to "grow" is the building (Ephesians 2:21).

In the context of Ephesians, the term "church" is not a local church, but rather the universal Church made up of both the Jews and the Gentiles in the united body of Christ (Ephesians 3:15 "from whom his whole family in heaven and on earth derives its name").

Through the church, the Gentiles became part of the "family of God." The believers in Ephesus were part of the "building" that had been constructed on the existing foundation of the apostles. The word "built" (*epoikodomethentes*) is an aorist passive participle, which indicates that the foundation had already been established before the building was constructed on it, just as with any other building construction. You cannot build the building until the foundation is carefully finalized. This is what the apostles and prophets accomplished.

Paul suggested that apostles would exist only for a limited amount of time in 1 Corinthians 4:9, "For it seems to me that God has put us apostles on display at the end of the procession, like men condemned to die in the arena." The apostles were not spread throughout the procession or the church, but would be martyred during the founding of the church. There is not indication that there would be additional apostles to replace the original group.

Paul described his participation in the apostleship when he described it as a limited group, which he was the last to join. In 1 Corinthians 15:8, he writes, "Last of all, as though I had been born at the wrong time, I also saw him." Paul describes his election as an apostle in the following terms:

(1) He was the "last of all" the apostles. The word implies a temporary aspect. In other words, in relation to the moment of his election to the apostleship, he was the last one to be put in that position. There were no more apostles after Paul.

(2) He was "born at the wrong time." This does not refer to the way in which Jesus appeared to Paul, but to the time of His appearing to Paul. The selection of Paul was somewhat abnormal, since it was out of the sequence with respect to the choosing of the other apostles. Many believers doubted Paul's authority because he was not one of the original Twelve.

Paul saw Jesus and received instruction and authority from Him after His resurrection for three years. Galatians 1:17-18, "nor did I go up to Jerusalem to see those who were apostles before me, but right away I departed to Arabia, and then returned to Damascus. Then after three years, I went up to Jerusalem to get acquainted with Peter and stayed with him fifteen days." From knowing nothing about Christ to being the leading authority in the foundation of the church, Paul had been taught directly by Jesus. He makes reference to this personal post-resurrection teaching in 1 Corinthians 11:23, "For I received

Chapter 14: *Fourteen areas of evidence for cessation of Gift of tongues*

from the Lord what I also passed on to you..." No one else received this kind of special instruction, only the apostles who were laying the foundation of the church for us today.

This foundation is evident in the history of the early church. In Acts 2:42 the church persevered in "the doctrine of the apostles," not what God was revealing to the whole church. Likewise, the supremacy of the authority of the apostles is seen in 1 Corinthians 14:37, in which Paul asserts his authority: "If anyone considers himself a prophet or spiritual person, he should acknowledge that what I write to you is the Lord's command." In other words, the prophets were to be subordinate to the apostles' teaching in the revelation of the Word, and they had to be submissive to the Word given by the Spirit to the apostles.

In addition to being the foundation of the church, Christ gave the apostles special authority to confirm the message of salvation once and for all for the church. In Hebrews 2:3-4 we see that Jesus announced the message to His followers and those that heard Jesus' message received the authority to confirm that message with "signs and wonders and diverse miracles." That ministry of miraculous "confirmation" was part of the foundation of the church.

Today we still depend on the confirmation made by the apostles in the first century. The only difference is that now we accept by faith the written evidence in the Bible without needing more foundation laying, or more revelation or confirmation. The existing apostolic evidence is sufficient for us to trust or believe to this day.

To believe that miracles are still needed to confirm the message would be to discredit the written evidence God gave us. The essence of 2 Corinthians 5:7, "For we walk by faith, not by sight," says that it is not necessary to continually reconfirm something that has already been confirmed. We can accept the apostolic evidence now by faith. Just as in a court of law, further proof is no longer needed once something has been proven. In the same way, the confirmation of the apostles does not have to be repeated, but rather accepted as sufficient evidence for individual faith. As Romans 10:17 says, genuine faith is born from confidence in the Word: "So then faith cometh by hearing, and hearing by the word of God." True faith does not need miracles, but rather understanding and confidence in God's Word.

Thus, the foundation of the Church was formed at the beginning of the church age, and when the apostles completed their work, the process of laying the foundation did not continue. As the apostles finished their task, so did the prophets, because if the gift of apostleship ceased, then the related gifts of prophecy, knowledge, and the confirming gifts of miracles and tongues ceased also.

Factor 6: The gift of tongues was an inferior gift even in the foundation of the church.

We can see that the gift of tongues was an inferior gift, thus its continuance was unnecessary. 1 Corinthians 12:28 lists five categories of gifts, in decreasing order of significance and emphasis; the gift of tongues fell in the fifth category. In fact, the principle purpose of 1 Corinthians 14 is to demonstrate the superiority of prophecy over the gift of tongues for use in the Church. The gift of tongues was inferior in the following three aspects:

1. It was inferior as a means of communicating the Truth.

In 1 Corinthians 14, Paul named at least four reasons why the gift of tongues is inferior as a means of communication:

(1) In 1 Corinthians 14:2, Paul writes, "For the one speaking in a tongue does not speak to people but to God, for no one understands; he is speaking mysteries by the Spirit," that is, he doesn't even attempt to speak to people, but in his mind he thinks he is speaking to God. This means that even the speaker of a tongue doesn't seek to communicate to or serve people.
(2) In 14:6, he says, "if I come to you speaking in tongues, how will I help you…?" with the implied answer, "it is absolutely no benefit to the hearer."
(3) He describes it in 14:9 as, "You will just be speaking into the air."
(4) In 14:14, he says "my mind (or understanding) is unfruitful." The gift of tongues is beneficial only when there is an interpreter present, whether in his natural tongue or through the gift of interpretation. The gift of tongues is so inefficient that without interpretation it is prohibited in the church (14:28). Therefore, if it does not serve as a way to communicate to anyone, then it is an inferior gift; it is impossible to edify others without communicating understanding (14:17, 19). It cannot be forgotten in this context that all the gifts must be exercised in love, that is, for the benefit of others.

2. It is inferior as a means of adoration, prayer and praise.

Paul declares this inferiority in 1 Corinthians 14:14-15, "If I pray in a tongue, my spirit prays, but my mind is unproductive. What should I do? I will pray with my spirit, but I will also pray with my mind. I will sing praises with my spirit, but I will also sing praises with my mind."

In the hypothetical example of attempting to pray or worship in song in a tongue, Paul perhaps wanted to communicate his "spirit" or feelings in prayer, but his mind or "understanding" was not associated with it. In order to pray effectively, Paul's entire person and understanding must be functioning. Isaiah 29:13 says it is impossible to pray and praise God without complete understanding, saying, "The Lord says: "These people come near to me with their mouth and honor me with their lips, but their hearts are far from me." In other words, if our minds are not functioning as we pray and praise God, then our actions are worthless. For this reason, Paul said: "I will pray with my spirit, but I will also pray with my mind. I will sing praises with my spirit, but I will also sing praises with my mind."

Chapter 14: Fourteen areas of evidence for cessation of Gift of tongues

Some say the expression, "praying always with all prayer and supplication in the Spirit, being watchful to this end with all perseverance and supplication for all the saints" (Eph 6:18 NKJ), is equivalent to praying in an unknown tongue. The problem with this view is that it implies any prayers spoken in a known tongue would be without or apart from the Spirit, yet Paul said that he prayed "with the spirit but also with understanding" (14:15). This is not a mystery language to Paul or utterances that he does not understand, since he is making specific "requests."

In other words, praying in a language and praying with self-control and understanding are not separate actions; he wanted his spirit and his mind to function simultaneously. Unless one speaks in a known tongue, both the mind and spirit cannot be involved. We should note that Paul never said that he prayed in an unknown tongue; therefore his proposal in 14:14 is simply a hypothetical circumstance. He did say, "I thank God that I speak in tongues more than all of you," (14:18), however; Paul spoke—not prayed—in other languages as a sign to the Jews (14:21).

The "spirit" of man is not mystical or unconscious. In 1 Corinthians 2:11, "For who among men knows the things of a man except the man's spirit within him? So too, no one knows the things of God except the Spirit of God." The way a man "knows" things is through his spirit. The way that men understand men is in their active spirit where intuition, perception and notions are part of the communication process.

Therefore the understanding (mental cognition) and the spirit of man are not two incompatible things; in fact, they are inseparable. They are expressions of the mind, the psychology of man, and his intelligence. The function of the spirit is to understand. It can sense the understanding from another human spirit. 1 Corinthians 2 is demonstrating that the unsaved man cannot understand God because he does not share the same Spirit.

Having contact with the Spirit of God is not a mystical experience; instead, it allows true understanding of God and His Word, which is communicated to our minds.

Paul continues, "So too, no one knows the things of God except the Spirit of God" (1 Cor 2:11 NET). In other words, the Spirit illuminates our understanding of God and His Word. If there is no understanding, then it is evident that the Holy Spirit is not working in our spirit to give us understanding.

Paul concluded his argument saying that he never prayed "in his spirit" without understanding (14:15). From this we can deduce that Paul never prayed in an unknown tongue, because he says he did not want his "understanding to be unfruitful" (14:14). It would have been a waste of time.

We know that in the ancient world many pagan devotees lost control of themselves in the worship of Diana in Corinth and spoke in ecstatic or "mystical" languages. This concept of a mystical or mystery language finds its origin in pagan religions of the first century.

Worship

The truth is that the spiritual gifts are not for worship. The idea that worship necessitates a certain gift would be inconsistent with other teachings. Paul had established the fact that no gift is common among all believers (1 Corinthians 12). Everyone has different gifts or combinations of gifts.

In addition, Paul said that the objective and the function of all the gifts was for the "edification of the church" (1 Corinthians 14:12). The first commandment with respect to the gifts is, "Everything must be done so that the church may be built up" (1Co 14:26 NIV). Therefore, all manifestation of the gifts must be for the edification of others.

This edification can provoke worship, but it is not directly the objective of the function of the gifts. In his argument, Paul shows that prayer can and does accomplish the objective of edifying, but it does not happen if the prayer is done in an unknown tongue. He says, "Otherwise, if you bless with the spirit, how will he who occupies the place of the uninformed say 'Amen' at your giving of thanks, since he does not understand what you say? For you indeed give thanks well, but the other is not edified." (1Cor 14:16-17 NKJ). Paul declared that the same person "remains without fruit," that is without any benefit (14:14) and "the other is not edified" (14:17). It is clear, therefore, that unknown tongues are not useful in prayer, worship or praise.

Think of this hypothetical situation: God wants to speak through the blank mind of a believer who has no idea what God wants to say or is saying through him. In the event that there is no interpreter then the tongue speaker is to "speak to God" in a language he does not understand. In essence this means that God is speaking back to Himself through the blank mind of a believer in a language that only God understands. Why would God ever need to do this? How could this unintelligible conversation of God speaking back to Himself have any effect on the vessel of the tongue speaker who is totally ignorant of anything that is being said? Does this make any sense?

3. It is inferior as a means of evangelism.

In 1 Corinthians 14:23, we see that the manifestation of tongues often results in the rejection of the message, even if everyone is speaking in tongues. If a gift is effective in evangelism, then we can conclude that the results will be greater effectiveness the more tongues is practiced. This is not the case with tongues, however; Paul argues that a universal manifestation of tongues would cause unbelievers to think that everyone was "crazy." The term, *mainomai*, refers to being out of control, out of your mind, or insane. If everyone is speaking a strange unknown language then 1) nothing is communicated for any intelligent basis of faith and 2) the respect for the speakers is totally destroyed.

In Acts 2 the crowd divided with respect to their response to hearing the tongues which were spoken. Some of the Jews marveled that the disciples of Galilee were speaking miraculously in foreign languages that they recognized from their countries of origin. The Hellenized Jews came from throughout the Roman Empire where these languages were spoken.

    The Hebrew Jews from Jerusalem made fun of the disciples because they thought they were "filled with wine" (Acts 2:13), since they did not understand anything that was spoken. As we have shown, one group probably understood their speech (16 different languages were identified) and the others from Israel could not understand anything, in fact, did not understand it to even be a language, but rather drunken slurs. Because the latter group, the Hebrews, did not understand the genuine languages, they rejected the idea of a miracle language. This is further proof that simply seeing a miracle convinces no one. Understanding the message is what convinced the unbelieving Hellenist Jews. As Peter says, "You have been born anew, not from perishable but from imperishable seed, through the living and enduring word of God." (1Pet 1:23 NET)

    As we have said, the gift of tongues was a sign for unbelievers and in particular unbelieving Jews. If a Jew heard his native tongue spoken by a foreigner who had no prior knowledge of the language, then his understanding of the prophecy of Israel's impending judgment could convince him that the message was true.

    A Gentile, on the other hand, would miss the significance and reject the speaker as "crazy." On the day of Pentecost, it was not the speaking in tongues that brought any conversions, but rather, the clearly understood preaching of Peter that brought conviction and conversion. Therefore, in general, speaking in tongues is not an effective means of evangelism.

    In the same context, Paul presents the other extreme of the exaggeration of the gift of prophecy, saying that, if all prophesied (an equally impossible manifestation according to 1 Cor 12:29), then the unbeliever would be convicted and would convert. Prophecy is much more effective in evangelism than a manifestation of tongues. Thus today we preach the revealed Word of God. For this reason, prophecy was to be emphasized over speaking in tongues.

Chapter 14 : *Gifts for Today*

CHAPTER 15

Tongues in Relation to the Confirmation of the Canon

In 1 Corinthians 13, the apostle Paul shows that spiritual gifts have to be exercised with an attitude of love, that is, seeking the benefit of others. The argument also shows that no gift is worth anything isolated from other people and exercised for their benefit. In addition, no gift is more important simply because it is more miraculous. These three gifts (prophecy, knowledge and tongues, along with some associated gifts) had to cease at some time because the text declares that they will ("they will cease"- 1 Cor 13:8). Charismatics maintain that all the gifts are fully in operation today and defend this position as though the credibility of the gospel and God's Word depend upon the validity today. Their special focus is on the revelatory or confirmation gifts of tongues, healing, word of wisdom, word of knowledge, prophecy and miracles. Robert Dean describes the "successful" aggressive attacks against those who hold to an early ceasing of the revelatory gifts:

> In the 1960s and 70s, charismatic defenders launched an effective counter-attack against the cessationist position utilizing the big lie technique of Goebbels—anything stated loudly enough and repeatedly will eventually become accepted as true despite the facts. The noncessationists continuously asserted that the "perfect" in 1 Corinthians 13:8 could not possibly refer to the canon of Scripture, yet later it became academically embarrassing to make such an assertion.
> This assault had become so effective that by the end of the century Richard Gaffin constructs his entire cessationist case without a single appeal to 1 Corinthians 13:8, for which he is lauded by Robert Saucy. (Dean 2005: 65)

Cessationists contend that the sign and revelatory gifts have not functioned in the church since the close of the apostolic age, leaving the church with only the edificatory gifts to build upon. Cleon Rogers' research on the Church Fathers (A.D. 100 to 400) concluded, "it is significant that the gift is nowhere alluded to, hinted at, or found in the Apostolic Fathers. (Rogers 1965: 133.)

One of the key issues is the timing of the ceasing of the gifts of prophecy, knowledge and tongues when "that which is perfect is come" (1 Cor 13:10). If the "perfect" refers to the glorious return of Christ, the coming kingdom or eternal state, then all of the gifts have never ceased. If the coming "perfect" refers to an event already past then these three gifts must have already ceased to function. What evidence indicates the time and the reasons for their cessation?

Factor 7: The gift of tongues would terminate before the coming of "that which is perfect"

1 Corinthians 13:10 "but when what is perfect comes, the partial will be set aside."

All exegetes agree that tongues, prophecies and knowledge were not meant for permanent use. In the context of the spiritual gifts Paul has demonstrated a balanced approach to the gifts without a focus on any one gift and the priority of benefiting others with the exercise of the gifts. Now he declares that some gifts he was exercising or witnessing would not be permanent implying that their purpose was temporary and when fulfilled they would cease. There are primarily two positions on the issue:

1. **Eschaton view:** The "perfect refers to a future time when an ideal, flawless, sinless Person or state is established on earth. This position takes the time or temporal indicators in the context as "now" referring to on earth, and the "then" to the end times presence of the Lord.
2. **Canonical or Completeness view**: The perfect refers to something that completed what had already existed in part. This view holds that the completion of the New Testament canon completed the function of the partial revelatory gifts ("in part") in 1 Cor 13:8-12. The temporal indicators "now" refer to the apostolic (pre-canonical) time and the "then" refers to the post apostolic (post canonical) period until the modern era.

Other views include the maturity of the church (Robert L. Thomas), meaning the independence and unity of the church attained by the application of the revealed biblical text to the church.

The context of the issue

Divisions were rampant in the church at Corinth (1 Cor 1-4), which is the issue addressed in chapters 12-14 where the misuse of the gifts was dividing the church. The primary issue was the exaggerated focus on the gift of tongues, which motivated Paul to write chapter 14, where ten reasons are given for its inferiority as a means of edification and ten rules for its manifestation.

Sandwiched between chapters 12 and 14 which give the proper perspective on the gifts, is chapter 13, sometimes called the "love chapter." This is not a description of "love" but a list of what love does. Paul is seeking to demonstrate that the gifts are to be exercised in an attitude of love rather than a selfish, elitism and divisiveness that was producing division in the Corinthian church (1 Cor 4:6, 18). Stanley D. Toussaint divides the chapter into three parts: the necessity of love (verses 1-3), the nature of love (verses 4-7) and the endurance of love (verses 8-13) (Troussaint 1963: 311).

The focus on love is set in contrast to the temporality of the revelatory gifts (vv. 8-10). Paul then illustrates the cessation of the revelatory gifts as a transition from an immature state to maturity (v. 11) and for limited sight to full sight (v. 12). Finally, Paul makes a the contrast of the triad of faith, hope, and love that will exist until Christ returns (v. 13a) with love alone remaining forever (v. 13b). Since faith will be replaced by sight at the coming of Christ (2 Cor 5:7) and hope will be realized as well at His coming (Rom 8:24) these virtues are not seen as permanent either. Love, however, will never end (v. 8a), thus is the greatest because it will last forever. (Thomas 1974: 84).

The text itself

The principle text on the theme is 1 Corinthians 13:8-13. The following is an outline of the grammatical structure of the passage with certain emphases added.

Definition	**Verse**	**Text**
Reason for the priority	1:8	Love never fails
Contrast to the false priority	1:8	**BUT** whether there are prophecies will fail; Whether there are tongues will cease; Whether there is knowledge, it will vanish away.
Principle of replacement	1:9	**BECAUSE** we know *in part* and we prophecy *in part*
	1:10	**BUT WHEN** that which is **perfect** has come **THEN** that which is in part will be done away.
Illustration 1 of principle	1:11	**WHEN** I was a child, I spoke as a child, I understood as a child I thought as a child **BUT WHEN** I became a man, I put away childish things.
Illustration 2 of principle	1:12	**NOW** we see in a mirror, dimly **BUT THEN** face to face. **NOW** I know in part **BUT THEN** shall I know just as I also am known.
Amplified priority	1:13	**AND NOW** abide faith, hope, love, these three; **BUT** the greatest of these is love.

Paul says that prophecies and knowledge will cease sometime in the future from the perspective of Paul's writing from Ephesus somewhere around 53 to 57 AD. We will examine the two views referred to above looking at their strengths and weaknesses.

Eschaton views

The Eschaton view interprets *teleion*, "perfect" in 1 Cor 13:10 as something absolute, ideal, unblemished or flawless. This becomes a qualitative meaning as derived from the English dictionary definition. Most of the adherents of this view see the fulfillment as being events around the second coming of Christ. The time is described as when "partial knowledge conveyed by the word of knowledge will be replaced by perfect knowledge; partial insight into God's wisdom through prophecy will be replaced by a face to face audience with Christ." (Thomas 1974: 83).

Criswell has enumerated the following five views in The Believer's Study Bible, other author noted give broader explanation of these views:

1) The perfect arrives when the believer dies and is brought into the presence of God (Edgar 1983: 333-344).
2) The perfect is the rapture of the church (Toussaint, 312-314).
3) The perfect arrives at Christ's second advent. (Johnson 1971: 633; Ryrie 1978: 1744, but he suggest the canon view in Balancing the Christian Life).
4) The perfect uses the general category of the end times as "Eschaton" to define the arrival of the perfect (Fee 1987: 645).
5) The perfect represents the eternal state as the arrival of the "perfect" (Morris 1958, p. 187; MacArthur 1992: 231). The phrase "face to face" in 1 Cor 13:10 and in Rev 22:4 seem to describe the believer's face to face relationship with God and it fits better with the neuter form of "the perfect."

Proponents of the Eschaton view also note that verse 12 further clarifies the time when the perfect comes. Grudem observes, "The word 'then' (Gk. tote) in verse 12 refers to the time 'when the perfect comes' in verse 10."(Grudem 1994: 1033) The phrase face to face of verse 12 coupled with the notion of knowing fully furnishes the weightiest evidence favoring the Eschaton view. (Thomas 1974: 83)

The Eschaton interpretations take the phrase "that which is perfect" as an absolute, that is to say, "perfection" or "the perfect," to refer in some way to Christ. The two phrases, seeing "face to face" and then "knowing fully" in verse 12 seem to describe the second coming or the *Parousia*. For these reasons the Eschaton view of *teleion* as the ideal condition after the second coming is the dominant view among commentators. (Ibid.).

Weaknesses of this view

Unfortunately, the strengths of this view are outweighed by its numerous problems. There are certain problems with all of these positions that deserve our study.

Problem 1: Paul never used the word "perfect," in the absolute sense of perfection (as defined as the absence of imperfection). (Delling 1972: 8:75–77).

The word "perfect" is *teleios*, which originally meant "goal, end of a development, fulfillment of a process." It refers to "totality, as opposed to partial or limited, that is, the opposite of this term is something partial or incomplete. It means 'things in full measure, undivided, complete, entire'" (Friberg Analytical Lexicon). The opposite is not something imperfect or sinful, but rather something that is incomplete or partial. In the LXX it is used 30 times and translated "the termination of a process," as in Ezra 9:1 where it means "done." In the New Testament, the word means "mature, adult." Six times *teleo*, the verb form of *teleios*, means "finish, or to be finished."

Therefore, if the meaning of *teleios* is relative, then the best interpretation of the coming of "that which is perfect" is the culmination of a process of gradual revelation, or "having attained the end or purpose, complete" (Bauer 2000), s.v. *teleios*).

Problem 2: The concept of qualitative perfection is lacking in the New Testament

The idea of utopian perfection was a philosophical rather than a New Testament concept (Ibid., 8:69-72). The relative sense is evident in Philippians 3:15, where Paul included himself when saying, "Let us therefore, as many as be perfect (*teleios*)..." Earlier he says, "Not as though I had already attained (in the absolute sense); either were already perfect (*teleios*): but I follow after" (Phil 3:12). In other words, Paul is saying that he was perfect (relatively), but he had not completed the total process of perfection, yet he considered himself to be mature (*teleios*).

Similarly, in Ephesians 4:13 he writes, "until we all reach unity in the faith and in the knowledge of the Son of God and become mature (*teleios*), attaining to the whole measure of the fullness of Christ..." (NIV). The "mature" man is contrasted to "children, tossed to and fro" (4:14), to show the emphasis on maturity in the context. The image of maturity (*teleios*) is in the sense of being obedient to God's commands.

This also conveys the relative use of perfect, or the idea of terminating a process or reaching a goal of being "complete" (Rom 12:2). Other uses of the term that indicate maturity or relative perfection can be found in Mathew 5:48 and 19:21; 1 Corinthians 2:6 and 14:20; Colossians 1:28 and 4:12; Hebrews 5:14; James 1:4 and 3:2; and 1 John 4:18.

Problem 3: The NT never uses *teleios* for the various eschatological events that the Eschaton view advocates typically for this word.

Is there any evidence that this word is ever used in an eschatological sense? Gromacki declared that *teleios* "never refers to the Second Coming, millennium or the eternal state" (Gromacki 1977: 123).

Problem 4: The Eschaton view fails to give an antithesis to "that which is in part" (*ek merous* with *to teleion* in 1 Cor 13:9-10).

In the context of 1 Corinthians 13, "that which is perfect" is the complement or goal of "that which is in part" (13:9-10). All prophets and even apostles were limited in the scope of their revelation, because they could reveal only a part or portion of the complete Word of God; the phrase "in part" limited the gift of revelation until "that which is perfect" came.

Ek merous is a quantitative phrase. It denotes the gifts' partial nature rather than their imperfection in quality. Thus, rendering *teleion* in verse 10 as "ideal," "flawless," or "unblemished" does not provide an appropriate opposite to the quantitative phrase *ek merous*. It is appropriate to contrast two qualitative phrases or two quantitative phrases, but not a quantitative phrase with a qualitative phrase (Woods 2004: 9).

As we have shown, the word "perfect" means the termination of a process or development thus can mean maturity or completion. The natural interpretation is that the prophets were giving the Word "in part," or little by little. At an appointed time all that God wanted to reveal to the Church would be completed and "that which is perfect" would be realized. If we were to interpret "that which is perfect" as the second coming or the eternal state, then it would have no direct relation to that which is "in part," referring to the progressive giving of prophecies and knowledge.

Problem 5: The Eschaton view of *teleion* would be unnatural with the illustration of this concept in verse 11.

"When I was a child, I spoke as a child, I understood as a child, I thought as a child; but when I became a man, I put away childish things." (1Co 13:11 NKJ)

Paul frequently referred to his imperfections in his adult stage. (Thomas 1998: 213) He refers to himself as the chief of sinners (1 Tim 1:15) and the least of the apostles (1 Cor 15:9). "Paul saw himself as being caught between the "already" of his initial soteriological benefits and the "not yet" of his future glorification, he recognized his own imperfections in his present adult state." (Woods 2004: 10). The comparison with Paul as a mature man and the Eschaton perfect state is hardly analogous.

Problem 6: The Eschaton view sees the church's transition from immaturity to maturity as something instantaneous at some eschatological event in the future (i.e., rapture, millennium, Second Coming, eternity).

The context describes the *teleios* as the passing of the partial things in a gradual process or transition. (Farnell 1993: 193). Woods gives two reasons for the passing of the partial things as a gradual process extending over a period of time. (Woods 2004: 10).

First, Paul uses the perfect tense of the word *gegona* rather than the aorist tense. On the one hand, the aorist tense communicates the idea "when I became a man, I put away childish things." On the other hand, the perfect tense communicates the idea of process: "when I have become a man, I put away childish things." The latter conveys the idea of a person looking back upon the process of doing away with immature behavior. Second, everyday experience "tells us that maturity is a gradual process of putting away childish habits." This notion of a gradual transition from immaturity to maturity is far more compatible with the canon and maturity views, which advocate the church's gradual weaning away from the apostolic revelatory gifts as the apostles died out and the New Testament canon was completed. The ideal view is incompatible with understanding maturity as a gradual process because it teaches an instantaneous transition from immaturity to maturity.(Woods, 2004: 10–11).

Problem 7: The phrase to *teleion* could hardly refer to the Rapture or the Second Coming since it is a neuter adjective.

It is not likely that a neuter adjective would refer to the personal coming of Christ, which would likely require a masculine adjective (MacArthur 1984: 365). If Paul had wanted the Second Coming to be the objective, he would have used a phrase with the masculine adjective, "he who is perfect," rather than the neuter word.

Problem 8: If *teleios* is the eternal state then the Christian will be years with Christ in heaven following the rapture and a thousand years during the millennium reign before the believer's limitations will be removed (Rev. 21-22).

The Scriptures never imply that the Lord will grant any additional capabilities or powers to the believer than what happens to him at the resurrection (Constable 2003:n.a.). All this manipulating the texts seems to deviate from the purpose of the passage itself, which is dealing with the activities within the local church, not some eternal transformation. Moving the subject line out of the immediate context of the issue seems out of context.

Problem 9: the Eschaton view leaves the canon open to addition throughout the church age.

Allowing the revelatory gifts of 1 Corinthians 12-14 to function throughout the church age contradicting the teaching that God's Word is completed (Jude 3; Rev 22:18-19). (Rothaar 2004: 37–38, 45). Dean describes the problem of an open canon having a negative effect by diluting the authority of the apostles (Dean 2005: 5), because the apostolic teachings would be continually modified by the "latest" prophetic utterances, as is being witnessed today.

An open canon is an open invitation to false teaching and heresy, with no way of verifying the legitimacy of the prophecy or prophet in today's pluralistic society. MacArthur describes a historical analysis documenting how the concept of continual revelations has allowed for heretical movements within the church (MacArthur 1992: 86–100).

To make matters worse allowing an open canon diverts attention and interest in the authority and value of biblical exposition within the local church. If new revelations are being practiced, why would anyone be interested in an exposition of the old revelations in the antiquated first century Scripture?

Why understand the Completeness View of *teleion* as correct?

This is the only view that combines a quantitative meaning to *teleion*, rather than a qualitative meaning. This view sees the New Testament canon as the completion of the partial and progressive revelations that are mentioned in 1 Cor 13:8-12. This view also understands the temporal indicators in 1 Cor 13:8-13, such as "now" to refer to the apostolic age (or precanonical period) and the "then" of the post apostolic age (or post canonical period). A number of contemporary commentators hold this view (Unger, Dean, Houghton, Gentry, and Vine). Woods describes three points to understand the canonical view (Woods 2004: 19).

Three pivotal points

First, the partial gifts (those that deliver the revelation of God's Word "in part") of knowledge, prophecy and tongues (1 Cor 13:8) are revelatory gifts, that is, God revealed His will and Word through the manifestation of these gifts. When Paul wrote 1 Corinthians the church had only two or three other Books of the NT (out of 27), sparsely scattered throughout thousands of churches on which to base their beliefs and teachings. In God's providence, special gifts of revelation (prophecy, knowledge, and tongues) were vital to guide the early church.

The nature of prophecy is revelatory in the NT as it was in the OT. He was one who received direct revelation from God (Deut 18:18) as Peter described prophecy in 2 Peter 1:20-21. Paul saw the major vehicle for revelation of and for the church as the apostles and prophets in Ephesians 3:5 (likewise in 1 Cor 14:29-30). Non-canonical prophets delivered God's revelations orally like the prophet Agabus (Acts 11:28; 21:10-11). (Boyer1960: 18).

The revelatory nature of the gift of knowledge can also be demonstrated by virtue of the fact that it is enumerated in 1 Corinthians 13:8–12 alongside prophecy. Paul places *gnsis* beside *mysteria* in 1 Corinthians 13:2 and between *apokalypsis* and *profteia* in 1 Corinthians 14:6, thus investing the term with "the significance of supernatural mystical knowledge." (BDAG, s.v. *gnsis*) Thus, "the gift of knowledge apparently involved unusual spiritual insight, including the supernatural guidance of the Holy Spirit, in determining the proper solution for the many practical problems which arose in the early church." (Smith 1970: 406).

The revelatory nature of tongues are evident in the requirement of an interpreter so the speaker's message can be understood by the congregation (1 Cor 14:26-27).

To appreciate the authority of these revelations and the great care in determining their validity one must see in the OT the price of ignoring what a prophet said, as in the case of Saul. Samuel had told Saul to wait 7 days for him so he could offer the sacrifice to honor the Lord. Under extreme threats from enemies Saul evidently took this lightly as he presumptuously offered the sacrifice himself (though not being a priest). "And Samuel said to Saul, "You have done foolishly. You have not kept the commandment of the LORD your God, which He commanded you. For now the LORD would have established your kingdom over Israel forever." (1 Sam 13:13 NKJ). Revelatory gifts are to be treated as the Word of God, infallible and inerrant.

Secondly, the revelatory gifts were designed to be partial and intended to be replaced by something more comprehensive or collected into a whole document. Paul's description of "prophecy in part" (*ek merous*) referred to the gifts of prophecy, knowledge and tongues (1 Cor 13:9-10, 12). Evidently variety of gifted individuals were scattered throughout the churches (perhaps as the Levites were scattered throughout the tribal locations in early history of Israel). These gifts were sporadic, now and then, short messages or if written an epistles or Gospel, but none gave the whole picture to any one church as did the eventual New Testament. "The various prophetic revelations offered at best partial insight into the will of God for the Church" (Gentry 2011: 53).

Another example of progressive revelation culminating in the completion of all the revelation that the Father wanted revealed to the early disciples. At the end of Jesus' ministry on the eve of His crucifixion, Jesus said, "…But I have called you friends, because I have revealed to you everything I heard from my Father" (John 15:15). Jesus progressively revealed to His disciples all they needed to understand the will of God. He would not need to reiterate what He had taught them. Jesus told them there was more to come, but they would need the Spirit in order to understand and apply it to their lives. Jesus said, "I have many more things to say to you, but you cannot bear them now. 13 But when he, the Spirit of truth, comes, he will guide you into all truth. For he will not speak on his own authority, but will speak whatever he hears, and will tell you what is to come" (John 16:12-13). This was a special promise to His disciples that they would receive additional revelations later, which would be for all the Church age.

The apostle Paul was conscious of his role in the maturity and development of the Church. He indicated that his epistles had scriptural authority (1 Corinthians 2:13; 14:36-37; 1 Thessalonians 2:13; 5:27), and Peter even observed that Paul had written inspired books (2 Peter 3:15-16), which he compared with the "rest of Scriptures." There is no reason to say that Paul did

Chapter 15: *Tongues and the Canon*

not know it.

He also knew that the Scriptures would not continue to be revealed indefinitely. If Christ did not return during his life, then a time would come when God would stop revealing His Word as He did at the end of the Old Testament, which was already a complete canon. The body of Christ would continue growing and receiving revelations through prophecy and the Word of knowledge until all revelation was completed. Of course, not even Paul knew how many epistles would be included in the Canon, but once it was finished, the final product would be indispensable for the maturity of the Church.

If "that which is in part" resulted in "that which is perfect," and the word "perfect" is the culmination of a process, then the most natural interpretation is that the prophets and those with the gift of the Word of knowledge contributed part by part to complete the perfect revelation of His Word. The second coming interpretation does not make sense.

Thirdly, if all the revelatory gifts were only "in part" (ek *merous*) for the early church, then *teleion* stands in antithesis to ek *merous*, therefore, it must refer to the NT canon when completed. The full collection of the partial revelations in a single document would render the partial revelations obsolete and unnecessary. Paul was anticipating the time when the full revelation of God for the church and everything necessary for the man of God to teach and exhort the churches (2 Tim 3:17, "that the man of God may be complete, thoroughly equipped for every good work").

Houghton similarly notes, "Is it possible to determine the nature of the partial gifts of prophecy, tongues, and knowledge? Yes. The answer is that they are revelational in quality. Since this is so, then 'the perfect' must also be revelational." (Houghton 1996:350).

It makes sense that Paul would use the term *teleion* to refer to something "complete" or "whole" as James had earlier used it in his epistle (James 1:25), referring to the "perfect law of liberty," a reference to the Word of God. Thus, this usage is not out of context historically and provides the best antithesis to the partial revelations of the gifts of knowledge, prophecy and tongues.

Meaning of the concluding verse

The phrase "And now" from 1 Cor 13:13 is *nuni de* in Greek. The conjunction de indicates a contrast to the anterior word and is better translated, "but now abides..." The word *nuni* emphasizes "the present time," a lapse between two temporary points of reference that denote an "epoch." The word is a "temporal marker with focus on a prevailing situation" (Bauer 2000), thus it introduces a distinct but long-term condition (as Rom 7:17).

Therefore, Paul is saying that after prophecy, tongues and knowledge have disappeared, faith, hope and love will continue on throughout the period of the church. Read the word *nuni* for the same sense in Romans 3:31; 6:22; 7:6 and 17; 1 Corinthians 15:20; Ephesians 2:13; and Hebrews 9:26.

The Greek words translated "now" in verses 12 and 13 are different. In verse 12; it is the word *arti*, which means "of the immediate present, presently, right now, at once," or "at this moment" (Friberg 2000: *arti*). The Latin word *artus* means "close, intimate." See the word *arti* in Matthew 9:18; 13:39; 26:29; John 2:10; 13:7 and 13:37; 14:7; 16:12; 1 Corinthians 4:11 and 13; Galatians 4:20; 2 Thessalonians 2:7; and 1 John 2:9. A comparison of the uses of these two words for "now" shows a difference in the measurement of time. One is imminent (*arti*), and the other (*nuni*) speaks of a longer period of time or a general condition. Therefore, the paraphrase is the following: "at this moment" I (Paul) know in part (verse 12); but "in this age" abides faith, hope and love (verse 13).

This trio of Christian attributes (faith, hope and love) occurs frequently in the New Testament (Romans 5:2-5; Galatians 5:5-6; Col. 1:4-5; 1 Thessalonians 1:3; 5:8; Hebrews 6:10-12; 10:22-24; and 1 Peter 1:21-22). It seems that they were a summary of the Early Church's concept of the Christian life. Of course, we should note that the "faith" in 13:13 should not be confused with the "faith" in 12:9 and 13:2, which refer to the spiritual gift of faith. In those two verses "faith" refers to the spiritual gift of "faith" that is given to only a few in the church.

At the end of the chapter (though it is the same word) in this context it refers to a common confidence for all believers and should be the principle that governs our lives (2 Corinthians 1:24) along with hope and love. This trio is the confident anticipation that equips the believer to suffer persecution (1 Thessalonians 1:3) in light of the coming of Christ. The theme of love has been dealt with in other chapters, but it is indispensable for the life of the body of Christ and the manifestation of the gifts in ministries of the entire Church.

Even among the last group (faith, hope and love) there is a distinction. Of the three, love is greater because it "never fails" (verse 8). The difference is in its relationship to time. Time is the emphasis of the entire paragraph starting with verse 8. Faith, hope and love are superior to prophecy, tongues and knowledge because the former (faith, hope and love) continue after the latter (prophecy, knowledge and tongues) have disappeared. Love is superior to the other two because even faith (2 Cor 5:7-8) and hope (Rom 8:24) are not permanent. Faith and hope will be unnecessary at a specific time when all is realized, possibly after the second coming of Christ. Only love will continue after that.

If everything refers to the Second Coming, then there is no time distinction meant by these temporal adverbs thus we have merely a meaning in the passage of superiority of value of love over everything else. As true as this is, the meaning of the passage in this context is focusing on the meaning of the temporal or the time-sense of the adverbs.

Faith is the anticipation of Christ's return. 2 Corinthians 5:6-8 says,

Chapter 15: *Tongues and the Canon*

"⁶Therefore we are always full of courage, and we know that as long as we are alive here on earth we are absent from the Lord—⁷ for we live by faith, not by sight. ⁸ Thus we are full of courage and would prefer to be away from the body and at home with the Lord."

A better definition of faith is found in Hebrews 11:1, which says, "Now faith is being sure of what we hope for, being convinced of what we do not see..." The phrases we emphasize show that when the Church is in the presence of the Lord after His return, it will not be necessary for us to walk by faith because everything will be seen. There will be nothing to anticipate, because all will be fulfilled. Therefore, after His return there will be no need for faith, at least as we define the meaning at this time.

The same is true of hope. In Romans 8:24-25, we read, "For in hope we were saved. Now hope that is seen is not hope, because who hopes for what he sees? 25 But if we hope for what we do not see, we eagerly wait for it with endurance.." The anterior verse refers to the hope of "the adoption, the redemption of our body." This event is fulfilled at the second coming of Christ. When we see with our own eyes the coming of Christ, His kingdom and the eternal state, there will be no need for hope because we will see everything we had hoped for. In addition, at what point in the future would faith and hope be superseded by love?

In the following chart we can see the periods of function and the time of the cessation of the gifts and virtues in 1 Corinthians 13.

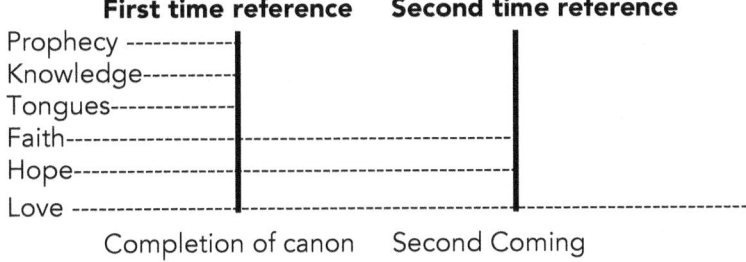

It seems that there are two points of time defined in chapter 13. We know that when the first period ends (verse 8), the gifts of prophecy, tongues and knowledge will cease. If we propose that this will occur at the Second Coming of Christ, then faith, hope and love must endure through the millennium, and we have shown that this is invalid. Therefore, the second coming of Christ cannot be the first point. If we propose that it is the second point of time, then the time line is seamless and its parts harmonize without conflict. Faith, hope and love reign as the greatest attributes during the age of the Church, exactly as Paul said, and the gifts of prophecy, knowledge and tongues cease when the foundation of the Church, the work of the apostles, is finished. Logically, then, the first point of time must be the coming of "that which is perfect," which we have shown marks the completion of the New Testament and God's revelation for this age. The second reference to time refers to the fulfillment of prophecy and the return of Christ to earth to establish His reign on earth.

As we have shown, faith, hope and love will replace the gifts of prophecy, tongues and knowledge. This poses a problem if "that which is perfect" refers to the second coming, because faith and hope would have to have an important function in the lives of believers after the return of the Lord. What purpose could they serve after Christ returns? None, and for this reason the Bible mentions faith and hope only with regard to the present time, that is to say, before the second coming of Christ.

Metaphors in context

The adult child analogy in 13:11-12 makes better sense with the progressive maturing of the early church until they had all the revelations that God intended for the foundation of the church other gifted men to build itself upon (1 Cor 3:10).

The child represents the incomplete knowledge available to the infant, precanon church. Just as a child has inadequate knowledge to live as a mature adult, so the precanon church lacked a sufficient canon and doctrine to lead the spiritual life of the new Church Age. An adult reaches maturity when he is complete with the knowledge and skills necessary for life. So, too the post canon church has the completed canon of Scripture, which is sufficient for every need, every problem, every difficulty in life. Through the learning of the doctrines of the Word under the filling of the Holy Spirit the believer is able to pursue spiritual maturity (Dean 2005: 9).

Gentry points out the intentional parallels between the three partial gifts in verse 8 (prophecy, knowledge and tongues) and the three characteristics of infancy in verse 11 (speaking, understanding and thinking as a child). Aligning them together tongues would be the equivalent to speaking as a child, knowledge would be understanding as a child and prophecy is like the reasoning of a child.(Gentry 2011: 55).

When Paul became a mature man he put away childish thoughts and mannerisms. Likewise the church would reach maturity (not perfection), when she ceased to be dependent on prophets for her piecemeal or partial delivery of God's Word, and had all the knowledge at her disposal to teach, exhort and edify each other, without the need of additional revelation.

The "dark glass" metaphor in 13:12 is usually translated "mirror." The other use of this word, *esoptron*, is used in James 1:23 where it is clearly referring to a mirror. Paul is comparing the partial revelations of the gifts at his time as looking into a dim or foggy mirror. The comparison is how the partial revelations gave an imperfect refection of God's will, but after the

NT canon was complete the viewer could see a reflection of God's will as clearly as a clear mirror reveals the viewer's face. Thus, the expression "face to face" refers to the clarity of the viewer seeing himself in a mirror being analogous to clearly seeing the will of God in the completed revelation of the canon. Now the reader of God's Word has a standard for an honest self-assessment (Woods 2004, 24).

It must be noted that there is no reference in the context to seeing God "face to face" though some commentators want to force this view (Ibid.: 57). It makes little sense to look into a mirror and see someone else looking back. The "face to face" motif is comparable to Numbers 12:6-8 where the face-to-face expression is not a focus on fellowship, but an illustration of the clarity with which God's revelation was delivered to Moses.

Challenges to cessationism

Knowing as known.

Some have been reluctant to accept the evidence of cessationism because of the seeming presumptuous nature of the phrase "but then I shall know just as I also am known" 1 Corinthians 13:12b to mean that the believers can know themselves through God's Word just as God knows them. It is said that this can only refer to the knowledge attainable in eternity. Rothaar stated, "It is pointed out that even today with a completed canon of Scripture we do not know fully. If we did, we would not be faced with the problem of interpreting the Scriptures as we are today." (Rothaar 2004: 37).

However, if one doubts the possibility of this level of knowledge referred to in 1 Corinthians 13:12b can be attained on this side of eternity Paul gives the promise that the Holy Spirit will reveal and illuminate even the "deep things of God" (1 Cor 2:10) and we have been given the Spirit "that we might know the things that have been freely given to us by God" (2:12).

Future prophets and prophecy

If revelatory gifts have ceased why are they operational in the Tribulation and millennium? (as in Joel 2:28-32 and Revelation 11). Likewise Isaiah spoke of a time when God's knowledge will fill the earth during the kingdom age (Isaiah 11:9).

The answer is seen in the different programs and objectives of God's plan for Israel and for the church. The context of 1 Cor 13 is the completion of the revelation for the church. "The operation of knowledge and prophecy in Isaiah 11, Joel 2, and Revelation 11 is set in the context of God's purposes for national Israel. Thus, the cessation of the gifts of prophecy and knowledge pertains explicitly to the church age." (Woods 2004: 28).

In 1 Corinthians 13, Paul clearly states that a time will come when "prophecy will cease," while Joel says that it will occur again after Christ comes. "And it shall come to pass afterward, that I will pour out my spirit upon all flesh; and your sons and your daughters shall prophesy, your old men shall dream dreams, your young men shall see visions" (2:28). This indicates that the second coming of Christ will mark the beginning of a new era of prophecy after a period of silence. For this reason, one age of prophecy must cease for a time before a new one can begin during the millennium. The coming of "that which is perfect" cannot be the second coming of Christ, because "that which is perfect" will terminate prophecy (1 Corinthians 13:8-13). Prophecy cannot begin and end at the same moment. An unknown span of time must pass between the cessation of prophecy that Paul establishes and the new age of prophecy that will begin at Christ's return.

```
              Ceasing of Prophecy        Reinstituting Prophecy
                       |                          |
Prophecy---------------|            ?             |---------------------
              Completion of canon          Second Coming
```

This shows that there are two points of time in the context: one that stops with the prophecies that were the Church's foundation, and the other when prophecies resume at the beginning of the millennium for a new age. Again, the first point of time aligns best with the time of the coming of "that which is perfect."

Conclusion of revelation

Believing that "that which is perfect" refers to the second coming requires that prophecy and knowledge (and by association, tongues) continue until His coming; but the Bible indicates that direct revelation, or prophecies, ceased when the New Testament was finished. In Revelation 22:18-19 we read, "I testify to the one who hears the words of the prophecy contained in this book: If anyone adds to them, God will add to him the plagues described in this book. 19 And if anyone takes away from the words of this book of prophecy, God will take away his share in the tree of life and in the holy city that are described in this book." With these words of warning against further prophecy being added to the prophecies of this book of Revelation, the author appears to be closing the New Testament era of prophetic revelations. To say that prophecies would continue until the second coming of Christ appears to contradict this passage.

The statement can have two meanings: 1) the warning against attempting to forge false prophecies to the end of the book of Revelation. This would hardly be a possibility since anyone could tell that John did not write it. 2) The warning against any further claim of prophetic revelations in general was to be considered false or spurious.

To "prophesize" is to reveal a truth that could not have been known naturally. For example, in Matthew 26:68 during the judgment and beatings of Jesus, His tormentors said to Him, "Prophesy for us, you Christ! Who hit you?"

Other Scriptures show that sometimes even the prophets did not understand the revelations they received. Peter writes, "Concerning this salvation, the prophets who predicted the grace that would come to you searched and investigated carefully" (1 Peter 1:10). Prophecy is not learned, but rather it is the result of direct revelation from God. It is certain that today we encourage believers (1 Corinthians 14:3) to lead unbelievers to a conviction of sin (1 Corinthians 14:24-25) by the preaching of prophecy, but today we do not receive revelation; we use what the prophets from other eras have written. People are edified, exhorted and consoled when biblical prophecies are preached today, so that there is no longer a need for direct prophecy from God.

Those who want prophecy to be a valid gift for today have to redefine it. They must interpret it as the gift of preaching or as acting with the boldness and conviction of a prophet. Preaching and boldness are aspects of the gift of teaching or exhortation as well, and not exclusively apply to prophecy. Inventing a brand of prophecy that relates to modern preaching, in order to maintain that the gift of prophecy is valid today, has no biblical basis. It is better to accept the evidence of its termination, along with the prohibition of adding any additional revelations or taking away from the finished Word of God. If prophecy ceased, then miraculously revealed knowledge ceased simultaneously. If both these gifts ceased, then it is highly likely that the gift of tongues did also, since Paul defined all three as temporal gifts.

Conclusion to Factor 7:

Taking the context into account, the most natural interpretation is that the first point of time corresponds to the completion ("that which is perfect") of the New Testament canon and/or the maturity of the Church. During this time the three gifts (as well as others) ceased, while the practical gifts of ministry along with faith, hope and love continue throughout the age of the Church. "That which is perfect" became part of the foundation of the Church (Eph 2:20). The coming of Christ is the second point of time in which faith and hope cease while love, the greatest of all, will never cease.

Factor 8: The ministries of Christ and the apostles ended 1,500 years of special revelation and signs.

An important question is whether or not God still communicates with men through special or additional revelation as he did during the period of biblical revelation. Four verses indicate that continual revelation was not to be God's plan, and they also affirm that when Christ's ministry ended and the apostles finished writing, the whole process of special revelation and the accompanying signs ceased at about the same time. Today we would dismiss anyone who would declare his writings to be the fruit of special revelation. However, many proclaim this very level of revelation and authority. This type of supposed revelations are the basis of the error among Catholics, Mormons, Adventists, Jehovah's Witnesses, Christian Scientists, and in a limited way, Charismatics. The false doctrines of these groups grow from the belief that special revelation continues just as in the age of the apostles.

The difference between Catholics and Evangelicals primarily comes from the theme of divine revelation. Most evangelicals believe that special revelation ceased with the completion of the New Testament, but Roman Catholics believe that it has continued throughout the tradition of the Roman Catholic Church. French Roman Catholic George Tavard says, "Tradition, then, was the overflow of the Word outside of the Sacred Scriptures. It was neither separate from the Sacred Scriptures nor identical to them. Its content was the 'other scripture' through which the Word was made known to Himself." (Tavard 1959:245)

Therefore, the doctrinal teaching of Roman Catholics has no limit, because they believe it is always possible to add more dogma by special revelation.

They also believe that their new revelations have equal authority to that of the Holy Scriptures. In the Council of Trent in 1546, the Roman Catholic Church made a declaration to contradict the doctrine of Martin Luther who said that "only the Bible" is the divine revelation. The Council declared,

> The "purity of the gospel of God" promised by the prophets was promulgated by Christ. It was preached by the apostles as the "rule of all saving truth and of all moral discipline." This "truth" is contained partially (*partim*) in written books, partially (*partim*) in traditions not written.
> These traditions are attributed to Christ and to the apostles, to whom it was dictated by the Holy Spirit. They have "come to us transmitted as by hand." The Council, therefore, recognizes the books of the Old and New Testaments and these traditions "as dictated orally by Christ himself or by the Holy spirit and maintained in the Catholic Church in continuous succession." The Council receives them as "sacred chronicles." It will use both to establish dogmas and restore morality in the Church. (Ibid.:246)

The continuation of apostolic revelation is the basis for the teaching of the infallibility of the Pope. In 1854, Pope Pios IX introduced the dogma of the Immaculate Conception, the doctrine declaring that Mary, the mother of Jesus, was born without original sin. He said, "This is a doctrine revealed by God and therefore, should be believed firmly and constantly by all the faithful." (Fremantle 1963:136)

This doctrine is neither found in the Bible nor consistent with its teachings, yet the Catholic Church adopted it based on the principle of continued apostolic revelation. Another similar example occurred in 1950, when Pope Pios XII proclaimed the dogma of the Ascension of Mary, claiming that Mary was carried corporally to Heaven and never died. He declared, "Therefore, if anyone, God forbid, dares to negate or intentionally doubt that which we have defined, he should know that he has become apostate from the divine Catholic faith." (Ibid.:299).

Almost all Catholics are conditioned to accept anything that the Roman Catholic Church declares, even when it clearly contradicts the Bible. It is as if the new revelations were more valid. This concept opens the door for all false doctrines, since there are no absolutes in a world of continuous revelation. God will not allow His true Church to accept anyone who says he has received new revelation, however; He left us His complete revelation, the Word of God, which is absolute and the only guide for our faith and practice.

There are four areas of evidence that demonstrate that continuous divine revelation is false:

Evidence 1: The action of speaking by inspiration is complete, once and for all (Hebrews 1:1-2) "God, who at various times and in various ways spoke in time past to the fathers by the prophets,:2 has in these last days spoken to us by His Son, whom He has appointed heir of all things, through whom also He made the worlds;"

Just as in Old Testament times, God revealed Himself to humanity, but this time through Jesus Christ. We can include the apostles in this because they revealed to us what Jesus taught them. The passage makes the following important points: (1) the only voice that we should listen to is the voice of God. (2) The reader should have the same respect for the words of the New Testament that Jesus and His apostles revealed as he has for the Old Testament.

The authority of the apostles is declared in Hebrews 2:3-4, because they are "those who heard" directly from the Lord. (3) Previously, God used many ways to communicate His Word, but now His method of communication is limited to the person of Jesus. The only way in which the Son speaks to us today is through His Word, insinuating that the other methods are no longer used to communicate God's revelation.

When Christ communicated His teachings, he completed His primary objective in coming. In John 17, Jesus prayed to the Father,

> "I have glorified You on the earth. I have finished the work which You have given Me to do.... Now they have known that all things which You have given Me are from You. For I have given to them the words which You have given Me; and they have received them, and have known surely that I came forth from You; and they have believed that You sent Me...I do not pray for these alone, but also for those who will believe in Me through their word... Neither pray I for these alone, but for them also which shall believe on me through their word." (17:4, 7-8, 20)

Christ came to communicate the God's message to the disciples so that they could transmit it to us. Both works, then, were completed and God still communicates to us through the words of Jesus and the apostles and not through any other contemporary means.

In addition, Hebrews 2:3-4 tells us the revelation of the Word of God was limited to a special group that was present with Jesus. Paul was the last person God permitted in this group. 1 Corinthians 15:8 says, "And last of all he was seen of me also"; in other words, He was the last to see Christ in person. If someone says Christ appeared to him, then he is lying, because He speaks to us today through His Words and those of His apostles, written in the Bible. Therefore, divine revelation terminated with the death of the apostles. Since speaking in tongues was an avenue for revelation and was associated with prophecy and the gift of knowledge (1 Corinthians 13:8), when one ceased, they all ceased.

Evidence 2: The message of Christ was given "once...to the saints" (Jude 3).

It seems that the tendency to add to God's revelation always existed. Jude confronted this very serious problem in the early Church; some had infiltrated into the Church and begun to add to the revelation given through the apostles. he phrase, "the faith which was once delivered unto the saints," found in Jude 3, refers to the body of truth the apostles taught. Jude assumed their acceptance and understanding in that body of truth.

Those who added to those teachings were false teachers; their "new" revelations obliged the Church to "earnestly contend (*epagonizesthai*, a heightened form of "struggle, or fight") for the faith." Evidently so many pagan ideas were creeping into the churches under the guise of new revelations that it was a fight to keep the doctrine pure. Note that in the Greek, the adverb describing the delivery of faith is emphasized. It is literally: "faith once delivered to the saints," meaning that there was already in existence a written record of the truth or the faith. During the Reformation, the leaders tried to rescue the Church from error using the theme of "Scriptures only." Now Charismatics are saying "Scriptures and more!" adding prophetic expressions, new revelations from God, and new tongues to the foundation of their belief. We must return to the truth of God's Word, that it was "once given" and cannot be added to or subtracted from.

Evidence 3: It was prohibited to add to the prophecies of Christ and the apostles (Revelation 22:18).

"For I testify to everyone who hears the words of the prophecy of this book: If anyone adds to these things, God will add to him the plagues that are written in this book."

The last sentences of the New Testament forbid us from adding to or taking away from the revelation or prophecy already given. Some want this to be exclusive to the modification of the Book of Revelation, but the warning is extremely serious for anyone to pretend to add additional revelations purportedly from God. Unless someone is writing or revealing an additional epistle for the canon, any additional revelations would be considered an addition to the last book of the Bible. f this text is insinuating that God be the source of any more prophecy, then it is because He has "completed" it (1 Corinthians 13:8). With the book of Revelation, written in 96 B.C., God completed His revelation to man and any additional revelations would be spurious or false.

As we have shown, if God ended prophecy at that time, then it is implicit that knowledge also ended because both are part of God's revelation; we can deduce that everything associated with the revelation from God ceased at that time, and history testifies that this is true.

Evidence 4: Jesus taught that all truth would be taught by the Holy Spirit and the apostles (John 14:26 and 16:13).

After three years of considerable teaching, it is probable that the disciples worried that they would forget all that He had said. If John 11-16 is any indication of one evening's teaching lessons, then three years of constant teaching must have covered a multitude of topics and truths. Before His crucifixion, however, Jesus assured the apostles that they would be able to remember all truth and also be able to write it for future generations. John 14:26 says, "But the Helper, the Holy Spirit, whom the Father will send in My name, He will teach you all things, and bring to your remembrance all things that I said to you.." The influence of the Spirit became the basis of apostolic authority and the confidence in the apostles' teaching.

In John 16:13 we read, "However, when He, the Spirit of truth, has come, He will guide you into all truth; for He will not speak on His own authority, but whatever He hears He will speak; and He will tell you things to come." Again, we have a promise given specifically to the apostles to establish their authority in the Church forever. The following two promises are inseparable and are not applicable to every believer: (1) "he will guide you into all truth," and (2) "he will tell you things to come." Today the Spirit teaches through the apostles' writing. The ministry of the Spirit today is not revelation, as is promised here, but rather illuminating and bring conviction in the spirit through what He previously revealed to the apostles. There is no way that these promises could continue, because there is no one alive whom Jesus taught personally.

Praise God that the Spirit brought back to the apostles' consciousness all that Jesus had taught them, thus they were guided to all truth and then could write it for us! The basis of our confidence in apostolic teaching is the authority with which they taught Jesus' teachings. Since speaking in tongues was also a way of communicating this truth, when interpreted, there would be no reason for their continuation once all Jesus' teaching had been revealed to the apostles. It is logical that this gift would cease. Similarly, if someone pretends today to have received a new revelation from the Spirit, then we should know that it comes only from his imagination or possibly from other deceiving spirits (1 Timothy 4:1; 1 John 4:1).

John MacArthur cites the following letter from a young Charismatic that shows us the tendencies toward mysticism, subjectivism and straying from the truth within that movement:

> The greatest experience of love that I have ever had was at the foot of the cross as the blood of Jesus Christ was poured out on me. He filled me with His Spirit. He brought me through the veil to the city of Jerusalem all the way to the Holy of Holies. There I contemplated myself in Him and Him in me. I received the baptism as by fire and since then, His love dwells in me. Because of this I have daily communion with Him. I do not feel the necessity of studying the Scriptures, because I know Jesus as He has revealed Himself in my interior; and while He dwells in me, there is the Word.
> I go to the Scriptures—and the Scriptures are vital and necessary--, but it is not central or crucial, because I have Him—in other words, He has me. The Scriptures are a secondary source of knowing Him.
> Through the baptism of the Holy Spirit, the Word in me (the body of Jesus Christ himself) is the most important—I say this as a live experience of that which He has given me to tell. (MacArthur, Jr. 1984: 38).

Factor 9: Speaking in tongues is mentioned only in the early books.

The gift of tongues appears in the book of Acts, where it is mentioned on three occasions. The manner in which it is written indicates that it was very rare, even in that period. Apart from Acts, the only reference to speaking in tongues is made in 1 Corinthians. In addition, the gift of tongues is not mentioned in other lists of the gifts of the Spirit, as we see in Romans 12:4-8, Ephesians 4:8-12 and in 1 Peter 4:10-11. In the later lists of spiritual gifts, the sign gifts, especially tongues and interpretation of tongues, are absent.

We should note that the word "wonder" (teras) occurs nine times in Acts; it is not found after 5:12, however, and even that passage refers to a previous occasion. The word "sign" (semeion) appears three times, but does not occur after 15:12, which also refers to a previous ministry. The word "miracle" (dynamis) appears ten times, but not after 19:11. Almost every time these words are used, they appear in the first half of the book of Acts. Of the thirty-two manifestations of miraculous signs in Acts, only six occurred after Acts 8. Considering the biblical evidence, we can conclude that the ministry of miracles declined after the early days of the Church because the frequency of miracles in the Bible declined during the life of the apostles.

Only the books of James and 1 and 2 Thessalonians were written before 1 Corinthians, which was written approximately in 55 A.D., 22 to 25 years after the resurrection. In this time the apostles and prophets were still very active, receiving and giving new revelations and also confirming the message of Jesus. During that time, people with the gifts of prophecy, knowledge and tongues were communicating to the churches new revelations from God. In the first years of the Church those gifts were very important, but they ceased to be useful when they fulfilled their purpose of giving to the Body of Christ all that Jesus had taught.

Chapter 15: *Gifts for Today*

CHAPTER 16

Tongues in relation to Christ and the Apostles

Chapter 16: Gifts for Today

Walking home with a close charismatic friend from language school in Guadalajara, Mexico as we both prepared for serving as missionaries, we engaged in the discussion about whether gifts were temporary or not. I made the assertion, "Well, surely we can agree that at least one of the gifts is temporary, that of apostles. Right?"

My friend responded, "Don't you know that in order for me to have been approved as a missionary with my agency, I had to prove that I was an apostle? I had to demonstrate the 'signs of an apostle' before I could be accepted. I had to show that I had raised the dead, performed healings, and spoken in tongues." My surprise at his response left me struggling to carry on any argument for temporary gifts.

It was very important in the beginning of the church for Christ to establish the authority of the apostles as being the unique representatives and messengers of Christ. Jesus personally spent little time on the earth and taught the message of the Father for only three years. The future of His message depended on those who would communicate it to the rest of the world.

Upon examining the evidence of the New Testament, we discover that the power to do miracles was not something given in general to all or even many believers, but rather it was exclusive to this group of apostles with very few exceptions. Miracles were never meant for the entire Church, which would have diluted the unique authority of the apostles, and thus, all that the apostles revealed for the church.

> That to be an apostle was itself a spiritual gift is clearly revealed in such passages as Ephesians 4:7–12 and 1 Corinthians 12:28–31, although through inattention to these Scriptures apostleship is often thought of as though it constituted a category entirely separate from the other spiritual gifts. But the inclusion of apostles along with prophets, teachers, miracles, and tongues in a list of charismata like that of 1 Corinthians 12:28 can leave no ground for question on this point. Accordingly, inasmuch as Protestant theology generally has clearly recognized the cessation of the apostolic gift in the first century, at the same time that it rightly denies any form of apostolic succession, all such Protestant theology becomes basically committed to the principle of temporary gift. For clearly the apostleship was itself temporary, and, if the principle be established, it is perfectly legitimate to inquire whether there may not be other first-century gifts which were likewise temporary. (Hodges 1963: 226–227).

We must understand the unique purpose of the miracles and signs in the Bible in order to be able to refute those who insist that miracles must occur today as in the days of the apostles. This position has many unintentional consequences that cannot be refuted if the premise of continual miraculous gifts, and thus apostolic authority, is accepted.

The use of the word "apostle" in literature outside the Bible in the sense of "representative" is used in a few passages as representatives of a local church;

Chapter 16: *Tongues in relation to Christ and the Apostles*

however, this is not the meaning of the NT gift of apostleship. Neither is this term used in the Bible as the contemporary title "missionary" (the Latin translation of the Greek apostle); nor is the meaning derived from the meaning of the parts of the word (etymology) as a "sent one." The meaning is determined by how it is used in the context.

> The only individuals in the New Testament who clearly possessed the miraculous gift of apostle of the Lord Jesus Christ and could perform miracles as required of an apostle (2 Cor 12:12) were the Twelve and Paul. Perhaps Barnabas and James can be included. Almost every branch of the church, including most Pentecostals, has held that apostles in this sense have not continued in the church. (Edgar 1988:381).

Those opposing a redefinition of the apostolic and prophetic gifts are called "too restrictive (Mallone 1988:19). These gifts can be defined in the Scripture and cannot be modified to match contemporary practices. The primary basis of the unique confirmation by the miraculous gifts of the apostles and prophets at the beginning of the church gave credibility to the new revelations of the NT for all the churches.

> The New Testament sets standards for an apostle that preclude the continuance of this gift. Not only must an apostle be able to perform miracles (2 Cor 12:12), not only was the early church very careful about granting anyone, even Paul, the title of "apostle" (Gal 2:1–10), but also an apostle must have seen the resurrected Lord (1 Cor 9:1–2; Acts 1:22–26). Paul explicitly stated that he was the last one to see the resurrected Lord (1 Cor 15:8), and he specifically connected this fact with his apostleship. This requirement for apostleship refers to genuine appearances of the resurrected Christ and not to "visions." There have been no resurrection appearances since the apostolic age. Paul clearly stated that the last appearance was to him. (Revelation 1:12–18 refers to a vision, and is not an appearance of the resurrected Lord in bodily form on earth.) Therefore apostles in the sense of the Twelve and Paul cannot occur today. (Ibid.: 382).

Factor 10: The gifts of tongues and miracles are not necessary today.

If the message of Christ were to be believed, then it would be necessary for His message and His messengers to be authenticated or confirmed. Miraculous powers were almost always the way a person proved that his message was true and that God had spoken to him. For instance, in the Old Testament, the "confirmation gifts" were used on several occasions to demonstrate the divine authority of the messenger. Moses was given three signs to convince Israel that he was their liberator: the leprous hand, the rod that became a snake and the power to change water into blood. In Exodus 4:8-9, we see the purpose of these miraculous gifts:

> "Then it will be, if they do not believe you, nor heed the message of the first sign, that they may believe the message of the latter sign. 9 "And it shall be, if they do not believe even these two signs, or listen to your voice, that you shall take water from the river and pour it on the dry land. And the water which you take from the river will become blood on the dry land."

In 4:1, Moses expressed the inevitable doubts that motivated the need for miraculous signs, "Then Moses answered and said, "But suppose they will not believe me or listen to my voice; suppose they say, 'The LORD has not appeared to you.'" The purpose of the miracles was specific: convince Israel that he was the messenger of God. It is significant that Moses had to use miracles only one time to convince his audience. No one ever doubted he was God's messenger thereafter.

> And Aaron spoke all the words, which the LORD had spoken to Moses. Then he did the signs in the sight of the people. 31 So the people believed; and when they heard that the LORD had visited the children of Israel and that He had looked on their affliction, then they bowed their heads and worshiped. (Exodus 4:30-31)

Two of the three signs were used before Pharaoh, but the people of Israel needed only one. Therefore, there was no need for further signs. The Israelites believed the first time, and a repetition would have served only to entertain them, as Herod wanted to do with Jesus (Luke 23:8).

This principle is seen also with respect to manna. For forty years God miraculously provided manna for Israel in the desert, but it suddenly ceased when they arrived at the Promised Land. In Joshua 5:11-12, we read that when "... they ate some of the produce of the land: unleavened bread and roasted grain. The manna stopped the day after they ate this food from the land; there was no longer any manna for the Israelites, but that year they ate of the produce of Canaan." The following principle seems to emerge in this circumstance: when something is no longer necessary for God's purpose, it ceases. Therefore, we can anticipate that miraculous gifts will cease when their purposes are fulfilled. What were the purposes of these gifts that have ceased?

Four purposes of the sign gifts:

Certain principles become evident when we analyze the passages related to the terms "miracle" (*dynamis*), "sign" (*semeion*) and "wonder" (*teras*). Today, when we speak of miracles, it is very common to hear references to healings instead of miracles. These are two different concepts in the Bible. However, it is rare that a miracle will occur unrelated to an act of healing.

(1) Miracles were used to introduce a new period of revelation.

In biblical narration we do not find periods of miracles centered on important people like Job, Abraham or Samuel. Even though they received individual revelations, they did not live in periods of biblical revelation. Their revelations were primarily for them personally, not revelations of the Word of God for all generations.

Miracles occurred in abundance when God began to reveal His Word through Moses and Joshua in the new period of the law, then through Elijah and Elisha in the period of the prophets and finally through Jesus and His apostles in the period of the Church. The Bible shows that these three eras of miracles were also the beginning of three periods of special revelation, which cannot be coincidental. In Exodus 33, when God gave the law to Moses, He authenticated it with His visible presence in a column of cloud over the Tabernacle (verses 9-10). This kind of manifestation occurred only one time.

Speaking in tongues, healings and miracles all served as signs to authenticate eras of new revelation. While the era of revelation came to an end, the signs also ended along with it. As theologian B.B. Warfield says,

> Miracles do not appear sporadically on the pages of the Scriptures, here and there without purpose or reason. They belong to periods of revelation and appear only when God is speaking to His people through credited messengers, who declared His magnanimous purposes. His abundant display in the apostolic Church is the sign of rich revelation during the apostolic era; and when this period of revelation was closed, the period of miraculous work also concluded, as merely a natural happening. (Warfield 1918:25-26)

In Acts 7, Stephen mentioned the marvelous signs that Moses did and that "he received words of life to give us" (verses 36-38). The miracles of Moses are tied to the "words of life," that is to say, the revelation of the Word of God. God always makes clear that His messenger is the carrier of a new revelation, and His way to verify it is through miracles and signs.

(2) Miracles were used to authenticate the messengers of the new periods of revelation.

When Moses proved his authenticity as the messenger of God in Exodus 4 through the signs of the leprous hand, the staff that turned into a snake and the water that changed to blood, he did not used these signs again to convince the Hebrews. It was not necessary, since they had already accepted him (Exodus 4:5-9). Similarly, when Elijah raised the widow's dead son in 1 Kings 17:17-23 the widow told him, "Now by this I know that you are a man of God, and that the word of the LORD in your mouth is the truth" (17:24). There was no further need to reconfirm his authenticity.

In the Gospel of John, the author chose precisely seven miracles from the life of Christ to prove His deity, which is the declared purpose of the book (John 20:31). He could have written about many other signs (John 20:31), but these seven were sufficient for his purpose.

(3) Miracles were used to authenticate the new message.

When God inaugurated the new revelation of His Word, He accompanied it with signs and wonders. God authenticated His message with signs in Acts 14:3, when the apostles were "speaking boldly in the Lord, which gave testimony unto the word of his grace, and granted signs and wonders to be done by their hands." This confirmation was not generally given to all believers but was special for those who carried the message directly from Jesus.

The message was so important that it required special confirmation from God after the ascension of Jesus. For this reason it says in Hebrews 2:4, "God also bearing them witness, both with signs and wonders." Joseph Dillow makes the following commentary:

> Note that this man (the author of Hebrews) was writing to the group of the second generation of believers, trying to encourage them to continue believing in their faith. The basis of his appeal is the confirmed testimony (through miraculous gifts of the spirit: tongues, miracles, etc.) from the first generation of believers. Since he is basing all his appeal on the confirmation of the testimony of the believers of the first generation through the sign gifts, it would be unbelievable to think that he was not referring to some miraculous manifestation from the second generation. If he could have cited some miraculous manifestations that continued into the second generation, he could have fortified even more his argument. However, he had to depend on the manifestations from the first generation. It seems that this apostle was not conscious of the continual presence of the sign gifts, so unusual in 70 A.D., when he wrote the epistle to the Hebrews. Possibly tongues had already ceased (1 Cor. 13:8). (Dillow 1975:146)

As we have shown, in each case in the New Testament the signs were used by very few people and principally by the apostles. The only three exceptions are as follows: Philip (Acts 9:6-7), Stephen (Acts 6:8) and Ananias (Acts 9:10-18), and each recorded only one experience. Because of their intimate association with the apostles and their ministries in the early Church of confirming the initial message to the Jews (Stephen) and the Samaritans (Philip), it is completely comprehensible. There were no other people involved in the confirmation of the biblical record, and even Phillip apparently did not continue with his ministry of confirmation. This confirmation became so exclusive that it was called "signs of an apostle" (2 Corinthians 12:12).

Chapter 16: *Tongues in relation to Christ and the Apostles* 261

(4) Miracles were used to give instruction to observers.

The miracles of Moses were directed against specific gods of the Egyptians. Archeologists have identified these gods as the Nile, frogs, fish, shrimp, serpents, etc. The Hebrews learned that Jehovah was stronger that any of the Egyptians' gods, and the miracles were so convincing that even many Egyptians accompanied them in the exodus.

When Elijah convened the priests of Baal at the "competition" of Mount Carmel, fire fell from heaven to consume the altar at his word. Israel learned not only that God was with Elijah, but also that Jehovah was stronger than Baal. Later, by the word of Elijah, it rained after three years of drought and again the people learned that only God could supply their needs and that Baal did not have any power.

While some were done out of compassion, the purpose of many of Jesus' miracles was also the teaching of a special lesson. In Luke 5:17-25 Jesus wanted to teach that it is easier to heal than to pardon. First, only God could forgive, and He was God. Second, it was more difficult to forgive than to heal because forgiving would cost Jesus His life, meaning that the price was much higher. Jesus took advantage of the opportunity of a healing to communicate this truth. No one could deny His divine authority.

God has left us His authenticated messengers, His message (the New Testament) and the new period of the Church, and He confirmed that they are from Him by the signs and miracles that followed them in the beginning. As always in the Bible, when the purpose of the miraculous gifts was finished, the gifts ceased.

Today the Word of God demands that we trust in the testimony of the 1st century biblical writers and in the testimony of the Spirit. In John 20:29, Jesus affirmed clearly that it is better to believe without having seen signs, and in 2 Corinthians 5:7 we are exhorted to live by faith, trusting in what is written in the Word rather than what we can see and feel in our time.

If anyone says that miracles are necessary today, then our first answer should be that miracles were used for a specific need: to authenticate a new period of revelation. What new era of special revelation is being introduced today? What new revelations or prophecies are being added to the prophecies of the book of Revelation? If the addition of new prophecies is prohibited (Revelation 22:18), then there is no need of more confirmation for new revelations.

Apparently there will be more revelations at the beginning of the millennium, when there will be more prophecies and signs again (Joel 2:38), but we are not living in those times. If miracles were to be continued during the era of the Church, their purpose would be different and a contradiction would exist as to the purpose of the signs found in the NT.

Our second answer should be that miracles are not a norm throughout the age of the Church. Jesus and Paul taught we should not depend on signs and miracles for our faith (John 20:29; 2 Corinthians 5:7). Only one period of signs and wonders, confirmed and authenticated Christ's message, and that was sufficient to establish the divine origin of God's message to the new era of the Church. It is never necessary to have an infinite series of witnesses to confirm a declaration is truthful. In the Bible, the norm is established by the word of two or three witnesses (Deuteronomy 17:6; Matthew 18:16). It is not necessary to continue proving a truth over and again. To insist now on more confirmation is to imply that the confirmation of the first century was insufficient or invalid.

The emphasis that is given to faith in the New Testament (239 references) indicates that in actuality, we should accept that Scriptural evidence declares that the apostles confirmed the message of Jesus in the first century, so there is no further need for confirmation today. This was the author's point in Hebrews in 2:3-4, and he insinuates that the message had already been confirmed when he wrote his epistle.

Factor 11: Only the apostles used the sign gifts.

Some Charismatic leaders insist that we need miracles every day. As a result, their congregations go around looking for miracles, and when they do not occur, blame and doubt grow to the point that they will do anything to have daily supernatural experiences.

Some leaders declare such things as, "God has a special miracle just for you today."

The truth is that Scripture does not affirm that the miracles that happened in the era of the apostles should occur in later times. In addition, none of Paul's letters say that believers should seek the manifestation of signs and wonders from the Spirit.

The Bible clearly indicates that the period of the revelation of the New Testament and the apostolic era were intimately connected. "I have made a fool of myself, but you drove me to it. I ought to have been commended by you, for I am not in the least inferior to the "super-apostles," even though I am nothing. The things that mark an apostle-- signs, wonders and miracles-- were done among you with great perseverance." (2 Cor. 12:11-12NLT).

> To argue that the New Testament gifts could occur today or that no verse rules out such a possibility is not enough; it must also be shown that the modern charismatic "gifts" are the same as in the New Testament. The proponents of the charismatic movement have been unsuccessful in proving either the first (the possibility of the gifts today) or the second (that these are the same phenomena). Are all phenomena automatically from the Holy Spirit simply because someone makes such an assertion, unless a verse can be found that directly states they are not? It is not enough merely to assert that charismatic phenomena are New Testament phenomena. There must be evidence that they are the same. (Edgar, 1988: 372).

In synthesis, Paul's argument to prove his apostleship is that he did miracles that none but apostles could do. It was the same thing that happened

Chapter 16: *Tongues in relation to Christ and the Apostles* 263

before Pharaoh: Moses had to prove his authenticity by signs that no one else could do. The Egyptian magicians imitated some signs, but not the last ones. Therefore, if everyone had been able to do miracles, there would not have been anything special about the apostles... and their revelations in the NT.

It was imperative that they do things that no one else could do. It is apparent that the gift of miracles was limited to the apostles. Some time before the out pouring of the Spirit and His gifts on the Day of Pentecost, Jesus gave to the 70 disciples authority to heal and cast out demons (Luke 10:9, 17), but this was a power given for a limited time and only to this group.

After that, only the apostles, and those commissioned by an apostle to share in his ministry (such as Phillip in Acts 8:6-7), manifested this power. Wherever signs and wonders occurred in the Scriptures after Pentecost, they all are directly related to the authentication of the apostles (Acts 4:30; 5:12; 14:3; Romans 15:18-19).

Three observations:

1. There is no evidence that the sign gifts were received apart from the ministry of an apostle.
2 Timothy 1:6, "Therefore I remind you to stir up the gift of God which is in you through the laying on of my hands."

The events in Acts 6:1-7 indicated that there was a problem between the "Hellenists" (Greek-speaking Jews from all over the empire) and Hebrew Jews from Judea in the early Church. The Hellenists widows were Jewish women born outside of Judah in the Roman colonies who had migrated to Jerusalem, probably after their husbands died; therefore, they spoke Greek, Aramaic, another dialect and had adopted many of the customs and philosophies of the Romans. Apparently the difference was notable and caused discrimination inside the early Church. Some thought that the Jewish widows had returned to Jerusalem in order to die in the Holy City, but did not have family members or financial support in Jerusalem. It is also possible that many of them had converted to Christianity, which isolated them from their Jewish families or friends.

Peter and the other eleven apostles, in order to find a solution to the problem, guided the congregation to select seven men to be responsible for this group within the church in Jerusalem. It seems that the apostles were going to continue to care for the Hebrew widows, and as a result the seven other men were given the responsibility to care for the Hellenist widows. In verse 5 we see that all the names of these chosen men are Greek, not Jewish. So the leaders of the Hellenist Jewish Church were all Greeks.

Many times the seven are called "deacons," because the noun "service" (*diaconia*) is used twice and the verb "serve" (*diakonein*) is used once. However, the word *diaconia* can refer to apostleship (Acts 1:17, 25), or to the ministry in general (Acts 12:25; 20:24; 21:19; 1 Corinthians 16:15; 2 Corinthians 5:18; Ephesians 4:12; Colossians 4:17; 2 Titus 4:5). The noun "minister" is *diakonos*, and it is used to refer to apostles and pastors (Romans 13:4; 1 Corinthians 3:5; 2 Corinthians 3:6; 6:4; 11:23; Ephesians 3:7; 6:21; Colossians 1:7, 23, 25; 4:7; 1 Thessalonians 3:2; 1 Ti. 4:6).

Only in Philippians 1:1 and 1 Timothy 3:8 and 12 do we see a reference to the office of deacon. Probably in Acts 6 the seven men were recognized by their faithfulness and service to others and, for this reason, they were constituted as ministers or leaders together with the apostles to help care for the people of God.

The apostles (Acts 6:6) lay hands on these men and gave them the authority of leading and, apparently, the power to perform signs and wonders (6:8). They immediately began to manifest apostolic powers. In Acts 6-8 we find a briefly related history of two of the seven, Stephen and Phillip. As we have shown, it seems that they received their power delegated directly from the apostles. In Acts 8:4 we read that the believers "went everywhere preaching the word," but there is no reference to miracles until Phillip arrived (8:5-8). Immediately there were signs, exorcisms and healings. No one else in the entire New Testament manifested such powers. These men could say that they did miracles by the commission and the authority of the apostles.

However, the delegation of the authority had limits. In Samaria many believed through Phillip's preaching, but they did not receive the Spirit (Acts 8:16) since this initially required the presence of an apostle, especially Peter. In Hebrews 2:4 we find that God was testifying "together with them" (those who heard Jesus in His earthly ministry in 2:3), with "...both with signs and wonders, and with divers miracles, and gifts of the Holy Ghost, according to his own will," in order to confirm the validity of the new message. In Acts 8:15 the Samaritans received the Spirit for the first time only when the apostles lay hands on them. This could not be delegated. But Paul exhorted Timothy to "...to stir up the gift of God which is in you through the laying on of my hands." (2 Tim. 1:6). If this indicates that the apostles could give gifts, then we can understand how some of the seven men in Acts 6 began to do apostolic-style miracles and signs immediately after receiving the laying on of hands from the apostles (6:6).

2. The sign gifts were given to the apostles and the non-miraculous gifts to the pastors and elders.

1 Timothy 4:14, "Do not neglect the gift that is in you, which was given to you by prophecy with the laying on of the hands of the eldership."

1 Timothy 4:14 also mentions the action of the laying on of hands, but in this case, it was not by the apostles but rather the "presbytery" (the group of elders or pastors). There is no indication that the elders had apostolic authority; for this reason the emphasis on "prophecy" indicates that the presbytery announced the quality and type of ministry that Timothy would have among them. It is like the recognition of a new pastor's gifts.

The mention of prophecy indicates that God revealed Timothy's gift to one of the presbyter-pastor-elders who had the gift of prophecy, which was still

Chapter 16: Tongues in relation to Christ and the Apostles

being exercised. The lesson of the passage is that we should not ignore our gift, once it is recognized. Acts 13:2-3 offers a similar illustration.

The Spirit communicated to the Church through a prophecy (13:1 indicated that there were several prophets in the church at Antioch) what the ministry of Paul and Barnabas would be. After praying and fasting over the decision, the other teachers and prophets laid hands on them and sent them out to minister.

At this point in the New Testament, they still depended on the revelation of God through prophets in their midst for how and what the local church was suppose to do. When the prophecies stopped, they had shed sufficient light on the theme of gifts for the people to recognize the gifts of the Spirit without the need of additional special revelation.

The description of the requirements for the pastorate in 1 Timothy 3:1-8 (Titus 1:7-9) provides us with sufficient criteria to approve or disapprove of a person who desires to be a pastor; no special revelation is needed. This was not the case with respect to the apostles and possibly prophets, since there had to be some miraculous indication in order to accept them as authentic.

It seems that through time church leadership shifted from apostles and prophets to evangelists, pastors and teachers. In the following chart we see the transition:

Eph 4:11

Provisional leadership	**Permanent leadership**
Apostles ⟶	Evangelists
Prophets	Pastors
	Teachers

> The apostolic office died with the first generation of Christians, there being no provision for successors, nor have there been in the history of the church any who could stand with the apostles. The fact that apostles were chosen from those who were eyewitnesses of the resurrected Christ in the nature of the case eliminates any possibility of later generations participating in the call to apostleship. The inventions of the Roman church in the attempt to continue the apostolic office have been often refuted. (Walvoord 1942: 40)

Evangelists replaced the apostles, and pastors and teachers replaced the prophets; but the ministry of edification, exhortation, consolation (1 Cor 14:3) and teaching continued the same. The change was in the authority of the revelation and the ministry of confirmation through signs and wonders that would become the text for preaching and teaching in the churches.

3. Paul's apostolic authority was proven with signs and miracles.

2 Corinthians 12:12, "Truly the signs of an apostle were accomplished among you with all perseverance, in signs and wonders and mighty deeds."

To be an Apostle of Jesus Christ was a singular privilege and responsibility. One had to be a personal witness of Christ's life, death, and resurrection (Acts 1:21-22). To prove that he had the authority only granted to apostles, God gave them power to perform miracles and wonders (Matt 10:1; 2 Cor 12:12). In the same manner, Paul's apostolic authority was confirmed by the supernatural miracles God worked through his hands (Acts 13:9-12; 14:8-10; 16:16-18; 19:11-12; 20:9-12).

MacArthur notes the apostolic authority was not to rule the church, but men were chosen vessels to speak God's revelation to the churches and to record those truths and revelations for all time (MacArthur 1997:1788).

If signs like tongues were common for all believers, then Paul's defense about his special position as an apostle would not have had value, leaving him without proof that he was unique as an apostle of Christ with unusual authority to reveal the Word of God for all the church. In 2 Corinthians 12:12 we see these signs are only for the apostles, since they are called the "signs of an apostle." Therefore the possession of the gifts of signs and wonders was related to the apostolic authority (in the New Testament) and occurred always in relation to the apostles.

> C. Peter Wagner, Gordon Fee, Oral Roberts, and others claim that miracles done by miracle workers have continued in the church and all available for the church today. Proponents of the modern faith healing movement base their position on the doctrine of healing in the atonement and/or they argue that God must work in the same way now as He did in the first-century church. (Bryan 1979: 3-4; Carlston 1971: 99-107; Williams 1980: 59)

> According to Wagner, "The power that worked in Jesus for His miraculous ministry not only is related to the power available to us today; it is exactly the same. As we relate to God in prayer, faith and obedience we have abundant resources to go forth in Jesus' name to preach everywhere 'with signs following' as did the early disciples." (Derickson, 1998:301). However, if this were the case then there would be no question about the nature of the contemporary "miracles."

> An examination of the New Testament reveals that the modern charismatic phenomena are not sufficiently similar to those of the apostolic age. Where are the tongues of fire and the rushing of a mighty wind as on the day of Pentecost? Do missionaries blind their opponents as Paul did? Do church leaders discern hypocrisy and pronounce the immediate death of members as in Acts 5:1–11? Do evangelists amaze an entire city with miracles as did Philip (8:5–8)? Are they then taken to another place of ministry by the Holy Spirit (vv. 39–40)? Are entire multitudes healed by merely being in the shadow of the healer (5:15)? Do prophets give specific prophecies, which come to pass soon after (11:27–28)? (Edgar 1988: 376).

Chapter 16: *Tongues in relation to Christ and the Apostles* 267

The observable and evident miracles of the apostolic age were undeniable. Little or no evidence has surfaced that questions the apostolic miracles. Most contemporary miracles are seldom instantaneous or visible; most today are internal disorders or "emotional healing" (Masters, 1988: 202-227).

Today's miracles are performed in special healing meetings with considerable preliminary screening and briefings and extremely limited to a few; on the other hand, in the NT the miracles occurred in the streets, virtual universal healings of everyone or at a distance. Often they occurred with people who had no idea of who the healer was or even that a healing was about to occur. Generally the healing had nothing to do with the faith of the recipient. No one today can duplicate the nature of the NT miracles.

The NT church was not characterized by perpetual miracles and supernatural manifestations as the charismatics want to duplicate. Rather, numerous problems, doctrinal errors, divisions and false teachers characterized the Early Church as described in Revelation 2-3. Primarily only the apostles performed miracles, with only a few exceptions of close associates to the apostles. The notion that the entire church performed or should perform miracles as the apostles is pure imagination.

Warfield associated miracles with the apostles and a few others from their generation. He clarified the purpose of their miracles as to authenticate the validity of the apostles and their witness to their generation. Warfield argued against modern miracle workers on the grounds that the gospel and its bearers no longer needed to prove they were unique and authentic messengers from God. He also argued that history indicates miracles ceased with the first-century generation of Christians. (Warfield 1972: 5–6) A belief in the closing of the biblical canon often includes an understanding that miracles must necessarily have ceased with its completion.

> Among cults and charismatics, apostleship is not limited to the beginning of the Church. Many are the modern day, self-appointed apostles who use their titles in an authoritarian, self-glorying fashion to declare new revelation and bring their followers to their knees before them. (Askins 1998: 310).

With the death of the apostles and the few who had received the laying on of hands from them, the era of miraculous gifts in the Church had passed. This occurred around the year 100 A.D. (70 years after the resurrection).

Factor 12: The past tense of Hebrews 2:3-4 indicates that the "confirmation" of the message of salvation through miracles was completed in the first century.

Hebrews 2:3, "how shall we escape if we neglect so great a salvation, which at the first began to be spoken by the Lord, and was confirmed to us by those who heard Him, 4 God also bearing witness both with signs and wonders, with various miracles."

Hebrews 2:3-4 shows a transition through three generations:
(1) Salvation was "announced first by the Lord" Jesus.
(2) "Those who heard" the announcement directly from Jesus were given the responsibility to confirmed the divine nature of the message.
(3) The others, including the author of Hebrews, received the confirmation of the second group ("it was confirmed to us" by them).

The tense of the verb "was confirmed" indicates that the confirmation was not in process at the moment when the author wrote Hebrews, but rather the author was looking back to a time when the apostles were confirming Jesus' message with miracles. In the Greek, the tense of the verb is aorist, or a kind of action that occurred at a determined moment or period in the past and did not continue. If he had wanted to say that the confirmation was still occurring, he would have said, "it is being confirmed." Obviously his argument might seem much stronger if he had been able to say that someone was still doing miracles to confirm the message, or that everyone through all the ages were to confirm the message with miracles. But this is not what was written. If there had been an apostle with such a ministry of confirming the message through miracles, then the author surely would have referred to him in the present tense.

When Paul wanted to confirm the resurrection, he cited present evidence at the time. For example, in 1 Corinthians 15 he said that still the majority of the 500 witnesses of the resurrection were alive to confirm the good news and validity of that event.

If we apply the Charismatic logic to the resurrection, then we would have to say, "We do not believe in the resurrection until we see the resurrected Lord personally today." (This is what Thomas said.) If they accept the evidence of Christ's resurrection because it is written in the Bible and insist on accepting it by faith, then why do they say that the confirmation by miracles is still necessary? Can't we say that the genuineness of Christ's message was confirmed by undisputed miracles, which we trust by faith in the record of the Word of God today?

For this reason the author of Hebrews 2 could not refer to anything in the present tense as a confirmation of the message, but rather he referred to the past confirmation, which he was willing to trust just as we are asked to trust their past confirmation as true.

An interesting note is that apart from 1 Corinthians 12-14, and merely two references in Acts, there are no other references to the sign of tongues. There are "signs, miracles and wonders" but never "signs, tongues, miracles, etc." It seems that the churches did not place much emphasis on tongues (except for the Corinthians), indicating that this sign must have disappeared very early. Later there were false manifestations of tongues that Paul was correcting in Corinth, but the miraculous sign of foreign tongues never was an important factor in the early church.

CHAPTER 17

Tongues in Relation to the Evidence from the History of the Church

Chapter 17: *Gifts for Today*

In the fifth category of evidence for the miraculous gifts is the history of the Church. The Bible says that tongues and other gifts ceased, and the implication is that tongues would cease in harmony with the other gifts. If some of the gifts were impermanent, then we can surmise that they disappeared simultaneously. Admittedly, this is not conclusive, but highly probable.

> As a sign, the purpose of tongues ended when that to which it pointed ended. A person driving to Los Angeles may see the first mileage sign about 300 miles away. Later he sees one that reads "200 miles to Los Angeles," and then "50 miles," and then "10 miles." After he passes through the city, however, the mileage signs to Los Angeles cease. They have no further purpose, because that to which they pointed has been reached and passed. The gift of tongues was attached irretrievably to one point in history, and that point has long been passed. (MacArthur 1984: 383).

Upon reading the book of Acts, we should note the difference between miraculous gifts at the beginning of the book and at the end; mention of them dwindles as if they were disappearing. This appraisal makes sense if we understand that the confirmation period of the message and of the messengers was coming to an end. Therefore, all of the practices of that earlier period are not the norm for subsequent generations of believers. The norm for each believer is to study and obey the Word of God, which was revealed and confirmed, and can make us wise and mature and effective in ministering to others. The norm is to live by faith, not by sight, in what God has revealed and previously confirmed.

MacArthur argues that the limited functions of the gift of tongues even during the time in history when it was operational, was misused and "became a hindrance to worship and to evangelism" (*Ibid.*:384).

Yet some cannot accept Christianity without apostolic miracles. They try to intimidate others by arguing such points as, "Who would want a God whose energy had run out? Could God do something in one century and not in another? Has God lost His power?" Others argue that anyone who negates the presence of apostolic-style miracles has a "faith that does not allow for Jesus Christ, who is the same yesterday, today and forever. They are perfectly comfortable with a distant God who has not done anything significant in 2,000 years." With such accusations, a person could be left trying to figure out whether he really was a believer or not. The Bible presents the apostolic era as something special and unique, however; it does not mention a Church Age when anyone could manifest the "signs of an apostle" (2 Cor 12:12).

In these two categories we will see the historic evidence both in the Bible and in secular history. If we find evidence of the ceasing of these sign gifts, then we can arrive at one of two conclusions: Either sin and lack of faith in the whole Church put to death the sign gifts, or they had completed their purpose in God's plan and were no longer needed. Charismatics choose the first conclusion, while non-charismatic evangelical believers believe the evidence supports the second option.

Factor 13: The cessation of other gifts and sudden divine judgments suggests that tongues also ceased.

Historically there were seven signs-gifts during the Early Church era that terminated by the end of the first century. Five of the seven are in relation to the gift of tongues (and interpretation of tongues); upon termination of one, we can anticipate the termination of the others also (Hunter 1976:74) Tongues has been discussed in other chapters so our present discussion will focus on the remaining five sign gifts, which include the following:

1. Miracles
2. Healings
3. Prophecy
4. Apostleship
5. Sudden judgment

(1) The gift of miracles.

The word "miracle" is *dynamis* or "power," meaning that the gift of miracles is the gift of power. It appears 120 times in the New Testament as a noun and another 100 times as a verb. This power is especially manifested in the Gospels to combat the reign of Satan (Matthew 8, 9, 12; Mark 5, 6, 7; Luke 9) and is principally the capacity of casting out demons. The apostles and Phillip had this power (Acts 13:10; 19:12 and Acts 8:6-7) in the initial era of the announcement of the Gospel of Jesus. Apart from these individuals, there is no evidence that the gift was more widely distributed in the church. To say that we need people who can do miracles today as the apostles did is to challenge God's purpose for those gifts.

For the generations that follow the apostles and that also had to fight against malignant spirits, the Scriptures tell us how to act (2 Corinthians 2:10-11; Ephesians 4:27; 6:11-18; 2 Timothy 2:25-26; 1 Peter 5:7-9). All these passages give us personal instructions on how to triumph over Satan. Today the authority is given to all believers to "resist the devil and he will flee from you" (James 4:7), but not to do miraculous manifestations.

Since it seems apparent that there were not going to be specially endued men to show miraculous powers over demons throughout the Church Age, the Church was given the general instruction in how to recognize and deal with subversive spirits. Frequently, the gift of miracles is strictly considered synonymous with healings, since Satan can produce sicknesses.

(2) Healings.

The gravest perceived physical problem that man suffers is physical sickness. The cost of researching new cures is enormous, and the number of modern procedures for healing the sick indicates the importance that they represent for society. Whether educated or not, people would be attracted to a religion or practice that promised healing, and the phrase that describes the desire for such a religion is, "A truth that heals."

There are five different branches of healing that are neither conventional nor chemical:

(1) Christian groups: Praying Christians who seek to see Jesus heal the sick as a result of answered prayer. This group is made up of all Christians, whether Charismatic or not. Probably as much prayer for healing occurs in non-Charismatic churches as it does in Charismatic.

(2) Metaphysical groups: members, like the Christian Scientists and the Unity Church, are philosophical in practice. These groups have many beliefs in common with psychic groups or the occult, like healing through telepathy. They organize in a church structure, the way a Christian denomination would.

(3) Natural practitioner groups: members are specialists in certain practices like shiatsu, iridology, acupuncture and reflexology. In this group we include homeopathy, naturopathy and other forms of natural or alternative medicine.

(4) Oriental Meditation and Human Potential Groups: members practice yoga, psychological synthesis, and ESP and believe in reincarnation. Included in this group are those who practice Transcendental Meditation and the Hindu Buddhist disciplines.

(5) Occult and Psychic Groups: This is the most diverse and difficult group to categorize because it includes all kinds of psychic healings and psychic healers. They emphasize the potential of the individual to acquire power to control his life. This potential is only possible through a special knowledge of the occult, which they communicate to their members. (Bixler 1970:59)

The theories of the five branches of healing are easier to identify than their practices, which tend to cross lines of distinction when forming a synthesis of healing. For example, we can observe the practices of psychics or Orientals in some Christian groups, and vice versa. Likewise, New Age philosophy, mysticism and oriental philosophies combine different elements of healing. The popularity of these groups is growing rapidly around the world, and they all promise similar healings, from bloodless surgery to the filling of teeth. Satan is the force behind many of these groups, and he has been able to attract the masses through false healings. A former spiritists medium who was converted to Christ said, "Today there are many spiritists who are gifted by Satan with this extraordinary power; and I myself, having been used in this way, can testify of having seen miraculous healings during 'healing meetings' of the spiritism movement." (Gasson 1966: 109).

In the some churches there is also much emphasis placed on the power

Chapter 17: Tongues in Relation to the History of the Church

to heal. Many of the assertions of such healings cannot be proved (declared internal or unobservable healings), but they are repeated and often exaggerated. All Christians believe that God can and does heal in response to our prayers in order to reveal His glory (James 5:16). Medicine, alternative or conventional, also heals. The question is not whether God heals today, but whether or not the gift of healing exists now as it did during the apostolic times.

There is a great difference between the healings we see today and those performed by Jesus and His disciples. Comparing Jesus' miracles of healing to those done by His disciples, we see that they are identical:

Jesus	**The apostles**
He healed with a word or a touch.	They healed with a word or a touch.
Matthew 8:6-8, 13; Mark 5:25-34	Acts 9:32-35; 28:8
He healed instantly.	They healed instantly.
Matthew 8:13; Mark 5:29; Luke 17:14	Acts 3:2-8
He healed totally.	They healed totally.
Luke 4:39	Acts 9:34
He healed everyone He meant to heal	They healed everyone they meant
Luke 9:11	to heal. Acts 5:12-16; 28:9
He healed organic sicknesses.	They healed organic sicknesses.
Matthew 9:20; John 9:2-7	Acts 3:6-9
He raised the dead.	They raised the dead.
Mark 5:22-24, 35-43; John 20:30-31	Acts 9:36-42; 20:9-12

Even though God may not give the gift of healing today, there are still healings that occur on a smaller scale and in different ways.

We must understand that in the Bible there are three kinds of healings. When we speak of healings, we should identify what type. The three kinds of healings are (1) healing by creation, (2) healing by exorcism of demons, and (3) Healing by prayer.

Healing by creation, for the lack of a better word, is the power to instantly "create" new body parts on command. In Mark 2:3-12, Jesus healed the paralytic whose muscles had degenerated and deteriorated, causing him to have no control over his body. Verse 12 states that when Jesus healed him, his body was restored "immediately." The healing was fully accomplished, not only in the instant restoration and re-creation of new muscles, nerves and skin, but also in that his coordination was restored. The apostles had the same capacity to create new physical members.

In Acts 3:1-8, the healing of a lame man from birth occurred "immediately," and the outcome was that, "his feet and ankle bones received strength."

In 2 Kings 5:14, the miraculous transformation of Naaman's leprous skin, "was restored like the flesh of a little child, and he was clean" was also immediate and completely effective. This kind of healing, which cannot be explained in terms of psychosomatic healing, psychological healing, autosuggestion, or natural remedy was most common during the time of Jesus and the apostles, but it is not seen today.

Healing by exorcism of demons removes demonic influences that can ail and even completely control someone. In Luke 13:10-17, we find a woman who was "bowed together and could in no wise lift up herself." Verse 11 says that she, "who had been crippled by a spirit for eighteen years," which is clarified in verse 16 when it says that she was "bound" by Satan. Jesus diagnosed her problem as satanic in nature instead of merely physical. When He cast out the demon, the woman was immediately healed.

Healing by prayer was distinct from the first kind of healing in the Early Church, which was usually accomplished by a command or order to be healed given by a voice of authority: "Be healed," or, "Stand up and walk." However, this third kind of healing is not based on authority, that is to say the request for healing was submitted to the will of God rather than the will of the one who had the gift of healing.

Apart from the manifestations of the miraculous gifts, God can respond to the prayer of individuals or groups. The first example of healing by prayer was when a person asks for his own healing. It is not a prayer of authority, but rather a petition subject to the will of God.

An example of this kind of prayer is found in 2 Corinthians 12:7-9, Paul prayed three times that God would heal his affliction, which was not defined in the text. In this case, God denied his petition of healing because He had a greater purpose for the sickness than to show His power in healing. He wanted to show His power as Paul was content with Christ even in the midst of a sickness.

The second example of healing by prayer is of elders pleading with God to heal a member of their congregation. James 5:14-16 discusses the ministry of praying for the sick in a church, which will be considered more fully later. It is important to note that this kind of healing is not a sign of confirmation to authenticate a messenger or his message, but rather was simply a ministry within a local church.

When the gift of healing was exercised through the first two kinds of healing, passages such as Acts 5:16 tell us "everyone was healed." It is evident that the gift of healing was passing away in the Church, even during the life of the apostles:

In 35 A.D., everyone was healed (Acts 5:14-16).
In 56 A.D., Paul could not heal himself (2 Corinthians 12:7-12).
In 60 A.D., Paul could not heal Epaphroditus (Philippians 2:25-28).
In 67 A.D., Paul could not heal Trophimus and had to leave him sick in Miletus (2 Timothy 4:20).

We should note that both Epaphroditus and Trophimus were filled with the Spirit and faith, but Paul could not heal them. Therefore, we cannot blame sin or lack of faith, but rather that Paul no longer had the authority to heal 25 to 30 years after the Ascension of the Lord. Sometimes God determines to receive more glory by showing His power in strengthening a believer to endure affliction with grace, contentment and peace.

It is evident that God does not heal today with the frequency that he did in the early Church. For a short time the apostles healed everyone with any sickness, but it seems that at the end of their lives even they could not do what today healers claims to do. If the gift of healing as a sign of an apostle had ended, then what remains is healing through the prayers for the sick especially by the elders and pastors.

(3) Prophecy.

The Prophets in the New Testament were very similar to those in the Old Testament. A prophet was an instrument of divine revelation, and occasionally becoming a writing prophet through inspiration, resulting in an inerrant, infallible text, which became part of the biblical record.

The only examples of the speaking prophets' ministries in the NT are predictions of the future through revelation. The gift had high priority and frequently belonged to the apostles. Since prophets were part of the foundation of the Church together with the apostleship (Eph 2:20), it would not continue during the building up period of the Church Age.

> Williams does not seem to place the application of the prophetic gift today on the same level with the Scriptures. "I do not intend in any way to place contemporary experience on the same level of authority as the Bible. Rather I do vigorously affirm the decisive authority of Scripture: hence, God does not speak just as authoritatively today as He spoke to the biblical authors. But He continues to speak (He did not stop with the close of the New Testament canon)" (Williams, 1977: 35).

If the gift of prophecy ended in the Early Church with the finishing of the book of Revelation, which prohibited that more prophecy be added to the last book of the New Testament, then the gifts associated with the prophets also had to disappear.

(4) Apostleship.

With all the requirements necessary to be an apostle, it would be foolish to insist that the gift of apostleship continues today. The apostles' capacity to work "signs of an apostle" was a mark that distinguished them from all other believers, and those who try to make the circle of apostles greater than the twelve and Paul base their beliefs on very shady interpretations. Almost no one else in the history of the Church has claimed to have this authority, and no one has been verified as having it. Similarly, no one can pretend to do miracles today in the same way that the apostles did in the New Testament. Scriptures indicate that the apostles were needed only for the Church in its beginning, and the gift of apostleship was not needed afterward.

(5) Divine judgments.

In the New Testament, God frequently judged sin among believers by death, and He sent it quickly. For example, in 32 A.D., Ananias and Saphira lied to the Spirit and were immediately killed (Acts 5:1-11). In 44 A.D., Herod accepted acclaim as if he were a god and was killed (Acts 12:20-25). In 56 A.D., Paul turned over a believer to be killed for having sexual relations with his stepmother (1 Corinthians 5:1, 5).

Sin was not taken lightly in the early Church. God controlled morality in the Church through periodic sudden judgments. In the following fifteen years (55-70 A.D.), however, it seems that this sudden judgment diminished until it was a rare occurrence.

By the end of the first century God was no longer dealing with men in such a drastic and immediate way. For example, in 64 A.D., Alexander, a blasphemer, was turned over to Satan for death (1 Timothy 1:19-20). In 67 A.D., Alexander still had not received his recompense for his actions against Paul (2 Timothy 4:14-15). This shows that God did not treat men the same at the end of Paul's life as he did in the beginning of the Church. Instead of a severe or fatal discipline on God's part, 1 Corinthians 6:2-5 places the responsibility to discipline on the churches.

It was important for God to use this method of dealing harshly with the early Church to demonstrate to the Jews that the God of the Old Testament was beginning a new era. As we have shown, special signs were promised to Israel (1 Corinthians 14:21) so they would recognize the Messiah and the new revelations.

During the time of the inauguration of the Law in the Old Testament similar events took place. In Leviticus 10:12, the judgment of God fell immediately on two of Aaron's four sons, Nadab and Abihu, for their disobedience to God's instructions.

Later in the history of Israel, God disciplined two other priests, Hophni and Phinehas, who caused Israel to sin and scorn the offerings. They were the sons of the high priest Ely (1 Samuel 2:12-17, 22). After God's judgment on them was announced, more than twenty years passed before it was fulfilled.

In the Old Testament, God's sudden judgment of sin ceased when God allowed Israel's judicial system to take its place. A similar transition occurred in the New Testament. In both the Old and New Testaments, discipline was accomplished when Israel or the Church judged themselves. In the Church, each believer is exhorted to examine himself (1 Corinthians 11:28-31) so as not to be disciplined by the Lord and to prove himself (2 Corinthians 13:5; Galatians 6:4), whether his faith be genuine or not. In difficult cases, the churches had to judge and discipline their own members (1 Corinthians 6:1-11; 5:7-8).

This change is the result of the relative maturity of the Church, which is now better able to judge itself through the completion of the revealed Word. Since the gifts of tongues and interpretation are related to the miracle gifts of

Chapter 17: *Tongues in Relation to the History of the Church*

healings, prophecy and sudden judgment, all of which disappeared in the first century, we can understand that tongues also ceased exactly as Paul said in 1 Corinthians 13:8.

Factor 14: Historically, tongues ceased completely.

The evidence of the first thirteen factors is in the Bible, but the secular history of the Church also indicates that the miraculous gifts terminated at the end of the first century. Even though this evidence is not compiled totally from the biblical record, it does confirm the prophecy in 1 Corinthians 13:8, which says, "Love never fails. But whether there are prophecies, they will fail; whether there are tongues, they will cease; whether there is knowledge, it will vanish away."

We should emphasize the fact that the Scriptures never show tongues ceasing and then reappearing. On the contrary, once they disappeared in the Church, they never appeared again in the Church Age.

If the gift of tongues were the principle gift among all believers throughout history, we should see it growing through time instead of diminishing along with the apostles as history indicates. This is not a surprise to those who know the Bible.

An investigator of the "Post-apostolic Fathers," or church leaders in the first 300 years of the Church, said, "it is significant that nowhere is there the allusion to or even a sign of tongues in the writings of these Post-apostolic Fathers." (Rogers 1965:135-136).

Although this might be considered an argument from silence, it is valuable evidence because of additional factors. (1) The Apostolic Fathers wrote from and to the churches where the gift of tongues had been practiced during the time of the apostles. (2) The widespread geographic locations around the Roman Empire of the Apostolic Fathers makes their silence significant. (3) The doctrinal characteristics of the Apostolic Fathers makes their silence remarkable because they covered practically every major doctrine taught in the NT yet no mention of tongues. (4) The purpose of their writings was to show the superiority of Christianity using every argument, but there is no mention of tongues, which could have been a supernatural argument had they existed.

There are five observations comprising the body of secular historical evidence, which show that tongues ceased.

Observation 1: Historically there are no references to tongues after Chrysostom in 380 A.D.

The great theologians of the ancient Church —Clement of Rome (d.101), Ignatius (d. 107), Justin Martyr (d.165), Origen (d.253), Chrysostom (d.407) and Augustine (d.430) — all considered tongues to be a remote practice that occurred in the early days of the Church. Contemporary historian Philip Schaff says that a similar but inferior phenomenon to the New Testamentary manifestation appeared at times during periods of religious emotion, but Augustine said in 407 A.D. that there were no longer authentic cases of tongues because the gift had ceased.

Clement of Rome wrote to the church at Corinth, yet he never mentioned the problem of tongues (that Paul had written three chapters to correct), yet many of the other problems Paul had corrected, were still persistent in the church. Evidently the tongues issue had been resolved by ceasing to exist, or possibly by practicing the principles of 1 Cor 14. The latter option seems out of character with the persistent carnality of the church.

Justin Martyr made reference to seven spiritual gifts, but tongues was not one of them (Rogers 1965:137). Since he was a teacher of the Christian faith, his silence on this issue speaks loudly. His writings were intended to prove that Christianity is the true religion by all the valid evidences, but he made no mention of speaking in tongues.

Origin who traveled widely and wrote prolifically "made no clear statement regarding the gift of tongues and his testimony indicates that the extraordinary gifts were gone" (*Ibid*:142). Later Origen added that "the Holy Spirit gave signs and outward demonstrations of His presence at the beginning of Christ's ministry and after His ascension, these things have diminished and are no longer widespread" (Origen, Against Celsus, VIII, 8). He refuted Celsus' description of contemporary prophets as false stating, "For no prophet bearing any resemblance to the ancient prophets has appeared in the time of Celsus." (*Ecclesiastical History*, VIII, 11)

In his commentary on 1 Corinthians, Chrysostom (345-407 A.D.) he confesses that the "whole place is very obscure," and goes on to add: "but the obscurity is produced by our ignorance of the facts referred to and by their cessation, being such as then used to occur, but now no longer take place." (Chrysostom, *Homilies on First Corinthians*, XXIX, 1). This great leader of the Greek Church declared that he saw no evidence of the gift of tongues in his day.

The only possible reference to tongues in the first 400 years of the Church is by Montanus (160 A.D.), and even this is not clear. Schaff describes Montanus and the two women who followed him, "All three left as prophets and reformers of the Christian life and proclaimed the immediate coming of the Holy Spirit and the Millennial Reign in Pepuza, a small town in Frygia, over which would come down the New Jerusalem." (Schaff 2006:n.a.)

Eusebius described Montanus as a false prophet with the following characteristics: he declared himself as a *Paracleto* or the Holy Spirit; he was legalistic; many sincere believers followed him; his movement was outside the majority of groups of believers. Eusebius wrote in Ecclesiastical History V, 16, "So that he was carried away in spirit, and was wrought up into a certain kind of frenzy and irregular ecstasy, raving, and speaking, and uttering strange things and proclaiming what was contrary to the institutions that had prevailed in the church...." (Rogers 1965: 141)

Since his prophecies did not come to pass, Montanus was a false prophet ipso facto; therefore, his experiences cannot be used as a faithful testimony

Chapter 17: *Tongues in Relation to the History of the Church* 279

that the gift of tongues was genuine throughout the history of the Church.

The single exception to this observation is the report of Irenaeus (d. 202) who gives some hearsay evidence stating, "we hear many brethren in the Church...who through the Spirit speak all kinds of languages" (Against Heresies V, 6. 1 quoted by Rogers 1965:138). However, it is known that Irenaeus was associated with Montanus so most see his statement was a reference to the Montanists of Asia Minor.

The bishop of Hipo in Africa, Augustine (345-430 A.D.), declared:

"In the early times 'the Spirit fell over those who believed and spoke in tongues.' These were signs adapted to the times. It seems that there was power of the Spirit in all tongues, to show that the gospel of God had to be told in all the tongues in all the world. That was done as a sign and ceased...If, then, the testimony of the presence of the Holy Spirit is not given through miracles, through what medium can one come to know if another has received the Spirit?" (Augustine: 497-498)

In the 300 years that followed the apostles, there is no evidence that any genuine believer had the gift of tongues or that anyone spoke in tongues at all. If the Bible says that tongues would cease and, in effect they did, then we can suspect that any manifestation of tongues today would be a false manifestation and not a biblical gift.

Observation 2: There is no evidence that the kind of "tongues" that appeared in Corinth were genuine; therefore, we can conclude that present manifestations are the false tongues that Paul spoke of in 1 Corinthians 14.

In today's world there are several manifestations of "tongues" or "mystical languages" practiced by pagans, and the same thing happened in the ancient world. Thomas Edgar cites Virgil, who referred to prophetesses who "spoke in tongues." Such practices of the Greek religions (the Tracian Dionisios, the Delfico Frygia and the Sibilas), as well as the animism of today's primitive religions speak in strange sounds as a supposed language with the gods. (Edgar, 1983: 253.) Many religious groups today have adopted universal practices related to glossolalia that have nothing to do with the movement of the Holy Spirit. Some of these include the following:
1. The speaker goes into a trance or ecstatic state.
2. The form and intonation of the voice is not normal.
3. The speaker is dominated or possessed by a strange force.
4. The verbal expressions are normally unintelligible to the speaker and listener, even though some pretend to have spoken in a real language.
5. The speaker comes to a peak of happiness or other emotion, a "high" during the experience, which frequently is followed by an emotional low.
6. The speaker normally is not conscious of his own words and actions.

7. It can be that other physical manifestations accompany the experience, such as accelerated respiration, foaming at the mouth, or convulsions.
8. Normally there is a procedure to provoke the experience.
9. The first experience is generally the most difficult or crucial and further experiences are easier to initiate. (Goodman 1972:121-123).

Another factor that indicates that these are not genuine tongues is that a linguistic analysis of the sounds shows it is not a genuine language. All languages have certain unique characteristics, distinct vowels or consonants that operate uniquely within it, different from every other language. To speak a language one must adapt his phonetics to that of the new language, because no two languages use the exact same phonetics or pronunciation of vowels and consonants in the same way.

There are seven linguistic tests that show a false or imaginary language:

Test 1: A lot of repeated syllables using similar sounds: "*ha, bah, beta, bata,*" etc. indicates a false language. Sounds vary greatly in a true language, and it is not very difficult to note the repetition of the same syllable. If there is little repetition and a lot of variety of sounds, it could be a true language.

Test 2: There is always a similarity between speaking in tongues and the language of the speaker. We know through linguistics that there are 350 distinct sounds among the world's languages. In a single language there can be 30 to 50 different sounds, and each language has its distinctions. There are sounds in English that do not appear in Spanish and vice versa. If a person speaks in "tongues" but only uses the phonetic sounds of his natural language, then that is merely a confusion of sounds or gibberish from his own native language, rather than a genuine miraculous tongue.

Test 3: The excessive use of one or two vowels is a characteristic of a false language. Languages usually have from 8 to 20 vowels. One Brazilian language has 26 vowels. The manifestation of "tongues" is almost always limited in vowels, and no genuine language ever uses so few vowels in any one sentence. In almost any group of 10 words in any language we find a minimum of 4 to 5 vowels. It is certain that one could invent a phrase with only one or two vowels, but it would be impossible to communicate effectively.

Test 4: The lack of grammatical structure is a telltale sign. Any amateur linguist can transcribe a recorded "tongue" for analysis. When an interpretation is given a comparison can easily determine if there is a consistent relationship between the sounds and the interpretation. The manifestation of the gift of tongues in many countries has been examined many times by experts and no one has ever found a "miraculous language" that contained a grammatical structure. One can visit any country, record the most primitive language and he will always find a well-defined grammar. If it does not have a grammatical structure, then it is not a language.

Test 5: Generally when an interpretation is given it is much longer than the message in a "tongue." It is certain that translating word-for-word is often difficult, but when the difference is disproportionate, something is not valid. When the "tongue" contains 15 to 20 groups of sounds or words and its interpretation is from 50 to 100 or more, something unnatural is happening. If there are more than 20% more words of interpretation, then the interpreter is inventing or adding his own ideas. If the difference is exaggerated, as is normally the case in such manifestations, then the interpreter is making it up.

Test 6: Interpretations of the same phrase or clause are usually inconsistent in a "tongue." In studies, a single group of sounds (morphemes) has been interpreted from 2 to 5 radically different ways, depending on the extent of the "interpretation." It is true that a word can have various meanings, but five totally different interpretations of the same word or phrase is unlikely, especially when tonal levels are not employed.

Test 7: The interpretation nearly always sounds as if it were a biblical reference, especially from Psalms. Sometimes it is a repetition of verses from the Bible already memorized with some added words. It is good that the heart of the interpreter is so full of the Bible that it flows so freely from his mouth, but it is strange that the interpretation would not be more natural. If the interpretation sounded like natural speech, then there would be more reason to accept it, because God always reveals His message in a way that makes it easy to understand. (Gromacki 1967: 5-22)

Note that in the cases of tongues in the Bible there was not a problem with these tests because they were always literal languages. If it is not a literal language spoken on the earth, then it is nothing but noise.

A final piece of evidence that today's gift of tongues is not genuine is the instruction that is given for entering into the experience; the procedure is completely contrary to the Bible. An author gave the following instructions for inducing a person to begin speaking in tongues: "To receive the Baptism of the Spirit, raise your hands and eyes to the heavens and begin to speak words, sounds or simple syllables; do it quickly, more quickly, more quickly and it will occur! You have received the baptism of the Spirit."

In his book, The Holy Spirit and You, the father of the charismatic movement Dennis Bennett, gave the following instructions:

Begin giving praises to the Lord such as "Glory!" "Hallelujah!", until it becomes difficult to say. Perhaps you will not recognize it, but the difficulty is the Spirit. He is pushing your mind to the contrary. The conflict between your will and that of the Spirit causes stuttering. People will sometimes experience such things as involuntary trembling, stammering lips, or chattering teeth… They probably arise out of our resistance to Him.
Since it is impossible to speak two languages at once, you must decide not to speak a word in your natural tongue. Your lips must be free to allow the Holy Spirit to move them. When the sounds begin, lift your voice without inhibitions, having faith in God for the result—that's it! Just as a child learning to talk for the first time, open your mouth and speak out the first

syllables and expressions that come to your lips...
It is necessary to discipline yourself not to speak a word in your own language. You can look up toward God and open your mouth, breathing deeply and by faith, drink from your interior the power of the spirit. Opening your mouth and breathing deeply constitutes a step of faith that God honors. If you do this, I can assure you that the Spirit will begin to move shortly. If you begin to follow your impulses, opening and closing your lips waiting for the guidance of the Spirit, speaking that which comes without thinking in how it sounds, you will be able to speak in a spiritual tongue.
Satan will try to make you believe that you are fabricating the words, or that you are imitating someone else, or perhaps he will say: "Now you are working in the flesh and that is dangerous." Do not pay attention to his suggestions. (Bennett, 1998: 65-68)

The Charismatic movement is an imitation of the genuine gift of tongues and deceives thousands of people, causing them to think that they are experiencing a "miracle" while biblical truth is ignored. Even when the spirit tries to make clear the truth of their false experience, his voice is rejected as the voice of Satan. The experience is all that matters.

Observation 3: There is no evidence that the occasional eruption of "gifts" has produced biblical revivals in history.

There is no evidence that anyone who manifested special gifts was responsible for revival or for any movement that lasted throughout the history of the Church. In addition, they were never accepted by Roman Catholics or by the churches of the Reformation; rather these radical expressions were rejected as heretics. They were not rejected for the "signs" they claimed to have but rather for their doctrines they introduced.

Only in the nineteenth and twentieth centuries were such manifestations accepted in evangelical communities. Is it possible that no one knew God intimately as some do (or, rather, claim to) today? Could it be that God kept the fulfillment of the promise of His Spirit for 1900 years a secret? These conclusions seem very extreme.

The claim that today's Charismatic movement is fulfilling the prophecy of Joel 2, which talks about the "latter rains" as an image of the outpouring of the Spirit in the end times before Jesus returns (the "former rains" are seen as the Apostolic Pentecost), is not biblically sound interpretation. Joel's prophecy describes the beginning of the millennial reign during the end times and cannot refer to anything prior to it. Joel 2 obviously describes real rain, meaning that the arid zones of Israel will become fertile again through the abundance of the promised rain at the beginning of the millennium.

If no biblical basis for Charismatic behavior exists, if all its historic antecedents are related to non-evangelical groups, and if "tongues" have not

Chapter 17: *Tongues in Relation to the History of the Church* 283

provoked any true revival throughout history, then there is reason to doubt the genuineness of the movement.

Observation 4: No great preacher, theologian, evangelist or missionary in Church history ever had tongues as part of his spiritual life.

The illogical implication of Pentecostal teaching condemns thousands and thousands of men of God throughout Church history to an inferior level of spirituality and power. If speaking in tongues is the sign of the "baptism of the Spirit," then most Christians have not experienced the fulfillment of the power of the Spirit. Could it be that the filling of the Spirit is only for the last days? And is it only for those inside the Pentecostal/Charismatic movement? Something is very wrong with this teaching.

On the contrary, church leaders and many others have been filled with the Spirit in marvelous ways, but they have not spoken in tongues because it was not necessary. God has used them in astonishing ways to impact the kingdom of God around the world.

John Wesley spoke of his experience of being filled with the Spirit and the second work of grace in Aldersgate (Wesley 1977:239), and Charles Finney said the "baptism of the Spirit" came over his soul like waves of the sea. However, neither suggested that he ever spoke in tongues!

Likewise, the evangelist D. L. Moody also described his fillings of the Spirit as marvelous, but never once indicated that he spoke in tongues. R. A. Torrey, in his book "Baptism of the Spirit", made it very clear that he never spoke in tongues, even though he was convinced that he had received the baptism of the Spirit. These men and many more manifested one of the principle signs of the filling of the Spirit that is mentioned in Acts 4:31: "they were all filled with the Holy Spirit, and they spoke the word of God with boldness."

It is inconsistent and dishonest for charismatic writers to cite these four men to prove their doctrine of speaking in "tongues," as if they had spoken in a tongue. It is even worse to say, as Bennett declared, that no one in the history of the Church has been filled with the Spirit without speaking in tongues! Bennett also says that these men actually did speak in tongues but did not reveal it to anyone for one of two reasons: (1) Fear of what others would say, or (2) They did not know that they had spoken in tongues! (Ibid.:65-66). How ridiculous! How is it possible that someone could speak in tongues and not know it? One of the main purposes of speaking in tongues, according to Charismatic believers, is to know that one has been "baptized" in the Spirit. What would be the value of speaking in tongues if the speaker were unaware of it? If there is a genuine experience, then it must be evident to the speaker as well as the listeners!

The truth is that no one since the first century has spoken in tongues. What is manifested today has nothing to do with the genuine gift of tongues.

Observation 5: The only evidence of the continuation of tongues in the history of the Church comes from heretical groups.

The few manifestations of "miraculous gifts" always came from non-evangelical groups: mystics, Catholics, Arians (who denied the deity of Christ), fanatic sects devoted to Mary, cults and pagan religions. These manifestations are identical to those seen in today's Charismatic Movement. Montanus, for example, said that he was the *"Paracleto"* (A Greek term translated "Comforter" in John 14:26). In other words, he said, the Spirit spoke to the churches through him, and his revelations were newer and thus even more authoritative than the Scriptures themselves. Sounds like some other false religions.

He said that Christ would return soon and establish His kingdom in Phrygia (Asia Minor) between 200 and 300 A.D. and that Montanus and his followers would have a prominent place in that kingdom. The name Montanus appears many times in Charismatic books as evidence of the continuation of the gift of tongues.

The following is a summary list of groups that claim to have miraculous gifts:

Montanus—a false prophet who said that he was the *Paracleto* incarnate. He did not say he had spoken in tongues, but he did claim to have experienced other manifestations.

Irenaeus – referred to different spoken tongues, but never to the gift of tongues. He left no evidence that tongues were used in his day.

Saints of the Roman Catholic Church in the Middle Ages — Many of them claimed to have spoken in tongues. These are references to actual tongues and do not have anything to do with unintelligible tongues, glossolalia, of today.

Camisard French prophets (Huguenots)—They spoke sounds from heaven and prophecies about children and other strange things. The disaster of their prophecies with respect to the second coming of Christ shows that they were not of the Spirit.

Radical segment of the Anabaptists—Their polygamy, ecstatic experiences and excesses provoked rejection from the reformists in the sixteenth century, and their unfulfilled prophecies indicate that they were not guided by the Holy Spirit. Some "babbled" with strange sounds.

Shakers—This was not a Christian group. Their founder said that she was the feminine equivalent to Jesus Christ. She said that she received revelation from God about the corruption of sexual relations even in marriage. With the purpose of "mortifying the flesh" and to help her followers to learn how to resist sexual tendencies, she instituted the practice of men and women dancing in the nude while speaking in "tongues." (Gromacki 1967:5-22). One historian shows that the origin of Pentecostalism comes from the Mormons and the Shakers. (Dollar, 1963: 320)

Irvingites—The spirit that motivated this group guided it to false doctrine. They declared that their revelations were superior to those of the Bible. They were the origin of the New Apostolic Church that still depends on prophecy from

Europe. Their doctrines indicate that the spirit that motivated them while speaking in tongues as well as their pretense of healings were not of the Holy Spirit.

Wesley—In his revivals there were people who manifested convulsions but were unsaved. Almost all of them declared that they needed salvation. The experiences were like those of demonic possession. Wesley did not believe that falling into unconscious trances or convulsions was of the Spirit. (Wesley 1977: 239) There was no evidence of *glossolalia* in his meetings.

When the group of believers in Kansas, began to speak in a "tongue" in 1901, it was the first time that evangelical believers accepted the speaking in tongues as a sign of the baptism of the Spirit. Various Pentecostal denominations resulted from that experience, which they all claimed was the sign of the baptism of the Spirit. The historic antecedents of that experience, discussed above, present a grave problem when trying to justify the existence of the Charismatics today.

Chapter 17: Gifts for Today

CHAPTER 18

Devotional Tongues

Chapter 18: Gifts for Today

In the practice of Charismatics today someone can exercise "his tongue" either in private or in the church, but it is more common for them to do it in private or in their personal devotional times. No one can know the number of people who seek and find some experience of speaking in "tongues" in the privacy of their devotions.

Around the turn of the century the thirst for holiness revivals and world evangelism drove many to seek the gift of tongues. Blumhofer's research on the beginnings of the Pentecostal movement reveals its unremarkable origin to become one of the dominant characteristics of Evangelical Christianity. The Azusa Street revival was to restore the church to her former place of favor and power in order to "fuel an unprecedented and swift world evangelization." (Blumhofer 2006:59). Some excerpts follow:

> The faithful expected that tongues speech would issue in the practical ability to speak languages useful for missionary work. Reports proliferated of tongues-enabled impromptu conversations with immigrants… Either external advice or internal conviction about what language one had be 'given,' then, prompted men and women to sail for remote places with little thought of mundane matters like financial support, firm destination, or suitable supplies…
> The expectation of miraculous speech in known languages soon faded: so-called missionary tongues, by most accounts, simply failed to deliver the expected language facility. Yet the anticipation of *xenolalia* suggests the aspiration of preaching the Gospel directly to every language and culture, their proclamation unencumbered by any traces of Western culture baggage, even language or accent. They did not articulate this aspiration; to their minds, the primary advantage of *xenolalia* was speedy evangelism.
> In place of *xenolalia*, participants in the "new Pentecost" came to focus on a phrase from Acts 1:8, "You will receive power when the Holy Spirit has come upon you." The baptism with the Holy Spirit was "enduement with power for service." If it did not deliver a tangible result like immediate linguistic fluency, it did testify to possession of the divine power necessary for effective Christian witness anywhere… Its personal meaning revolved around themes of power, purity, and spiritual gifts. The baptism with the Holy Spirit transformed the meaning of life by heightening sensitivity to the spiritual world… Early Pentecostals thought their religious experience brought a touch of heaven into their ordinary lives: 'I have found a heaven below, living in the glory of the Lord,' one of their choruses ran…
> Results were mixed at best, and complaints trickled back that Pentecostals seemed more anxious to pray than to work, more eager to persuade missionaries than to commit to the task of evangelizing native populations… Despite their hyperbolic rhetoric in 1906 and later, Azusa Street participants did not immediately change Christian practice in the West or abroad… Their hopes to promote Christian unity under a restorationist banner faded quickly as within months their internal unity ruptured. At the

Chapter 18: *Devotional Tongues* 289

end of 1906 a Los Angeles pastor noted, 'In the city there are already four hostile camps of those who unduly magnify the tongues, which prove that the tongues have not brought Pentecost to Los Angeles.'(*Ibid.*:61-62).

For fifty years the Pentecostal movement was marginalized but continued spreading around the world as it adapted to different contexts, but the original thrust continues: a desire for spiritual renewal and energy for evangelistic work. The original ideal of miraculous languages for immediately preaching the gospel in earthly languages failed to materialize so a redefinition of the purpose and practice of tongues became universally accepted. A second focus became the power for serving Christ and reaching sanctification could primarily be reached through speaking in tongues. A third focus became dominant with the advent of the Charismatic movement outside the Pentecostal movement in the 1960's, and is called "devotional tongues" for self-edification.

The classical Pentecostal theologian, Ernest Swing Williams, has stated, "Those who have spoken in tongues in private worship and devotion can testify to the enriching, spiritual rest, and refreshing to the soul that results from such communion with God." (Burns 1975: 243).

As new manifestations of the gift of tongues began to be practiced, it became apparent that it was distinct from how it was practiced in the Book of Acts, so a new definition of the gift became necessary and collaborating biblical evidence made to appear in support of the new definition.

There are devotional tongues, or prayer language, for times when the human intellect falls short of knowing what to ask for in prayer. At such a time, the Spirit prays through the Spirit-filled believer with groans and tongues that cannot be expressed in human language (Romans 8:26). Devotional tongues, of course, do not happen without a first-time initial evidence of tongues. We believe this devotional use of tongues is what Paul was referring to when he told the Corinthians: "I thank my God that I speak with in tongues more than all of you all" (1 Corinthians 14:18). Certainly, Paul was not speaking in tongues more than the Corinthians in public worship services, because he was giving instructions on regulating the public use of tongues (Bicket, 2010:74)

According to Charismatic teaching, the language is a gift for praising God in a supernatural form. To be sure, they say, in order to communicate only with God and with no one else, you must speak in a heavenly tongue. It is the most intimate way to come near to God. With all our human shortcomings they say it would be impossible to get close to God in our nature; adding that a supernatural tongue allows an intimacy with God that is impossible to achieve through a human tongue.

Some hold to a possibility of tongues of angels being unique: Barrett 1968: 299–300; Dautzenberg 1971; Dunn 1975: 244; Ellis 1978: 70–71; Fee 1987: 598–99; D. Martin 1991: 574; Witherington 1995: 258; Wolff 1996: 293–94;

Hays 1997: 212; R. Collins 1999: 456; Schrage 1999: 159. Thiselton (2000: 973) considers this the least plausible view; see also Grudem 1982: 120–29. (cited by David E. Garland, in "1 Corinthians" in Baker Exegetical Commentary on the New Testament (Grand Rapids, MI: Baker Academic, 2003).

They also assert that everything the Bible says about tongues has to do with its use in the congregation or the church. Therefore, it is not necessary to apply the rules or priorities of 1 Corinthians 14 when tongues are practiced in private. They think that they can do what they want in private, since only their experience guides them and does not need to be revealed to others. This means that many people can be participating in the use of tongues without saying so.

As one Pentecostal work explains: "Every Spirit-filled Christian can and should pray frequently in tongues for self-edification (1 Cor. 14:2, 4, 5, 18), building himself up by praying in the Holy Ghost." (Barnett and McGregor 1986: 327)

Dr. Palma highlights the value of this prayer language: "When done in private, it [tongues] builds up the one praying, in a manner not explicitly stated in Scripture. Since tongues is a means of spiritual upbuilding (what some would call a means of grace), it is available to all God's children." (Palma 2001: 168). Now the primary function of tongues is seen as self-edification, renewal and private religious experience.

Reasons why devotional tongues is not encouraged as a biblical practice:

The argument for the need of a special language due to human limitations requiring a special intimate language that transcends human frailties does not come from a biblical perspective. This is the same argument that motivated the mistaken need for special mediators, saints or angels to intercede for us or to interpret our prayers to God since we cannot approach him directly. The idea that we are inadequate ignores the biblical effect of justification, which makes us perfectly acceptable in Christ ("…His grace, by which He has made us accepted in the Beloved" Eph 1:7). The notion that something extra is necessary to be intimate with God ignores the implication of our new position in Christ (Ephesians 3:12 "Because of Christ and our faith in him, we can now come boldly and confidently into God's presence"). Nothing can make this relationship more intimate. The following arguments will attempt to deal with the issues that are frequently mentioned in regards to devotional tongues.

1. The biblical evidence of devotional tongues is only an inference, not a declaration

1 Corinthians 14:2, "For he who speaks in a tongue does not speak to men but to God, for no one understands him; however, in the spirit he speaks mysteries."

The New Testament does not say that tongues are for devotional use. Why did the apostles use them in another way? Why do the only examples correspond to their use in public? Why do all the rules pertain to their use in public, with no mention of their use in private? The reference to speaking to God in 1 Cor 14:2 is taken to mean a private language, but the reference to "no one understands him" implies that this tongue is spoken in public or at least where someone else can hear him.

The only other possible reference to a devotional use in this context would be the statements by Paul that when he states that he always prays or sings with understanding and not just in his unconscious spirit in an unknown language tongue. This, of course, is Paul's denial of using tongues in any private prayer or worship singing, because worship is meaningless when the speaker cannot speak from his heart or mind to express his love and devotion to God. If he is saying anything, his mind has no idea what is being expressed so he cannot know if he means what is being expressed or not.

If the gift is for private use, then why does the Bible permit its use with limitations in public? If the evidence of the New Testament has value, then tongues should be used only in the churches and never in private.

2. Devotional tongues are contrary to the purpose of the spiritual gifts.

If such a gift existed for use in private, then it would be in a category that would make it the only selfish gift. As we have shown, all the spiritual gifts are for ministering to others, as their names suggest—giving, helps, exhortation, teaching, etc. Does God need to hear a special language to understand man? Is God limited to an intimate language if we want to communicate with Him? Is this spiritual gift somehow ministering to God's needs? If this language comes from God, is God using this language that the recipient does not understand to speak back to Himself? Does that make any sense? If no one else can be edified or helped by hearing someone speak in tongues (1 Cor 14:6), how could the speaker be biblically "edified" since he does not understand any more of what he is saying than the one listening? Something does not seem congruent with the intent and function of the spiritual gifts with the practice of devotional tongues.

> Thus *glossolalia* was a gift given by God, not primarily as a special language for worship; not primarily to facilitate the spread of the gospel; and certainly not as a sign that a believer has experienced a second "baptism in the Holy Spirit." It was given primarily for an evidential purpose to authenticate and substantiate some facet of God's truth, This purpose is always distorted by those who shift the emphasis from objective sign to subjective experience. (Gerlach 1973: 251).

On the other hand, devotional tongues would mean that a small group of believers would have an advantage in prayer and communion with God through their special gift, rather than their standing in Christ by faith. No other gift is given to the believer in order to have a better or more intimate relationship with God. The Pentecostal theologian, Ernest Swing Williams, has stated,

"Those who have spoken in tongues in private worship and devotion can testify to the enriching, spiritual rest, and refreshing to the soul that results from such communion with God." (Williams 1953, 3:50). This misguided emphasis is totally selfish, and self-centered, since it supposedly benefits only the gifted person emotionally. The idea that an emotional feeling is the meaning of edification is foreign to the biblical and historical concept. Nathan Busentiz gives an exhaustive comparison to the Patristic Fathers of their view of the gift of tongues in the Early Church.

> Ambrosiaster believes spiritual gifts should be "conducive to the good of the brotherhood." (Ambrosiaster, Commentary on Paul's Epistles, cited from 1–2 Corinthians, ACCS 142). Chrysostom agrees, arguing that tongues was to be "used for the edification of the whole church." (Chrysostom, Homilies on 1 Corinthians 36.5, cited from 1–2 Corinthians, ACCS 144). John Cassian emphasizes the importance of love over any type of spiritual gift. (John Cassian, The First Conference of Abbot Chaeromon 12). And Theodoret of Cyrus sums up the Corinthian error like this: "The Corinthians also did these things, but they did not use the gifts as they should have done. They were more interested in showing off than in using them for the edification of the church."(Theodoret of Cyrus, Commentary on the First Epistle to the Corinthians 240, cited from 1–2 Corinthians, ACCS 117). (Busentz 2006: 66)

Furthermore, the discipline of a daily devotion is not for the generation of a "warm and fuzzy" feeling. A devotional time is for acknowledging the glory of the Lord in worship, confession of sin, thanksgiving for all that God has done in your life and circumstances and especially intercession for others. A daily time in the Word to allow God to speak especially through the commands, keeps one in tune with God.

If devotional tongues were real, it would be logical to think that such a gift should be given to everyone; however, this would be a contradiction of 1 Corinthians 12:7, "To each person the manifestation of the Spirit is given for the benefit of all". First, the gifts are not given for the individual, but so the individual can benefit everyone else through his empowered service to meet their needs.

Second, it is not God's plan that everyone speak in tongues. It is His plan that all pray and that others who understand what is being prayed be edified even through our prayers (1 Cor 14:17), but the Bible declares unequivocally that not everyone will receive the same gift—even, the gift of tongues.

Gifts exercised in love seek the benefit of others (1 Corinthians 13:1-7). Love is not an emotion, but rather a giving attitude toward others. The commands in the context of 1 Corinthians 12-14 suggest that some early believers exercised their gifts selfishly or without love, which annulled what they did. Paul made it clear that there is no profit or recognition from God for the possessor of a gift when he acts without love (13:1; 14:1), that is, serving others. If the gift is exercised in love, the possessor is recompensed with the rewards, recognition and approval from God plus the joy of serving others. If we speak in tongues without love, it is only noise (13:1). If it is done in love, then it will not be done for personal benefit but for the good of others. By this definition, it is impossible to exercise a gift in private as a ministry of love to others.

If devotional tongues do not benefit others (because no one else is present), they are not exercised in love and have no value for the speaker. It is imperative that the gift be expressed in love benefiting others, but the one who ministers is never the direct recipient. Paul said, "I am nothing," if others do not benefit in love (13:2); and "I receive no benefit." (1Co 13:3 NET). When there is no benefit for others, as in the case of devotional tongues, Paul declares that the language is as "a noisy gong or a clanging cymbal" (1Co 13:1 NAS), or merely meaningless noise. The necessity of exercising the gifts in love for others negates the possibility that tongues have a private function. Devotional tongues cannot accomplish this requisite; therefore, they have no value for the individual, even though they may generate a feeling of intimacy.

3. They are contrary to the purpose of "tongues."

In Mark 16:15-17, Jesus sent the eleven with special gifts as a "sign for unbelievers" (1 Corinthians 14:22NKJ). The expression "for a sign" is *eis semeion*. The preposition *eis* is an expression of purpose. The clearest description of this purpose in the New Testament is in Acts 2:4-11, where tongues functioned as signs for the unbelieving Hellenistic Jewish audience who needed no interpretation, and this was in public.

As we have shown, signs do not have to be repeated since they are for pointing out the beginning of a new era or for authenticating messengers or a message. In addition, devotional tongues cannot serve as a sign since no one is there to convince. The private use, devotional or in prayer, eliminates its biblical use as a sign for unbelievers.

The existence of the required gift of interpretation implies that tongues are not for devotional use. God does not need an interpreter. The interpretation is for communicating the message to men. If the tongues speaker wants to be edified, he "should pray that he may interpret" (14:13), because only the interpretation edifies. God provided the gift of interpretation so that an unknown tongue could be communicated as a sign for men, suggesting that He never intended that tongues be used in private.

4. Tongues are not a sign for the speaker.

1 Corinthians 14:22, "Therefore tongues are for a sign, not to those who believe but to unbelievers; but prophesying is not for unbelievers but for those who believe."

What is the purpose or benefit of speaking in a private tongue? Since it is impossible to minister to others, there are only four other possibilities:

1. Prayer
2. Worship
3. Self-edification
4. A sign

Paul declared that he only prayed in a known language that he understood with his mind (1 Cor 14:15). Even when he gave thanks in prayer it was always in a known language that he understood (14:16) and he commanded this to be the practice by obligating the edification of others in all things (14:12). When he sang (worship?) he always sang in a known language that he understood so there could be meaning in what he expressed (14:15).

All biblical passages indicate that tongues are signs for unbelievers (Mark 16:17; 1 Corinthians 14:22), not for the believer himself. It is not a sign to prove that one is spiritual or has received the Spirit baptism. This sign purpose to unbelievers would be impossible in the practice of devotional tongues.

A private sign would be an indication that God is dealing with the person speaking in a special or supernatural manner. The problem with this focus on tongues is that when any spiritual gift becomes evident it proves the same thing: when God gives a gift, it is because the Spirit wants to use that person in a special way to benefit others, not himself. It is not reasonable to say that God gives a gift with the purpose of showing the person that he has a gift. The gift would have no purpose in ministry.

The sign of the gift of tongues is not for the speaker, but for the hearers (1 Corinthians 14:22, "Therefore tongues are for a sign, not to those who believe but to unbelievers"). There is no sign-purpose of tongues according to the Scriptures that is to indicate anything to the speaker of the tongue. Some have wanted the tongues to indicate a special insider relationship with God or be a sign that the person has received the Baptism of the Spirit. Neither of these concepts is taught in Scriptures. They are wrongly deduced from a couple of passages where they are associated.

Acts 2 refers to the filling of the Spirit (though the Baptism is implied only the filling is stated) and to speaking in tongues, but nowhere is tongues mentioned as a sign to the believer himself that he had received the baptism of the Spirit. Making deductions that are not declared in the biblical text is a dangerous way to interpret the Bible.

There were three signs associated with the Spirit outpouring in Acts 2: a mighty sound, appearance of small tongues of fire, and then the speaking in foreign languages. The only one that was repeated in Acts 10 and 19 was the gift of tongues. These are all declared to be the same gift manifested in Acts 2 (Acts 11:15). In all cases the signs were for the observers, not the speakers.

5. Tongues are not for self-edification (14:3-4)
1 Corinthians 14:3-4, "But he who prophesies speaks edification and

exhortation and comfort to men. 4 He who speaks in a tongue edifies himself, but he who prophesies edifies the church."

The argument from the phrase, "edifies himself," explains why tongues should receive less emphasis than prophecy. This self-edification is a negative effect from the excessive emphasis on tongues and is not God's purpose for tongues; it is more of a detriment and, therefore, does not serve the congregation. The whole argument of the passage is to downplay and discourage this prideful self-serving practice that was common in the Corinthian church.

When tongues were used correctly they edified others, but only when they were interpreted. This shows that the only way speaker could be edified, according to the Bible, was as he listened to the interpretation of his own tongue message. In other words, the speaker is edified only in his own mother-tongue. When tongues were used without an interpreter, they were only for supposed selfish edification, and Paul discouraged it. Why would anyone emphasize what Paul discourages?

Verses 3 and 4 describe the erroneous use of tongues in the congregation. If the purpose was to be a sign to unbelieving Jews, then speaking in tongues for personal benefit was alien to that purpose.

Some people would say that even though it is not the purpose, speaking in devotional tongues is indeed an advantage. There are two possible interpretations to the expression "edifies himself." The verb "edify," *oikodomeo* in the Greek, means to "construct or develop"; normally it has a beneficial sense, but in 1 Corinthians 8:10 it is used in a negative form. The conscience can be "edified" in a negative way, for example, to continue sinning with idols. So the meaning of the edification (positive or negative) depends on the context. In this context it seems apparent that the use of devotional tongues is a negative concept to be avoided.

Reasons why self-edification in 1 Corinthians 14:4 is negative (self-edification means to boast).

1. Self-edification is to make oneself important in the eyes of other people.

Pride and self-glory were problems in the church (1:26-29; 3:3-7, 18, 21; 4:6-7). It is evident that they were boasting in their gifts and exalting themselves, which are contrary to the principles of Christian ethics and the purposes of the spiritual gifts.

2. The theme of 1 Corinthians 14 is the impossibility of being edified by a language which is not understood.
1 Co 14:6 NKJ, "But now, brethren, if I come to you speaking with tongues, what shall I profit you unless I speak to you either by revelation, by knowledge, by prophesying, or by teaching?"

Greater is the one who is speaking about the revelation of God's Word in an understandable language in verse 5, otherwise no one is edified. Then in verse 6 the speaker himself does not benefit because he does not understand. Paul said that he who speaks in a tongue that no one understands, "speaks to the air" (14:9) and is personally "unfruitful" (14:14, meaning that it does not produce any benefit to anyone). Paul indicated that tongues, in themselves, were impossible to edify anyone. They were designed to be dependent on either being understood by the listener in their language or being interpreted into their language in order to be beneficial to both the speaker and the listener. Otherwise the experience was meaningless.

3. Paul made very clear that without understanding it is impossible that there be any positive edification.

Paul said that the speaker should know what he has said in prayer or it was no benefit to anyone. If not, then there is no edification; his prayer is "unfruitful," (14:14) that is, with no edification.

Verses 15 and 19 indicate that the mind was not involved when they spoke in tongues. Therefore, there was no benefit or positive result in the speaker. The speaker did not understand anything. To be edified, it is indispensable to understand what is said about a truth to be able to decide to believe or obey it, thus being edified.

"Love [always] edifies" (1 Cor 8:1, brackets indicate the meaning of the present tense), that is, it always acts by seeking to benefit others or meet others' needs for understanding truth and living in the light of His Word, without personal interest.

In a discussion on Christian rights to eating and drinking Paul applies the principle of edification as the guideline for living: "all things are lawful for me, but not all things edify. Let no one seek his own, but each one the other's well-being." (1Co 10:23-24 NKJ) The believer is commanded not to seek his own benefit or "well-being," but that of others. To emphasize the self-benefiting of tongues creates a direct contradiction in Scriptures for the use of the gifts.

Paul affirmed that prayer to God was without fruit or without edification for the hearer or the speaker when there is no understanding. To pray without understanding was a negative action and, therefore, Paul exhorted them not to practice that kind of prayer. (1 Cor 14:15)

If the speaker is edified by anything other than understanding, then we should ask ourselves: "If he is spiritually stimulated through hearing himself make sounds he does not understand, why are others not stimulated spiritually by hearing the same sounds?"

No one has offered an explanation of how an unknown tongue can edify. There is no other reference in the Bible that shows the term "*oikodomeo*" used positively for self-edification. In Ephesians 4:16, the verb "edifying of itself" is reflexive, giving the idea that the Body of Christ is edified, but in the sense that each one of its members edifies others—that is to say, each member edifies other members but never himself.

It is impossible to conceptualize how someone can edify himself without understanding; edification always comes through understanding more of His Word.

Suggestions of why edification without understanding has no foundation in the light of serious investigation.

1) Some say that they receive spiritual truths when they speak in miraculous tongues. However, the need to learn spiritual truths in order to be edified cannot be supplied by speaking in tongues because the mind "is unfruitful" (14:14). The speaker cannot receive spiritual truth without understanding God's Word.

2) To be conscious or to realize that God has given you a gift and is using you is a blessing. In the opinion of some, this blessing is "edification"; but even though one tries to give it a different appearance, the blessing is only an emotion. As author F.L. Godet said: "as a power deep in the soul" (Godet 1971: 268). Because there is no understanding, this "edification" has nothing to do with exhortation, consolation, instruction or learning; the only possibility left is that it is mere emotion.

However, generating emotional responses is not the purpose of the gift of tongues. For example, a prophet could know that God had given him a gift and was speaking through him. But the self-edification or self-confidence of the gifted, produced by the knowledge that God used him, was not the purpose of the gift of prophecy. It was possible that the prophet experienced some emotional benefits, but this was not the purpose of his gift. The only purpose was edification, consolation and exhortation of his brothers and sisters.

All concepts related to spiritual edification of a believer depend on the Word, its understanding or knowledge, exhortation or consolation. The New Testament is full of information telling believers what they must first know and later what they are to act on as a result of the fundamental of understanding what God has said.

In no part of the New Testament are we exhorted to experience a feeling or grow spiritually based on emotion. It is common in paganism, however, to desire to be used by supernatural forces and to seek emotions or feelings that accompany such an experience and generate a self-assurance of a supposed divine presence. This is called mysticism. Considering an emotion—coming as a consequence of an act of power within oneself—to be the same as "edification," or to think that there has been some spiritual benefit, is not a biblical concept.

6. God gave the gifts of prophecy, apostleship, teaching and exhortation for the edification of the believers.

The gifts of the word of knowledge and the word of wisdom both depend on understanding to produce edification. It would be impossible for the gift of tongues to edify without understanding, since it would be converted into a singular gift; and it would be very subjective to think that God would give a gift that edifies without understanding, while all the other gifts require it. It is said that it is a "blessing" for those who have felt themselves "touched." Even though such experiences existed in the Bible, they have nothing to do with edification. Feeling blessed is only an emotion and is not biblical edification.

One can only imagine the thrill of being in the presence of Jesus when He walked on this earth and many were astonished at seeing what He did. However, no one was benefited by seeing and feeling His presence unless they understood what He said and were willing to act in faith on their understanding.

7. No biblical passage exhorts believers to grow spiritually through self-edification produced by tongues.

If it had been so important for edification, then we would expect at least one reference or one command, but there is none. In Ephesians 4:11 the main gifts that produce edification are listed, and the gift of tongues is not mentioned. These gifts (apostleship, prophecy, evangelism, pasturing and teaching) are "for the edifying of the body of Christ" (4:12).

The only self-reflective reference is in Eph 4:16, "causes growth of the body for the edifying of itself in love." This is not a reference to individual self-edification, but to individual members of the body edifying each other in love or care for the maturity of each other. The goal of edification is stated in Eph 4:13, "till we all come to the unity of the faith and of the knowledge of the Son of God, to a perfect man, to the measure of the stature of the fullness of Christ" (Eph 4:13 NKJ). This is not a mystical or emotional experience, but a conscious "renewing of the mind" (Rom 12:2) and a commitment to each other "for building up one another" (Rom 14:19; also 1 Thes 5:11).

We grow spiritually as others edify us, not as we edify ourselves mystically.

8. If it were true that tongues edify, this would create an elite group of a few believers gifted with the ability to grow spiritually by their own actions; this means it would be impossible for those without the gift to grow.

Since the gifts are given by a sovereign God, according to His will (1 Cor 12:7, 11) apart from any decision or participation of the individual, the supposition that tongues by themselves can edify would make us think that God decides to give to a select group of believers a miraculous power for spiritual growth. If one never received the gift of tongues he would forever be limited in his potential growth. This is totally contrary to the teaching of the New Testament. God never intended that tongues be used for self-edification.

9. If tongues could edify a person independently from others, the design of God for the unity and interdependence of the body of Christ would

be voided.
1 Thessalonians 5:11, "Therefore comfort each other and edify one another"

Every positive reference to exhortation refers to what one member of the Body of Christ does to another. This makes each of the Body of Christ interdependent on the ministry of others. There is a healthy bonding and unity that takes place when there is a mutual need only met as each part of the Body ministers to others. The way a person matures is when "the members have the same care for one another" (1 Cor 12:25). If there were a way a person could self-edify he would not need the rest of the Body of Christ. God never intended us to be able to grow independently.

The Corinthians were practicing tongues in order to edify themselves negatively, in order to enjoy an emotion, instead of seeking the truth from other gifted speakers and teachers, they began to stray from the way of the Lord without realizing it. The revealed Word of God had less importance to them as they preferred their experiences to learning His Word. The purpose of the chapter 14 was to lead them out of their emotionalism and cause them to pay attention to the revealed Word of God.

Is there a special language that only God understands, which the gift of tongues transmits?
1 Corinthians 14:2 NKJ, "For he who speaks in a tongue does not speak to men but to God, for no one understands him; however, in the spirit he speaks mysteries"
1 Corinthians 14:28 NKJ, "But if there is no interpreter, let him keep silent in church, and let him speak to himself and to God."

What would it mean if there were a language unknown to any human being and only used within the Godhead to communicate within the trinity? Since the speaker has no notion of what is being said, and it is the intimate communication directly between the Holy Spirit and the Father, which permits the human speaker to be a participant of the divine communication, what is the purpose? Why does God need, want or allow a human to be a link in such a communication within the Godhead?

The most vivid depiction of the "heavenly language" is evident in Isaiah's vision of the scene in heaven of the angels saying, "Holy, holy, holy is the Lord of hosts; The whole earth if full of His glory!" (Isa 6:3), which Isaiah perfectly understood without interpretation. Then he hears the Lord saying, "Whom will I send? And who will go for us?" in a language that was perfectly understood as the Godhead communicated within itself. There is no mystery language in heaven, or within the Godhead, rather a perfectly understandable language that communicates intelligence and understanding. Isaiah communicated back in his language and God responded in his language (6:9). Nothing could be more intimate. The only thing that was required to be in his presence was described as "Your iniquity is taken away, and your sin is forgiven" (6:7NAS).

Every born-again believer has this privilege. There is no mystery language in heaven.

No other place in the Bible teaches that there is a special communication through a miraculous tongue from the Spirit through a man's tongue and the Father. Could it be that these verses are teaching that tongues are for prayer and worship "to God"? (14:2). Is this a positive statement or a negative statement? Is Paul encouraging this practice or discourage it as it was being practiced?

In 1 Corinthians 14, Paul is writing in favor of the superiority of prophecy. The believers needed to be zealous in emphasizing prophecy because it became the means to edify each other. Tongues were inferior because they could supposedly be used only to speak to God.

In the first place, in the assembly speaking to men has superiority over speaking to God. Prayer and worship are important in the meetings, however; according to 1 Corinthians 14:15-16 even prayer to God was to be a blessing to others (irrespective of the blessing to God) and produces edification when it is understood (see also Ephesians 6:18; Philippians 4:4-6; Colossians 4:2; 1 Thessalonians:1:7; 1 Timothy 2:1-8).

The edification takes place in learning how to minister to others by praying for them, by worshiping in "spirit and in truth" (John 4:23) and in the demonstration of genuine thankfulness for all circumstances of life. Without understanding what was being said none of these phases of edification can take place.

In second place, the problem in 14:2 has nothing to do with prayer or worship to God. The second part of the verse is introduced by the Greek conjunction *gar* ("for [or because] no one understands him"), which is the reason it says that he spoke "to God." In other words, the reason it says that he spoke to God is not because he actually spoke privately to God, but because no one understood him.

The idea of "speaking to God" is equivalent to saying "only God can understand him." (Obviously we are referring to an actual language, not mere babbling that not even God can understand.) The phrase "to God" does not indicate that a special language is used in prayer or worship, but that only God could understand when the language is expressed without the correspondent interpretation. Speaking without an interpreter, as we have shown, is the same as speaking "to the air" (verse 9), that is "speaking to the wall." Paul preferred prophecy because everyone can understand it.

In third place, if the primary purpose of the gift of tongues is to communicate a message from God to men, as in Acts 2, it makes no sense that the message would not be communicated to men through an interpreter, but rather privately repeated back to God. Why would He need the message He is sending to men to be spoken back to Himself?

Chapter 18: *Devotional Tongues*

Other reasons that the phrase "speaks to God" does not indicate that the purpose of tongues was prayer or worship.

1. The phrase "speaks to God" is not an absolute declaration of the function of tongues.

Given that the genuine gift of tongues could be understood in certain occasions, as at Pentecost, the declaration that only God can understand is not absolute. When a stranger was present and his language was used, he immediately understood it. 1 Corinthians 14:2 was fulfilled only when those present did not understand the language being spoken, whether it is because it was not their native language or because they had not learned it.

It would be like preaching a message in an empty hall. The only one hearing him would be God, the only other One present. This does not mean that the purpose of preaching is to preach to God in private, just because He can hear when no one else is present.

2. The prohibition of the use of an unknown language in the congregation would not make sense if the purpose of tongues were prayer and worship.

The congregation meets precisely to pray and worship and be edified. It would be contradictory, then, to prohibit a gift that would make prayer and worship more effective. Obviously, Paul was not restricting prayer and worship in the congregation, but rather he was restricting the exercise of an unknown language that had no inherent use in worship and prayer.

The only utility for an unknown tongue would occur when it was interpreted. If a tongue genuinely made worship more effective Paul would have encouraged it to be practiced.

3. The gift of interpretation of tongues would not have had any utility if tongues were used in prayer or in expressions of worship.

On the contrary, the giving of the gift of interpretation indicates that the purpose of an unknown tongue was to speak to men, not to God, through the interpreter. The interpreter was given so that men could understand and be blessed by the spoken word.

In 1 Corinthians 14:28, tongues speakers were restricted in the congregation without an interpreter. It seems odd that such a supposed gift for speaking to God would be prohibited without an interpreter if it were the epitome of the worship experience.

The phrase "speaks to himself and to God," is parallel to the phrase "be quiet in the church." Without an interpreter, he who speaks in an unknown tongue must be quiet. He can speak to himself or pray to God in silence.

Obviously, he could not speak to himself if he did not understand what he was saying, because this is not communication. It would be ridiculous to think that the gift of tongues was given so that the people could speak to themselves, since this does not require a gift. Paul is politely suggesting they keep quiet without being too frank. The main issue in this context was that Paul wanted no interruptions in the meetings.

On the other hand, if this verse were supporting devotional tongues (in personal, private prayer or worship) it also would be supporting speaking to oneself in an unknown tongue (without understanding, or "without fruit" of edification) in the same way that he speaks to God (supposedly in tongues). He would be speaking to himself, without any "fruit" of understanding or edification.

However, the phrase "to himself" can also mean, "so that only he and God can hear." It is merely an expression to demand that they speak their sounds in absolute silence so that no one can hear whatever they may be saying. There is no implied effect of being able to speak a special wave-length language that only the God-head is tuned into.

The verse is similar to Romans 14:22, "Do you have faith? Have it to yourself before God." It is obvious that Paul did not say that one should direct his faith to himself or experience a private devotional faith. Paul is referring to someone who has faith that permits him to eat anything and not have to be concerned about anyone else. Paul tells him that he should act with the motivation for edifying others, not just by however he feels. He should keep his faith to himself and act for the benefit of others.

Paul is saying that one should not flaunt his liberty while destroying his brother, who may believe that Christians should not do such a thing. The mature man has faith to eat with liberty, but he does not have to exercise that liberty in public. It is better to deny one's liberty and abstain for the benefit of others than to offend or cause someone to stumble.

In the same way, he who has the gift of tongues should keep it to himself and not exercise it if there are no interpreters present. There is no requirement or need to manifest it. On the contrary, he must keep quiet before God. Only He can hear what happens in one's mind.

Paul had indicated that speaking in an unknown tongue was like "speaking to the air" (14:6). In other words, there is no advantage in speaking to oneself, just as there is no advantage in "speaking to God" in a tongue. If there were some benefit to such speaking Paul would have encouraged it for everyone.

In 14:14-16, Paul declares that tongues are useless as a vehicle of prayer. They are useful only when they are spoken with understanding. For this reason Paul always prayed in his spirit and with understanding, that is to say, in a language that he understood. If it is impossible to interpret a prayer, then the mind remains "without fruit" and without any spiritual advantage. Any "blessing" is fictitious, imaginary or invented; it is not from God.

Because the only benefit of tongues is in the interpretation, 1 Corinthians 14:14 begins with the Greek word *gar* ("for or because") and connects 14:13 with 14 (14:13 "Therefore let him who speaks in a tongue pray that he may interpret. 14 For if I pray in a tongue, my spirit prays, but my understanding is unfruitful").

Chapter 18: *Devotional Tongues* 303

From this we know that 14:14 is not an argument for praying in an unknown tongue, but rather it is the reason why there must be an interpreter in order to experience fruit and why Paul never prayed in a tongue!

As we have discussed, Paul declared that speaking in an unknown tongue does not produce fruit (verse 14) in the mind of the speaker; the hearer can receive fruit only if the message is interpreted for understanding. Therefore, when Paul says that he prayed "in the spirit...and also with understanding" (verse 15), he is referring to a language that he understood. He is not saying that sometimes he prayed in an unknown tongue while on other occasions he prayed with understanding. Paul prayed with the spirit and with understanding simultaneously, which is not possible in an unknown tongue. Therefore, when Paul prayed, he did not do it in an unknown tongue; he wanted both his mind and his spirit to be involved.

The introduction, "What, then?" (*ti oun estin*), from verse 15 indicates a conclusion to the section, in which he had just said that prayer in an unknown tongue does not produce fruit. Prayer that can be understood is preferable to incomprehensible prayer. Since it is practically impossible for a private prayer to be interpreted, the mind of the speaker would remain without fruit or benefit. As we see, there is not one biblical reason to pray in an unknown tongue; the gift of tongues was not for prayer.

Additional reasons:
1) The idea that an unknown tongue communicates unconsciously with God (without the participation of the mind of the individual) is contrary to the teachings of Jesus.

Matthew 6:7-8 "And when you pray, do not use vain repetitions as the heathen do. For they think that they will be heard for their many words. Therefore do not be like them. For your Father knows the things you have need of before you ask Him."

Later the Lord gave them the example of an intelligible, understandable prayer to imitate.

The phrase "vain repetitions" is *battalogeo*. It does not appear in the Septuagint (the Greek translation of the OT, also referred to as LXX) and is used only here in the New Testament. It is defined as "babbling" and is used in relation to stuttering expressions or frequent repetitions.

Frequent repetition (such as "glory," "hallelujah," "glory to God," etc.) is disobedience because it goes against the instruction of Jesus. It is especially so when the phrases become incoherent, mindlessly repeated or become syllable sounds instead of words. This is the pagan practice of unintelligible and ecstatic prayer that Jesus prohibited. It is and was the pagan medium of communication with their gods.

Jesus prayed and taught us to pray clearly and intelligibly. He never taught prayer in an unknown or unintelligible tongue, especially by repeating a phrase over and again at an ever-faster rate of repetition until the syllables become blurred into babble-type sounds.

2) The groans of the Spirit are not a prayer in glossolalia; the expression in Romans 8:26 is not a language.
Romans 8:26 NJV, "Likewise the Spirit also helps in our weaknesses. For we do not know what we should pray for as we ought, but the Spirit Himself makes intercession for us with groanings which cannot be uttered."

First, the passage refers to all believers. Romans 8:23 says, "...but ourselves also, which have the firstfruits of the Spirit, even we ourselves groan within ourselves, waiting for the adoption, to wit, the redemption of our body." The following context refers to the foreknowledge, predestination, call, justification and the permanence of the love of Christ. The entire context refers to the universe of believers, so that verse 26 also refers to all believers, without condition.

In second place, the phrase, "groanings that cannot be uttered" (stenagmois alaletois) does not mean speaking in tongues. The word alaletois is something "without expression, without words," or "that which cannot be expressed in a language," any kind of language. It is a "groan or sigh," not a word. Apparently it is not a reference to any audible sound in any form. It is not a language at all. It is a feeling from a perspective that only God can understand.

What is this groan?

3) It is the same groan that the Spirit makes between the creation and God.
Romans 8:22 NKJ, "For we know that the whole creation groans and labors with birth pangs together until now."

The use of "also" in 8:23 indicates that the groaning of the fallen creation and the groaning of all sinful but forgiven believers is the same expression. The only thing that makes us acceptable to a holy God is the amazing grace that granted sinners like us the covering of God's perfect righteousness as a result of our faith in His Word (Gen 15:6; 2 Cor 5:21). Nothing in us makes us acceptable or ever could. Our pride, envy, lust, greed, hatred, unforgiving spirit, bitterness, anger, ambition, selfishness, ego, etc. etc., all make the Spirit within us groan and long for the day when we are finally transformed into His glorious likeness. Then the groanings will cease and the creation and all the created beings will be restored to perfection at creation.

Therefore, if the groaning is the gift of tongues, then all of creation would have the gift of tongues—which would be ridiculous.

On the contrary, the groan is the desire for something meant to be or the tension between the fallen creation and its potential to be the way God planned the perfect creation to be, and one day will be realized. Until that day the groanings of creation will continue. This tension will be alleviated when "the redemption of our bodies" is realized (8:23).

4) It is evident that the groans are made by the Spirit, not by the believer (8:26)

Romans 8:26 NKJ, "Likewise the Spirit also helps in our weaknesses. For we do not know what we should pray for as we ought, but the Spirit Himself makes intercession for us with groanings which cannot be uttered."

We have no idea what God's plan for the universe and for man will be. Isaiah 55:9 NKJ, "For as the heavens are higher than the earth, So are My ways higher than your ways, And My thoughts than your thoughts." When God thinks of how the world and man could be as He designed them, He groans at how far we are from His plan. How He will transform everything one day into an amazing existence beyond human imagination.

At the present time only He knows this great difference or dissonance between the sinful creation and the eventual transformation of all things as He originally intended. This difference provokes the groaning of the Spirit who lives within the body of sinful believers who are covered with His righteousness by grace, but too gradually are being transformed into His sanctified image. Since we cannot imagine what God's plan is for us and all creation, we have no idea how to pray for its realization and the consummation of time.

This groaning has nothing to do with a special divine language that communicates anything more than the agony of fallen man who someday will be glorified and transformed into His likeness. "He chose [us] to become like his Son…" Rom 8:29 NLT is the great plan of God for all believers. He groans in agony until this transformation is realized.

5) Since the gift of tongues is an actual language, it would be difficult to categorize such a language as "groanings that cannot be uttered."

The phrase "cannot be uttered" is *alaletos*, means it is inexpressible, without words, not spoken. It is an inaudible communication of an emotion. The word is a+*laletos* (not + spoken). Essentially, it is not a language in any form. It is just a groan of agony or the heart cry of God for the new creature and the new heavens and new earth to begin where Adam left off.

10. The concept of needing a special gift to communicate in prayer and worship to God violates all the teachings of the New Testament about prayer.

We have complete access to God through Jesus Christ. It was obtained for the believer by Christ's death on the cross (John 14:13-14), as illustrated in Ephesians 3:12, "in whom we have boldness and access with confidence through faith in Him." This assures us that we will always have entrance directly to the throne, "Let us therefore come boldly to the throne of grace, that we may obtain mercy and find grace to help in time of need." (Hebrews 4:16) No special language is needed in God's presence, only the redemption of our souls by His blood on Calvary.

If we say that there is yet a special gift language that makes our prayer more effective than the blood of Jesus, this would imply that simply talking to God in our mother tongue is deficient and that without such a gift we would not have absolute access to God the Father.

Such a supposed debility of the believer would render these prayer promises as partial, limited or worse, exaggerated. In no part of the Bible do we find such an idea that we need a special language to talk to the heart of God. He never demands a special gift in order to speak intimately with Him. This whole notion is imported from paganism or someone's imagination for an elite spirituality beyond work of the cross.

The teaching that a special tongue is needed to communicate with God is similar to the teaching of the need for special mediators in the Catholic Church. Both teach that man is weak, without merit to be in the presence of God and requires a mediator who would permit a special and more intimate communication with the Father. This concept is not biblical.

The Catholic Church has invented the virgin Mary and the Saints as intercessors, while the Charismatics have the gift of tongues to take them into the presence of the Father. But the gift of tongues never has this function in the New Testament, and saying otherwise is contrary to the teaching of prayer in the New Testament. It is through Christ alone that every believer has complete, full and permanent access to the heart of God.

The help of the Spirit referred to in Romans 8:26 is not a gift of tongues, because all believers have this intercession of the Spirit. His gives us help that we do not realize or understand, a level of communication through the Trinity on our behalf. Just as the Son "always lives forever to intercede with God on [believer's] behalf" (Heb 7:25 KJV), so the Spirit likewise never ceases to intercede for us.

We do not understand what God's intentions are for man and creation, so we do not know what to pray for. Too often we are only asking for selfish things and short-sighted plans, so God has to put them into His perspective and respond in ways that bring His purpose about.

If there existed a tongue in which God prefers to hear his worship, one would have been specified. How is it possible for a particular language like Chinese or German to be better to worship God than in English? It is even more illogical to imagine how God could prefer worship in an unknown tongue, when the speaker does not understand what he is saying. Why would worship from Himself (the Spirit without man's understanding) mean more than a man who fully understands the truth that he is thrilled about and express to Him his full surrender and appreciation for what He has shown him about Himself in His Word? How could an expression that makes no sense whatsoever to the speaker mean more to God than a person who in total transparency and commitment to Christ shares in total awareness the most intimate of his desires for God's will?

Intelligent beings want mutually intelligent communication, something expressed out of our own feelings, something we understand and are intentional on saying. God does not want robots, or to listen to Himself, but rather wants His creatures who respond to Him in true understanding because they voluntarily choose to love Him and want to tell him so in their own words.

In addition, there is no indication that the worship of God by the angels is better than that of men (Revelation 4:11-5:14), but if the angels had a special language—something that the Bible does not teach—then the worship of men in their own tongues would be inferior. Angels are not redeemed. If they had a distinct language, they could not express the depth and heart-felt praise of a redeemed sinner in their language. That can only come from redeemed sinners saved by grace.

In 1 Corinthians 13:8, Paul said that the gift of tongues would cease. If the idea has to do with a special language to communicate with God, then would the ceasing of the tongues indicate that the angels would stop speaking this special language in Heaven as well? Why would a language that produces a more intimate communication and more effective worship ever have to cease? In Heaven, will the believers have to worship God in an inferior language as well, since tongues had ceased? None of this makes any sense; the whole concept of a special prayer communication language with God is a false notion.

In Acts 10:46, when the Jews heard Cornelius and his family, "speak with tongues, and magnify God," this does not necessarily mean that they spoke in an unknown tongue to the hearers. It is possible that there were two actions: speaking in a tongue as a sign to the Jews who accompanied Peter and, later, in magnifying God. The Jews spoke Aramaic and Hebrew. It is likely that a resident Gentile might have learned Aramaic, but it is doubtful that he would have learned Hebrew as well. More than likely Cornelius' family only spoke Greek or possibly Latin. A reasonable solution would be that these Gentiles spoke miraculously in fluent Hebrew, a language only the Jews present would have known.

How could they know that the Gentiles were magnifying God if they were speaking in an unknown or mystery language? There is no mention of a interpreter being necessary. Could they have know it by the expressions on their faces? Not likely. It was most probably an expression of worship after having received the Holy Spirit, then they spoke in an unknown language to Peter, but a language known to the hearers from Jerusalem that did not need translation. Given the record that they praised God in an unknown language before the Jewish observers; therefore, it would have had to be a language understood by the Jews, but not know to Cornelius or his household, so that they could know what had been said.

Also, the purpose of a sign could be accomplished whether through worship or preaching. Here it was worship, but such worship was not the purpose in itself. The purpose of the language was to make it clear that the Gentiles had received the same Spirit, in the same manner that the Jews had received the Spirit some 10 years before. (Acts 11:15, 17).

So there is no basis to presume that the gift of tongues is for personal use or that it permits a more intimate access to God. The possessor of any gift can know that God is using him without a special gift to tell him so. No gift, especially one that would cease, was given for prayer and worship to God. This gift was a sign to the Jews and fulfilled its purpose with indisputable clarity (Acts 11:15).

When it is understood that the gift of tongues is a manifestation of an actual language, there remains positively no reason for its use in private. How could one language be better than another for speaking to God? This is a pagan concept, not a biblical one. The use of devotional tongues is completely contrary to the teachings of the New Testament and is in opposition to the declared purpose of the gift of tongues in 1 Corinthians 14:22, which is a sign to unbelievers. Therefore, the teaching and practice of devotional tongues is not biblical.

CHAPTER 19

A Possible Explanation

With all the scriptural evidence against the manifestation of tongues in our day, how do we explain the modern phenomenon of tongues? The members of the Charismatic Movement declare that their experience is genuine and makes them feel nearer to God. They tell us of more power in their lives to testify of Christ and to live for Him and they are doing just that.

I do not want to be unkind, but what the modern Charismatic movement around the world has done is to integrate and synthesize many pagan worldview concepts into Christianity. Admittedly many phenomena occur in their churches and meetings, but when the Word is ignored and not obeyed, the results do not come from God. The Pentecostals and Charismatics are wrong about the nature, purpose and practice of tongues. They are wrong about who receives them and how and when they are received. They exaggerate what the Scriptures say about tongues, invent a heavenly language and disobey the principles of 1 Corinthians 14. They distort the text to prove their viewpoints, as in their emphasis on women who preach and speak in tongues that is clearly contrary to the teaching of the New Testament (1 Cor 14:34-35).

The evolution of the movement is continuing to develop new doctrines that are dangerously close to pagan practices. Those who do not believe in and/or rely on the Bible as their only authority of faith and practice are willing to accept all kind of phenomenon as something divine, while evangelists who are well-taught in the Word and are spiritually mature do not see these apparent miracles as biblical. Something is wrong. If they are wrong in aspects related to the gift of tongues, then they are wrong even in the basis of their experiences.

As we showed in chapter 1, the Charismatic Movement has roots in Pentecostalism, which did not originate among fundamentalists well founded in the Word, but rather among those who were disenchanted with their churches and their own spiritual lives. They found an experience that made them feel that they had true contact with God, even though their ecstatic experiences were not defined in the Bible. The benefit of such an ecstatic experience must be repeated continually and even exaggerated to reach the same euphoria or satisfaction each time; however, many have become disillusioned and frustrated because of this empty experience that cannot perpetually satisfy.

What are some of the possible explanations of what is happening in the Charismatic Movement?

Possibility 1: Is it possible that demons are involved?

Regrettably one of the explanations for supernatural phenomena originates from demonic sources. This would apply to any deceiving spiritual activity that seeks to attract people to any worship or submission that turns the focus away from the Person of Jesus Christ as the preeminent manifestation of God. The comments made here by no means wish to attribute any or all of the Charismatic Movement to demonic sources. However, some of the extreme

Chapter 19: *A Possible Explanation*

practices of the movement some of the spiritistic, animistic and mystical practices have infiltrated the Christian churches unrecognized and, in fact, encouraged as though they were divine.

The modern Charismatic Movement is similar to the biblical manifestation of the gift of tongues. Similarity does not imply identical. A phenomenon occurred in the biblical descriptions of demon possession as we see in Luke 9:38-39 and 42, "Suddenly a man from the multitude cried out, saying, 'Teacher, I implore You, look on my son, for he is my only child.' And behold, a spirit seizes him, and he suddenly cries out; it convulses him so that he foams at the mouth, and it departs from him with great difficulty, bruising him.... And as he was still coming, the demon threw him down and convulsed him. Then Jesus rebuked the unclean spirit, healed the child, and gave him back to his father." Notice that the (demon) spirit suddenly takes control (*lambano*) of the boy making him go into convulsions and throwing him to the ground. This kind of spirit passion activity was evident as demonic.

In Mark 9:18-20, we find similar and additional details on demonic activity: Mark 9:18 "And wherever it seizes him, it throws him down; he foams at the mouth, gnashes his teeth, and becomes rigid. So I spoke to Your disciples, that they should cast it out, but they could not." 19 He answered him and said, "O faithless generation, how long shall I be with you? How long shall I bear with you? Bring him to Me." 20 Then they brought him to Him. And when he saw Him, immediately the spirit convulsed him, and he fell on the ground and wallowed ["rolled around"], foaming at the mouth."

Some of these characteristics are very similar to what often happens in spiritistic and Charismatic meetings. Falling to the floor and rolling around, shaking unconsciously, supposedly from the "Spirit," speaking in different voices, becoming rigid or immoveable, etc., are typical experiences among many Pentecostal gatherings. They defend their activities saying that the Spirit of God is controlling them. They admit that similar activities are caused by demons, but argue that it is the demonic activities that are imitations of the genuine activities of God. Where do we find in the Bible a genuine example of such an experience given by the Spirit? It does not exist! In the Bible, any such activity is provoked by demons.

The Bible does not suggest that tongues would be active in later days, but it does strongly indicate that satanic activity and even demonic miracles would be performed and the Spirit would not be the source. The passage in Matthew 7:22-23 refers to people who, in the name of Christ, prophesied, cast out demons and performed many miracles. When these imposters said that they did these signs "in your name," it means that they used the name of Jesus probably repeatedly.

Arnold Fruchtenbaum in his thorough analysis of the Toronto Phenomenon stated, "The name of Jesus is heavily used in almost ritual-mantra style, all kinds of signs and wonders are claimed to occur, and yet, by themselves, these things do not prove anything because Satan can duplicate these." (Fruchtenbaum, 1996: 10). Since Christ did not know them, their power could not have come from the Spirit, but from Satan, who deceives the simple.

They were deceived into thinking that their power came from Christ, when it really came from the fountain of demonic powers. They thought that they were genuine believers because of the power they manifested. Surely if they could perform a miracle they had to belong to Christ. What a terrible error! Christ will declare, "I never knew you" (Matt 7:23).

A genuine relationship to Christ is not based on experiences, feelings or signs, regardless of how supernatural they may appear, but rather is based on a trust in the biblical revelation of truth in the Word of God.

Another example of this same area is 2 Corinthians 11:3-4 and 13-15:

> "But I fear, lest by any means, as the serpent beguiled Eve in his craftiness, your minds should be corrupted from the simplicity and the purity that is toward Christ. For if he that comes preaches another Jesus, whom we did not preach, or if ye receive another spirit, which ye did not receive, or another gospel, which ye did not accept, ye do well to bear with him. For such men are false apostles, deceitful workers, fashioning themselves into apostles of Christ. And no marvel; for even Satan fashions himself into an angel of light. It is no great thing therefore if his ministers also fashion themselves as ministers of righteousness; whose end shall be according to their works."

Just as Satan was able to deceive Eve, even the believers in the Corinthian church were deceived by Satan, not as directly, but in a more subtle manner. It cannot be forgotten that sensationalism, signs and wonders and unusual experiences captivated the Corinthian church. As a result of their openness to phenomena and the unexplainable supernatural, they opened their minds to deception by false teachers.

In 1 Timothy 4:1, Paul taught that "in the last days" (or the end of the church age), it would be common to find "deceiving spirits" and "doctrines of demons," teachings that demons have planted in the minds of false teachers to make them appear as coming from the Holy Spirit. These do not have to be demon possessed false teachers, just those who are open to receive "spirit" guidance, voices and new revelations. In the passage in 2 Corinthians 11 Satan can appear as an "angel of light." How many cultic ideas and false notions have come from "angelic messengers" in false religions?

The book of Revelation declares that there will be people who worship demons and that the demons will do miracles (Revelation 9:20; 16:14). Paul warned that the devil and his demons can disguise themselves as an "angel of light" or as "ministers of righteousness" (2 Corinthians 12:1-2; 2 Thessalonians 2:9; 2 Peter 2; Revelation 2:20), but the believers had the responsibility of discerning if the person was speaking by the Holy Spirit by another spirit. In other words, they could never accept a phenomenon as divine simply because it was supernatural. It had to stem from conformity to all the revealed truth known to the Church.

False religions are known by euphoric experiences, which can include speaking in tongues, that is to say, ecstatic utterances or babbling sounds. The founder of the Mormons, Joseph Smith, said, "Stand up, speak or make a sound, continue making the sound and the Lord will make a language out of it." (Smith 1978: n.a.). The seventh Article of Faith, one of the thirteen "creeds" of Mormonism, reads in part: "We believe in the gift of tongues."

The author's experience of witnessing shamans among tribes in the Amazon jungle who manifest a strange language while in a trance to communicate with the spirit world is remarkably similar to what he has witnessed in Pentecostal meetings in various countries. Spiritism, Macumbas of Brazil and Argentina, Voodoos of Haiti, and gurus, sadhus and sufi ascetics in India all practice a similar mystical babbling language to what is practiced in the Pentecostal/Charismatic churches.

These are practically the same instructions Charismatics give to those who seek to speak in tongues. Also, speaking in tongues is found among the Muslims, Jehovah's Witnesses, Eskimos and among the occult and the mystics. Spiritists in Brazil often fall to the ground in unconsciousness and make babbling sounds said to be from the spirits. I have seen tribal witch doctors in the Amazon showing their powers of speaking in mystical languages. They are supposedly communicating to the spirits in a way that no one else can. This gives them their spiritual edge or authority.

Whoever is willing to depend on his experiences and to submit himself to whatever power or spirit that comes over him is open to satanic influence. This is not the same as demonic possession; rather is an openness to the seductive influence of demonic suggestion (1 Tim 4:1). It is the same method that witch doctors, Spiritists and shamans use to submit to the spirits of the underworld to communicate with them and let the spirits speak through them to the people.

It is irresponsible and dangerous to allow your mind and spirit to be open to any other powers. Because of their ignorance, many have submitted to forces outside their comprehension and control. Such powers are subtle and deceptive. They try to imitate the Holy Spirit and/or angles, in order to deceive as many as possible with supernatural manifestations instead of the truth of the Word.

Do not take this section to say that all those who are in the Charismatic Movement are influenced by demons, but it is a possibility that all believers should seriously consider. Demons do not wave flags announcing their presence, but rather they pretend to be spiritual and can deceive any believer to keep him from knowing and obeying the Word.

Possibility 2: It is something learned.

If the actual experience of speaking in a tongue is not biblical, then it is not produced by the Spirit and is not a miracle of God. If it is not produced by demons (Possibility 1), then it is possible that the person has learned it, whether consciously or unconsciously. We would like to believe that this is the most common explanation in the contemporary movement.

> One easy way for a person to learn is to pretend that he is speaking a foreign language. He starts speaking, slowly and deliberately producing syllables. Then be speeds up, consciously trying to make it sound like a language would sound. Once he is doing well, he just relaxes and does not worry any longer about what comes out. (Poythress 1979: 370).

Tongues speaking may be associated with considerable peer pressure and need of approval/acceptance for those who wish to speak in tongues. (Kildahl 1972: 2-5). Pentecostal authors Charles and Frances Hunter give this encouragement to their readers: "Many of you will be hearing little sounds right now running through your mind. Strange little parts of words. Strange little syllables. You don't understand them, but listen for them, because this is the beginning of your Spirit language. Some of you may not hear anything, but will just begin to speak in a moment."(Hunter 1976: 185). Then he adds the following description for how to begin to speak in a tongue:

> You may start off with a little baby language, but just keep on. Remember when your children were small they started out with a very small vocabulary, and then as they added new letters to it, they were capable of making more words. The same thing is sometimes true of your Spirit language. The Spirit can only give back to you what you give to him, so put those extra sounds of the alphabet in and see what he does with them! Don't keep on speaking a baby language, but allow the Holy Spirit to develop a full language in and through you. (Hunter 1976: 188).

Another analyst William Samarin answers the question, "Can the average person be taught to produce tongues speaking or free vocalization?

> Yes. Learning to free vocalize is easier than learning to ride a bicycle. As with the bicycle, the practitioner may feel foolish and awkward at first. But practice makes perfect. Moreover, though at first a person may feel self-conscious, after he has learned he may sometimes forget that he is doing it. It is something that he can start or stop at will without difficulty. (Samarin 1969 :44-149)

Clinical psychologist John Kildhal and his coworker Paul Qualben, a psychiatrist, were commissioned by the American Lutheran Church and the National Institute of Mental Health to investigate the cause of the manifestation of tongues in Charismatic churches. After their long and extensive investigation, they arrived at the conclusion that "it was no more than a learned behavior." (Kildhal 1972: 54)

Those who are involved in the movement support a gigantic pressure to participate in the common experience of speaking in an unknown tongue.

When there are problems in their lives, the first question is, "Have you spoken in tongues today?" For them, it is the secret of the entire Christian life. They say that until one has spoken in tongues, he will have unconquerable problems and little power to overcome the evil nature.

When a sincere person submits to the pressure and babbles something, but later recognizes that there was nothing supernatural in the experience, he can suffer a great disillusion. Kildhal and Qualben discovered that the more sincere the person when he began to speak in tongues, the greater was his disillusion upon realizing the error.

Every linguistic analysis of tongues speaking are assured that their samples represent no known natural language or any kind of language at all.

> These facts—especially the fact that free vocalization is so easy to produce and that most [tongues]-speech is not a natural language—have become one of the main grounds for a certain amount of debunking on the part of social scientists. To them, it appears that [tongues]-speech has nothing to do with the Holy Spirit. ... What the research does show is that free vocalization is not an intrinsically miraculous and therefore infallible sign of the working of the Holy Spirit. (Poythress 1979: 373).

Some become involved in the movement for carnal reasons, seeking to fill a void in their lives, and wanting "instant spirituality," and are satisfied upon speaking in tongues. It is my belief that these are people who never have examined the Bible to see if there is any truth in this teaching.

Possibility 3: It is possible that there is something psychological.

Psychologists have been studying the phenomenon of *glossalalia* for several years and have suggested the possible existence of capabilities in the human psyche that could produce this ecstatic speaking. If the experience is not from the Spirit or from demons and is not learned, then it is probable that some psychological mechanism could produce it.

In the psychological structure of man there is a condition that, in certain circumstances, makes it possible for the person to lose control of himself momentarily. The author has explained this psychological experience as something similar to that of many young people during an intense music concert.

> In the emotion, fervor and noise, they literally abandon voluntary control of their vocal cords and their muscles. They may fall to the floor and begin to shake.
> Almost everyone, in a given moment, can experience moments in which they feel a little disassociated, a little light headed and somewhat faint. Since the correct combination of conditions, particularly where there is much fervor and emotion, as happens sometimes in the Charismatic meetings, a person can easily fall into this kind of experience.(MacArthur

1978:176)

The mental preparation that is part of Charismatic teaching to psychologically prepare the person consists in sayings such as "Ignore your inhibitions," "Do not resist your impulses," "Let go of your soul," or "Release control of your voice." The person must submit himself to a "passive renunciation through the loss of intentional control." He should not think about what he is saying, abandoning self-control. (Ibid.:177)

Psychological capacity 1: ecstasy

The person finds himself in a state charged with emotion, unconscious of his actions and sometimes produces passionate and unknown sounds. He may arrive at this point in an atmosphere of emotional music, moving his body with the music and concentrating on something outside himself, whether it is the rhythm, lights or a compelling person. Suddenly, he is almost in a trance and later does not even remember what he did! This type of experience does not come from God because 1 Corinthians 14:32 says, "the spirits of the prophets (or whatever person dominated by the Spirit) are subject to the prophets"; in other words, they are always in control of themselves.

Some testimonies of Charismatics indicate that their spirits left their bodies and traveled to other places. They can also see visions during these trances. It is interesting that almost all the witch doctors in the Amazon tribal people have the same experience! Sometimes, the shaman's body is immobile for days while his spirit travels, sometimes in the bodies of animals such as the jaguar or a bird. His body can also tremble, fall to the ground tossing and turning, etc. The manifestation of the indigenous people is similar in many aspects to that which the author has seen among charismatic believers. In reality, however, having a rare experience is not enough evidence to say that the phenomenon is from the Spirit.

Psychological capacity 2: auto-hypnosis

The result of auto-hypnosis is very similar to that of an ecstasy, although auto-hypnosis is more controlled by the will of the individual.

Ecstasy can be the result of taking drugs or of an atmosphere charged by emotion, but auto-hypnosis comes when the person is persuaded to seek a specific experience such as becoming euphoric or speaking in ecstatic tongues. The emotional atmosphere is not a factor. Kildhal and Qualben concluded that, "the ability to be auto-hypnotized constitutes the sine qua non of the experience of *glossalalia*." (Kildal, 1972:54)

Even though it would be impossible to analyze each person who speaks in tongues and describe his symptoms, it is possible to compare what psychology has learned with the experiences of charismatic believers. There are four steps that produce auto-hypnosis:

(1) A sense of frustration and inner conflict. When the life of the believer does not reach the level that the Bible indicates is the ideal, he feels frustration. Personal sin, the lack of miracles and other manifestations in his life all make him think that something is lacking in his Christian life. The person is psychologically prepared for any promise of relief.
(2) This frustration motivates a secret quest for the "abundant life." The goal of speaking in tongues is taught to be the end of this empty feeling of frustration; then, unconsciously the person begins to seek to speak in tongues. The person is persuaded that some day he will achieve the goal. However, the impediments to the "abundant" life are not the lack of experiences, but false concepts, hidden sin, or refusing to obey what is known to be the will of God. An emotional experience will merely cover the problem rather than eradicate it.
(3) Speaking in tongues is presented as the greatest reward in the Christian life. It is taught that speaking in tongues will bring prestige, the sense of acceptance by the congregation and by God.
(4) Everyone assures the person seeking tongues that this is the solution to his problems. These suggestions are very effective for some people and they suddenly speak in an ecstatic language. Once they arrive at step four, their will is so controlled by this desire that some can have the experience whenever they want. They are so convinced by the experience that it is impossible to reason with them. They become totally closed and will not consider analyzing their experience in the light of the Scriptures. (Goodman 1972:n.a.).

The difference between ecstasy and auto-hypnosis is mainly the will of the individual. Not everyone who speaks in tongues can be categorized this way, but many do fit here. When emotions grow and pressure rises, the result can easily be speaking in tongues. They submit themselves to the power of suggestion and will do anything asked of them.

Observation 1: The genuine believers that accept the charismatic teaching of tongues are completely normal and love the Lord.

God works in our lives through manifold means that are not always stereotyped as we might prefer. The idea that tongues speakers are more emotional, mentally ill or more easily swayed is evidence of prejudice. It is true that in some cases there may be a temporary emotional need, but the great majority of the people involved in speaking in tongues are completely normal and sincere in their devotion to the Lord.

Our exemplary charismatic, then, receives benefits of three main kinds from T-speech. First, his T-speech reinforces belief in the power and presence of the Holy Spirit. The T-speaker believes that in T-speech God the Holy Spirit

> is speaking through him. When uttering a T-speech, or when reflecting on the fact that he has done this in the past, he may marvel at the fact that the Holy Spirit could thus speak through him. He is convinced more thoroughly than ever, and more deeply than ever, how wonderful and powerful God the Holy Spirit is. He also has a peace and assurance that the Holy Spirit is dwelling in him and can help him to do God's will. God's will no longer seems burdensome, but something that God himself will cause him to fulfill with joy. What a marvelous blessing!
> Now, what is happening? Our T-speaker is being taught by God the biblical doctrine of the indwelling of the Holy Spirit in believers. He is being taught the power of the resurrected Christ who comes to dwell in him and give him joy and victory in the Holy Spirit. No wonder he is filled with joy! (Poythress 1979: 379–380).

The potential problem here arises because the believer has based his convictions about the Holy Spirit on his experiences, rather than first of all on what the Bible says. If his experiences later begin to fade in emotional impact in his mind, he may lose his confidence in the reality of the Spirit and thus his emotional stability. However, the tongues speaker attempts to speak to God in random syllables that make no sense to him, but in his heart/spirit he is agonizing over an issue or need that he wants to communicate to God. He may believe that his special tongue is approaching God much better than he can by merely speaking, but the truth is that God knows the heart and needs of his children and knows what we want to communicate before we even say anything. He reads our heart as readily as our lips. Our prayers are effective no matter how we are communicating them to the Father (Phil 4:6-7; Rom 8:26; Ps 139).

Not just learning how to pray, but even deeper aspects of the Christian life can be understood through the experience.

> He may have become interested in T-speech because he felt dissatisfaction with his own Christian life. He felt an emptiness, a lack of power, a lack of vital and fresh communion with God. He wanted to be filled with the Holy Spirit. So he began to pray, to seek God, to repent, and to seek instruction from the Bible about the Holy Spirit. He found that he was holding back certain things in his life. He found areas that he was keeping to himself rather than surrendering to God. So he began saying to God, "Yes, I will follow you in this and that area too." Earlier he had thought to himself, "If I surrender everything, God may ask me to do something foolish or humiliating." He was afraid. Perhaps for him the area of the use of language was one such area. So tongues symbolized for him the question of whether everything was given to God. Finally, he said, "All right, I am willing to speak in tongues if that is what God wants for me." We will suppose that he in some way misunderstood the meaning of modern T-speech. Still, many of his prayers and desires were genuine, and God answered them. Since his first experience with T-speech, his life has been transformed.

Chapter 19: *A Possible Explanation*

He has awakened to the reality of the work of the Spirit in his life. He has started to believe that God still does remarkable things today. He has come to trust that God knows and understands his deepest concerns. He has started to look to the Bible for answers to his daily problems. He finds now that the Bible is a living book where God speaks. The intensive fellowship that he has experienced with other charismatics has further strengthened his Christian life. (*Ibid.*, 132-136).

These are great lessons in the Christian life to have learned, but how much more solid the believer's life would be had these lessons been learned from applying the biblical commands and principles to his life. The end result for now can be similar, but the long-term results either will require more and rarer experiences or, turning to the Scripture, he begins to ground his life on the truths and instructions given for transformation.

Observation 2: The majority of those who speak in tongues think that they are speaking in a literal language.

Analysis has proved that 60% of charismatic believers think that they have spoken in a real language whether angelic or human. However, Pew Forum Polls from a hundred countries have shown that "40% of Pentecostals say that they have never spoken in tongues" (Banks 2006: n.a.). Until now, there is still no concrete evidence that any modern manifestation of tongues has any characteristics of a real language previously unknown to the speaker. There is no reason for the speakers' conviction that he is speaking a real language. They simply convince themselves to believe it to be so.

It seems that those who speak in tongues believe "by faith" that what they are speaking is a foreign language, and that the whole world will believe it as well. "If you believe, it is so," seems to be their theme. As Dennis Bennett said: "Any sound can and should be accepted by faith as the gift of tongues."

In Hebrews 11:1, ("Now faith is the substance of things hoped for, the evidence of things not seen") the word "substance" in the original language means "evidence." True faith is not based on mere imagined beliefs, but rather is based on biblical evidence. Just because a person believes something to be true, does not make it true, nor will God accept a person's beliefs just because he is sincere in his beliefs. Faith does not believe in something that is not so, in order to make it real. Either it is real or it is not.

Sometimes, the report of foreign languages being spoken is a perhaps exaggerated and the objectivity of the reporter is wishful thinking that seems real. Speaking several syllables or producing a sound or word that is similar to a word in some foreign language is not speaking in that language.

We are still looking for evidence to accept these declarations of a language of whatever kind. In conclusion, we see that the phenomenon of the tongues of today is not comparable to the gift of tongues in the Scriptures. Speaking in tongues today is a likely psychological experience with random sounds, while that which occurred in the first century was the precise expression of foreign languages spoken in their contemporary world. What we see manifested today as speaking in tongues is an imitation.

It is possible today that God could give a literal language should He choose to, but that is not the norm within the Pentecostal/Charismatic Movement. Universally we find spoken "tongues" actually are ecstatic utterances (glossolalia), which has no parallel in the New Testament. When Paul used the term for the gift of tongues in 1 Corinthians 14:10, he referred to them as "languages [that are] are surely in the world."

If the "tongues" of the Charismatics were earthly languages, then we should be able to analyze them linguistically, immediately ending all controversy. However, the *glossalalia* of today fails every examination when it is written, analyzed and compared with the interpretation, if there is one. If the tongue spoken is not miraculous in every sense, then are we left with no sign of the initial baptism of the Spirit? Do we need a miraculous sign to prove a truth that the Bible clearly states "all" believers have been baptized by the Spirit (1 Cor 12:13)? Should not the clear statement of the Bible be all the evidence needed to believe that all believers have the power of God indwelling them?

In conclusion, Paul called on his readers to recognize that everything he has written about the glossolalia error and the corrective action to be taken was the command of the Lord (1 Cor 14:37). Anyone who failed to obey his authority, especially in this theme, was not to be recognized (14:38). Our task is to clearly understand all that Paul wrote and receive it as spoken directly from the Lord Himself. When 1 Corinthians 12-14 is understood clearly then so many of the differences and values can be shared throughout the Body of Christ creating a deeper unity that will honor His name.

# CHAPTER 20

One Last Word about Charismatics

Chapter 20: *Gifts for Today*

From which sectors of society do the greatest numbers of people come into the Charismatic Movement? Do they have a background of biblical teaching with which to evaluate the teachings of the charismatic teachers in order to distinguish whether or not they are biblical?

Once the Pentecostal experience spread into other denominations and churches, the movement continued to grow beyond the early adaptors of the Pentecostal movement into the mainline denominations. The focus and characteristics of the whole of evangelical Christianity began to change after the 1960's. Music, worship concepts, bands, lyrics, singing groups, solos, style of church meetings and many other practices of the popular churches today knowingly or unknowingly are taking their cues from the Charismatic movement (esp., Vineyard movement model). The popularity of the movement has motivated a "I-could-care-less" attitude about the doctrinal differences among many, if not most, conservative evangelical churches.

For the average churchgoer there seems to be little difference between many conservative non-charismatic worship services and charismatic worship services. This similarity of worship has led many church members to believe that there are no doctrinal differences. Any comment that raises questions about the charismatics raises questions about the entire conservative Christian biblical perspective. Few can discern any differences, or even care anymore.

Pope Frances expressed a common attitude when he said, "At the end of the 70s, early 80s, I couldn't see them. I once said they must confuse liturgical celebration with samba lessons! Then I got to know them better and I was won over. I saw the work that they did and I said mass for them in Buenos Aires every year. I think movements are necessary; they are a gift from the Holy Spirit. The Church is free; the Holy Spirit does what it wants." (http://vaticaninsider.lastampa.it/en/the-vatican/detail/articolo/gmg-26831//pag/1/).

A question that was asked to Doctor Why in Yahoo! Answers, though not exactly a credible theological source it was interesting from a secular position: "What are the pros and cons of charismatic worship?" The answer in part was:

> The advantages of a charismatic movement are that they are very relevant and personal. You can interact with the center and the center can interact with the world. This makes it seem to involved people that they are really part of something that's going on, that they are in contact with the energetic source though that central figure. (http://answers.yahoo.com/question/index?qid=20080127065556AAY5hE4)

In most large churches or ministries the number of people with Charismatic backgrounds or tendencies is so significant that it would be suicidal to teach against the basic tenants of the movement for fear of loosing constituents or your job. The majority of evangelicals will seldom ever hear a message or a study that contradicts any of the Charismatic teachings. Publishers are extremely hesitant to publish anything negative about the Charismatics for fear of loosing buyers or being boycotted. The end result will be that soon all

Christians will increasingly believe that the Charismatic teaching is the only biblical viewpoint.

Donald E. Miller's book *Global Pentecostalism: The new Face of Christian Social Engagement* describes the reasons why Pentecostalism is growing so rapidly around the world. He calls them the "Progressive Pentecostals," but he makes a distinction between the Pentecostal holistic mission and theology and that of the Social Gospel and Liberation theology. (Miller and Yamamori 2007). Miller points to four major benefits:

1. Charismatic Christians have been a sign of eschatological faith in the church. It describes the restoration of the manifestations of the Day of Pentecost. Chaplain Mike on the Internet Monk describes what he appreciates about the Charismatic Movement:

> "challenged the church of their day with outside the box thinking and practice that implicitly or explicitly criticized the status quo and called people to wake up for a new day was coming. Such renewed visions of Jesus and new creation have always been accompanied by a lot of silliness, overblown enthusiasm, and wild fire. What the wind and fire do is not always tame and pretty. But it bespeaks a power of exciting new possibilities." (Mike, Internet Monk, June 25, 2012)

2. Charismatic Christians have been a force for worship renewal. Those who responded to the new worship model that the Charismatics brought to the church have a sense of anticipation, joy, personal testimony and heartfelt sincerity to worship that was a new spirit in the church.

3. Charismatic Christians have given testimony to the joy of the Lord. Instead of a cold, traditional and antiquated music (the opinion of the Charismatics) they brought the freedom to express joy and celebration with freedom and abandon. This would include singing and playing loud music, and dance.

4. Charismatic Christians have modeled radical inclusiveness and social concern. The movement brought a renewed focus on the poor and disenfranchised. Their congregations would be inclusive both ethnically and socio-economically. Their works are often in the inner city, seeking the street people, drug addicts and dysfunctional. (http://www.internetmonk.com/archive/what-i-appreciate-about-the-charismatic-movement).

Some of the reasons for the exploding growth of the charismatic movement is the experience by many of healing and miracles, which attracts many people. In 2006 Pew Forum survey found that 34% of Brazil's population claims to be charismatic. Nearly every country is making increasing claims of Charismatic growth at astounding rates.

The Charismatic movement is amazingly effective in reaching out to lost individuals, especially with personal witnesses of friend to friends. The number of charismatics has grown phenomenally in Latin America. In 1900 there were approximately 50,000 Protestants in Latin America. In 1980 they were approximately 50,000,0000. And by 2012 there were more than 100,000,000. This is impressive because 75 percent of these Protestants in Latin America are charismatic.

Barna Research (2008) indicated a number of interesting facts about American Christianity: 36% of Americans claim to be Charismatic or Pentecostal. Thought only 8% of the American population is evangelical, half of the evangelicals (49%) are charismatic. One out of every four Protestant churches in the US (23%) is a charismatic congregation. The non-traditional Pentecostal/charismatic denominations are growing the fastest. Four out of every ten non-denominational churches are charismatic.

The phenomenon is not exclusively Protestant. One-third (36%) of all US Roman Catholics claim to be charismatic, making up 22% of all US charismatics are Catholic.

Other denominational borders have been crossed in the US, for example in 2008 7% of Southern Baptist churches and 6% of other mainline churches are charismatic according to the senior pastor's position.

In America only 16% of the white Protestant congregations are Pentecostal, but 65% of the African-American Protestant churches are Pentecostal.

David Barnett states that the Pentecostal and Charismatic Christianity is second in size on to the Roman Catholic Church; however, the Charismatic statistics include 120 million Catholic Charismatics who are also counted as part of Roman Catholicism. (Barrett January 2009, 31).

The Pew Research Center's Forum on Religion & Public Life reports the global explosion of Pentecostal believers is even more significant in 2010. In Brazil, the Protestant population in 1940 was 2.6 percent of the population and in 2010 it was 21 percent, which is "overwhelmingly Pentecostal" and over half of Brazilian Catholics identify with the charismatic movement. In Sub-Saharan Africa 44% of the world's Pentecostals reside.

Smith quotes David Roozen of the Hartford Institute for Religion Research saying, ""If someone is going to be religious in today's world, it (Pentecostalism) has a lot more pizzazz than sitting around reading an old book. With Pentecostalism [you] can call on the spirit; there is an element of control." (Smith 2010). Roozen stated that the "Pentecostal and charismatic movement is spreading among the middle class Americans – a phenomenon that has puzzled many academics" (*Ibid.*)

> "The charismatic orientation is most popular among the non-white population - which is, of course, the sector of the population that is growing most rapidly. Also, the freedom of emotional and spiritual expression typical of charismatic assemblies parallels the cultural trend toward personal expression, accepting diverse emotions and allowing people to interpret their experiences in ways that make sense to them," Barna explained. "It is not surprising that the Pentecostal community in America has been growing - nor do we expect it to stop making headway."
> "We are moving toward a future in which the charismatic-fundamentalist

split will be an historical footnote rather than a dividing line within the body of believers. Young Christians, in particular, have little energy for the arguments that have traditionally separated charismatics and non-charismatics. Increasing numbers of people are recognizing that there are more significant arenas in which to invest their resources." (Retrieved 9/29/13 from https://www.barna.org/barna-update/congregations/52-is-american-christianity-turning-charismatic#.UkFmamRgbhM)

If this latter statement is true, it will make this book irrelevant. It is the hope of this author that the serious study of God's Word will never lose its influence and authority in the life of the church.

In general, the following is a list of the different groups that make up the core of the movement in America:

Classic Pentecostalism

The Pentecostal movement began in 1901. Several Pentecostal denominations have grown into a majority among fundamental evangelical believers. However, the classic Pentecostals are a minority within the overall Charismatic Movement and are mainly made up of those who were born into the Pentecostal denomination, the Assemblies of God, Church of God or other Pentecostal denominations.

Liberal churches

Neither human philosophers nor the negation of biblical truths can satisfy the spiritual hunger of the soul. In the world there is a great philosophical transition from atheistic humanism toward mystical humanism. This indicates that atheism does not satisfy real needs of humanity. On the contrary it is imperative that man has some contact with the transcendental or the supernatural. In the same way, the naturalism of the liberal churches has not satisfied the needs of its members, since they are still seeking contact with the supernatural that confirms to them His reality. Since truth is seen as relative and not absolute, and man's experience as the center of all reality, it was natural that a personal experience oriented evangelical message would meet with acceptance in the liberal churches.

Once the spiritual experience is seen as possible and respectable, there are no intellectual restrictions for those who desire something more than social action, that is, something real in their own religious experience.

Evangelical churches

In many evangelical churches the Bible is preached without the power of the Spirit in the lives of the leaders because legalism and Phariseeism have destroyed the heart and passion of many evangelical churches. Spiritual maturity is measured as conformity to rigid dress and behavioral standards instead of biblical obedience to just the commands in Scripture, which does not lead to legalistic, critical self-righteousness.

As a result, the hearers do not receive personal growth or blessings. Their hearts become as judgmental and cold as their churches. No one is converted to Christ; there are no transformed lives and no one grows spiritually. People feel they are only accepted if they conform and contribute to the superficial reputation of the church. In many churches there are arguments over insignificant themes, leaders who are more political than godly, and hypocritical pretending to be better than others. All this creates an atmosphere of rejection and an attack on the confidence in the church.

As a result, many become frustrated sensing the shallowness of their church, the lack of teaching the whole counsel of God, thus gravitating toward Charismatic churches because they believe that there is something more to Christianity.

The evangelical world is agonizing to see a genuine Christianity that is characterized by practical teaching, passion for Jesus Christ and the lost around the world, and where the Body-life of the local church is genuine.

Young people

Many young people have begun to reject formal religion and the institution of the church, both Catholic and Evangelical, as filled with ritualism, formalism and superficiality without heart or feeling. They are seeking experiences that excite their emotions, make them feel something real. Many experiment with drugs and sex without lasting satisfaction, giving up on all the institutions of society. Now some are turning to Charismatic churches looking for another kind of "trip." They find unconditional acceptance among Charismatics, and they believe that they are experiencing the meaningful emotional highs that they are looking for.

What a shame that all believers are not known for their joy and enthusiasm in serving the Lord! However, the "worship experience" is becoming the definition of contemporary Christianity. It is a very feeling oriented, participatory and subjectively meaningful experience. This sense-based worship has replaced personal inductive Bible study and commitment to a global mission for Christ as the highest value in the Christian life.

All of these groups have something in common: They want to know or feel the reality of an encounter with God. If they can be led to "feel" that encounter, their enthusiasm is contagious. This feeling-based religion is the core concept of mysticism.

In one large meeting, a Charismatic leader closed his Bible and said, "We are not going to be in agreement on the interpretation, so let me tell you of my own experience to give you a solid base." But true experience and "real" religion is found exactly in the opposite way: first, know the truth, and then practice it in an experience of joy and peace as consequences of following His commands.

Chapter 20: *One Last Word about Charismatics*

Three results of the emphasis of tongues in the Church of Corinth

Every doctrine has its own consequence, both positive and negative, whether taught from the biblical perspective or distorted from its original intent. In the Church of Corinth the emphasis on tongues and supernatural gifts resulted in a number of negative consequences, which provoked the writing of 1 Corinthians as a corrective text. It is interesting to compare the Corinthian church to the modern Charismatic Movement, because we often see similar consequences. Keep in mind that this problem was never regarding the existence of such gifts, but rather with the inordinate emphasis on them.

(1) The emphasis on ecstasy.

In 1 Corinthians 12:2 NLT Paul says they are, "...you were led astray and swept along in worshiping speechless idols..." Paul is describing a type of ecstasy without control, especially in the demonstration of the presence of a supernatural power. In pagan mystic religions, this practice was and is the norm. Paul also said that it was a common experience they shared as participants in pagan religions. In addition, historians tell us that in Greek religions, the devout trembled in an ecstasy and fell to the floor, speaking in ecstatic tongues. Both Plato, the philosopher, and Virgil, the poet, described such experiences.

In referring to these ecstatic experiences, Paul was saying that this kind of manifestation was not a sign of spirituality, but rather that it was something common to the Gentiles or pagans, which had evidently infiltrated into the practice of worship in the Corinthian church.

The Spirit does not cause a trance or ecstasy in which the person is unconscious of what is happening or loses control in any way. The following verses show that an ecstasy is not the result of the filling of the Spirit:

1 Corinthians 14:32, "And the spirits of the prophets are subject to the prophets,"
1 Corinthians 14:40, "Let all things be done decently and in order ['disciplined']."
Gal 5: 22-23, "But the fruit of the Spirit is love, joy, peace, ... self-control."

(2) The exaggerated focus on speaking in tongues.

It seems that Paul's purpose in writing 1 Corinthians 12:4-11 was to redirect this focus. Several times he emphasized having a variety of gifts instead of only one gift. The incorrect teaching that the baptism of the Spirit helps a Christian achieve an additional power after the indwelling of the Spirit a regeneration, or is a sign that one has received the power of the Spirit, coupled with the false teaching that tongues are the sign of the baptism of the Spirit, has produced this abuse of tongues. Remember, the Bible does not command us to pray, beg, cry or fast in order to receive a particular gift. They are all sovereignly distributed to every believer as God sees fit (1 Cor 12:7, 11, 18).

Our responsibility is simply to discover our gifts, develop them and use them in the church for the edification of others, not ourselves, and for the glory of the Lord. The emphasis on one gift is a perversion, as if a human body had only one member. 1 Corinthians 12:12-14 states that the Corinthians' use of the gifts was a perversion because it is not the plan of God. His plan is unity in the diversity of the gifts, not unity in the emphasis on one gift or in a common experience.

It is also a perversion because it overshadows Christ! It is easy to do, especially when there are sensational events, but it cannot be condoned. The emphasis must be on the preeminence of Christ (Colossians 1:18-19). The fact that most Charismatic churches portray drawings of doves on windows, pews and pulpits calls into question the figure of prominence in their churches. Is it the Spirit? Jesus did not say that the Spirit would exalt itself, but that the Spirit would exalt Jesus (John 16:14).

How many excuses we hear today when Charismatics negate Paul's doctrines with respect to the practice of tongues in their churches! We see hysteria, confusion, mystical sayings, inappropriate conduct, women speaking and giving direction in the churches and individuals seeking their own edification. Paul said it should not be like this.

(3) The emphasis on signs and revelations as evidence of spiritual reality.

False teachers in Corinth tried to teach that Paul had no authority because he did not perform many signs and miracles, perhaps as they did. Paul declared, "Do you look at things according to the outward appearance?" (2 Corinthians 10:7). They wanted some outward evidence that Paul was genuine and a true apostle. Later he comes back to this issue: "since you seek a proof of Christ speaking in me..." (2 Corinthians 13:3). They wanted visible proof of his authority.

Those teachers were completely wrapped up in external (visible) and mystical (apparently spiritual) manifestations. These experiences made people appear to be more spiritual, leaving the Corinthians with a false idea of what constitutes spirituality. The preoccupation with spiritual signs and wonders resulted in the negation of the authority of Paul's teachings. It is evident that the Corinthians did not want to completely obey the first letter because they were no longer impressed with Paul's authority and spirituality.

In 2 Corinthians, Paul wrote four chapters (10-13) defending his authority as an apostle. We can suppose that the false teachers had convinced the Corinthians with their spirituality by signs and miracles.

Note the attitude of the Apostle Paul when he related his experiences in 2 Corinthians 12:1-5. Paul did not like to do it, but it was necessary: "It is doubtless not profitable for me to boast..." (12:1). There is no elaboration or exaggeration, and he did not want to refer to himself. To avoid this, in his testimony he refers to himself saying, "I knew a man in Christ above fourteen years ago" (12:2).

God is so sensible to people who seek their own glory that he gave Paul a "thorn" in the flesh to humble him so that he would depend on His grace (12:7) instead of on his own experiences or abilities. God wanted to teach Paul,

"My grace is sufficient for thee" (12:9). No matter how important you may be or think you are, no matter what miracles you have done, none of it makes you spiritual. God is saying, "Only my grace makes you acceptable to me, not your appearance or performance, no matter how miraculous. My grace makes you as acceptable to me as my Son, the Lord Jesus. Seek no other approval."

The "love of Christ" (12:10) was the cause of his joy "in infirmities, in reproaches, in necessities, in persecutions." Therefore, he did not delight in his experiences or miracles, but in the love and presence of God as promised in the Word.

While Paul preferred to joy in his debilities or weaknesses in order to make more evident the power of the Spirit, the Corinthians were glorying in their spiritual experiences as proof that they possessed spiritual powers. And they received reproach.

We see that seeking special spiritual experiences is an improper motivation. Paul says that it should not be necessary for a man to glory in his experiences in order to prove his spirituality. The Corinthians wanted proof "according to appearances" (12:7), that is to say, something visible in order to accept Paul's authority. However, this only showed their immaturity. Their false doctrine caused them to accept a concept that was not biblical.

Six suspect consequences of the Charismatic Movement

The arguments that we have presented in this book are not personal opinions but teachings derived from the biblical text and scores of other scholars. Resolving this problem before the Lord in light of the Scriptures is necessary, because the movement's significance merits the question of whether or not it aligns with God's truth. We have shown that all evidences presented as fundamental to the movement have errors mixed with good teachings, and yet without a solid biblical foundation there will not be good, long-lasting results. Beyond a doubt there are many good things that have accompanied this movement, millions of lives have been impacted and the gospel of Jesus Christ has spread throughout the world.

As has been discussed, the Pentecostal Movement began in 1901 with the Charismatic Movement emerging 60 years later. The trends of these movements are becoming more and more evident as they continue to evolve. When Wesley said that the only way to be sure of your salvation was through a second work of grace, thus achieving sanctification, he did not know that the consequences would be a new definition of sin and an exaggerated emphasis on works to make sure of one's salvation.

In the same way, the Charismatic Movement has certain tendencies that are more and more evident as time passes. The fundamentals of the movement need to be verified. It is worthwhile to evaluate and compare the claims of the experiences of thousands who have come under the influence of Charismatics to the Scriptures. It is also certain that some "good" consequences have occurred (many have been converted and healed), but still these have come at the cost of the erroneous teaching and neglect of God's Word. This moves us to ask if it would not be better to achieve the good results in another way, avoiding the bad consequences. The answer: faithfulness to the Scriptures produces wonderful results. Some of the negative consequences are listed below.

Consequence 1: Living by experiences instead of by the Word

Teaching that believers need to have an additional "experience" after salvation has caused many to base their beliefs on feelings rather than on the clear promises of the Scriptures. One should ask: "How do I know where my confidence is?" Disregard your experience; the possibility of another experience should not affect your confidence or your relationship with God. If you can say: "It cannot affect me because I am trusting in the Word, not in my experience," then you are correct. However, if you say, "I need the experience for my confidence and my security, such as the assurance of the baptism of the Spirit, so my feeling of power can be real, etc.," then your basis is an experience, not the Word.

The beginning of error in the Christian life begins when a personal experience (as emotional and real as it may be) replaces the direction from the Word of God or serious study of the Bible. The teaching that tells us to forget inhibitions in order to achieve an experience can be dangerous, as it is certain to produce all kinds of unpredictable responses, euphoria, excitation or a sense of liberation from self. This kind of experience is mysticism, and is not biblical.

A Charismatic pastor, who has since left the movement, said, "Give me a group of people who will follow my instructions to sing, work up their emotions and give up their inhibitions, and, in a short time, some of them will be speaking in tongues." When we ask Charismatic teachers why they do not subject their experiences to the ten New Testament requirements for true tongues, it is not rare that they prefer their experiences to the Truth. When someone thinks this way, the basis for their Christian life is their experience, not the Word. Pentecostal author Melvin Hodges writes in his book Spiritual Gifts:

We should not lose the fact that in the New Testament, the baptism of the Spirit (through tongues) is considered an essential requirement, and is supremely important for a totally developed spiritual life and ministry (Hodges 1964:16).

Consequence 2: Divisions among the churches

In any part of the world we find the same testimonies that the Pentecostals are destroying the work or that the evangelical churches have divided because of Charismatic teachers. They produce division instead of unity. To avoid division the people must forget or ignore what they understand of the Word and blindly accept the new teachings. Now there numbers are so great that those who are holding to the study of God's Word are the minority and are causing the problem. The pressure to conform to the ever changing and evolving majority is overwhelming.

Chapter 20: *One Last Word about Charismatics*

Paul wrote strongly against those who caused divisions in Romans 16:17, "Now I beseech you, brethren, mark them which cause divisions and offences contrary to the doctrine which ye have learned; and avoid them." Put simply, brethren who cause divisions in the church should be separated from the congregation. Now the problem is arising that a significant majority of many churches are quietly persuaded toward tongues experiences and that to raise the issue at all, or teach the Scriptures on the issue, will cause division. The division is undercover already and no one will deal with it without causing conflicts.

Literally thousands of churches have been divided because of Charismatic teaching. They infiltrate into the membership without stating their belief, but, little by little, they begin to communicate their doctrines behind the backs of the leaders. When a confrontation becomes inevitable, many leave the church because a part of the congregation already has been subjugated by Charismatic ideas.

The church or denomination that does not take a firm, public position will likely be infiltrated and eventually divided. Even with a firm position, it is necessary that the leaders live a life of victory and teach the truths for victorious living to their congregations. This type of division is not a temptation for those who are living in the victory and joy of the Lord.

Consequence 3: a weak testimony to those who do not know Christ

In the minds of many unbelievers, Pentecostalism is identified by the fanatic experiences resulting from biblical ignorance. The movement has become so dominant that evangelical Christianity is identified globally as Charismatic. It was the same during the time of Paul; because of this he said that he would not use tongues in the churches. In 1 Corinthians 14:23, Paul said that the opinion of the unbelievers that entered into a church where they were speaking in tongues was: "will they not say that you are out of your mind?" That is a weak testimony.

It is difficult to identify Christ with a movement that produces spells, fainting, convulsions, incoherent speech, babblings and emotional excesses. It is certain that there are many sincere believers among them, but, generally, they are thought to be strange.

On the other hand, in 1 Corinthians 14:24, if the unbeliever were to enter into the congregation and listen to the preaching of prophecy [the revealed Word of God], he would understand and perhaps would come under conviction of the Spirit, then be saved. When the Word is taught about the sinfulness of man, the unbeliever senses that the speaker knows his deepest secrets when the truth is, the speaker is merely teaching what the Bible says about all sinners.

Consequence 4: It generates pride

Among some Charismatics we see pride in the execution of the gifts. When tongues become the goal for the Christian life, pride is inevitable. They have something that other Christians do not have; they think that non-Charismatic Christians are somehow below them because they have a gift that non-Charismatics do not. Pride moves among these believers because they use tongues as a sign to prove that they now have the baptism or the filling of the Spirit that others do not. However, the purpose of tongues was as a sign to unbelievers, especially Jewish unbelievers, not to other believers, and it was never used as a mark of spirituality.

Pride is very subtle and can be seen in any believer. But among non-Charismatic Christians there is no experience or doctrine that makes then immediately "spiritual," mature or filled with the Spirit. The idea that a person achieves a second level of spirituality or instantly receives an anointing of extraordinary power through an experience of speaking in tongues inevitably will produce pride.

The non-Charismatic believers often get confused by subtle legalism concepts that give them a false sense of acceptance before God because of their approved dress, music, behavior, discipline or life-style. This deviation generates a bitter, self-righteous, critical and a superficial "joy" of being the only ones right. Neither extreme is healthy. Unbelievers need to see a balance and genuine walk with God in a clear understanding of all of His Word, especially through the commands that we are to obey.

If the gift is for unbelievers, then it should be used where unbelievers are. This explains why Paul said that he did not use tongues in the churches, in his private prayers or in his private worship, but rather with unbelievers, apparently in the synagogues or other evangelistic outreaches. It had a great impact on the day of Pentecost when unbelieving Hellenist Jews heard God's Word proclaimed in their languages (16 are mentioned in Acts 2). If missionaries and evangelists could do this today there would undoubtedly be a great turning to Christ. This was the expectation of the Azusa Street Revival of 1906 in Los Angeles, but it never came about.

Consequence 5: It is a pagan concept among the churches

Never, since the creation, has God used a special method for man to communicate with Him. It is not necessary. However, pagan tribes and false religions throughout the world have been speaking in tongues, just the same as the Charismatics, for centuries. Paul warned the church in Corinth that spiritual gifts were completely different from the pagan manifestations (1 Corinthians 12:2), but even today Charismatic teachers continue to introduce the ecstasy and mystical language as the pagans practice. Genuine tongues, as we have shown, were true earthly languages, not a special tool for communicating with God. On the contrary, an unknown language would be a hindrance to spiritual understanding because the person would not know what he was saying.

Consequence 6: It leads to superstition

Many people in the movement believe they have visions and direct revelations from God. To them, each dream is a vision. In each circumstance, each minute of the life, they believe they see the hand of God or the hand of Satan in action. Frequently this road leads to the extreme of seeing demons

Chapter 20: *One Last Word about Charismatics* — 333

everywhere. The Charismatic believer can become paranoid from seeing so many visions, to the point of having to continually cast out demons from himself and from others in order to have victory. This is how the animist live in the jungle.

Pagan superstition is evident when people think that they will have "good luck" or be blessed after speaking in tongues. Because of having had this mystical experience, they feel secure that all will go well that day. They think that blessings and prosperity are assured for those who speak in tongues.

If the person thinks that these mystical encounters are genuine, then he will take the instructions that he receives in the vision or trance as truly inspired by God. The need to hear the Word of God revealed in the Bible becomes less valuable (and too complicated) so the need to have more visions, direct contacts with the spirit world or to speak in tongues grows.

When this lifestyle surfaces, the main problem is that the Bible loses its central position in the believer's life. If it is used at all, it is to defend these new beliefs. It is replaced by emotional experiences or "spiritual" impulses, visions and revelations. There are now Charismatic books that prophecy about the end of time that add details of new revelation to the biblical prophecy—exactly what is prohibited in Revelation 22:18. These visions cannot be from God since they violate His own Word.

This circumstance is similar to the simple tale about the dog and his bone. A dog with a bone in his mouth was crossing a bridge, and as he crossed he looked into the water and saw his reflection. As he examined the water's surface, the bone he saw reflected in the water seemed better looking than the one he had in his mouth, so he let it fall into the water in order to retrieve the other one. In the end, the dog ended up with nothing, having given up what he already had in order to chase the imaginary.

Similarly, if all believers have already received the baptism of the Spirit at salvation, and begin the continual filling of the Spirit as they walk in obedience, which the Scriptures affirm, why should they throw away something real in order to seek an illusion of something supposedly more sensational or impressive? What an error!

FOUR DANGERS IN THE CHARISMATIC MOVEMENT

1. It causes confusion.

The expression in 1 Corinthians 14, "God is not the God of confusion" (14:33), indicates that the abuse of the Corinthian tongues produced confusion rather than peace. The word "confusion" is *akatastasia*, or "instability" (a = negative + kata = "under" + stasis = "ended/stopped), and is used to indicate a disorderly state, disturbance, translated "perturbation" (James 3:16), "sedition" (Luke 21:9) and "disorder" (2 Corinthians 12:20).

When we see the result of a momentary Charismatic exposition and the confusion that it produces in the believer and even in the meetings, we note that God is not the origin of the experience.

Recently in Argentina a new gift was promoted, that of running without tiring, taken from Isaiah 40:31. Those who receive this gift begin to run around the meeting place during the church service. The pastor continues to preach. What a ridiculous confusion! The very same verse in Isaiah says, "...they will rise up on wings as eagles." Now that would certainly be interesting to see!

The people are accustomed to believing anything they are told without discernment. Another gift that is gaining popularity is that of becoming like a baby. The Scriptures say "unless you are converted and become as little children, you will by no means enter the kingdom of heaven." (Matthew 18:3). With this "gift" the people begin to slobber and babble, and they even give up control of their biological systems as if they were babies, wearing diapers. This is the gift of humiliation (Matthew 18:4).

They believe all of this should manifest itself in the meetings. What confusion! Some are running, others imitating babies and still others speaking in tongue, all while someone else tries to preach. How can anything be accomplished here?

2. It causes people to become closed to the declarations of the Scriptures.

Those who have had the experience of speaking in tongues, or other experiences, are generally not open to the teaching of the Scriptures, since they had the experience before knowing the Scriptures. Now they have a "divine" touch, and no verse will take away from them the reality of that experience. What will he believe if he finds that the Bible does not teach that the baptism of the Spirit accomplishes a second work of grace or that speaking in tongues is not the sign of the baptism? He will feel obligated to form an interpretation that permits and backs up his experience. Anyone who disagrees will be called a "heretic" for intimidation. It is rare that someone with such an experience accepts that it does not come from the Scriptures.

Many have disobeyed the teaching of the Apostle Paul, especially regarding the rules of practicing speaking in tongues. They say that the Holy Spirit directed them to do it, defying the Scriptures! Or it is said that Paul was only giving his opinion, not God's. As harsh as this may sound, when a woman speaks in tongues in a church and says that the Holy Spirit is guiding her, she is closed to the Scriptures because the Bible contradicts this practice (1 Corinthians 14:34).

3. It distorts the Christian life.

For many, the Christian life is no more than the quest for another mystical experience of speaking in tongues or for another miracle. Instead of having their focus on Christ and His desires for the Church, the center of their expectation is a miracle or another experience.

If the Spirit is not manifested in such a way, the believer is unsatisfied, disillusioned and frustrated. To assure that miracles happen, a system of prohibitions is introduced and people are intimidated with the loss of their salvation if they do not happen. Suddenly, everything depends primarily on the believer and very little on God. The tranquility that can be felt in such a system only comes as the person fulfills his requirements to achieve spirituality and miracles. He is convinced of the genuineness of the miracle, and he believes that this qualifies him as a spiritual believer.

The motivation for evangelism and missions often is only secondarily the gospel and salvation, rather primarily, it the sharing of the blessings of the miracles and tongues.

4. It exalts the Spirit instead of Christ.

In Charismatic meetings it is common to see the emphasis directed toward the Holy Spirit instead of toward Jesus, but the Lord said that the Spirit "shall not speak of himself...he shall glorify me" (John 16:13-14). The Spirit never calls attention to Himself, but he always exalts Christ. It is true, however, that the Spirit should be exalted as God, but in turn He will exalt Christ.

The problem with this danger is that it robs Jesus of the glory that belongs to Him. The result of a bad focus is always extremism, fanaticism or disobedience of the Word. When we sing and pray exclusively to the Spirit, when we follow our own impulses as if they were the voice of the Spirit and when we think almost exclusively about the Spirit, our focus is in error.

Two defenses against the Charismatic Movement

The majority of people who are attracted to the Charismatics are not seeing genuine faith in fundamentalist Christianity. It is sad to have a good doctrine but a cold life that is inconsistent or even hypocritical. Some who leave the fundamentalist camp may have superior biblical understanding over Charismatic believers and do not accept all their doctrines, but the illusion of a power, victory and encouragement in the things of the Lord motivate them to ignore the excesses and accept the parts that seem real to them. It is necessary that fundamentalists have the following two characteristics in their personal lives as well as in the corporate life of the Church:

(1) Understanding of our glorious salvation

It is interesting that when the churches understand the glorious simplicity of the Gospel, our total unworthiness and the consequences of a sufficient salvation through Christ and in addition, all that we receive at the moment we trust in Christ, the attraction of the Charismatic camp will be diminish. If the believer is sure his salvation is complete and that in Christ he has all he needs, the fullness of God in Christ, he feels no need to seek more than that. Why would he seek what he already has?

When a believer does not understand his position in Christ and has lost the sense of security or completeness of that position, Pentecostalism seems to have something to offer. Even Paul had to learn the concept: "My grace is sufficient for thee" (2 Corinthians 12:9). There is sufficient satisfaction in the grace of God to allow us to rejoice forever.

(2) To experience perpetual growth in power and knowledge of Christ.

The second defense is to experience personal growth and gain knowledge of Christ. The mature believer can participate in endless precious experiences, growing in power and knowledge of Christ as he experiences a deeper intimacy with Him, and only then can he rest in the position that he has by faith in Christ.

If the believer is faithful in his quiet time with the Lord each day, enjoys his relationship with Christ searching for daily instruction from the Word, learns how to testify to others and practices his gifts of the Spirit in service to others, and catches a vision of his life's purpose in expanding the knowledge of Christ around the world, then he will have many satisfying and genuine Christian experiences.

When the believer does not follow through in these four areas of Christian discipline, he will feel a great lack in his Christian life. For some, the alternative option of an emotional experience fills them. This substitute promises instantaneous satisfaction, but genuine satisfaction is not there.

Even though the cost of being disciplined in our walk with the Lord seems great, we must realize that only through these disciplines are we truly transformed into the image and lifestyle of Jesus. Pouring out our lives for others, especially the lost, as Jesus did, becomes our passion empowered by the filling of the Spirit to carry us to even greater acts of self-sacrifice for others.

Our life should be attractive to others, because it reflects the beauty of our Lord. Peter said that we must be prepared to defend our doctrine if anyone asks: "always be ready to give a defense to everyone who asks you a reason for the hope that is in you, with meekness and fear;" (1 Peter 3:15).

Our hope should be so obvious that others want to know why we can be so confident in the face of adversity and loss. Unfortunately, many believers are bad publicity for the Gospel. Paul was satisfied in knowing Christ and in the power of His resurrection and the joy of suffering with other believers (Philippians 3:10). Genuine contentment with what we have in Christ must be our testimony and message.

CHAPTER 21
The Gifts of the Spirit

The term "noncessationist" refers to those who believe that all of the spiritual gifts are continuing today as they were originally in the Early Church. This movement is spreading rapidly around the world and is categorized in three groups: Classic Pentecostalism, The Charismatic movement, and Third Wave Theology. Another group called "cessationist" represent the fourth alternative to a position on the spiritual gifts. These four positions can be reduced to two basic positions on the gifts: those that hold that some of the gifts were temporary and those that hold the gifts were all permanent throughout the Church Age.

Those who hold to temporary gifts see apostleship, prophecy, knowledge, miracles, healing, tongues, and interpretation of tongues, and some add faith and wisdom, among the temporary gifts. The permanent gifts that both positions agree upon are evangelism, pastors and teachers, and those with gifts of helps, administration, exhortation, giving and showing mercy. The objective of all the gifts is the edifying or building up of the body of Christ.

The subject of spiritual gifts has high interest in every Christian circle. Charismatic theology has influenced or been accepted in almost all theological and religious institutions and missions. In 2010 there were approximately 2.18 billion Christians in 232 countries, nearly a third of the world population according to the Pew Research study dated December, 2011. (Pew Research, "Global Christianity"). This number was 600 million in 1910, so it has quadrupled in the past 100 years. It should be noted that 11.3% of this global Christian population is within the continental United States (Brazil and Mexico are second and third by percentage).

Statistics are now distinguishing among Protestant, evangelical and Charismatic; likewise, some polls distinguish Pentecostal and Charismatic groups. According to the Center for the Study of Global Christianity, there are about 279 million Pentecostal Christians and 305 million charismatic Christians worldwide for a total of 584 million. Charismatic Christians refer to non-Pentecostal denominations yet engage in the same spiritual practices as the Pentecostals, especially speaking in tongues and public healings.

In addition to these groups there are 285 million evangelical Christians who do not practice the Pentecostal gifts. Naturally the Pentecostal/Charismatic groups are also evangelical, some of the numbers overlap.

From basically zero population in 1900 growing now to twice the population of the evangelicals and every branch of evangelical Christianity embracing some form of Charismatic theology, discerning evangelical Christians are either giving up in acquiescence or are attempting to clarify the issue where it is possible.

The Four Groups that promote the Spiritual Gifts

Classic Pentecostalism: This is a group that began in Topeka, Kansas in 1900 by Charles Parham (d. 1929), who taught his students to seek the apostolic baptism of the Spirit as evidenced by speaking in tongues. When one of his students spoke in Chinese it was declared that the Pentecostal power of Acts was restored to the churches (Nichol 1966: 28). Parham was invited to Houston to teach his new doctrine where he met William Seymour, a black pastor in training, who soon was invited to Los Angels to head the Azusa Street Mission. This small church started a revival that swept the world, leading to the founding of the Assemblies of God, The Church of God in Christ, and the International Church of the Foursquare Gospel. The Pentecostal Movement remained marginalized from dominant Protestant/evangelical circles until the 1960's when the Pentecostal experience broke the denominational barrier.

Charismatic Movement: In the late 1950's the Full Gospel Business Men's Fellowship International began reaching out to non-Pentecostal denominations. In August, 1960, Dennis Bennett, a pastor of an Anglican church in Van Nuys, California announced he had spoken in tongues. He was so criticized that he resigned after the third Sunday morning service the same day. This day is considered the birth of the Charismatic Movement when the Pentecostal experience crossed into major denominations and across all theological barriers (*Ibid.*, 59-67). The movement spread worldwide with great focus on Spirit baptism and speaking in tongues after salvation. Trinity Broadcasting Network began by Paul Crouch in 1973, the International Catholic Charismatic Conference in Rome in 1975 and the after 1980 of prominent televangelists like Oral Roberts and Richard Hagin, Pat Robertson, Rex Humbard, Jimmy Swaggart, Kenneth Copeland, Jim Bakker and Benny Hinn, gave rise through enormous visibility and awareness to the Charismatic movement.

Third Wave Movement: Not everyone was successful at speaking in tongues or wanted to be associated with the Charismatic movement, but many wanted to believe in the miraculous gifts, tongues and healing for today. Their biblical differences regarding the baptism of the Spirit led them into a new direction. The Third wavers teach that the new birth and Spirit baptism occur at the same time, empowering the believers for the miraculous gifts, which they claim had been buried in neglect throughout the church age. Peter Wagner, who taught missions at Fuller Theological Seminary along with John Wimber of the Vineyard Christian Fellowship in Anaheim, California, along with Jack Deere, former professor at Dallas Theological Seminary launched this new movement. The primary focus is on healing and spiritual warfare against demonic activity. A loosely associated group to this position is the "open but cautious" position (Grudem 1996:13, 97–148). Other notables in this group include Martyn Lloyd-Jones, Robert Saucy, John Piper, and Wayne Grudem himself, along with Chuck Smith and his Calvary Chapel movement. (Stitzinger 2003: 147). This whole movement is becoming the basis of a new ecumenical movement uniting all churches.

Cessationism: It has been the historic view of the church that the miraculous gifts ceased with the death of the apostles to whom, and only to whom, the miraculous gifts were given. The miraculous and non-miraculous gifts are given together at a time when they were operational under apostolic leadership. It recognizes that all the gifts were given by God's power to different persons and in different mixes of the gifts to equip every believer for their unique purpose in God's plan. "The view rests on a careful, non-speculative exegetical study of the Scriptures. It minimizes the element of human experience by not allowing experience to influence decisions of biblical interpretation." (Stitzinger 2003: 148). Stitzinger lists some of the prominent writers of this position as Benjamine B. Warfield, Richard B. Gaffin, Edgar Thomas, Anthony Hoekema, Robert Gromacki, Peter Masters, John Whitcomb and John MacArthur Jr.

Views will vary on the definitions of the gifts primarily because of the lack of clear explanations in the biblical text and the attempts to fill in the gaps with logical deductions from the word meaning, and assumptions from experience or emotions. It is difficult to stay within the bounds of the information revealed in Scriptures concerning the spiritual gifts, so many authors take liberties to define what is not expressed in the biblical text with their ideas (or revelations). The undiscerning public seldom recognizes when the author has crossed the line into speculation.

A working definition of the gifts

James Boyer gives a clear definition of the spiritual gifts.

A spiritual gift, then, is any ability and accompanying spiritual ministry and effect that God, through Christ, enables a believer to use, or motivates him to use, for His glory, in the body of Christ, through the energizing work of the Spirit. God may grace the believer with a gift or gifts, or bring them to light, at salvation or later, but these abilities are only gifts when used for edification in the church. Today, as in biblical times, these enablings differ among churches according to the needs of the church and vary greatly as the needs vary.(Boyer 1960:17).

Two ways to divide spiritual gifts

There are various ways of dividing the spiritual gifts in order to distinguish them and their uses in the ministry.

Miraculous and non-miraculous. The first kind of spiritual gift would be the miraculous (or sign) gift and the non-miraculous gifts. By definition a miraculous gift enables a person to perform an act that involves God's supernatural power to be evident in contrary to the natural order. Such an event involves "a suspension, a bypassing, or even an outright contravention of the natural order." (McCune 1976:15). John Whitcomb described the miracles of Christ and His apostles as "fantastically abundant, utterly spectacular, and totally undeniable." (Whitcomb 1971:6).

On the other hand the majority of the gifts operate in the non-miraculous realm, as helps, administrations, pastor and teachers and most of those of mentioned in Rom 12. God works through the natural realm in a providential manner to bless others. However, when Paul lists the gifts there is no attempt to distinguish between the miraculous and non-miraculous implying that all gifts are demonstrations of God's grace and power, just in a different manner.

Speaking and Serving. Another means of distinction is found in 1 Peter 4:11 which divides the gifts between the speaking gifts and the serving gifts: "If anyone speaks, they should do so as one who speaks the very words of God. "Whoever speaks, let it be with God's words. Whoever serves, do so with the strength that God supplies, so that in everything God will be glorified through Jesus Christ" (1Pe 4:11 NET).

Peter had just described the purpose of the spiritual gifts in verse 10: "Just as each one has received a gift, use it to serve one another as good stewards of the varied grace of God" (1Pe 4:10 NET). Everyone has one of these kinds of spiritual gifts; therefore, they are to be used to "serve one another." The gifts are for the benefit of others, not ourselves.

The speaking gifts are to be exercised under the guideline "let it be with God's words." This is not saying that every speaking gift receives a new revelation from God, nor that every word spoken is "God's words," but the content of what is spoken and explained is to be limited to "God's words," that is what God has supplied, previously revealed and recorded for all time.

The serving gifts are to be exercised according to "the strength that God supplies," implies limits and enablement to a multitude of services rendered to the body of Christ and others with the goal of glorifying Christ, that is to "cause the dignity and worth of some person to become manifest and acknowledged" (Strong, 1392). The word "strength" (*ischus*) means "ability, force, or might." God equips everyone to be able to give of themselves sacrificially for the benefit of others.

Four principles to consider in respect to the gifts

First, thank the Lord for treating every believer in particular and individually. It is not a coincidence that every believer has the gift that he does. In 1 Cor 12:11-18 Paul declared the importance of every function of all the gifts. God is directly involved in every believer's life in a particular form to equip us precisely to accomplish His purpose. This is what He prepared before the foundation of the earth for our lives (Eph 2:10). To be dissatisfied with His selection of our gifts is to thwart God's plans from eternity past!

Second, no believer should have pride or brag about his gifts. Paul said, "For who makes you differ from another? And what do you have that you did not receive? Now if you did indeed receive it, why do you boast as if you had not received it?" (1Co 4:7 NKJ) The gifts did not come to us because we deserve them. The reason the gifts are distributed is "according to the grace that is given to us" (Rom 12:6 NKJ), that is, there is nothing in us that merited the gifts that we have, nor is it because of our faith.

Third, do not idolize a human leader through the admiration for his gifts. The Corinthian church was divided among the followers of their specially gifted leaders (1 Cor 3:3-7, 21-23): Paul, Apollos and Cefas (Peter). None of the three were present in the church when the division occurred and certainly had nothing to do with these divisions, but it was the believers who wanted their leader or idol to have the last word. They exaggerated the differences, compared their gifts and capacities making one superior to another, in stead of appreciating the contribution of each one to the unity of the church. This is the carnal reactions when one wants to appear more important than others.

Fourth, do not envy the gifts of others. Everyone must learn to be content with the selection of gifts that God has given him. Discontentment, in reality, is a critical attitude toward Christ's distribution of the gifts, and also against how He governs and manages His Church. Your satisfaction comes from the ministry of the gifts that He has given. No one needs any more gifts or anything else to be content. In the list of the fruit of the flesh (Gal 5:19-21) appears the manifestation of envy.

Two key questions

Is the list of gifts complete? It is difficult to answer this questions because there is no agreement among biblical scholars. Some believe that the gifts are complete; others say that the listed gifts are examples of the possible gifts. At times those who want to add to the list of the gifts, add natural gifts as though they were spiritual gifts (i.e., music ability, art, sports, etc.) It is better to see the gifts as a completed list as given in the Bible. Every gifted person can be explained by the combination of the multiple gifts or variations of the gifts. There is no stereotype of the gifts, each one can be manifested in a distinct form (1 Cor 12:4-6). The gifts are not limited to a single function, but are broad enough to cover whatever ministry is necessary.

Every believer receives gifts that are "diversities" or distinct or unique in its distribution to every believer from the implanting of the Spirit within the believer at regeneration (1 Cor 12:4) This is the general area of the ministries. Then this distinction of how the gifts are blended uniquely to every believer equips each one for a unique or "differences of ministries" (*diakonia*, "services") (12:5). Thus one gift has many different service or ministry possibilities. This is the quality of the ministries. Finally, each possible ministry has "different results" (12:6 NET). This is the quantity or broadness of the ministries.

Are there more gifts mentioned in the Bible outside 1 Cor 12-14 and Romans 12? There are possibly two additional gifts mentioned in the Scripture:
1. Celibacy (1 Cor 7:7). Although the text calls celibacy a gift, it also

implies that to be married is a gift as well, because it says, "each one has his own gift from God, one in this manner (celibacy) and another in that (married). (1Co 7:7 NKJ) Thus everyone has either the gift of celibacy or the gift of marriage. Although this is a "gift," it is not a spiritual gift in the sense of an ability to serve others in the church.

2. Hospitality (1 Pet 4:9-10). This gift is very similar to the gift of service/helps and is considered related by Bible scholars. This is a requirement of an elder (Titus 1:8). It would be out of the norm for a spiritual gift to be a requirement for an elder.

Two important observations:

First, no gift is exclusive to one gender or another, although certain offices in the church are limited to males. The Bible puts certain restrictions on positions of leadership. These restrictions are not to discriminate between genders, but to place the responsibility of the churches on the shoulders of godly men alone. The Bible limits the ministry of the women in the area of exercising dominion over men (1 Tim 2:12) and of teaching publicly in the church. The requirements for pastor are all concerning men (married to one woman that governs his house well, etc.)

The fact that to be a pastor one must be a man does not signify that any man can be a pastor. There are nineteen requirements in 1 Tim 3:2-8 and Tit 1:5-9 that limit the men who can be pastors. It is evident that limitations in Scripture are not just for women.

Although there are restrictions concerning leadership in the church. This does not indicate such a person does not have certain gifts. Also the ministries of evangelism, counseling, helps, mercy, exhortation, giving or faith, do not have to be exercised only in the congregation before men, rather they can be used with women and children, allowing for a wide field of possibilities of vital ministries in the churches.

Second, if someone does not have a certain gift, it does not give that person an excuse for disobeying related commands. A gifted person has an extraordinary capacity for a particular ministry. It is interesting that there are commands related to every one of the gifts that must be obeyed by all believers. However, there are no commands with regard to the sign or miracle gifts. The Bible commands us to give (1 Cor 16:1-2), but do not think that if we do not have the gift of giving (Rom 12:8), we can avoid being generous. Other commands that we are obligated to practice in the area of the gifts: evangelize (Acts 1:8); giving (1 Cor 16:1-2; exhort (1 Thes 5:14; Col 3:16); serve/help to others (Gal 5:13); discerning of spirits (1 Thes 5:21; 1 Jn 4:1) and teaching (Col 3:16).

Since there are commands for every spiritual gift, it is possible that the Spirit capacitates the believer to be sufficiently obedient to accomplish the edification of the church and its growth. The special gifts that each one has received are something extraordinary in order to serve in an extraordinary form and be an example in that respective area of service. The power of the Spirit and the example of the gifted people in each church, enables the believers to fulfill the plan of God for every work in the area of their gifts (Eph 2:10).

Description of the Gifts described in the NT

The fact that some gifts are described in 1 Cor 13:8NET as going to be "set aside," "cease" (*katargeo*, "render idle, inactive, inoperative" in the passive form) and tongues will "cease" (*pauo*, "make to cease, stop, make an end of" in a form meaning "of itself"), indicates that some gifts are temporary. Other gifts are permanent. The distinction appears to be made because of their purpose in establishing the church. Although the distinction of the gifts in this manner is widely held, there is not a consensus on which gifts are temporary and which are permanent. The biblical text does not distinguish clearly between which are miraculous and which are not. Though they may all appear in the same list, "that does not indicate that they all have the same purpose or reflect the same amount of divine empowerment." (Stitzinger 2003: 166).

For a more detailed description of the spiritual gifts see the author's book, "Gifts of the Spirit" by Branches Publications (www.branchespublications.com).

Temporary gifts

Apostles. The meaning of the word is "envoy or messenger," but in the NT, the Early Church applies it to a select few as supreme delegates or representatives of Christ who were specially gifted and recognized. They were "apostles of Jesus Christ." They were special and unique in various ways. They followed Christ all through His ministry and were witnesses of the resurrected Lord (Acts 1:22; 1 Cor 9:1).

Theirs was a multifunctional ministry specifically appointed by Jesus Christ. 2 Tim 1:10b-11, "through the gospel, to which I was appointed a preacher, an apostle, and a teacher of the Gentiles."

The nature of their gift made it unrepeatable and untransferable. Paul knew he was the last apostle (1 Cor 15:8; cf. 3:10). Those men were God's special gift in founding of the church. No biblical basis exists for diminishing the qualifications and miraculous powers of apostles (2 Cor12:12) to allow anyone to claim this gift today. (Stitzinger 2003:166-167)

The Early Church followed the apostles as being the final word in doctrinal and practical decisions of life. The early picture of this authority is seen in Acts 2:42, "And they continued steadfastly in the apostles' doctrine and fellowship, in the breaking of bread, and in prayers." (Acts 2:42). Once their teachings were recorded the churches continued to remain faithful to the founding apostles through their writings in the NT.

There is no biblical basis for redefining the requirements for apostleship (Acts 1 and 2 Cor 12:12) to open the door for attempting to restore the apostleship today.

Prophets. James Boyer declares, "Prophecy in the New Testament is the same as prophecy in the OT; it is a continuation of the same office and function." (Boyer 1960 :13). As in certain periods of the OT, the NT was the apostolic age of revelation. A prophet was chosen and gifted with the formidable task of receiving the revelation of God's Word from God, then declare it either in the form of a prediction of the future or by preaching this newly revealed knowledge to a people for whom it was meant as Paul was revealed the knowledge of the church (Eph 3:3-5).

Attempting to either declare that contemporary renewed "prophets" are the same as biblical prophets who delivered infallible messages and predictions has no biblical basis. Furthermore, to redefine the gift of prophecy to mean enthusiastic preaching is to distort the NT concept of prophet.

Discerning of spirits. In the age of prophets in the Early Church before there were any written records of the apostolic teachings, whenever a prophet spoke in a congregation the church was to "judge" ("the others should evaluate what is said" – 1 Cor 14:29). The word for "discerning" or judging or evaluating, are all the same (*diakrino*, meaning "to separate" or "differentiate."). This gift is closely associated with prophecy in practice and appears to have been practiced widely (1 Cor 12:10; 1 John 4:1-6). This was a deterrent to protect the early church from false teachers who were deceived by thoughts originating from demons (1 Tim 4:1). Possibly there might have been an application when the Early Church practiced internal judgments among the church members (1 Cor 6:5).

There is no indication that this gift is either a gift of clairvoyance or determination of demon possession.

Word of Wisdom and Knowledge. Though there may have been some distinction between these words, Scripture does not give a clear definition between the two. Knowledge (*gnosis*) is associated with the miraculous gift of prophecy in 1 Cor 13:8. Both of these two actions (prophecy and knowledge) will cease or "be de-energized," implying that both were revelatory gifts. The close association between wisdom and knowledge and their association with other revelatory gifts would indicate that they are both (wisdom and knowledge) means of early revelations of God's will and Word to the early church.

All believers are to "walk in wisdom toward outsiders" (Col 4:5), but this refers to practical application of already revealed wisdom. Paul described how God "lavished on us in all wisdom and insight, He did this when he revealed to us the secret of his will," (Eph 1:8-9 NET). Of the multiple gifts of an apostle Paul was given wisdom and knowledge to reveal it to us to study and learn for our lives. Later Paul wrote, "The purpose of this enlightenment is that through the church the multifaceted wisdom of God should now be disclosed" (Eph 3:10 NET).

The wisdom and knowledge revealed in the recorded Word of God will be declared and clarified through the ministry of the church. We are commanded to "Let the word of Christ dwell in you richly, teaching and exhorting one another with all wisdom," (Col 3:16 NET). We are to learn the knowledge already revealed through the gifts of knowledge and wisdom, then teach and exhort one another to live out its wisdom.

These gifts brought us the Word of God that now we are to teach and exhort.

Faith. The gift of faith is a little difficult to pin point in the Scripture. There are illustrations of saving faith (Rom 3:25, 26, 28; 4:11; 5:1, etc.), faith as a compendium of doctrine (Tit 1:13; 1 Tim 4:6; 5:8; 6:21), faith in the sense of faithfulness (1 Tim 6:11; 2 Tim 2:22), and faith as unquestionable trust (Matt 9:2, 29; 15:28; 17:20).

Paul used the exaggeration of the gift of faith in 1 Cor 13:2 to demonstrate how the gift of faith could trust in the miraculous power of God to do impossible signs through believers. This same illustration is used by Jesus (Matt 17:20; Mark 11:22-24) to encourage his apostles to trust God for the impossible.

Stitzinger quotes J. Oliver Buswell, in his *A Systematic Theology of the Christian Religion* 1:117, saying,

> "It is a great mistake for Christians to distort their reports of answered prayer so as to make out 'sign' miracles where nothing comparable to the Biblical 'signs' has occurred. God gives us abundant evidence of His love and care without any exaggeration on our part." (*Ibid.*, 168).

Miracles and healings. These gifts include a wide range of supernatural demonstrations of God's power. These words are used as signs of an apostle (2 Cor 12:12) and the confirmation signs of those who directly heard the message of salvation from the lips of Jesus (Heb 2:3-4).

Closely associated with miracles is the gift of healings (plural), described as "this miracle of healing" (Acts 4:22). The miracle element is described as "healing all kinds of sickness" (Matt 4:23), "healing every sickness and every disease" (Matt 9:35).

Contemporary attempts to imitate this level of miraculous signs fail to be comparable. As the confirmation ministries decreased following the authentication of the new revelations of the NT, so the miraculous healings diminished. The ministry of praying for healing continues throughout the church age, but this is distinct from the early miraculous instantaneous healing of the NT.

Tongues and Interpretation of tongues. As has been discussed throughout this book the miraculous (i.e. unexplainable by any natural phenomena) nature of the original gift of tongues, which enabled Galileans to speak Mesopotamian languages they had never heard, has never been linguistically demonstrated in the contemporary movement. The gift of interpretation of tongues is obviously closely related to the gift of tongues in 1 Cor 14.

The miracle of speaking in a complex language (every language is extremely complex no matter how "primitive") is only equaled by the miraculous ability to interpret the spoken tongue (*diermeneuo*, "translate or interpret"). Again no one has demonstrated an accurate interpretation of either an ecstatic utterance tongue or a literal language tongue, though several attempts have been made.

Tongues are said to "stop" (*pauo*, in the future middle indicative means "stop of itself"). History describes how this gift ceased to function. (See the development of Thomas R. Edgar, *Miraculous Gifts: Are They for Today?* (Neptune, N.J.: Loizeaux, 1983) 223-59).

The Permanent Gifts

As the church received the full revelation that it would need to be "rooted and built up in Him and established in the faith, as you have been taught" (Col 2:7). Additional revelations are not necessary because all the Scripture God has given to us is "profitable for doctrine, for reproof, for correction, for instruction in righteousness, that the man of God may be complete, thoroughly equipped for every good work. (2Ti 3:16b-17 NKJ).

The non-miraculous gifts appear to be almost generic in their descriptions, depicting ministries of many different possibilities and applications.

Speaking gifts

Evangelist. No one doubts the continuation and practice of the work of the evangelist today. Though the term only occurs three times in the NT (Acts 21:8; Eph 4:11; 2 Tim 4:5), many more evangelists were engaged in the ministry than are mentioned specifically, like Philip, "...passing through, he preached in all the cities..." (Acts 8:40). Paul instructs Timothy to "do the work of an evangelist" (2 Tim 4:5), which probably indicated that Timothy did not have the "gift" of evangelism, but it was his responsibility anyway.

Paul was the model for this evangelistic activity (Rom 1:9, 16:25; 1 Cor 15:3, 4; 2 Tim 2:8). In the absence of the apostles, the evangelist took their place in the on-going advance of the gospel around the world. Professional evangelists and missionaries are the contemporary function of the evangelist.

The gift is recognized by the evident passion for the lost and the capacity to speak clearly and effectively the message of salvation, as in Acts 14:1, "...so spoke that a great multitude both of the Jews and of the Greeks believed." This is the goal of the "evangelist," the apostle Paul, "I have made myself a servant to all, that I might win the more." (1Co 9:19 NKJ)

Pastor. The word "pastor" (*poimen*) is the word for the pastor of sheep.

It is used eighteen times in the NT, six times with reference to Christ. Only in Ephesians 4:11 is it used as the leader of a church, but without description as to what it does. The function evidently is similar to the agrarian model among the sheep. For example:

1. "He was moved with compassion for them, because they were weary and scattered, like sheep having no shepherd." (Matt 9:36 NKJ) Reversing this scene, with a pastor the sheep will be secure, comforted and united.

2. "Now there were in the same country shepherds living out in the fields, keeping watch over their flock by night." (Luke 2:8 NKJ) Thus pastors guard and protect their flock.

3. John 10 is a long description of a good pastor who is willing to sacrifice himself for his sheep, and he knows them and they know him, because he lives to protect them from their enemies.

Jesus was called the "great Shepherd [pastor] of the sheep…" (Heb 13:20) and the "Shepherd [pastor] and Overseer [bishop] of your souls" (1 Peter 2:25).

Christ confirmed the apostles and prophets by giving them revelations and miracles, but the pastors have to be confirmed by their local churches when they present evidences of their maturity: above reproach, husband of one wife, temperate, self-controlled, respectable, hospitable, an able teacher, etc." (1 Tim 3:1-6)

Teacher. Many see the gifts of pastors and teachers united as one gifting, and it is certainly the requirement in 1 Tim 3:2 ("an able teacher"). Certainly this is a lifetime goal and for those who are willing to work hard, can win "double honor" (1 Tim 5:17). The concept appears 147 times in the NT as one of the major activities of the church. As with an evangelist, it appears that many should be teaching who may not be specially gifted to teach: all disciples are taught to be able to teach other disciples; after a period of time in a ministry everyone is expected to be able to teach what they have been taught (Heb 5:12).

Exhortation. The word (*paraklesis*) refers to "encouragement" (1 Thes 2:3), "appeal, request" (2 Cor 8:4) and "comfort, consolation" (2 Cor 1:4-7). The practice can include motivating unbelievers to come to Christ (Acts 2:40) as a powerful mix with the gift of evangelism.

Like most of the gifts we are commanded to practice the ministry function whether we have the gift or not. The strength of the church depends on the practice of mutual exhortation as seen in Heb 3:13, "but exhort one another daily, while it is called "Today," lest any of you be hardened through the deceitfulness of sin."

Serving gifts

Service, helps. Two gifts that are very close in meaning may represent one area of caring for one another. In the list of gifts in 1 Corinthians 12 the gift of "helps" (*antilempsis*, "laying hold of, hence help, assistance; plural helpful deeds") is the only mention in the NT.

The second word is "service" (*diakonia*, "ministry, aid, support"), which can have a variety of meanings depending on the context. *Diakonia* can be used for spiritual ministry (Acts 1:25; 6:4), physical aid ministry (Acts 6:1), hospitality (1 Cor 16:15), giving (2 Cor 8:4), and general preaching and teaching ministry (Acts 20:24). In general, the gift refers to a wide range of caring and loving benefit to others. It is used for helping the sick (Acts 10:35) to slaves serving their Christian masters (1 Tim 6:2a). Such service we are to "teach and exhort these things." (6:2b).

Peter exhorts serving others: "If anyone ministers, let him do it as with the ability [*ischus*, "force, strength, might"] which God supplies, that in all things God may be glorified" (1Pe 4:11 NKJ). This implies that considerable energy and effort is extended to benefit others. The same word is used in Acts 6:1NAS for "the daily serving of food" and in Acts 6:4, for "the ministry of the word." This implies the same motivation and same effort in both areas of service.

Administration. Likewise, two words appear to have similar meanings in this gifted area of service. In Romans 12:8, "he who leads, with diligence" is the word *proistemi* ("to place before; to be over, superintend, preside over"). The meaning is to "put oneself (responsibly) at the head, lead, direct, rule (1 T 5:17); (2) active, of a protective leadership, care for, help, give aid (1 Th 5:12)" (*Friberg Lexicon* 23066). The giftedness becomes evident as others want this person to be their leader.

The second similar word "administrations" (*kubernesis*, "literally, the skill with which a pilot guides a ship; figuratively, of leadership skill, administrative ability, gift of leadership, managerial skill") (*Friberg Lexicon* 16776). From this original word we have the English word "government." This word only appears once in the NT in 1 Cor 12:28.

This characteristic is first to become evident in the family (1 Tim 3:4-5), then can be beneficial to the church; however, the restriction of this service is the prohibition: "do not lord it over those entrusted to you, but being examples to the flock" (1 Pet 5:3NET).

Giving. The list of gifts in Romans 12:8 lists the gift and a guiding exhortation: "he who gives, with liberality" (Rom 12:8 NKJ). The main idea of metadidomi is "to share with someone else what one has" (Louw-Nida Lexicon, 57.96). Jesus gave the command, "a person who has two shirts must share with another who doesn't have any" (Luke 3:11). In Rom 1:11 it is used of Paul imparting a spiritual gift or benefit; in Eph 4:28 of sharing of money; and 1 Thess 2:8 of sharing the gospel and one's own soul. The major focus seems to be in the area of physical giving (e.g., 1 Cor 13:3, giving to the poor).

The Romans 12 reference gives the accompanying exhortation, "with liberality" (*alotes*, "singleness, sincerity, mental honesty, not self seeking, openness of heart, manifesting itself by generosity") (Strong's Lexicon 572).

Those gifted as givers become models and motivation for others.

The danger in this area of service is illustrated in Acts 5 where a donor was seeking personal benefit and recognition by giving, such that he was seduced into lying about how much he had sacrificed to be appreciated even more.

Showing mercy. Romans 12:8 describes the gift of mercy as "he who shows mercy, with cheerfulness" as a gifted area of service (12:6). "Showing mercy" (*eleeo*, "help one afflicted or seeking aid") (Strong 1653). Vine amplifies this definition: "the outward manifestation of pity; it assumes need on the part of him who receives it, and resources adequate to meet the need on the part of him who shows it." (Vine 1976, 9). Thayer describes it as "kindness or good will towards the miserable and afflicted, joined with a desire to relieve them." (Thayer, *Greek English Lexicon*, 203).

Mercy is more than a feeling of compassion; it is the commitment to act sacrificially to benefit the hopeless and needy with the accompanying attitude of "cheerfulness" (hilarotes, "graciousness, without reluctance") (Gingrich Lexicon 3200). The English word hilarious is derived from this Greek word. God demonstrates this quality toward me (Luke 1:58) and the "mercy of our Lord Jesus Christ unto eternal life" (Jude 21) becomes our attitude toward the undeserved.

Conclusion

The non-miraculous gifts are uniquely given to individuals for the purpose of benefiting the body of Christ both from their extraordinary service and by being a model for other believers to imitate. All of these areas of ministry are commanded to be practiced throughout the church. Notice how the activity involved in a given spiritual gift is elsewhere commanded of all believers in the following instances; Evangelism (Acts 1:8, "you shall be My witnesses"); Pastoring (1 Thess 5:11, "build up one another"); Teaching (Matt 28:19, "teaching them"); Exhortation (Heb 10:25, "encouraging one another"). (Stitzinger 2003:175).

As the Word of God was completed and the body of Christ established on the revelations given in the NT, the ongoing ministries are to put into practice everything that was revealed to us by the apostles and prophets of the Early Church. Always the focus is on the building up or edifying of the believers from the initial comment in 1 Corinthians 12:7 that the gifts are given for the common good of others, not the individual benefit (1 Cor 14:3, 4, 5, 12, 17, 26).

Mutual edification (not the self-centered self-edification) is the major thrust of the New Testament (1 Cor 14:26; 1 Thess 5:11; 2 Cor 10:8; 12:19; 13:10; Rom 14:19; 15:2; Eph 4:12, 16, 29). The body of Christ is designed to be interdependently edifying itself, not independently edified. We need each other by design. This is the bond of body life. Our relationship is not just with

Christ, but it is equally our bond to each other.

Furthermore, the only way we can serve the Lord is by serving each other. Jesus gave the principle that "just as you did it for one of the least of these brothers or sisters of mine, you did it for me" (Matt 25:40 NET). Likewise, our relationship with the Lord is no better than our relationship with each other. For example, if a husband and wife are not in harmony, their prayers are hindered before the Lord (1 Pet 3:7). Thus, our commitment to the body of Christ in service and sacrifice is our commitment to our Lord in serving His people and He empowers every believer to be able to make a unique contribution.

Paul's final exhortation to the elders at Ephesus was to "shepherd the church of God that he obtained with the blood of his own Son." (Act 20:28 NET) May we care for each other as precious properties of our Savior to build up and protect, especially as God has gifted and enabled each one of us to serve each other.

Chapter 21: *Gifts for Today*

CHAPTER 22
Conclusions

As we conclude, we should clarify certain concepts, since an exaggerated focus on the gifts becomes a panacea or a magic solution for many Christians.

Spiritual gifts do not make a person spiritual.

The church in Corinth lacked none of the gifts, but there was little spirituality among the members. They were very carnal. Not even the miracle gifts guarantee spirituality (e.g., Samson). It seems that the Corinthians placed so much importance on the gifts that they ignored their spiritual problems and personal relations.

It is true that each one of the believers had a spiritual gift, but it is also obvious that their gifts did not make them spiritual. Some Christians are blessed in extraordinary ways and still lack the qualities of a spiritual life. It is absurd for a person to think that his service to the Lord is effective simply because he is exercising his spiritual gifts.

Spirituality is related to our biblical knowledge and our willingness to obey what we learn and understand from the Word. We need others to minister to us in order to help us mature in the faith and our Christian lives because we all have blind spots. While others minister to us, we in turn minister to them and in this way the Body of Christ will "edify" itself. We are a team in the battle against sin, ignorance and deception.

Therefore, the gifts of the Spirit are not given to make us spiritual, but rather to enable and motivate us to function in the Body of Christ as part of a ministering team to others. The effectiveness of that ministry depends on the motivation of love that guides Christians to use their gifts to serve and benefit one another.

The recognition of your gift is not vital in order to serve God.

It is true that each believer has a spiritual gift given by God as He wills. In 1 Corinthians 12, not all the believers possessed the gifts they might have selfishly preferred, but an individual cannot choose his spiritual gift. Each of us should know that we have at least one gift, and we should try to identify it, then develop in that area of ministry to benefit others. The gift will function whether the believer knows what it is or not; however, often other people will recognize the gift before the owner identifies it in himself. Thus we are to help each other discover how God has made us for His kingdom purposes. We cannot be fighting and criticizing each other, and build each other up at the same time.

If a person is sensitive to practicing the will of God, his gifts will become evident. Almost all the gifts in use today have related commandments (giving, evangelization, teaching, exhorting, showing mercy, etc.) If we are practicing these commands, one or more of them will emerge in our lives as a high personal motivation and result in blessing and encouragement to others.

That said, it is not a priority for the believer to discover his gift because, out of all of the commands regarding the Christian life, there is no biblical command for the Christian to find his particular gift. In fact, if it were not for the problem that arose with tongues in Corinth, we would know very little about the spiritual gifts.

The gifts make it easier to carry out certain ministries. It is much more important to follow the commands of the Word regarding ministry than to identify our gifts. There is even a danger in discovering our gift, because we may even use it as a pretext to ignore or disobey other biblical responsibilities using our gift as an excuse not to engage in other mandatory areas of ministry.

If we know our gift and have the opportunity to make a decision about a ministry, we can choose the one that best fits the way we perceive God has made us. It is possible that our gifts could be an indication of the direction God wants for our lives.

Gifts are a means, not an end.

Gifts are a means by which we may edify and serve the Body of Christ. Having a gift is not the purpose of the Christian life, however; some believers have made the discovery and manifestation of their preferred gift their main goal in life. This is unbiblical. We should not covet certain gifts or use our gifts selfishly; we should use them only to serve others (1 Corinthians 13).

When we compare the discovery of our gifts with other principles of the New Testament, it is evident that the manifestation of the fruit of the Spirit (Galatians 5:22-23) is more important than the manifestation of the gift of the Spirit. Knowledge of the Bible is more important than knowledge of our gifts.

It is possible that emphasizing certain gifts can cause tremendous negligence of other vital truths for the Christian life. Therefore, the focus should be on the knowledge of God's revealed will in His Word and how to obey it on a daily basis. The gifts are given so that Christians can minister to one another. Therefore, when the Spirit uses others to speak to us by the Word we should receive the exhortation humbly and gratefully.

The gifts are not mystic secrets that only certain people can know; they are God-given capacities to supply practical needs and to be a blessing, encouragement and help to others. The knowledge of our gift does not guarantee success nor is it a magical power, because gifts do not make people infallible or better than anyone else.

A gifted person is simply someone who has a special motivation, energy and desire to serve others in a particular way. Seeking power rather than service to others through giftedness is a pagan, selfish motivation. Simon the sorcerer (Acts 8) sought more power and was not motivated by biblical love for anyone but himself; in the same way, some people today are motivated to seek gifts because of selfish desires or ambition.

Gifts do not just surface completely in one's life all at once. Only the sign gifts were completely developed at the beginning of their manifestation. (After all, it is nearly impossible to heal a person partially or to perform half of a miracle.) The other gifts must be developed by exercising them and by following instructions from other believers in order for us to become perfected or equipped in "the work of the ministry" (Ephesians 4:12).

Essentially, no believer should live under tension or worry about discovering his gifts. Many serve the Lord for years before they really manifest their spiritual gifts. The more we are committed to serve each other in the church, the more effective and useful we will be for God. He will take charge of helping us discover our gifts when He determines that it is important. In the meantime, we have much to do in the work of God.

The miracle gifts marked the beginning of the Church and the confirmation of the New Testament.

The purpose of this study has been to analyze spiritual gifts that were said to cease at some point, paying special attention to the excessive importance many Christians place on these miracle gifts. The abuses, which are the product of a deviation from biblical teaching, are not insignificant and should not be ignored. Small deviations today become extremes tomorrow. When a teaching is not according to the Word of God, eventually there will be serious problems in the churches.

We hope that this study has clarified the following truths:

First, there is no similarity between the today's charismatic gifts (prophecy, miracles, healings and tongues) and the genuine gifts mentioned in the New Testament. Biblical evidence, as well as historical evidence, proves that such gifts were temporary. For this reason, we do not believe that the phenomena that we see today are from the Spirit.

Second, the description of the gifts in the Gospels and in Acts indicates an undoubtedly divine quality of character. It is impossible to explain what happened in those days as merely psychological or "put on." The innumerable miracles that Jesus (John 21:25) and his apostles performed show that the only possible source was the miraculous power of the living God. The substitutes and imitations today are, in comparison, mere imitations of those true acts.

Finally, God gave these miraculous gifts to establish His Church. They were never seen before or after that time. Our confidence in the value of our faith is that God confirmed the work and words of those men through undeniable miraculous signs and the internal evidence of the written revelations themselves. Today we trust in the evidence recorded in the Word of God. The apostles' miraculous gifts achieved identical results to those of Jesus, confirming that their communication of God's Word to the church, especially what is written in the Bible, has the very authority of Jesus himself.

Finally, throughout this book the writer has sought to carefully examine the biblical and related evidences regarding the spiritual gifts. If the discussion of spiritual gifts could focus on the biblical text itself, rather than on a multitude of experiences, then many differences could be resolved.

There are two types of spiritual gifts that become evident in the NT: miraculous gifts that characterized the apostolic age for the purpose of delivering the new revelations of the NT Church, and gifts for the authentication of those foundational revelations. It seems evident that these miraculous gifts were limited to the apostles and a few close associates who were part of their ministries.

Attempts to restore those miraculous gifts and prove their validity by experiences, visions and new revelations must be rejected as bogus. The foundation was laid by the apostles and prophets in association with the chief cornerstone, Jesus Christ, in the first century (Eph 2:20). Now our task is to "persevere in the doctrine of the apostles" (Acts 2:42), not invent new teachings just to be novel.

The temporary gifts of the apostolic age were amazing and undeniable so we can trust in every word they delivered to us today. Paul said he laid the foundation and now we are to "build upon it. But let each man be careful how he builds upon it for no man can lay a foundation other than the one which is laid" (1 Cor 3:10-11a).

The non-miraculous gifts are given for the "building up" of the church on the foundation of the miraculous gifts of the apostles and prophets. Evangelists, pastors and teachers take the "faith which was once for all delivered to the saints" (Jude 3) by the apostles and prophets to teach and apply to every believer's life throughout the time of the church. There is no need to reprove or reconfirm anything again that has already been proven.

By faith in the biblical evidence of the NT we believe in every word, seeking to know it and live it out in our daily lives. May this objective bring a oneness of mind and heart to all believers.

Chapter 22: *Gifts for Today*

Bibliography

Abbot-Smith, G. (1905). *A Manual Greek Lexicon of the New Testament.* New York: Charles Scribner's Sons,.

Aldrich, R. L. (1957, July). *Bibliotheca Sacra,* Vol. 114(455), pp. 235-242.

Alford, D. (2006, January). "Tongues Tied." *Christianity Today.* Carol Stream, IL, 50:2.

Anderson, A. (2007). "Spreading Fires: The Globalization of Pentecostalism in the Twentieth Century." *International Bulletin of Missionary Research.* Denville, NJ, 31(January), 8-14.

Anthony C. Thiselton, (2000). *The First Epistle to the Corinthians: a Commentary on the Greek Text, New International Greek Testament Commentary.* Grand Rapids, MI: W.B. Eerdmans.

Aristotle. "Poetics." *Loeb Classical Library.*

Arndt, William F. and Gingrich, F. Wilbur. (1947). *A Greek-English Lexicon of the New Testament.* Chicago: University of Chicago Press.

Ashcraft, J. Morris. (1971). "Glossolalia in the First Epistle to the Corinthians" in *Tongues,* ed. Luther B. Dyer. Jefferson City, Mo.: Le Roi.

Askins, Alan. (1998): "Paul's Defense of His Apostolic Authority to the Galatians." *Conservative Theological Journal* 2, no. 6: 310.

Augustine, "The Epistle of St. John," VI, 10, *Nicene and Post-Nicene Fathers,* vol. VII.

Babcox, Neil. (1985). *A Search for Charismatic Reality.* Portland, Ore.: Multnomah.

Bailey, M. L. (1998, January). "Guidelines for Interpreting Jesus' Parables." *Bibliotheca Sacra,* Vol. 155(617), 29-38.

Bales, James D. (1970). *Pat Boone and the Gift of Tongues.* Searcy, Arkansas: published by the author.

Banks, Adell M., *Religion News Service, Christianity Today,* retrieved 9/16/13 from www.christianitytoday.com/ct/2006/octoberweb-only/140-53.0.html.

Barclay, W. (1959). *The Daily Study Bible Series: The Letters to the Philippians, Colossians, and Thessalonians* (2d ed.). Philadelphia: Westminister Press.

Barna Research, retrireved 9/29/13 from https://www.barna.org/barna-update/congregations/52-is-american-christianity-turning-charismatic#.UkFmamRgbhM

Barnett, Donald Lee and Jeffrey P. McGregor. (1986). *Speaking in Other Tongues.* Seattle: Community Chapel.

Barrett, C. K. (1993). *First Epistle to Corinthians, Black's New Testament Commentary.* Peabody, MA.:Hendrickson Publishers, Inc.

Barrett. David. (2009). "Christian World Communions: Five Overviews of Global Christianity, AD 1800-2025," *International Bulletin of Missionary Research,* Volume 33, No. 1, January 2009, 31.

Basham, D. (1969). *A Handbook on the Holy Spirit Baptism.* Monroeville: Whitaker.

Bassler, J. M. (1992). "1 Corinthians." *The Women's Bible Commentary.* Edited by C. A. Newson and S. H. Ringe. Louisville: Westminster/John Knox.

Bauer, Walter. (2000). *A Greek-English Lexicon of the New Testament and Other Early Christian Literature,* rev. and ed. Frederick William Danker, 3rd ed. Chicago: University of Chicago Press s.v. teleios.

Bauman, Louis, S. (1963). *The Tongues Movement.* Winona Lake, IN.: The Brethren Missionary Herald Company

Behm, Johannes. (1964-1974). "Glössa." *Theological Dictionary of the New Testament.* Edited by Gerhard Kittel and Gerhard Friedrich, translated and edited by Geoffrey W. Bromiley. 10 vols. Grand Rapids: Wm. B. Eerdmans Publishing Co., 1964-1974, 1:719-26.

Behm, Johannes. (1964-1974). "Kainos." *Theological Dictionary of the New Testament.* Edited by Gerhard Kittel and Gerhard Friedrich, translated and edited by Geoffrey W. Bromiley. 10 vols. Grand Rapids: Wm. B. Eerdmans Publishing Co. 3:447-450.

Bellshaw, William G. (1963). "The Confusion of Tongues." *Bibliotheca Sacra* 120, no. 478: 144.

Bennett, Dennis and Rita. (1971). *The Holy Spirit and You.* Plainfield, New Jersey: Logos International,.

Bennett, Dennis. (1975). *The Holy Spirit and You.* Grand Rapids: Zondervan Publishing House.

Bevan, Edwin R. (1966). *The House of Seleucus.* Routledge & Kegan Paul PLC.

Biblical Studies Press. (2006). The NET Bible First Edition Notes. Biblical Studies Press. Joe 2:28.

Bicket, Zenas, (2010). *Introduction to Pentecostal Doctrine: An Independent-study Textbook,* Third Edition. Springfield, MO: Global University.

Bigalke Jr., Ron, (2006). "The latest Postmodern Trend: The Emerging Church." *Journal of Dispensational Theology.* 10, no. 31.

Birch, Desmond. (1996). *Trial, Tribulation and Triumph.* Queenship Pub Co.

Bixler, R. Russell. (1970). *It can happen to anybody.* New Kensington, PA: Whitaker House.

Blumhofer, E. L. (2006, 2nd Quarter). "Revisiting Azusa Street: A Centennial Retrospect." *International Bulletin of Missionary Research.* New Haven, CN, 30(2), 59-64.

Blunt, J. H. (1990). *Dictionary of Sects, Heresies, Ecclesiastical Parties, and Schools of Religious Thought* (John Henry Blunt, Ed.). Detroit: Omnigraphics.

Booth, (1998): "The Purpose of Miracles," *Bibliotheca Sacra.* Volume 155: 202–3.

Boyer, James L. (1960). "The Office of the Prophet in New Testament Times," *Grace Journal* 1

Bromiley, G. W. (1976). Theological Dictionary of the New Testament, Edited by G. Kittel and G. Friedrich; translated and edited by G. W. Bromiley, 10 vols. Grand Rapids: Eerdmans.

Brown, Francis; Driver, S.R.; and Briggs, Charles A. (1962). A Hebrew and English Lexicon of the Old Testament. Oxford: Clarendon Press.

Bruce B. Barton and Grant R. Osborne, (1999). 1 & 2 Corinthians. Life Application Bible Commentary. Wheaton, IL: Tyndale House, 174.

Bruce, F. F. (1951). *The Acts of the Apostles*. London: Tyndale Press.

Bruce, F. F., (1980). *1 and 2 Corinthians, NCB*. Grand Rapids: Eerdmans, 128.

Bruner, F. D. (1970). *A Theology of the Holy Spirit*. Grand Rapids: Eerdmans.

Bruner, F., Dale. (1970). *A Theology of the Holy Spirit*. Grand Rapids: William B. Erdmann's Publishing Company.

Bryan, William F. (1979). "Miraculous Continuity," *Alliance Witness*, January 24, , 3–4.

Burgess, S. M. (2001). *The New International Dictionary of Pentecostal and Charismatic Movements*. (2001) (S. M. Burgess, Ed.). Grand Rapids: Zondervan.

Burgon, John William. (1871). *The Last Twelve Verses of the Gospel According to S. Mark*. Oxford: London.

Burns, J. Lanier. (1975). "A Reemphasis on the Purpose of the Sign Gifts." *Bibliotheca Sacra* 132, no. 527 243.

Busentz, Nathan. (2006). "The Gift of Tongues: Comparing the Church Fathers with Contemporary Pentecostalism," *Master's Seminary Journal* 17:1.

Carlston, Charles E. (November 1971). "The Question of Miracles," *Andover Newton Quarterly* 12 99-107.

Carroll, Leonard, R. Conn, Charles W. and Horton, Wade H. (1966, 2008). *The Glossolalia Phenomenon*. Gilsum, N.H.:Pathway Books.

Carson, D. (1994). *New Bible Commentary 21st Century Edition* (4th ed.). Downers Grove, Ill.: Inter-Varsity Press.

Cate, B. F. (1965). *The Nine Gifts of the Spirit*. Des Plaines, Illinois:Regular Baptist Press.

Chisholm, Robert B., Jr. (1985). Joel. Edited by J. F. Walvoord and R. B. Zuck. *The Bible Knowledge Commentary: An Exposition of the Scriptures*. Wheaton, IL: Victor Books,

Christenson, L. (1968). *Speaking in Tongues*. Minneapolis, MN.: Dimension Books.

Christie-Murray, D. (1978). *Voices From the Gods*. London: Routledge and Kegan Paul.

Chrysostom, *Homilies on First Corinthians*, XXIX, 1.

Clapp, Rodney. (1983). "Faith Healing: A Look at What's Happening." *Christianity Today*. 16 December.

Clark, Elmer T. (1949). *The Small Sects in America: Their Historical, Theological, and Psychological Background*. Nashville, Tennessee: Abingdon Press

Collins, K. J. (1997). *The Scripture Way of Salvation: The Heart of John Wesley's Theology*. Nashville, TN.: Abington Press.

Comfort, Ray. (2006). *The Way of the Master*. Orlando, FL.: Bridge-Logos Publishers.

Conn, C. W. (1979). *Pillars of Pentecost*. Cleveland, TN.: Pathway Press

Constable, Thomas L., (2003). "Notes on 1 Corinthians," 143, http://www.soniclight.com/constable/notes/pdf/1corinthians.pdf (accessed November 24, 2003).

Cox, H. (1995). *Fire From Heaven*. Cambridge, MA: Da Capo Press.

Criswell, W. A., ed. (1991). *The Believer's Study Bible*. Nashville: Nelson.

Culpepper, Robert H. (1977). *Evaluating the Charismatic Movement*. Valley Forge, PA.:Judson Press

Dalton, R. C. (1945). *Tongues Like as of Fire*. Springfield, MO.: Gospel Publishing House.

Damboriena, Prudencio (1969). *Tongues as of Fire*. n.a.:Corpus Books.

Dayton Donald. (1987). *Theological Roots of Pentecostalism*. Grand Rapids: Zondervan Publishing House.

Dean, Jr., Robert. (2005) "Three Arguments for the Cessation of Tongues." *Conservative Theological Journal* Volume 9, no. 26.

Delitzsch, Franz and C. F. Keil. (1967). *Biblical Commentary on the Prophecies of Isaiah in Biblical Commentary on the Old Testament*. Reprint ed. Grand Rapids: Wm. B. Eerdmans Publishing Co.

Delling, Gerhard. (1964-1974). "Battalogeö." *Theological Dictionary of the New Testament*. Edited by Gerhard Kittel and Gerhard Friedrich, translated and edited by Geoffrey W. Bromiley. 10 vols. Grand Rapids: Wm. B. Eerdmans Publishing Co. 1:597.

Delling, Halle Gerhard. (1972) "*Teleios*," in *Theological Dictionary of the New Testament*, ed. G. Kittel, trans. G.W. Bromiley (Grand Rapids: Eerdmans,), 8:75–77.

Derickson, Gary W. (1998). "The Cessation of Healing Miracles in Paul's Ministry." *Bibliotheca Sacra* 155, no. 618: 298.

Dillow, J. (1975). *Speaking in Tongues: Seven crucial questions*. Grand Rapids: Zondervan Publishing House.

Dillow, Joseph. (1972). *A Biblical Evaluation of the Twentieth Century Tongues Movement*. Garland, Texas: published by the author.

Dollar, George W. (October 1963): "Church History and the Tongues Movement." *Bibliotheca Sacra* 120 316-21.

Duffield, G. P. a. V. C., Nathaniel M. (1987). *Foundations of Pentecostal Theology*. San

Dimas, CA.: L.I.F.E. Bible College at Los Angeles.

Eadie, John. (1977). *Commentary on the Epistles to the Ephesians.* Reprint ed. Minneapolis, Minnesota: James and Kloch Christian Publishing Co.

Eckhart, Meister, "Mysticism." Retrieved 1/3/2007, from http://en.wikipedia.org/wiki/Mysticism.

Edgar, Thomas R. (1988). "The Cessation of the Sign Gifts," *Bibliotheca Sacra* 145, no. 580: 372.

Edgar, Thomas. (1996). *Satisfied by the Promise of the Spirit.* Grand Rapids: Kregel Publications.

Edgar, Thomas. (1998, Sept). "The Sufficiency of Our Justification." *Conservative Theological Journal,* 6, Vol 2, pp. 226-246.

Edgar, Thomas. (2001). *Miraculous Gifts: Are They for Today?* Eugene, OR.:Wipf & Stock Publishers.

Enns, P. (1989). *The Moody Handbook of Theology.* Chicago: Moody Press.

Ervin, Howard M. (1968). *These Are Not Drunken, As Ye Suppose.* Plainfield, New Jersey: Logos, International.

Eusebius. (1952). *Ecclesiastical History, The Nicene and Post-Nicene Fathers,* 2d series. 14 vols. (Grand Rapids: Wm. B. Eerdmans Publishing Co. Vol. VII, p. 486.

Farnell, F. David. (April-June 1993). "When Will the Gift of Prophecy Cease?" *Bibliotheca Sacra* 150:191-93.

Farnell, F. David. (1993). "Does the New Testament Teach Two Prophetic Gifts?" *Bibliotheca Sacra* 150, no. 597: 61.

Fee, Gordon D. (1987). "The First Epistle to the Corinthians." *The New International Commentary on the New Testament.* Grand Rapids: Wm. B. Eerdmans Publishing Co.

Fee, Gordon D. (1996). *Paul, the Spirit and the People of God.* Grand Rapids: Baker Academic.

Ferm, Virgilius. (1959). *Encyclopedia of Religion.* Escondido, CA.: The Philosophical Library

Finney, C. G. (1994). *Finney's Systematic Theology* (B. N. Bill Nicely, Dennis Carroll, and L. G. Parkhurst, Ed.) [New Expanded Edition]. Minneapolis, MN.: Bethany House Publishers.

Foster, L. (1992) *Women, Family, and Utopia.* Syracuse, NY: Syracuse University Press.

Fremantle, Anne. (1963). *The Papal Encyclicals in the Historical Context,* exp. Ed. New York: New American Library.

Friberg, Timothy, Barbara Friberg, and Neva F. Miller. (2000). Analytical Lexicon to the Greek New Testament. Baker's Greek New Testament Library. Grand Rapids: Baker.

Fruchtenbaum, Arnold G. (1996). "The Toronto Phenomenon" *Chafer Theological Seminary Journal* 2, no. 2:10.

Gaffin, Jr., Richard. (1993) *Perspectives on Pentecost*. Phillipsburg, N.J.: P&R Publishing. 59.

Garland, David E. (2003). "1 Corinthians." *Baker Evangelical Commentary on the New Testament*. Grand Rapids, MI.: Baker Academic,.

Garrett, Duane A. (1997). "Hosea, Joel." Vol. 19A. *The New American Commentary*. Nashville: Broadman & Holman Publishers,.

Gasson, Raphael. (1969). *The Challenging Counterfeit: An Expose of Psychic Phenomena*. Plainfield, NJ: Logos International.

Gentry Jr., Kenneth L. (2011). *The charismatic Gift of Prophecy*. Carol Stream, IL.:Victorious Hope Publishing,.

George, T. (1994). "Galatians." (Vol. Volume 30). *The New American Commentary*. Nashville, TN.: Broadman Press.

Gerlach, Joel C., (October 1973). "Glossolalia," *Wisconsin Lutheran Quarterly* 70: 251.

Godet, Frederic Louis, (1977). *Commentary on First Corinthians* (Edinburgh: T. & T. Clark, 1898; reprint, Grand Rapids: Kregel.

Goodman, Felicitas D. (1972). *Speaking in Tongues: A Cross Cultural Study of Glossolalia*. Chicago: University of Chicago Press.

Gordon, A. J. (1882). *The Ministry of Healing*. New York: Revell.

Grant, Heber J. and Durham, G. Homer (compiler). (1976). *Gospel Standards*. Salt Lake City, UT.: Deseret Book.

Green, M. (1975). *I believe in the Holy Spirit*. Grand Rapids: William B. Eerdmans Publishing Company.

Gromacki, Robert G. (1977). *The Modern Tongues Movement* (Philadelphia: Presbyterian and Reformed.

Grudem, Wayne, ed., (1996) *Are Miraculous Gifts for Today?* (Grand Rapids: Zondervan.

Grudem, Wayne, Gaffin Jr., Richard B., Saucy, Robert L., and Storms, C. Samuel (2011) "An Open But Cautious View." *Are Miraculous Gifts for Today?*, Grand Rapids: Zondervan.

Grudem, Wayne. (1994). *Systematic Theology*. Grand Rapids: Zondervan.

Hamilton, Michael Pollock. (1975). *The Charismatic Movement*. Grand Rapids: Eerdmans Publishing Co.

Hanegraaff , Hank. (1997). *Counterfeit Revival*. Nashville: Word Publishing,

Hannah, J. D. (1992). *The History of the Pentecostal Movement*. Unpublished classnotes, 28 lessons, Dallas Theological Seminary, Dallas, TX.

Harper, M. (1965). *As At the Beginning; the Twentieth Century Pentecostal Revival*.

London: Hodder and Stoughton.

Harris, W. H. (1994). *A Biblical Theology of the New Testament*. Roy B. Zuck, Ed. Chicago: Moody Press.

Hasel, Gerhard F. (1991). *Speaking in Tongues: Biblical Speaking in Tongues and Contemporary Glossolalia*. Berrien Springs, MI.:Adventist Theological Society Publications.

Hayford, Jack W. and Gary Matsdorf. (1993). *People of the Spirit: Gifts, Fruit and Fullness of the Holy Spirit. Spirit-Filled Life Kingdom Dynamics Study Guides*. Nashville: Thomas Nelson.

Hayford, Jack W. and. Bauer, Rebecca Hayford. (1996). *Heavenly Resources for Praise and Intercession: Praying in the Spirit*. Nashville, TN.: Thomas Nelson Pubs.

Hays, Richard B. (1997). *1 Corinthians*. Louisville, KY: John Knox Press,.

Hodge, Charles (1857). "Finney's Lectures on Theology." *Essays & Reviews*. New York: University of California Libraries.

Hodges, Zane C. (1963). "A Symposium on the Tongues Movement" *Bibliotheca Sacra* 120, no. 479: 226.

Hoekema, Anthony A. (1966). *What About Tongue speaking?* Grand Rapids: Eerdmans.

Hoekema, Anthony A. (1972). *Holy Spirit Baptism*. Grand Rapids: William B. Erdmann's Publishing Company.

Houghton, George . (1996). "A Reexamination of 1 Corinthians 13:8-13." *Bibliotheca Sacra* (July-September).

Hughes, R. B. and Laney, J. Carl. (1990). *Tyndale Concise Bible Commentary*. Wheaton, Ill.: Tyndale House Publishers, Inc.

Hummel, Charles. (1982). "Healing: Our Double Standard?" *Christian Life,* November: 33.

Hunter, Charles y Frances. (1976). *Why Should I Speak in Tongues?* Houston: Hunter Ministries Publishing Co.

J. Rodman Williams. (1971). *The Era of Spirit*. Plainfield, N.J.: Logos.

J. Rodman Williams. (1977). "Opinion," *Logos Journal* 7. May-June.

Jamieson, Robert, A. R. Fausset, and David Brown. (1997). *Commentary Critical and Explanatory on the Whole Bible*. Oak Harbor, WA: Logos Research Systems, Inc.

Jenkins, P. (2000). *Mystics and Messiahs: Cults and New Religions in American* History. New York: Oxford University Press.

Johnson, S. Lewis. (1971). "1 Corinthians." *The Wycliffe Bible Commentary*. Ed. Everett F. Harrison. Chicago: Moody.

Johnson, Todd M. (2009). *Atlas of Global Christianity. Center for the Study of Global Christianity*, Gordon-Conwell Theological Seminary, South Hamilton, MA: Edinburgh University Press.

Joseph Smith. (1978). *History of the Church.* Volume 2, 2nd edition. Salt Lake City: Deseret Book Company.

Kelsey, Morton, T. (1981). *Tongue Speaking.* New York: Crossroad Pub. Co.

Kildahl, John P. (1972). *The Psychology of Speaking in Tongues.* New York: Harper & Row.

Kistemaker, Simon J., and William Hendriksen. (1953–2001). "Exposition of the First Epistle to the Corinthians." Vol. 18. *New Testament Commentary.* Grand Rapids: Baker Book House.

Kittel, Gerhard, Geoffrey W. Bromiley, and Gerhard Friedrich, eds. (1964). *Theological Dictionary of the New Testament.* Grand Rapids, MI: Eerdmans.

Knox, Ronald A. (1950). *Enthusiasm: A Chapter in the History of Religion.* Notre Dame, IN.: University of Notre Dame Press.

Knuteson, Roy E. (1998). "Are You Waiting for a Miracle?" *Bibliotheca Sacra* Volume 155:22.

Kole, Andre, and Janssen, Al. (1984). *Miracles or Magic?* Eugene, OR: Harvest House.

Kurian, G. T. (2001). *Nelson's New Christian Dictionary.* Nashville, TN.: Thomas Nelson.

Laurentin, Rene. (1977). *Catholic Pentecostalism.* New York:Doubleday.

Liddell Henry George, (1935). *Liddell-Scott Greek-English Lexicon,* Oxford: Oxford University Press.

Liddell, H.G. and R. Scott, (1900). *An Intermediate Greek-English Lexicon,* 7th ed. New York: Harper and Brothers.

Liddell, Henry George and Scott, Robert. (1968). *A Greek-English Lexicon.* Revised by Henry Stuart Jones. Oxford: Clarendon Press.

Liddell, Henry George and Scott, Robert. (1996). *A Greek-English Lexicon.* Oxford: Clarendon Press.

Lloyd-Jones, D. Martyn, (1984). *The Baptism and Gifts of the Spirit.* Grand Rapids: Baker.

Logan, James C. (1975). "Controversial Aspects of the Movement." The *Charismatic Movement.* Ed. Michael P. Hamilton. Grand Rapids: Eerdmans.

Longenecke, R. N. (1990) *Word Biblical Commentary: Galatians* (B. M. Metzger, Hubbard, Ed.) (Vol. 41). Dallas, TX.: Word Books, Publisher.

MacArthur Jr., John. (1984). "1 Corinthians." *MacArthur New Testament Commentary.* Chicago: Moody Press,

MacArthur, J. F., Jr. (1978). *The Charismatics.* Grand Rapids: Zondervan.

MacArthur, John F. (1992). *Charismatic Chaos.* Grand Rapids: Zondervan.

MacArthur, John F., Jr. gen. ed. (1978). *The MacArthur Study Bible.* Nashville: Word.

MacDonald, W. (1995). *Believer's Bible Commentary*. Nashville, TN.: Thomas Nelson Publishers.

Mackie, Alexander. (1921). *The Gift of Tongues*. New York: George H. Doran Co.

Mallone, George (1983). *Those Controversial Gifts*. Downers Grove, IL.: InterVarsity Press.

Malone, George and Michael Green. (1988). *Those Controversial Gifts: Prophecy, Dreams, Visions, Tongues, Interpretation, Healing*. Arlington, TX.: Grace Vineyard of Arlington.

Martin, L. E. (1997). "Charles Fox Parham: Father of the Twentieth Century." In L. E. Martin (Ed.), *The Topeka Outpouring of 1901*. Joplin, MO.: Christian Life Books.

Masters, Peter. (1988). *The Healing Epidemic*. London: Wakeman Trust.

McClung, G. (2006, April). "Pentecostals: The Sequel." *Christianity Today*. Carol Stream, IL.

McCune, Rolland D. (1976). "A Biblical Study of Tongues and Miracles," *Central Bible Quarterly* 19:15.

McDonnell, Kilian. (1976) *Charismatic Renewal*, Toranto, ON.:Seabury Press.

McGee, J. V. (1998). *Through the Bible with J. Vernon McGree*. Pasadena, CA.: Thru the Bible Radio.

Meadors, G. T. (2003). *Decision Making God's Way*. Grand Rapids: Baker Book House.

Meyer, Wilhelm. (2009). *Critical and Exegetical Handbook to the Epistles to the Corinthians*. New York: BiblioBazaar (Barns and Nobles).

Michel, Otto. (1964-1974). "*Oikodomeö*" *Theological Dictionary of the New Testament*. Edited by Gerhard Kittel and Gerhard Friedrich, translated and edited by Geoffrey W. Bromiley. 10 vols. Grand Rapids: Wm. B. Eerdmans Publishing Co., 5:136-144.

Miller, C. A. (2002, July). "Did Peter's Vision in Acts 10 Pertain to Men or the Menu?" *Bibliotheca Sacra*, 635, Vol 159, p. 302-317.

Miller, Donald E. and Yamamori, Tetsunao. (2007). *Global Pentecostalism: The New Face of Christian Social Engagement*. Berkeley, CA.: University of California Press

Montanism. (2001-2005). *The Columbia Encyclopedia. [Encyclopedia Britannica]*. Sixth Edition. New York: Columbia University Press.

Morris, Leon, (1958). *The First Epistle of Paul to the Corinthians, TNTC*. Grand Rapids: Eerdmans.

Morrison, Alan. *The Evangelical Attraction to Mysticism*. Retrieved 1/3/2007, from http://www.evangelicalresources.org/mysticism.shtml

Moulton, J. H. a. M., George. (1930-33). *The Vocabulary of the Greek New Testament*. London: Hodder and Stoughton.

Moulton, J. H., Wilbert Francis Howard, and Nigel Turner, (2000) *Grammar of New

Testament Greek. Edinburgh:Bloomsbury T&T Clark.

Moulton, W. F. and Geden, A. S. (1963). *A Concordance to the Greek Testament.* Edinburgh: T. & T. Clark.

Nichol, John Thomas. (1966). *Pentecostalism.* New York: Harper and Row Publishers.

North, Gary. (1976). *None Dare Call It Witchcraft.* New Rochelle, N.Y.: Arlington House.

O'Connor, E. D. (1971). *The Pentecostal Movement in the Catholic Church.* Notre Dame, IN.: Ave Maria Press.

Oates, Wayne E, Frank Hinson, and Wayne E. Stagg. (1967) *Glossolalia Tongue speaking in the Bible, Historical and Psychological Perspective*, Nashville, TN.:Abingdon Press.

Palma, Anthony D. (2001). *The Holy Spirit: A Pentecostal Perspective.* Springfield MO.: Gospel Pub House.

Parry, John, (1957). *The First Epistle of Paul the Apostle to the Corinthians, CGTSC* (Colchester, England: Spottiswoode & Ballantyne, 1916; reprint, Cambridge: University Press.

Peters, George W. (1968). "The Church in Missions." *Bibliotheca Sacra* 125, no. 497: 44.

Peterson, Brian G.. (1976). "The Significance of Miracles within the Transitional Framework of the Book of Acts" (Th.M. thesis, Dallas Theological Seminary, 30;

Pew Reserch, (2011). *"Global Christianity,"* retrieved 9/18/13 from http://christianity.about.com/gi/o.htm?zi=1/XJ&zTi=1&sdn=christianity&cdn=religion&tm=219&f=10&tt=11&bt=7&bts=7&zu=http%3A//www.pewforum.org/Christian/Global-Christianity-exec.aspx.

Piper, John A. (1991). "Signs and Wonders: Then and Now," *Desiring God Ministries*, http://www.desiringgod.org/library/topics/spiritual_gifts/signs_wonders.html (retrieved 31 Oct. 2003).

Powell, C. E. (1997). "Questions Cessationists Should Ask: A Biblical Examination of Cessationism." In 48th Annual Meeting of the Evangelical Theological Society. Jackson, MS.

Poythress, Vern S. (1980). "Linguistic and Sociological Analyses of Modern Tongue Speaking." *Westminster Theological Journal*, Vol. XLII.

Poythress, Vern S. and Watson E. Mills (1986). *Speaking in Tongues: A Guide to Research on Glossolalia.* Grand Rapids: Eerdmans.

Quebedeaux, Richard. (1976). *The New Charismatics.* New York: Doubleday.

Rengstorf, K. H. (1964-1974). *"Didaktikos." Theological Dictionary of the New Testament.* Edited by Gerhard Kittel and Gerhard Friedrich, translated and edited by Geoffrey W. Bromiley. 10 vols. Grand Rapids: Wm. B. Eerdmans Publishing Co., 2:165.

Rescher, Nicholas. "Reductio ad absurdum". *The Internet Encyclopedia of Philosophy.*

Retrieved 21 July 2009.

Ricciotti, Giuseppi. (1958). *The History of Israel. Volume II: From the Exile to A.D. 135.* Pittsburgh, PA.:Bruce Publishing Company-Caliban Books.

Riggs, R. M. (1949). *The Spirit Himself.* Springfield, MO.: Gospel Publishing House.

Robert D. Hales, (2002). "Gifts of the Spirit," *Ensign*, February.

Robert Jamieson, A. R. Fausset, and David Brown. (1997). *Commentary Critical and Explanatory on the Whole Bible.* Oak Harbor, WA: Logos Research Systems, Inc., 1997.

Roberts, D. (2004.). "The Baptism in the Holy Spirit." *Conservative Theological Journal*, 8:2 (August).

Robertson, Archibald and Alfred Plummer. (1911). *A Critical and Exegetical Commentary on the First Epistles of St. Paul to the Corinthians, International Critical Commentary.* New York: Scribners.

Robinson, D. W. B. (1972). "Charismata versus Pneumaticka: Paul's Method of discussion," *Reformed Theological Review* 2.1 (May-August).

Rogers, Jr., Cleon L. (1965). "The Gift of Tongues in the Post Apostolic Church (A. D. 100-400), *Bibliotheca Sacra*, Volume 122, no. 486.

Rothaar, James E. (2004). "An Exegetical Investigation of 1 Corinthians 13:10," *Chafer Theological Seminary Journal.* Volume 10:6.

Ruble, R. L. (1964). "A Scriptural Evaluation of Tongues in Contemporary Theology." Unpublished doctoral dissertation, Dallas Theological Seminary.

Russell, W. (1986, Spring). "The Anointing with the Holy spirit in Luke-Acts." Trinity Journal, Vol. 7(1):47-63.

Ryrie, Charles C. (1978). *The Ryrie Study Bible.* Chicago: Moody.

Samarin, William J. (1968). "The Linguisticality of Glossolalia." *The Harford Quarterly*, vol 8, no. 4 (Summer): 49-75.

Samarin, William J. (1969). "Glossolalia as Learned Behavior, *Canadian Journal of Theology* 15:60-64.

Samarin, William J. (1970). *Tongues of Men and Angels.* New York: The Macmillan Co.

Samarin, William J. (1973). "Glossolalia as Regressive Speech," *Language and Speech* 16:77-89.

Sarles, Ken L. (1988). "An Appraisal of the Signs and Wonders Movement," *Bibliotheca Sacra* 145 (January-March): 70).

Saucy, Robert L., (1974). *The Church in God's Program* Chicago: Moody Publishers.

Schaff, Philip, (Ed.), (1956). "Homilies on First Corinthians" by Chrysostom, J. *The Nicene and Post-Nicene Fathers.* Homily 24: 12:168. Grand Rapids: William B. Erdmann's Publishing Company.

Schaff, Philip, (Ed.), (1956). Eusebius, "Ecclesiastical History." *The Nicene and Post-Nicene Fathers,* 2d series. 14 vols. Grand Rapids: Wm. B. Eerdmans Publishing Co. Vol. VII.

Schaff, Philip. (2006). *History of the Christian Church,* 8 vols., Reprint ed., (Grand Rapids: Hendrickson Publishers.

Sharp, Granville. (1807). *Remarks on the Uses of the Definitive Article in the Greek Texts of the New Testament,* 3d. ed. Philadelphia: B. B. Hopkins and Co.

Shelley, B. L. (1995). *Church history in plain language.* Dallas, Tex: Word Pub.

Sherrill, John L. (1965). *They Speak in Other Tongues.* Utica, NY.:Pryamid.

Shulman, Albert M. (1981). *The Religious Heritage of America.* South Brunswick, New Jersey: A. S. Barnes.

Smith, Brittany, (2011), *Chriatian Post.* Retrieved 9/24/13 from http://www.christianpost.com/news/more-than-1-in-4-christians-are-pentecostal-charismatic-65358/.

Smith, Charles R. (1970). "Biblical Conclusions Concerning Tongues." Ph.D. diss., *Grace Theological Seminary.*

Smith, Charles R. (1972). *Tongues in Biblical Perspective.* Winona Lake, Indiana: BMH Books.

Spittler, R. P. (2002). "Glossolalia," *The New International Dictionary of Pentecostal and Charismatic Movements.* Ed. Stanley M. Burgess. Grand Rapids: Zondervan.

Stagg, Frank E., Glenn Hinson, and Wayne E. Oates. (1967). *Glossolalia.* Nashville: Abingdon Press.

Stendahl, (1976). "*Glossolalia: The NT Evidence,*" *Paul among Jews and Gentiles,* Minneapolis, MN.: Fortress Press, 1976.

Stitzinger, James F. (2003). "Spiritual Gifts: Definitions and kinds" *Master's Seminary Journal* 14.

Stonehouse, N. B. (1950 Nov). "Repentance, Baptism and the Gift of the Holy Spirit." *Westminister Theological Journal,* Vol 13(1).

Stott, J. R. W. (1972). T*he Baptism and Fullness of the Holy Spirit.* Downers Grove, Ill.: Inter-Varsity Press.

Strachan, G. (1973). *The Pentecostal Theology of Edward Irving.* London: Darton, Longman & Todd Publishers.

Strong, James. (1890). *The Exhaustive Concordance of the Bible.* Nashville: Abingdon Press.

Strong, James. (1988). *Strong's Exhaustive Concordance of the Bible.* Peabody, MA.: Hendrickson Publishers.

Synan, V. (1971). *The Holiness Pentecostal Movement in the United States.* Grand Rapids: William B. Erdmans Publishing Company.

Tauler, J. (1985). *Sermons* (Maria Shrady, Trans.). Paulist Press.

Tavard, George. (1959). *Holy Writ and Holy Church*. New York: Harper and Brothers.

Thayer, Joseph Henry. (1962). *Greek-English Lexicon of the New Testament*. Grand Rapids: Zondervan Publishing House.

Theissen, Gerd and Galvin, John. (1994). *Psychological Aspects of Pauline Theology*, Edinburgh: T. & T. Clark Publishers.

Thomas, Robert L. (1974). "Tongues. .. Will Cease," *JETS* 17 (Spring): 84.

Thomas, Robert L., (1998). "A Revisit: An Exegetical Update." *The Master's Perspective on Difficult Passages*, ed. Robert L. Thomas (Grand Rapids: Kregel.

Toussaint, Stanley D., (1963) "First Corinthians 13 and the Tongues Question," Bibliotheca Sacra 120 (October-December).

Turner, Nigel. (1963). *Syntax.* Vol. 3. A Grammar of New Testament Greek. James H. Moulton. 4 vols. Edinburg: T. & T. Clark.

Unger, M. F. (1944). "The Baptism with the Holy Spirit, Part 1." *Bibliotheca Sacra*, Vol 101(No. 402): 232-247.

Unger, M. F. (1971). *New Testament Teaching on Tongues*. Grand Rapids: Zondervan Publishing House.

Van Elderen, Vastian, (1964) "Glossolalia in the New Testament" *Journal of the Evangelical Theological Society* Volume 7 7, no. 2.

Vine, W. E. (1952). *An Expository Dictionary of New Testament Words*, 4 volumes in one. Westwood, N.J.: Revell.

Wacker, Grant. (2003). *Heaven Below: Early Pentecostals and American Culture*. Cambridge, Massachusetts: Harvard University Press.

Wagner, C. Peter, (1983). "The Power of God and Your Power," *Christian Life*, July 1983, 46.

Walston, Rick. (2003).*The Speaking in Tongues Controversy*. Maitland, FL.:Xulon Press.

Walvoord, John F. (1942). "The Person of the Holy Spirit, The Work of the Holy Spirit in the Believer." *Bibliotheca Sacra* 99, no. 393:40.

Walvoord, John F. (1973). *The Holy Spirit at Work Today*. Chicago: Moody Press.

Walvoord, John F. (1986). "The Holy Spirit and Spiritual Gifts." *Bibliotheca Sacra* Volume 143, no. 570.

Ward, Wayne E., "Various Views of Tongue Speaking," in *Tongues* 21. .

Warfield, Benjamin B., (1918, 1972). *Counterfeit Miracles* (New York: Scribner's Sons. Reprint, London: Banner of Truth Trust, 1972), 5–6.

Wesley, John. (1959, 1977). *The Journal of John Wesley*. Chicago: Moody Press.

Whitcomb, John C. (1998). "Does God Want Christians to Perform Miracles Today?

Bibliotheca Sacra Volume 155:7.

Whitcomb, John C., (1971). "Does God Want Christians to Perform Miracles Today?" *Grace Journal* 12:6.

Wiersbe, W. W. (1989). *The Bible Exposition Commentary*. Wheaton, Ill.: Victor Book Publishers.

Williams, J. R. (1984). "Charismatic Movement," in *Evangelical Dictionary of Theology*, ed., Walter A. Elwell. Grand Rapids: Baker.

Williams, J. Rodman, (1980). *The Gift of the Holy Spirit Today*. Plainfield, NJ: Logos International.

Windisch, Hans.(1974). *"Barbaros," Theological Dictionary of the New Testament*. Edited by Gerhard Kittel and Gerhard Friedrich, translated and edited by Geoffrey W. Bromiley. 10 vols. Grand Rapids: Wm. B. Eerdmans Publishing Co. (1:546-553).

Woodbridge, J. D. (1988). *Great Leaders of the Christian Church*. Chicago.: Moody Press.

Woods, Andy M. (2004). "The meaning of the perfect in 1 Corinthians 13:8-13" *Chafer Theological Seminary Journal* Volume 10, no. 2.

Gifts for Today

www.ingramcontent.com/pod-product-compliance
Lightning Source LLC
Chambersburg PA
CBHW071647090426
42738CB00009B/1448